THE EVOLUTION OF CULTURE

D081369b

The Evolution of Culture

THE DEVELOPMENT OF CIVILIZATION TO THE FALL OF ROME

Leslie A. White

Foreword by
Robert L. Carneiro and Burton J. Brown

Left Coast Press inc.

Walnut Creek, CA

Left
Coast
Press
inc.

Left Coast Press, Inc.
1630 North Main Street, #400
Walnut Creek, California 94596
http://www.LCoastPress.co

Copyright © 2007 by Left Coast Press, Inc.

All rights reserved. No part of this publication may be reproduced, stored in a retrieval system, or transmitted in any form or by any means, electronic, mechanical, photocopying, recording, or otherwise, without the prior permission of the publisher.

Originally published in 1959 by McGraw-Hill Book Company, Inc., New York

Library of Congress Cataloging-in-Publication Data
White, Leslie A., 1900-1975.
  The evolution of culture : the development of civilization to the fall of Rome / Leslie A. White ; foreword by Robert L. Carneiro and Burton J. Brown.
    p. cm.
  Originally published: New York : McGraw-Hill Book, 1959.
  Includes bibliographical references and index.
  ISBN-13: 978-1-59874-144-5 (pbk. : alk. paper)
  1. Civilization, Ancient. I. Title.
  CB311.W55 2007
  930.1--dc22

                                        2007000279

07 08 09 5 4 3 2 1

Printed in the United States of America

The paper used in this publication meets the minimum requirements of American National Standard for Information Sciences—Permanence of Paper for Printed Library Materials, ANSI/NISO Z39.48—1992.

Cover design by Joanna Ebenstein

To the Memory of My Father
ALVIN LINCOLN WHITE
1866–1934

It is indeed hardly too much to say that Civilization, being a process of long and complex growth, can only be thoroughly understood when studied through its entire range; that the past is continually needed to explain the present, and the whole to explain the part.

Edward Burnett Tylor

Researches into the Early History of Mankind and the Development of Civilization, 1865, p. 2.

Contents

vii

Foreword

Robert L. Carneiro and Burton J. Brown

Leslie White (1900–1975) was clearly one of the leading anthropologists of the mid-twentieth century. We believe that he remains one of the most important and pivotal figures in the whole of anthropological history. White stood at the forefront of that small group of anthropologists who helped redirect anthropology from a cautious particularism to vigorous and far-ranging theorizing. He thus served to restore the discipline to its place among the generalizing sciences.

When White first entered the profession in the late 1920s, anthropology had fallen into the grip of the "particularists," who had themselves fallen prey to a great skepticism as to whether anthropology could or even should attempt to formulate large ideas. They possessed a narrow concern with the facts—a "barefoot empiricism," Elman Service (1971:9) called it, reigned. The search for regularities and the erection of grand syntheses were carefully avoided.

Indeed, theory of any kind was not only suspect, it was openly disdained. To show how strongly this attitude prevailed, White was fond of quoting a passage from Berthold Laufer, a disciple of Franz Boas. "I must confess," wrote Laufer, "that I am in a state of mind where I would no longer give a dime to anyone for a new theory, but I am always enthusiastic about new facts . . ." (Laufer 1930:162). One of the authors to this foreword (Brown) calls this the "Dragnet" period in anthropology after actor Jack Webb's immortal radio and television catch phrase, "The facts, Ma'am, just the facts."

What was true of theorizing in general was especially true with regard to the theory of cultural evolution in particular. Ignored by most anthropologists, it was dismissed out of hand by others. White again looked to Berthold Laufer to exemplify the hostility to it. Cultural evolution, Laufer said, was "the most inane, sterile, and pernicious theory ever conceived in the history of science" (Laufer 1918:90). Thus, when Leslie White became an anthropologist, cultural evolutionism found itself at a very low ebb: denounced by almost all and practiced—let alone championed—by none. By the time White died in 1975, though, evolution had arisen from the depths, recaptured most of its lost ground, and become once more recognized as a major approach to the study of culture. And it was White himself, more than any other anthropologist, who was instrumental in this resuscitation.

Few persons outside the field of anthropology are fully aware that the concept of evolution, the guiding principle of so many of the other natural sciences, was for decades rejected and decried by cultural anthropologists. However, it was not always so. Propelled by the work of such men as Edward B. Tylor, Lewis H. Morgan, and Herbert Spencer, ethnology had begun its life with a strong evolutionary bent. Indeed, in the nineteenth century, evolutionary anthropology made many fruitful and enduring contributions to our knowledge of the origin and development of human societies. True, some of the early evolutionists did commit errors of the sort characteristic of any science in its pioneer stages. Morgan's now-discredited theory that primitive promiscuity and group marriage had preceded monogamy in the history of human marriage was an instance of this.

By the middle of the 1890s, a movement had begun, led by Franz Boas, to expunge from ethnology those theories of the early evolutionists that, like Morgan's views about the succession of forms of the family, had proved untenable. The movement, however, did not stop with pointing out errors. By the time it reached its high-water mark in the 1930s, antievolutionism had engulfed most of the profession. Almost universally, anthropologists had turned their backs on virtually every evolutionary formulation. Instead, they concerned themselves with the findings of their own fieldwork, with studies of distribution, diffusion, acculturation, and similar matters.

It is not well known—indeed, it seems anomalous in retrospect—that Leslie White was raised in this antievolutionary environment and for a time embraced its tenets. But, as he tells us in the preface of this volume, there came a time when he could not maintain his allegiance to this philosophy: "The author absorbed the antievolutionary doctrines of the Boas School as a graduate student. But as he began to teach, he found, first, that he could not defend this point of view, and later that he could no longer hold it." White was being questioned and challenged by his students and discovered that he could no longer defend these antievolutionary doctrines against their criticisms.

It was during his three years of teaching at the University of Buffalo (1927–1930) that White began to turn against antievolutionism. But not until after he had been teaching at the University of Michigan, from 1930 on, did he totally change direction and begin a concerted effort to rehabilitate the theory of cultural evolution. The rehabilitation began in a modest way in 1939 with a paper read at the meeting of the American Anthropological Association and continued with an article published in the *American Anthropologist* in 1943. White then went on to write a series of trenchant essays, published in the 1940s and 1950s, in which he systematically undertook the reconquest of the field of evolutionary theory for ethnology.

White's best-known work, *The Science of Culture,* was published in 1949 and consisted of a number of his previously published influential essays, only one of which dealt with cultural evolution. This essay, which formed the concluding article of the book, was entitled "Energy and the Evolution of Culture." Of it, he wrote in the "Author's Note," this essay "was written in its entirety for this volume although based upon the thesis of an earlier article by the same title in the *American Anthropologist* . . ." (White 1949:xiv).

The fact that only one of White's articles in *The Science of Culture* dealt with cultural evolution suggests that he intended to withhold the others and publish them in a separate volume. He was never able to do so during his lifetime, but he did assemble twenty-four articles he meant to appear in this projected volume, eight of which were devoted to cultural evolution. After White's death in 1975, his literary executors were able to see to their publication under the title of *Ethnological Essays* (White 1987).

When White launched his campaign on behalf of evolutionism, he had to face, and overcome, formidable opposition, for in those days antievolutionism was in full throttle in American anthropology. He felt strongly that the negativism thus reflected was intellectually stifling and that its influence was highly prejudicial to the proper growth of the entire discipline. With undisguised vehemence, he gave vent to this feeling, writing in 1945:

> The repudiation of evolutionism is an error in logical analysis, a blind spot in philosophy, and worst of all a great injury to anthropology as a science. It has done much to emasculate cultural anthropology and to deprive it of its most valuable function: that of pointing out the course of cultural development in the past and its probable course in the future. (White 1987:38)

As difficult as the struggle to reestablish cultural evolutionism promised to be, White was nonetheless optimistic, assured of its eventual success. As he noted years later, "The concept of evolution has proved itself to be too fundamental and fruitful to be ignored indefinitely by anything calling itself a science" (White 1960:vii).

White began his campaign by attempting to refute what he deemed to be the errors and misrepresentations of the antievolutionists. While admitting the mistakes and imperfections of the classical evolutionists, White argued that much of what they had written still remained valid and fruitful.

Gradually, his colleagues began to show a greater receptivity and a fuller appreciation of the central role of cultural evolution in the domain of anthropology. But the long climb back was slow and tortuous, its progress hard won. Its advance was marked by a number of significant mileposts. White's first major article on the subject, "Energy and the Evolution of Culture," appeared, as we have noted, in the *American Anthropologist* in 1943. Its publication may be taken as the first major step on the road back. The "re-arrival" of cultural evolution back to something approaching general acceptance may be dated to 1959. That was the year of the Darwin Centennial, during which the celebration of the occasion was followed by an outpouring of published writings marking the event. Anthropologists were made to feel that a principle so warmly embraced and fruitfully pursued by all the other natural sciences was worthy of serious reconsideration by their own science. And, of course, 1959 was the original date of publication of the present volume.

While a few other anthropologists—notably V. Gordon Childe in England and Julian H. Steward in the United States—played a role in redirecting the attention of their colleagues to the reality and importance of cultural evolution, the resurgence of interest in this field, and its ultimate reacceptance, was due first and foremost to Leslie White.

The Evolution of Culture was not originally meant to stand alone. Rather, it was intended to be the first of three volumes, which together would not only survey human cultural development from the Paleolithic to the present, but also extrapolate existing trends into the future. As White wrote, "The present volume will take the reader to the collapse of the Roman state. We propose to follow this work with a study of the Fuel Revolution and its institutional concomitants. And, finally, we hope to project the curve of a million years of cultural development in a modest way and to a limited extent in a third volume on *Recent Trends and Future Probabilities: 1958–2058*."

The Fuel Revolution, while completed, has never been published. The third volume of the trilogy, on which White continued to work up to the time of his death, grew beyond the author's original expectation, reaching a total of some 1,400 manuscript pages. White retitled it *Modern Capitalist Culture*, and under that name it will appear in 2007 as a companion volume to this one.[1]

With this much as a background, let us see what manner of book White brought forth under the title of *The Evolution of Culture*. Described succinctly, this volume can be said to be a treatise on the structure, function, and evolution of human sociocultural systems. It is not, however, an episodic account of the history of human cultural achievements. In fact, throughout most of the book, persons, places, and events are not highlighted and usually not identified. Rather, this work is meant to be a description and analysis of the general principles, processes, and mechanisms involved in cultural evolution. Its focus is on the *general course* of development of human society, and it attempts to explain this progression in terms of the motive forces White believed gave it impetus and direction.

However, despite the title of the book, evolution does not dominate it to the extent one might have supposed. Part One, entitled "Primitive Culture," which comprises nearly three-quarters of the volume, is essentially a presentation of many of the more important customs and institutions of primitive society. But it is no mere description. It contains an analysis of how they contribute to the struggle of societies for survival and security. This section is concerned more with the origin, nature, and function of such things as the incest taboo, kinship systems, the clan, and the division of labor than it is with tracing their development over a million years or more of culture history. Not until Part Two of the book, "The Agricultural Revolution and Its Consequences," does the exposition become fully evolutionary.

---

[1] For further information about White's life and career, the reader may consult the biography of him by William J. Peace (2004) as well as the following briefer treatments: Barnes (1960) and Carneiro (1979, 1981, 2005).

Above and beyond his concern with cultural development, White was a major theorist in anthropology generally. He held the view that culture was a distinct class of phenomena and as such required a separate science to study it. This science he christened *culturology*. The opening chapters of this book contain a clear statement of White's views regarding the place of culture in nature and that of the science of culture among the sciences. One of White's major premises was that cultural phenomena, being part of the natural world, must be interpreted from the viewpoint of science. Thus, he wrote, "Uniformities, regularities, and continuities are found everywhere, in systems of all kinds. Custom is merely the name of these attributes within the class of *cultural* systems. The concept *custom* thus serves to place sociocultural systems in a context as broad as science itself."

Furthermore, he observed, "The problems of the social scientist in general and of the culturologist in particular do not differ in nature from those of scientists in the physical and biological realms. The basic problems of all science are those of structure and function, of differentiation and integration. The astronomer's objective is to discover the structure of the cosmos, galaxies, star clusters, and the stars and to interpret their behavior. The physicist is concerned with the structure of the atom and the interrelationship of its parts. The biologist wants to know how living things are constructed and how they behave. Like his fellow scientists in other fields, the culturologist analyzes the structures of cultures in general and of social systems in particular and interprets their behavior."

It follows from this view of culture that human behavior and institutions, like other elements in the domain of nature, are subject to natural laws: "The culturologist wants to work out the laws of behavior of cultural systems . . . just as the physicist has worked out laws for falling bodies."

White makes a convincing case for the primacy of technological factors in determining the form a society will assume. "[A] social system," he writes, "might well be defined as the way in which a society makes use of its particular technology in the various life-sustaining processes: subsistence, protection from the elements, defense from enemies, combating of disease. . . ."

While White considered the technological system of society as comprising both tools and ways of applying energy, ultimately, he believed, it was the utilization of energy that was the dominating fact in cultural evolution. Indeed, he expressed the relationship between energy and cultural growth in the form of a law:

Culture advances as the amount of energy harnessed per capita per year increases, or as the efficiency or economy of the means of controlling energy is increased, or both. (Italics original)

Despite the importance he ascribed to the use of energy, White was not a "reductionist"; that is, he did not hold that cultural phenomena are to be interpreted primarily in terms of physical, biological, or psychological properties. On the contrary, he defended the position he had vigorously championed in *The*

Science of Culture, namely, that culture constitutes a distinct level or domain of phenomena and that cultural phenomena are to be explained in terms of other cultural phenomena.

White proceeded to examine a number of practices and institutions of primitive societies, both as to their internal workings and as to their contribution to the operation of social systems in their entirety. This portion of the book is an excellent introduction to human social organization. It is clear, penetrating, and illuminating. The following passage is typical of the way in which White seized on a relationship only dimly apprehended or vaguely expressed by others and turned it into an enlightening and far-reaching principle:

> The effectiveness of a group in the struggle for existence and survival depends both upon its size and upon its solidarity. These factors are variable and stand in an inverse ratio to each other. Other factors being constant, the degree of solidarity varies inversely with the size: the larger the group the less the solidarity; an intensification of solidarity would mean a diminution of size.

But size by itself is advantageous to a society, especially if it faces hostile neighbors. Thus, "The desirable goal of social evolution, from the standpoint of success in the competitive struggle for existence, is therefore *increase in size without loss of solidarity*" (italics original).

In White's day, anthropologists were usually classified as belonging to a historical, a functionalist, or an evolutionist school. Members of the historical school studied series of events, as particular and unique. Functionalists concerned themselves with the ways that cultural elements functioned in relation to one another in the societies they studied. Evolutionists focused their attention on tracing the development of cultural forms over time. Persons identified with a particular school tended to work within the limits of theory and method characteristic of that school. Thus, anthropologists of the functionalist school were largely indifferent to problems of the history and development of institutions. They studied intensively how societies worked within a narrow range of time but did not concern themselves particularly with how and why large-scale change in sociocultural systems came about.

Accordingly, the belief arose in many quarters that evolutionism and functionalism were antagonistic and mutually exclusive. However, while White was an evolutionist *par excellence*, he argued against this misconception. Not only did he reconcile evolutionism and functionalism as *approaches,* but he made it clear that evolution and function, as *processes,* actually entail each other. After an innovation in one sphere of culture has taken place, changes often begin to occur in other spheres of culture and may eventually ramify throughout an entire social system precisely because there tends to be a *functional* relation among all its component parts. Because all parts of the system are geared more or less closely to one another, when, by an inner dynamic of its own, the technological aspect of a culture, let us say, initiates a change, it starts in motion a series of successive transformations that ultimately affect every part of the system. Cultural evolution is, essentially, this process writ large.

As already mentioned, the second part of this book deals with the invention of agriculture and with the ensuing revolution that occurred in economic, social, political, and religious institutions. One important chapter describes the processes and steps by which simple, Paleolithic bands were transformed into complex states. It is here that White concentrates most of his evolutionism. Especially illuminating are some of his observations about the sequence of cause and effect that led from early agricultural beginnings to the rise of great empires. Traditionally, anthropologists had told this story somewhat as follows: By making it possible—technologically—for a man to produce more food than he and his family could consume, agriculture "automatically" gave rise to food surpluses. And once these surpluses were in place to be drawn on, certain individuals were withdrawn from primary food production and devoted their time and energies to the elaboration of the arts and crafts, political organization, and religious institutions—in short, to building states and civilizations.

The difficulty with this view of the matter, White pointed out, is that many agricultural peoples exist today who have the tools and the time to produce a surplus of food—and therefore, so the theory runs, to give rise to complex cultures. Yet the fact remains that many of these peoples produce no food surplus at all and persist in staying simple! Evidently, then, the technical means of producing an agricultural surplus are not by themselves sufficient to bring such a surplus into being. Additional factors—economic incentives or, more especially, political compulsion—seem to be required before a food surplus, with all its attendant social consequences, will actually emerge.

We have already noted that White is not concerned here in the detailed sequence of cultural development of any particular people or region of the world. Instead, his focus is on the evolution of culture *as a whole*. In pursuing this "universal evolution," as it is sometimes called, White takes pains to avoid the pitfalls attributed to the classical evolutionists. For example, he is careful to state that no particular society had to go through any fixed series of stages. The fact that the Bantu tribes of Africa went directly from a Stone Age to an Iron Age, without passing through an intermediate Bronze Age, for example, does not invalidate the existence of such a sequence. This is so because only in the evolution of *culture as a whole* does a Bronze Age necessarily precede an Iron Age. The process of diffusion renders it unnecessary for each individual society to recapitulate every stage in the development of culture as a whole.

When he does refer to the culture histories of particular peoples, White neither ignores nor minimizes their differences. Thus he notes that, in addition to diffusion, different environmental conditions may give rise to variations in the course of development of particular societies. Accordingly, in discussing the origin of agriculture he writes:

> We are still faced with such questions as, "Why did agriculture begin, in the Old World, about 8000 B.C. rather than 50,000?" . . . and "Why did it begin where it did rather than in other places?" We must look . . . to environmental—climatic and physiographic—factors . . . for the answers to these questions.

This recognition of the influence of particulars raises no theoretical difficulties for White:

> The culturologist is trying to formulate laws of behavior of cultural systems in general. Like the physicist, he wants valid universals. If one wishes to deal with particulars, with particular cultures or particular falling bodies, then allowance must of course be made for particular conditions in each instance.

Readers familiar with White's earlier writings on cultural evolution and expecting to find in this volume new advances in evolutionary formulations did not find their expectations met. Some felt that, although the contrast presented between primitive societies on the one hand, and early civilizations on the other, was most vivid and enlightening, the *process* by which the transformation from one to the other took place might have been spelled out in greater detail. It is probably fair to say that in his earlier articles White went as far in developing evolutionary interpretations as he was prepared to go. This book, then, may be said to be a summation and consolidation of the gains previously made, not an attempt to break new ground or conquer new heights.

White seems to have felt this to be the case, to judge from his foreword to Sahlins and Service's influential little volume *Evolution and Culture,* which appeared a year after White's own *The Evolution of Culture.* After lauding the advances in evolutionary theory he thought had been made by the authors of that book, he went on to explain, somewhat ruefully, it would seem, why he himself had not advanced the interpretation of cultural evolution even further:

> A few decades ago the opponent of antievolutionism [meaning himself] had to fight a series of propositions designed to refute evolutionist theory such as "the facts of diffusion negate evolutionism." . . . The opponent of these theories had to adapt himself to the propositions advanced by the Boasian antievolutionists and was therefore restricted in his scope and perspective. (White 1960:xi)

Nevertheless, whatever regrets White might have felt that he was no longer at the very cutting edge of evolutionary theory were probably more than tempered by the satisfaction of knowing that his lonely and heroic struggle had been crowned with success. With a justifiable sense of triumph, he proclaimed in the foreword to the Sahlins and Service volume, "antievolutionism has run its course and once more the theory of evolution is on the march" (White 1960:vii).

Still, though perhaps making no further evolutionary advances, the present volume firmly secures the ground already won. Moreover, as an introduction to human societies as working systems and as an exposition of the motive forces underlying the great transformations in the history of culture, this book has stood the test of time. Written in the lucid and forceful prose for which White was well known, the book remains as incisive and illuminating today as when it was written.

Leslie White died in 1975, too soon to have witnessed the reemergence—one might even say the *recrudescence*—of antievolutionism. This time, though, antievolutionism is not a narrow movement, sharply focused on a single issue as it was in the days of Franz Boas and his disciples. Today's antievolutionism is part of an all-encompassing oceanic doctrine denying that cultural anthropology—the whole of it—can be practiced as a science. Evolution is thus just one of the many targets in its gun sights.

This general movement in anthropology is no indigenous development. It derives from the antiscientific intellectual revolt known as postmodernism. Born out of French literary criticism, the movement quickly metastasized and invaded many other parts of the body intellectual. Working assiduously within a profession that White once led with rigor and discipline, postmodernism has spawned a kind of New Age anthropology. "Spawned" is perhaps not the right word; "reanimated" may be more precise, since anthropology always had a cadre of practitioners who felt more comfortable pursuing their profession as a humanity rather than as a science.

Still, as White argued half a century ago, anthropology cannot long turn its back on an approach that has proved so stimulating and rewarding in all the other sciences. And, in fact, cultural evolutionism has never really died in anthropology. Abandoned in large part by ethnologists, who were once its strongest practitioners, cultural evolutionism has continued to be championed and advanced by a stalwart and dedicated few. But—let it be noted—archaeologists have now replaced ethnologists as the principal standard bearers of cultural evolution. Nonetheless, when the day finally comes that the anthropological profession as a whole is ready to reembrace cultural evolution, it will find in *The Evolution of Culture* a primer—vivid and pungent—of what evolutionism is and how it has illuminated our understanding of human society.

It is against this current backdrop of postmodernism and anti-science that *The Evolution of Culture* returns to print for the first time in nearly a half century. It is our sincerest hope that the next generation of readers will find this book as insightful as we do and that it may contribute, at least in a small way, to the return of science and evolutionism to the forefront of cultural anthropology where they belong.

REFERENCES CITED

Barnes, Harry Elmer
1960   "Foreword" to *Essays in the Science of Culture in Honor of Leslie A. White*, ed. by Gertrude E. Dole and Robert L. Carneiro, pp. xi–xlvi. Thomas Y. Crowell, New York.

Carneiro, Robert L.
1979   "White, Leslie Alvin." *International Encyclopedia of the Social Sciences; Biographical Supplement*, ed. by David L. Sills, Vol. 18, pp. 803–807. The Free Press, New York.
1981   "Leslie A. White." In *Totems and Teachers*, ed. by Sydel Silverman, pp. 209–251, 293–297. Columbia University Press, New York.
2005   "Prologue" to *The Science of Culture*, by Leslie A. White, pp. v–xxiii. Percheron Press, Clinton Corners, New York.

Laufer, Berthold
1918   Review of *Culture and Ethnology*, by Robert H. Lowie. *American Anthropologist*, Vol. 20, pp. 87–91.
1930   Review of *Are We Civilized?* by Robert H. Lowie. *American Anthropologist*, Vol. 32, pp. 161–165.

Peace, William J.
2004   *Leslie A. White: Evolution and Revolution in Anthropology.* University of Nebraska Press, Lincoln, Nebraska.

Service, Elman R.
1971   *Cultural Evolution: Theory in Practice.* Holt, Rinehart and Winston, New York.

White, Leslie A.
1939   "A Problem in Kinship Terminology." *American Anthropologist*, Vol. 41, pp. 566–673.
1943   "Energy and the Evolution of Culture." *American Anthropologist*, Vol. 45, pp. 335–356.
1949   *The Science of Culture*, Farrar, Straus and Company, New York. (Reprinted by Percheron Press, 2005).
1959   *The Evolution of Culture.* McGraw-Hill Book Company, New York.
1960   Foreword to *Evolution and Culture*, by Thomas W. Harding, David Kaplan, Marshall D. Sahlins, and Elman R. Service, ed. by Marshall D. Sahlins and Elman R. Service, pp. v–xii. University of Michigan Press, Ann Arbor, Michigan.
1987   *Ethnological Essays*, ed. by Beth Dillingham and Robert L. Carneiro. University of New Mexico Press, Albuquerque, New Mexico.

Preface

In this work we present and demonstrate a theory of the evolution of culture from its origins on anthropoid levels to relatively modern times. The theory of cultural evolution inspired and dominated most of cultural anthropology during the last three or four decades of the nineteenth century. Evolution "is the great principle which every scholar must lay firm hold of," said England's great pioneer, Edward Burnett Tylor, "if he intends to understand either the world he lives in or the history of the past."[1] The theory of cultural evolution was science's answer to the question, "How are the civilizations, or cultures, of the world to be explained?" It was advanced by science to replace the theory of creation as provided by Judeo-Christian theology.

The theory of cultural evolution enjoyed great success in England and the United States during the 1870s and 1880s. But during the closing years of the nineteenth century, a reaction against evolutionism set in both in America and in Germany. The American attack upon cultural evolutionism was led by Franz Boas (1858–1942; born, reared, and educated in Germany), who dominated much of anthropological thinking in the United States for a quarter of a century. Numerous members of the Boas school opposed *any* theory of cultural evolution, not merely those expounded by Lewis H. Morgan, Herbert Spencer, or others.[2] This reactionary attitude received its most picturesque expression at the hands of Berthold Laufer in a laudatory review of a book by Robert H. Lowie, a staunch opponent of evolutionism. "The theory of cultural evolution [is] to my mind," said Laufer, "the most inane, sterile, and pernicious theory ever conceived in the history of science."[3] William Jennings Bryan could have said no more.

In Germany, a nonevolutionist interpretation of culture became prominent around the turn of the century among a group of scholars—Friedrich Ratzel, Bernhard Ankermann, Leo Frobenius, and Fritz Graebner—of which Graebner

---

[1] E. B. Tylor, *Anthropology*, 1881, p. 20.

[2] This statement has been disputed. For supporting evidence see Leslie A. White, "Evolutionism in Cultural Anthropology: A Rejoinder," *American Anthropologist*, vol. 49, pp. 402–404, 1947.

[3] B. Laufer, review of Lowie's *Culture and Ethnology* in *American Anthropologist*, vol. 20, p. 90, 1918.

was the leader. This was a historical type of interpretation, the so-called *Kulturkreislehre*. In some respects it was merely nonevolutionist in point of view. But it was obliged to take issue with evolutionism at some points, i.e., to argue that similarities of cultures in noncontiguous areas were due to diffusion rather than to independent development, and in this respect it was antievolutionist. The German Diffusionist school of Graebner was eventually taken over by a Roman Catholic priest, Father Wilhelm Schmidt, S.V.D. (1868–1954), who with Father Wilhelm Koppers and their clerical workers became an influential school of ethnology. As might be surmised, these clerical anthropologists have been vigorously antievolutionist in outlook and action.[4]

A nonevolutionist, and sometimes antievolutionist, school of ethnology became prominent in Great Britain and the United States during the 1930s under the leadership of Bronislaw Malinowski and A. R. Radcliffe-Brown, namely, the Functionalist school. "Social anthropology," the prevailing type of interpretation in Great Britain today (1958), is nonevolutionist in point of view.

Antievolutionism reached its peak during the 1920s, and much of this point of view still persists. But there are numerous indications that the theory of cultural evolution is staging a comeback. The *News Bulletin* of the American Anthropological Association[5] observed that at the annual meeting of the Association at Albuquerque in December, 1947, "a reawakening of interest in the problem of cultural evolution . . . was noticeable." A number of articles have been published since that time in which the theory of cultural evolution has been reconsidered.[6] Recently, Julian Huxley has presented, as a matter of course, as a thesis that does not need to be defended, the theory of evolution as being as relevant to culturology as to biology and quite as necessary to its development.[7] It would be curious indeed—more, it would be incomprehensible—if this theory, which has been so fundamental in the biological sciences, so fruitful and illuminating in the physical sciences, where it is coming to be used more and more in astronomy and physics, and in many of the social sciences, should not find a place in cultural anthropology.

The author absorbed the antievolutionist doctrines of the Boas school as a graduate student. But as he began to teach, he found, first, that he could not

[4] See "Catholic Anthropologists and Evolution" in White, *op. cit.*, pp. 408–410.

[5] Vol. 2, no. 1, p. 2, February, 1948.

[6] Melville Jacobs, "Further Comments on Evolutionism in Cultural Anthropology," *American Anthropologist*, vol. 50, pp. 564–568, 1948; E. Adamson Hoebel, "Evolution," *Man in the Primitive World*, 1958; Alexander Lesser, "Evolution in Social Anthropology," *Southwestern Journal of Anthropology*, vol. 8, pp.134–146, 1952; Julian H. Steward, "Evolution and Process," in *Anthropology Today*, A. L. Kroeber (ed.), 1953, pp. 313–326, and various essays in his *Theory of Culture Change*, 1955. In Great Britain, V. Gordon Childe has published *Social Evolution*, 1951.

[7] "Evolution: Biological and Culture," the editorial of the first *Yearbook of Anthropology*, vol. 1, published by the Wenner-Gren Foundation for Anthropological Research, 1955.

defend this point of view, and later that he could no longer hold it. In due time he cultivated the theory of evolution in a course called Evolution of Culture, which he has taught at the University of Michigan for many years.[8] He has attacked the position of the antievolutionists in a number of articles.[9] The present work is an attempt to present a modern, mid-twentieth-century exposition of evolutionist theory.

But let it be said, and with emphasis, that the theory set forth here cannot properly be called "neoevolutionism," a term proposed by Lowie, Goldenweiser, Bennart, Nunomura (in Japan), and others.[10] Neoevolutionism is a misleading term: it has been used to imply that the theory of evolution today is somehow different from the theory of eighty years ago. We reject any such notion. The *theory* of evolution set forth in this work does not differ one whit in principle from that expressed in Tylor's *Anthropology* in 1881, although of course the development, expression, and demonstration of the theory may—and does—differ at some points. "Neo-Lamarckism," "neoplatonism," etc., are valid terms, but "neoevolutionism," "neogravitationism," "neoerosionism," etc., are not.

Although anthropologists lay claim to the whole field of culture, few if any have undertaken to cultivate this domain in its entirety. Most cultural anthropologists have confined their works to nonliterate cultures; some include the great urban cultures of the Bronze and Iron Ages; but we know of none who has grappled with modern Western civilization—although a few have established beachheads with community studies. We have committed ourselves to do this. The present volume will take the reader up to the collapse of the Roman state. We propose to follow this work with a study of the Fuel Revolution and its institutional con-

[8] He also offered this course in the Department of Anthropology at Yale University in the fall semester of 1947–1948, in the Department of Social Relations, Harvard University, in the fall semester of 1949–1950, and in the Department of Anthropology, University of California, Berkeley, spring semester of 1957.

[9] Cf. "Energy and the Evolution of Culture," *American Anthropologist,* vol. 45, pp. 335–356, 1943; "History, Evolutionism and Functionalism: Three Types of Interpretation of Culture," *Southwestern Journal of Anthropology,* vol. 1, pp. 221–248, 1945; "Diffusion vs. Evolution: An Anti-evolutionist Fallacy," *American Anthropologist,* vol. 47, pp. 339–356, 1945; "Evolutionism in Cultural Anthropology: A Rejoinder," *ibid.,* vol. 49, pp. 400–413, 1947; "Evolutionary Staves, Progress and the Evaluation of Cultures," *Southwestern Journal of Anthropology,* vol. 3, pp. 165–192, 1947; "Evolutionism and Anti-evolutionism in American Ethnological Theory," *The Calcutta Review,* vol. 104, pp. 147–159, and vol. 105, pp. 29–40 and 161–174, 1947 [published also in Portuguese translation in *Sociologia* (São Paulo), vol. 10, pp. 1–39, 1948, and in Japanese translation in *The Japanese Journal of Ethnology,* vol. 15, pp. 1–22, 1950].

[10] R. H. Lowie, *History of Ethnological Theory,* 1937, p. 289; Alexander Goldenweiser, "Four Phases of Anthropological Thought," *Papers and Proceedings, American Sociological Society,* vol. 16, pp. 66, 1921; John W. Bennett, review in *American Anthropologist,* vol. 47, p. 451, 1945; Kazuo Nunomura, "On the 'Neo-evolutionist' School," *Japanese Journal of Ethnology,* vol. 14, no. 4, 1949.

comitants. And finally, we hope to project the curve of a million years of cultural development in a modest way and to a limited extent in a third volume on *Recent Trends and Future Probabilities: 1958–2058.*

The author is indebted to many people for assistance and encouragement during the years that he has labored on this book. It would be impossible to mention here everyone who has helped in one way or another. Scores of students in the author's courses during the past twenty-five years have helped him to formulate and to express the ideas here set forth. Dr. Harry Elmer Barnes's inspiration and encouragement and his encyclopedic knowledge have been of inestimable value. The author wishes to express his gratitude to a number of institutions for aid or hospitality or both: to the University of Michigan for granting him leaves of absence in order to devote full time to writing; to the Department of Anthropology at Yale University for their hospitality during the fall semester of 1947–1948, and for helpful discussions with the late Professor Ralph Linton and with Professor George P. Murdock; to the Department of Social Relations and the Department of Anthropology at Harvard University for their hospitality during the fall semester of 1949–1950, and for kindness shown him by the late Professor Earnest A. Hooton, Professor Clyde Kluckhohn, and Professor J. O. Brew; to the Laboratory of Anthropology, Museum of New Mexico, the Honorable Boaz Long, Director, and to Mr. Stanley Stubbs for their hospitality and many kindnesses in the fall semester of 1954–1955; and to the Wenner-Gren Foundation for Anthropological Research and to Dr. Paul Fejos, Director of Research, for encouragement and financial assistance. Betty Ann Wilder (Mrs. Harry C. Dillingham) and Grace Louise Wood (Mrs. Frank Moore) have been most helpful as research assistants. And finally, the author wishes to express his most grateful thanks to his wife Mary, who typed the entire manuscript, in addition to sustaining the author with patience, encouragement, and understanding.

Leslie A. White

P A R T O N E   *Primitive Culture*

Chapter 1 MAN AND CULTURE

Man is unique: he is the only living species that has a culture. By *culture* we mean an extrasomatic, temporal continuum of things and events dependent upon symboling. Specifically and concretely, culture consists of tools, implements, utensils, clothing, ornaments, customs, institutions, beliefs, rituals, games, works of art, language, etc. All peoples in all times and places have possessed culture; no other species has or has had culture. In the course of the evolution of primates *man* appeared when the ability to symbol had been developed and become capable of expression. We thus define man in terms of the ability to symbol and the consequent ability to produce culture.

Man, as an animal, possesses a number of characteristics which qualify him for culture. Among these may be mentioned erect posture, which frees the forelimbs for nonlocomotory activities; an opposable thumb, which makes the hand an effective grasping organ; stereoscopic, chromatic vision; gregariousness; and possibly a few other traits. But the most important qualification of all is the ability to symbol.

We call the ability freely and arbitrarily to originate and bestow meaning upon a thing or event, and, correspondingly, the ability to grasp and appreciate such meaning, *the ability to symbol*. Holy water provides us with a good example of this. Holy water is a liquid that exists in nature *plus* a meaning or value derived from man. This meaning or value cannot be grasped or appreciated with the senses. Symboling, therefore, consists of trafficking in meanings by nonsensory means. Keepsakes and fetishes provide us with other examples of symboling. But perhaps the best example of all is articulate speech or language; at any rate, we may well regard articulate speech as the most characteristic and the most important form of expression of the ability to symbol.

Dogs "can understand words and sentences," as Darwin observed long ago. And today laboratory rats can distinguish the food meaning of green circles from the electric-shock meaning of red triangles. But this is not symboling. In neither case does the animal originate and bestow the meaning; it is man who does this. And in each case dog and rat grasp the meanings with their senses because these meanings have become

3

so identified with their physical bases through the operation of the conditioned reflex that sensory comprehension becomes possible.

Darwin declared that "there is no fundamental difference between man and the higher mammals in their mental faculties," that the difference between them consists "*solely* in his [man's] almost infinitely larger power of associating together the most diversified sounds and ideas . . . the mental powers of higher animals do not differ *in kind*, though greatly *in degree*, from the corresponding powers of man" [italics supplied]."[1] This view has been held by many psychologists, anthropologists, and sociologists down to the present day.[2] It can be readily demonstrated, however, that this is not the case; that the difference between the mind of man and that of subman is indeed one of kind, not merely one of degree; that man's mind is unique among all species of living beings.

There are many things that man can do that no other creature is capable of. Only man can appreciate the difference between holy water and ordinary water; no ape, rat, dog, or any other subhuman animal can have the slightest conception of the meaning of holy water. Many primitive peoples distinguish parallel cousins from cross-cousins; all peoples classify their relatives, distinguishing cousin from sibling, uncle from grandfather, etc. No subhuman animal can do this; no monkey can tell an uncle from a cousin. No nonhuman animal can remember the Sabbath to keep it holy; in fact, he cannot distinguish the Sabbath from any other day, and he can have no conception whatsoever of holiness. No animal other than man can grasp the meaning or value of fetishes. The lower animals can ascertain the intrinsic properties of commodities, but they can know nothing at all about their prices. Incest and adultery exist for man alone; all other animals must remain forever innocent. Human beings can be killed by magical practices; no other animal can suffer this kind of death. Only man has gods and demons, heavens and hells, and immortality. Only man knows death.

All the above examples of behavior are "either-or" situations; one is either capable of the kind of behavior in question, or he is not; there are no intermediate stages. It is not that man has a greater, the ape a lesser, conception of sin, or that man has merely a superior appreciation of the significance of holy water, or a better understanding of prices. The lower animals are utterly and completely incapable of any of the acts and conceptions cited above. No one, so far as we know, has brought forth convincing or even plausible evidence to indicate or prove that any of the lower animals are capable of the sort of behavior illustrated above, even to the slightest extent. No one, so far as we know, has even

[1] Charles Darwin, *The Descent of Man*, 1904, Chaps. 3, 18.

[2] Some examples are cited in Leslie A. White, "The Symbol: The Origin and Basis of Human Behavior," *The Science of Culture*, 1949.

tried to argue that rats, apes, or any other subhuman animal can have any comprehension whatever of holy water, fetishes, prices, uncles, sin, Sabbaths—or Wednesdays—incest, adultery, etc. None of the lower animals can enter the world of *human* beings and share their lives. Nothing demonstrates the "great gulf"—as Tylor put it—that separates man from subman more dramatically and convincingly than the life of Helen Keller. Prior to her association with her teacher, Miss Sullivan, Helen Keller lived on a subsymbolic plane. Under the tutelage of Miss Sullivan, she crossed the threshold between subsymbolic and symbolic and entered the world of human beings. And she did this *instantly*.[3]

The fundamental, qualitative difference between the mind of man and that of lower species has, of course, been recognized for centuries. Descartes[4] identified and characterized it. John Locke[5] recognized a "perfect distinction between man and brutes." Edward B. Tylor,[6] one of the great founders of modern anthropology, discoursed upon the "great gulf that divides the lowest savage from the highest ape." And today distinguished neurologists like C. Judson Herrick,[7] biologists like Julian Huxley[8] and George G. Simpson,[9] and anthropologists such as A. L. Kroeber[10] see the distinction clearly. Since the author has discussed this matter at some length in his essay "The Symbol: The Origin and Basis of Human Behavior," and since this essay has been reprinted a number of times,[11] we shall not deal with it further here.

Man and culture originated simultaneously; this by definition. Where they originated and whether there were many origins, a few, or only a single origin are questions that are not relevant to our discussion here, since we are not writing a historical treatise, and hence are not concerned with particular events in time and place. The time of origin, however, is very significant since it will provide us with a temporal perspective necessary to an appreciation of the evolution of culture. The time of

[2] See review of this point in White, *op. cit.*, pp. 36–39.

[4] *Discourse on Method*, pt. 5, 1637.

[5] *An Essay Concerning the Human Understanding*, book 3, chap. 9, 1689.

[6] *Anthropology*, 1881, p. 54.

[7] *Brains of Rats and Men*, 1926.

[8] *Man Stands Alone*, 1941, and "The Uniqueness of Man," *Man in the Modern World*, 1948.

[9] *The Meaning of Evolution*, 1949.

[10] *Anthropology*, rev. ed., 1948.

[11] It was originally published in *Philosophy of Science*, vol. 7, pp. 451–463, 1940. It has been reprinted in *ETC., a Journal of General Semantics*, vol. 1, pp. 229–237, 1944; in *Language, Meaning, and Reality*, S. I. Hayakawa (ed.), 1954; in *Readings in Anthropology*, E. Adamson Hoebel (ed.), 1955; in *Readings in Introductory Anthropology*, Elman R. Service (ed.), 1956; in *Sociological Theory*, Lewis A. Coser and Bernard Rosenberg (eds.), 1957; and, in slightly revised form, in Leslie A. White, *The Science of Culture*, 1949.

man's and culture's origin cannot be fixed with precision, of course, but one million years ago represents a fair consensus among authorities of the date of their beginning.

We may assume that culture came into being in the following way: Neurological evolution in a certain line, or lines, of anthropoids culminated eventually in the ability to symbol. The exercise of this ability brought culture into existence and then perpetuated it. We may elucidate and justify this conception by showing that culture in all its parts and aspects is dependent upon symboling, or, more specifically, upon articulate speech. For this purpose we may divide the components of culture into four categories: ideological, sociological, sentimental or attitudinal, and technological.

The ideological sector of culture is composed of beliefs, and all beliefs —at least all beliefs of man as a human being—are dependent upon symboling, or articulate speech, for their origin and for their perpetuation. A belief that the world is round or flat, that owls bring bad luck, that when tempering material is added to clay better pottery can be made, that man has a soul, or that all men are mortal would be impossible without articulate speech. All the philosophies of mankind—or as components of cultural systems—are therefore dependent upon symboling.

The sociological component—i.e., the customs, institutions, rules and patterns of interpersonal behavior, etc.—of cultural systems likewise is dependent upon articulate speech. How could one know without speech that two mates are permissible if possessed one at a time but not if held simultaneously? Or that marriage with a cross-cousin is permissible, or even obligatory, but marriage with a parallel cousin is incestuous and therefore criminal? How, indeed, could one tell a cousin from an uncle without language? How could one distinguish between mine and thine, or right and wrong, or know what is a polite and acceptable way to behave toward one's mother-in-law, or how to dispose of the dead, etc., without verbal expression and communication? It is plain, therefore, that the behavior of man as a human being [12] in his social life is dependent upon symboling.

With regard to sentiments, or attitudes, as components of culture, we find the same situation. The feelings or attitudes that constitute the subjective aspect of the mother-in-law taboo, for example, require symboling for their existence. No ape, dog, or rat is capable of feelings cast in such form, or attitudes so organized and directed. The loathing of milk, attitudes toward chastity, snakes, bats, death, etc., are all pro-

[12] A portion of the behavior of man is not symboled and is therefore not human. Coughing, scratching, yawning, etc., are examples of this.

duced and given form and expression in human society by the exercise of the ability to symbol; without it man would not differ from beasts. But how is it with the technological sector of culture, the manufacture and use of tools and implements? The definition of man as the tool-using animal, often attributed to Benjamin Franklin—but with a justification open to question—is obsolete. Apes not only use tools with ease, skill, and versatility; they make or "invent" them as well.[13] They seem to be almost as much at home with tools that require a fine and delicate touch as with those requiring great muscular strength. One ape may learn the use of a tool from another by observation and imitation. But for all this, there is a profound difference between man's use of tools and the technology of anthropoid apes. The use of tools in the human species is, on the whole, a cumulative and progressive process; it is this that distinguishes neolithic from paleolithic cultures, and the Age of Coal and Steel from the Middle Ages. In the human tool process, one generation may begin where the preceding generation left off. It is otherwise with the anthropoids. Tool using with them is not a cumulative or progressive process; each generation begins where its predecessor began. There is no reason to believe that apes are any farther along technologically today than they were ten, or a hundred, thousand years ago. Why this great difference?

A simple exercise in logic suggests the answer. We shall write two equations, thus:

Primate organism (Ape) = use of tools

Primate organism (Man) = use of tools + cumulation and progress

We must assume that the difference between the use of tools, as indicated on the right side of the equations, is due to a difference in primate organisms as set forth on the left side of the equations. And since the *human* use of tools is equal to the anthropoid use *plus* the characteristics of accumulation and progress, we must assume that the human organism is equal to the ape organism *plus* an additional characteristic that is responsible for the difference in use of tools. This reasoning is simple and sound enough. And, of course, we know precisely what this additional characteristic is that distinguishes man from ape: it is the symbolic faculty. The distinctive feature of the tool process in the human species is due, therefore, to the ability to symbol. In the author's essay "On the Use of Tools by Primates," [14] he has gone to considerable length to show, specifically and concretely, how symboling and language have transformed the nonprogressive, noncumulative tool process of anthro-

[13] See Leslie A. White, "Use and Manufacture of Tools by the Lower Primates," *Antiquity*, vol. 22, pp. 210–211, 1948.

[14] *Journal of Comparative Psychology*, vol. 34, pp. 369–374, 1942.

poids into a cumulative and progressive process in the human species. Since this essay has been reprinted in *The Science of Culture* and elsewhere,[15] we shall not repeat the argument here.

We see, then, that everything comprising *culture* has been made possible by and is dependent upon the symbolic faculty: the knowledge, lore, and beliefs of man; his social systems; his institutions, political and economic; his rituals, paraphernalia, and forms of art; his traditional attitudes and sentiments; his codes of ethics and etiquette; and, finally, his technology.

The function of culture. The purpose and function of culture are to make life secure and enduring for the human species. All species of living beings behave in such a way as to perpetuate their kind. Subhuman species execute this behavior by somatic means, i.e., with their bodies, muscles, organs, etc. Man, as a mere animal, also employs his bodily organs in life-sustaining behavior. But as a human being man employs the extrasomatic tradition that we call culture in order to sustain and perpetuate his existence and give it full expression. We may think of culture, then, as an extrasomatic mechanism employed by a particular animal species in order to make its life secure and continuous.

Specifically, the functions of culture are to relate man to his environment—his terrestrial habitat and the circumambient cosmos—on the one hand, and to relate man to man, on the other. Man is related to his habitat by means of tools, techniques, attitudes, and beliefs. Tools are employed to exploit the resources of nature; clothing and dwellings provide shelter from the elements; and utensils of many kinds are used in the processes of living and survival. The life process in the human species is carried on collectively, as well as individually, and it is the business of culture to organize human beings for this purpose. The exploitation of natural resources and defensive-offensive relations with neighbors, or enemies, may require concerted action. Communal hunts, house building, irrigation enterprises may require organization into groups, and warfare is almost always a collective enterprise. But apart from direct relationship to habitat, the effective conduct of life requires the social organization of human beings into groups of various kinds: families, lineages, guilds of artisans, priesthoods, etc. All the various parts of society must be organized into a coherent whole, and this whole must be regulated and administered in order to function effectively. In short, social organization is as necessary for the effective conduct of life and for survival of the human species as technological adjustment to and control over the

---

[15] In *Man in Contemporary Society*, Contemporary Civilization Staff, Columbia University, 1955, and in *Readings in Introductory Anthropology*, Elman R. Service (ed.), 1956.

natural habitat. And embracing everything is a philosophy, a system of beliefs, weighted with emotion or attitude or "values," which serves to relate man to both earth and cosmos and to organize and orient his life, collectively and individually.

We might express the functions of culture in another way: the purpose of culture is to serve the needs of man. These needs may be divided into two categories: (1) those that can be served only by exploiting the resources of the external world; and (2) those that can be served by drawing upon the resources of the human organism only. Man needs food and materials of many kinds for clothing, utensils, ornaments, etc.; these must be obtained, of course, from the external world. But man has inner, psychic, social, and "spiritual" needs that can be fed and nourished without drawing upon the external world at all. Man needs courage, comfort, consolation, confidence, companionship, a feeling of consequence in the scheme of things that life is worthwhile, and some assurance of success. It is the business of culture to serve these needs of the "spirit" as well as the needs of the body.

Life is continued only by effort. Pain, suffering, lonesomeness, fear, frustration, and boredom dog man's steps at almost every turn. He requires companionship, courage, inspiration, hope, comfort, reassu ance, and consolation to enable him to continue the struggle of life. Cultural devices serve man here. Mythologies flatter, encourage, and reassure him. By means of magic and ritual he can capture the illusion of power and control over things and events: he can "control" the weather, cure disease, foresee the future, increase his food supply, overcome his enemies. Various devices relate him to the spirit world so that he may enjoy the blessings and avoid the wrath of the gods. Cosmologies give him answers to all fundamental questions, of life and death and the nature of all things. Thus culture gives man a sense of power and of confidence. It assures him that life is worth living and gives him the courage to endure it. It comforts and sustains him when he meets defeat or frustration. It provides him with companions, divine as well as human. It attacks boredom and manages at times to make life pleasurably exciting and of fine flavor. In short, culture gives man the illusion of importance, omnipotence, and omniscience. These inner spiritual—or *intraorganismal*—needs of man are of course as real as those for food, shelter, and defense; in fact, they might be felt even more keenly. And these needs must be served if man is to succeed in the struggle of life.

There are institutions or customary practices in virtually every culture that have as their prime, if not sole, purpose association among members of the community or some members of it. There are tribal or community feasts and festivals. There are clubs and societies, both secret and nonsecret. Groupings of this sort are, perhaps, especially conspicuous in a culture like our own where the individual would be lost in the vast structures of government, economics, and industry without some small group within which he may have intimate and personal association with his fellows. The almost innumerable fraternal orders, lodges, and clubs of all kinds in our culture testify to the ubiquity and magnitude of the need for the annihilation of solitude and loneliness, the need for the moral and psychological support that comes from membership in a relatively small, intimate, personal group. The sociological sector of cultural systems thus serves the "inner," psychic, "spiritual"—or "moral" as Durkheim would put it—needs of man just as the ideological—the mythological, theological, philosophical, and even the scientific—sector does.

And even the technological sector is not immune; it, too, provides satisfactions that are not utilitarian or technological in character. Craftsmanship, the process of doing or making something, can and often does provide the craftsman with pleasures and satisfactions quite apart from the product made or the fruits of its use. Carving a perfect canoe paddle, grinding a symmetrical stone ax, weaving a basket, making a spear, a cradle board, etc., as technological processes can yield psychic satisfactions in and by themselves. It is significant to observe, in this connection, that beauty and use are often united in handicrafts. Weapons—even modern six-shooters—may be highly ornamented, shields may be decorated with designs, canoes may have intricately carved prows, saddles and bridles may be decorated with beads or silver mountings, etc. Craftsmanship can provide beauty as well as use, can provide needed nourishment for the human psyche, as well as articles to serve material needs.

Thus we see that culture in all its aspects—ideological, sociological, and technological—serves man's inner, spiritual needs as well as his outer, material needs.

It might be well to reiterate, in order to avoid misunderstanding, that these two "classes" of needs are not separate and distinct in actuality. They are rather *aspects* of the needs of man, intraorganismal and extraorganismal aspects, so to speak. The thing of which they are aspects is the life process itself. In serving these two classes of needs culture is doing but one thing: contributing to the security, fullness, and continuity of life within the human species.

Relationship between man and culture. We have taken considerable pains to distinguish culture as a class of phenomena from man as another class. To separate culture from man in logical analysis and for certain scientific purposes is, of course, justified. But this intellectual procedure should not be permitted to obscure the fact that man and culture are inseparable in actuality, and that therefore a significant relationship obtains between the two. We shall discuss this relationship in its generic and specific aspects. First the generic.

Culture was brought into being by the actions of man; it is supported and maintained in the same way. It could not be otherwise, then, that culture should be determined *in a general way*, in its structure and behavior as a system, by the nature—the bodily structure and capabilities—of man. Had culture been produced by a race of supercats, supercows, or superants, instead of a race of supersimians,[16] it would have been quite different from what it is with us, because cats, cows, and ants are fundamentally different in their natures from simians—as well as from each other. The nature of man, i.e., his bodily structure and functions, makes possible certain developments within, and also imposes certain limitations upon, the culture-building process. Our culture would be quite different if man could subsist only upon plants, or upon a single genus of plant, instead of being omnivorous. Our culture is a function of our vision to a certain extent; it would be otherwise if our vision were achromatic and nonstereoscopic. The continuous activity of our sexual life, instead of a rutting season, has a profound effect upon our social organization, as we shall see later. If the offspring of *Homo sapiens* were born in litters, like pigs or puppies, instead of singly, as a rule, kinship systems would undoubtedly differ from those that have been realized. If adult men and women were 10 inches or 10 feet high, there would be corresponding differences in culture. The necessity of hibernation or estivation would require a culture different from our own. Even such a minor biological difference as the possession of tactile hairs—man is the only mammal without them—might make a significant difference in our culture. It is clear, then, that culture is, in a general sense, a function of the structure and properties of the human organism. Certain properties and capabilities of man make certain developments of culture possible. But certain limitations are placed upon the scope and content of culture by these same structures and properties of man.

But if there is a significant and fundamental generic relationship between man and culture, there is no instance of a specific relationship between a grouping—a physical type, race, tribe, or nation—of mankind and a type of culture. Few people would wish to argue that the physical type of the Chinese disposes them to eat with chopsticks or to write with a brush rather than with a pen. But there are many who believe that a people's "temperament" shapes their political, social, or economic system—they are by nature aggressive, submissive, individualistic, communistic, etc. These beliefs receive no support, however, from scientific evidence.

[16] As Clarence Day has so cleverly pointed out in his deceptively simple but profound little book *This Simian World*, 1920.

Peoples differ in physical type, of course, and they may differ temperamentally, also. But we do not know what these differences may be, nor how to identify and measure them, and much less to determine their effect upon cultural differences. We do know that the influence of culture upon the behavior of peoples is so powerful, so overriding, that we may be sure that such temperamental differences as may exist among peoples is slight and insignificant in comparison. And there is good reason to believe that the phenomena, or qualities, called temperament are not innate, or biologically determined, at all, but are produced by cultural influence.

In the man-culture situation, therefore, we may consider man, the biological factor, to be a constant; [17] culture the variable. There is an intimate generic relationship between man as a whole and culture as a whole. But no correlation, i.e., in the sense of a cause-and-effect relationship, can be established between particular peoples and particular cultures. This means that the biological factor of man is irrelevant to various problems of cultural interpretation such as diversities among cultures, and processes of culture change in general and the evolution of culture in particular.

Extrasomatic character of culture. We have already spoken of culture as an extrasomatic tradition, as having an extrasomatic, or suprabiological, character. This conception is very important, if not essential, to a science of culture, and we must therefore make fully clear what we mean by it. We mean that although culture is produced and perpetuated only by the human species and therefore has its origin and basis in the biological make-up of man, in its relation to human beings after it has come into existence and become established as a tradition, culture exists and behaves and is related to man as if it were *nonbiological in character.*

The suprabiological, extrasomatic character of cultural phenomena is easily demonstrated. A baby is born into a group of human beings. It has the capacity—a potentiality at first which will be realized as the infant becomes a child—for symbolic, cultural behavior, but it has no culture. The baby is not born with culture—with a language, beliefs, patterns of human behavior, etc.—nor does he acquire these things automatically as a function of the development of his nervous system. He acquires his

[17] This does not mean that man has undergone no change biologically since his origin; he has, unquestionably, at least in physical type. But man has undergone no significant change even physically since the appearance of *Homo sapiens* tens of thousands of years ago. And, quantitatively considered, most of his cultural development has taken place within the past thirty thousand, or perhaps even the past ten thousand, years. For all practical and even theoretical purposes, therefore, we may treat man as a constant factor with reference to cultural diversities and processes of culture change.

culture from the world outside himself, from his human, cultured associates. This is of course obvious. If the baby is born into one cultural setting, he will acquire a certain language, certain patterns of behavior, beliefs, attitudes, and so on. If born into another and different kind of setting, he will acquire another kind of cultural equipment. We see, therefore, that offspring in the human species are born cultureless; they acquire their culture from the world outside their organisms. Cultural forces impinge upon them from the outside, as Durkheim once put it, just as cosmic forces do.[18] The growing infant and child becomes humanized, culturized, as a consequence of cultural influences exerted upon him from the world outside his own organism. From his standpoint the origin and locus of culture are definitely extrasomatic.

The extrasomatic character of culture is well illustrated by another example: one group acquires culture traits from another. This phenomenon is too well known to require much elucidation. The transfer of culture from one group to another may be occasional and insignificant, or it may take place on a grand scale. It may be fortuitous or deliberately planned and executed. In any event, we witness the relationship between human organisms, on the one hand, and culture traits, on the other, a relationship in which the culture borrowed has definitely an external position with reference to the human organisms.

The independence of culture from its human carriers in logical analysis may be shown by two kinds of examples. First, let us consider a number of groups of human beings, tribes or nations, of the same general physical type, such as a number of North American Indian tribes. Their cultures, including languages, vary. In a comparison and contrast of these cultures and languages, in an inquiry into the reasons for their similarities and differences, we are not aided by taking the biological carriers of these cultures into consideration. On the contrary, to do so would only obstruct or confuse the solution of our problem. The fact that the individuals in all tribes considered have straight black hair, copper-hued skins, and prominent cheek bones, whereas some tend to be long-headed, others short-headed, does not help us at all in our study of their linguistic and other cultural similarities and differences. On the contrary, to introduce these irrelevant elements into the problem would only make the solution more difficult, if indeed it did not, through the confusion thus caused, make it impossible.

Some anthropologists would readily grant the irrelevance of *anatomical* traits to an interpretation of cultural differences, but would insist upon not only the relevance but the importance of psychological factors.

---

[18] "Les tendances collectives ont une existence qui leur est propre; ce sont des forces aussi réelles que les forces cosmique,...elles agissent également sur l'individu du dehors...." Émile Durkheim, *Le Suicide*, 1897, p. 348.

The personalities, character structures, minds, egos, or ids of peoples or individuals will, they argue, shape their cultures. But if *personality, mind,* etc., be defined as biological phenomena, as functions of the neuro-sensory-muscular-glandular-etcetera system, then their argument is wholly lacking in scientific support.[19] If, however, they define personality and mind as products of human social experience, i.e., as culturally determined, then they are saying that culture causes or determines culture, but through the medium of human biological organisms, which is precisely what we are maintaining here.

Secondly, let us consider a large population, a tribe or nation, for example, over a considerable period of time, such as the people of England between A.D. 1066 and 1866, or the people of Honshu between A.D. 1850 and 1940. We observe in each case that the culture has changed greatly. The populations, as biological organisms, have, however, undergone no appreciable change, either anatomically or psychologically. We cannot, therefore, explain the cultural changes by invoking the biological factor; we cannot explain a cultural variable in terms of a constant, biological or otherwise. Nor would we be aided in the slightest degree by taking the human organism into consideration. Here as before the biological factor is irrelevant, and consequently it should be disregarded. In both of these examples, therefore, the independence of culture from its biological carriers, or substratum, from the standpoint of logical analysis and for purposes of scientific interpretation, is again demonstrated.

The extrasomatic character of an ax or an amulet is fairly obvious, one might say; it has its existence outside the human organism. But what about sentiments and attitudes, it may be asked; are they not so deep-seated, so integrally a part of the human organism, as to preclude the possibility of an extrasomatic role? To reason thus is to be guilty of error, on the one hand, and of superficiality, on the other.

The error is the failure to distinguish between things and logical analysis, between things and the interpretation of things. To be sure, sentiments are imbedded in human organisms in reality. But they may be

---

[19] We have no proof, or even significant evidence, that peoples vary appreciably in their innate, biologically determined mental characteristics. Since peoples vary somatically, sometimes considerably, we may infer that they differ psychologically also. But what these differences are and how to measure them, and how to ascertain their distinctive effects upon culture, if any, we do not know. There is much evidence, however, that indicates that such innate psychological differences as may exist among peoples are insignificant, if not negligible, in their effect upon culture when compared with the power and influence of the cultural factor itself. The uniformity of cultural expression within a population of diverse physical make-up is one indication of the validity of this proposition. The marked changes in the culture of a biologically constant population over a period of time are another.

separated from it in logical analysis; no terrestrial vehicle moves without friction, but the physicist can and does divorce the momentum of vehicles from the friction that impedes their motion. Similarly, we can divorce sentiments and attitudes from their biological matrixes. The English language has no existence apart from human organisms, but it is a commonplace that we can treat it scientifically without reference to its human carriers; glands, nerves, "organs of speech" are irrelevant to philology. In exactly the same way we can divorce a customary loathing of milk, a taboo against eating pork, an attitude of respect for the aged and consider it as an element of a social tradition, quite apart from human organisms. So considered, it has an extrasomatic character just as truly as an ax has.

The superficiality of the view expressed above lies in a confusion of subjective and objective aspects of any culture trait, i.e., any thing or event dependent upon symboling. An ax has its locus outside the human organism, and therefore it may be thought to be "objective" in character; in fact, we call it an *object*. A sentiment, or attitude, has its locus within the human organism, and therefore it may be regarded as "subjective" in nature. But this is to fail to recognize the fact, as we have just observed, that every culture trait, or element, has both subjective and objective aspects; indeed, the one implies and requires the other. An ax is indeed an object, with its locus outside the organism. But, as a culture trait, it is meaningless without an idea, a conception of its nature and use. It is inseparable, too, from an attitude, or sentiment, with regard to its use. On the other hand, a sentiment or attitude is meaningless without overt expression in speech, gesture, or socially significant behavior of some kind. The expression of a sentiment or attitude is a physical event and, as such, is as perceptible as an ax. A sentiment or attitude becomes an object; i.e., it is objectified, in its expression; it becomes a thing or an event just as truly as an ax is. Thus we see that every cultural element, every culture trait, without exception, has both subjective and objective aspects. And all may be regarded as things, or events.[20]

We see, then, that culture may be considered as an extrasomatic class of things and events, as a nonbiological tradition. It is always present wherever man is. It has its origin in the organisms of human beings; it could not exist or be perpetuated without the existence and action of human beings. But from the standpoint of scientific explanation of cul-

[20] This is what Émile Durkheim means when he says, "the first and most fundamental rule [for the observation of social facts] is: *Consider social facts as things.*" This proposition, he tells us, lies at "the very basis of ... [his] method." In *The Rules of Sociological Method*, George E. G. Catlin (ed.), University of Chicago Press, Chicago, 1938, pp. 14, xliii. It will be recalled, too, that William James pointed out that minds themselves may be considered "as *objects*, in a world of other objects." *Principles of Psychology*, vol. I, Henry Holt and Company, Inc., 1918, p. 183.

tural diversities and of processes of change (but not of the nature of culture in general), culture may be treated as if it had an existence of its own, independently of the human species. The "as if" factor does not render explanations made on the basis of this assumption fictitious or nonscientific. The science of linguistics proceeds upon this assumption, and it is the closest approximation to a mature science that we have on the level of *human* affairs. Man, the human species or human organism, is irrelevant to the science of linguistics. He, or it, is likewise irrelevant to the science of culture. "Science must abstract some elements and neglect others," says Morris Cohen, "because not all things that exist together are relevant together." [21]

Culture as a temporal flow, or stream. Culture may be viewed in a number of significant ways for purposes of scientific interpretation. We may think of the culture of mankind as a whole, or of any distinguishable portion thereof, as a stream flowing down through time. Tools, implements, utensils, customs, codes, beliefs, rituals, art forms, etc., comprise this temporal flow, or process. It is an interactive process: each culture trait, or constellation of traits, acts and reacts upon others, forming from time to time new combinations and permutations. Novel syntheses of cultural elements we call inventions; they are events which take place when the culture process places certain elements in juxtaposition or in conjunction with one another. When an invention becomes possible it becomes inevitable also. It is meaningless to say that an invention was possible but that it did not occur; if it did not take place, in what sense was it possible? An invention is like a shower of rain. When certain meteorological factors and conditions are present and in proper conjunction rain will fall; when they are not present or in proper conjunction it will not rain. There is no difference here between possibility and inevitability. It is the same with inventions. When certain cultural elements and conditions are present and in proper conjunction, an invention will take place; when they are not, the invention will not occur. The numerous instances of inventions or discoveries being made simultaneously by persons working independently of one another illustrate this point: when the interactive stream of cultural development has reached a certain point certain syntheses of cultural elements become not only possible but inevitable, and if culture is advancing upon a broad front, these syntheses will find multiple and simultaneous expressions.

The stream of culture undergoes changes of content as well as alterations of form as it flows. New elements may be added; old elements may drop out. Metals, coal, or petroleum may be introduced into the culture

[21] Morris Cohen, "Fiction," in *Encyclopaedia of the Social Sciences*, vol. 6, The Macmillan Company, New York, 1931, p. 226.

stream at stages of development that make the stream receptive to such introductions. Stone axes, ox carts, and spinning wheels may drop out as they become incompatible with their respective contexts in the stream of culture.

Culture as a nontemporal system. We may view the culture of mankind as a whole, or any distinguishable portion thereof, as a nontemporal system; i.e., we may consider it merely as an organization of cultural elements without regard to chronological sequences. A system is an organization of things and events so interrelated that the relationship of part to part is determined by the relationship of part to whole. An atom, a molecule, or living organism is a system. Culture, too, has systemic organization. System implies both parts and interrelationships among parts, or structure and function, or process. We have already distinguished four categories of cultural,elements: technological, social, ideological, and attitudinal. These may be thought of as the structure of a cultural system. The interrelationship of these elements and classes of elements and their integration into a single, coherent whole comprise the functions, or processes, of the cultural system.

Culture and cultures. When we think of culture in general, or of the culture of mankind as a whole, we call it simply *culture*. But when we think of the culture possessed by a tribe, nation, or region, we speak of *a* culture, or of cultures.

The culture of mankind in actuality is a one, a single system; all the so-called cultures are merely distinguishable portions of a single fabric.[22] The culture of mankind as a whole may be considered temporally as a flowing stream, or nontemporally as a system, or as both, i.e., as a system in a temporal continuum.

For certain purposes and within certain limits, the culture of a particular tribe, or group of tribes, or the culture of a region may be considered as a system. Thus one might think of the culture of the Seneca tribe, or of the Iroquoian tribes, or of the Great Plains, or of western Europe as constituting a system. Actually, of course, Seneca culture is but a distinguishable portion of Iroquoian culture, just as Iroquoian culture is a distinguishable portion of aboriginal North American culture, and that in turn a portion of the culture of mankind as a whole. The culture of all mankind does indeed constitute a self-contained, closed system. But the cultures of tribes or regions are not self-contained, closed

[22] "...A specific culture is an abstraction, an arbitrarily selected fragment.... There is only one cultural reality that is not artificial, to wit: the culture of all humanity at all periods and in all places." Robert H. Lowie, "Cultural Anthropology: A Science," *American Journal of Sociology*, vol. 42, p. 305, 1936.

systems in actuality, at all; they are constantly exposed to cultural influences, flowing in both directions, with other cultures. But for certain purposes, and within certain limits, these cultures can be treated as systems. The culture of any distinguishable group of people at any given time is complete; i.e., it contains all the kinds of elements that culture as a whole contains, and it has systemic organization. Thus, the culture of the pueblo of Zuni at any given time and regardless of its affinities and contacts with the cultures of neighboring tribes does exist and function as a system. The same might be said for the cultures of the Iroquoian tribes, or of the Great Plains, or of western Europe.

In short, it is only when and in so far as cultures can be considered significantly apart from their relations and contacts with other cultures that they can be treated as systems. Failure to realize this has led to serious error in the past in ethnological theory. Thus it was pointed out by opponents of the theory of cultural evolution that "a given culture" did not have to pass through certain stages of development in order to reach a certain point because this point could be reached as a consequence of cultural diffusion. The fact that certain African tribes went directly from a stone age to an iron age without passing through an age of copper or of bronze was the favorite illustration of this thesis. The error here consisted in treating these cultures as systems while at the same time extrasystemic factors were introduced. Actually, of course, the evolutionists did not say that every culture, or every people, had to pass through a certain sequence of stages, but that processes of cultural development had to go through a certain series of stages. The opponents of cultural evolutionism were confusing the culture history of peoples with evolutionary sequences of culture.[23]

We may, then, consider the culture of mankind as a whole as a system. We may also think of the cultures of distinguishable groups of people, or of regions, as systems, but only in so far as they are uninfluenced by contact with other cultures. To the extent that we can think realistically of the culture of Zuni or of western Europe or of aboriginal America as not significantly influenced by other cultures, to that extent can we think of them as systems.

Technology: The Basis and Determinant of Cultural Systems

Through logical analysis we have distinguished four kinds of components of cultural systems: technological, sociological, ideological, and sentimental, or attitudinal. Viewed statically, these classes of cultural phenomena may be considered as parts of a whole, as different

[23] See Leslie A. White, "Diffusion vs. Evolution: An Anti-Evolutionist Fallacy," *American Anthropologist*, vol. 47, pp. 339–356, 1945, for fuller treatment of this point.

sectors or areas of a culture. From a dynamic standpoint, however, technology, social organization, and philosophy are to be considered as *aspects* of any cultural system, or as kinds of behavior of the cultural system as an organic whole—as breathing, metabolizing, procreating, etc., are processes carried on by a biological organism as a whole. This means, of course, an intimate interrelationship between traits distinguished as technological, social, philosophic, etc., as we have already seen. But the fact that these four cultural categories are interrelated, that each is related to the other three, does not mean that their respective roles in the culture process are equal, for they are not. The technological factor is the basic one; all others are dependent upon it. Furthermore, the technological factor determines, in a general way at least, the form and content of the social, philosophic, and sentimental sectors.

The technological basis of cultural systems is rather easily demonstrated. All living organisms can maintain themselves as individuals and perpetuate themselves as species only if a certain minimum adjustment to the external world is achieved and maintained. There must be food, protection from the elements, and defense from enemies. These life-sustaining, life-perpetuating processes are technological in a broad, but valid, sense; i.e., they are carried on by material, mechanical, biophysical, and biochemical means.

If it be argued that technologies could not exist without ideas—and it is of course a matter of empirical observation that technologies do not exist apart from ideas—and that therefore tools are dependent upon ideas, it may be countered, first, that ideas can be significant and effective in the maintenance of life only by receiving expression through technological means, and hence are dependent upon them, whereas the technological culture is significant directly. Secondly, in associations of technologies and ideas, one can account for idea systems in terms of technologies, and technologies can be explained in terms of the physico-chemical, mechanical means of adjustment of one material body to another. But if one explains technologies in terms of ideas, the ideas are either unexplained or are accounted for by appeal to other ideas, which amounts to the same thing.

It is fairly obvious that the social organization of a people is not only dependent upon their technology but is determined to a great extent, if not wholly, by it, both in form and content. As a matter of fact, a social system might well be defined as the way in which a society makes use of its particular technology in the various life-sustaining processes: subsistence, protection from the elements, defense from enemies, combating disease, etc. The activities of hunting, fishing, gathering, farming, tending herds and flocks, mining, and all the processes by means of which raw materials are transformed and made ready for human consumption are not merely technological processes; they are social processes as well.[24] And *as* social processes they are functions of their respective technological processes; as the latter change, so will the former. The processes of combating disease, "controlling" the weather, providing protection against the elements and defense against enemies are likewise social processes. Social systems have, therefore, like technological systems, subsistence, health, protection, and defense coordinates. Of these, the subsistence function is the most important because all others are dependent upon it. Thus, hunting, herding, gathering, fishing, farming, mining, manufacturing, and transportation will influence, each in its own way, and in proportion to its magnitude, the form and content of a social system. Any society will have more than one of these technological determinants; some will have many. In addition to the exploitation and processing of materials taken from nature, any social system will be determined by medical, protectional, and military technological factors as well. Each of these is capable of considerable variation. A social system, even the simplest, is therefore a fairly complex affair, complex in the sense that it is the resultant of a number of factors, each of which may vary considerably. We may express this by means of the following formula: $T(Sb \times Pr \times D) \rightarrow$ *society*, or *social system*, in which the technological factor, T, exercised and expressed in the tools and processes of subsistence, Sb, protection from the elements, Pr, and defense from enemies, D, determines the social system. Each of the three subfactors—the technologies of subsistence, protection, and defense—may vary enormously in its range of specific expression, from the digging stick and club to modern agricultural techniques and guided missiles, producing a corresponding result in the social system.

The propositions set forth here are neither abstruse nor radical. On the contrary, they are little more than recognition of the obvious. A hunting people will have one type of social organization as a consequence of this kind of activity, i.e., the use of certain technological implements; an agricultural, pastoral, or industrial people will have another cast to

[24] "The ship and the tools employed in its production symbolize a whole economic and social system," says V. Gordon Childe; "the canoe ... also implies an economy, a social organization.... The bronze axe which replaces [a stone ax] is not only a superior implement, it also presupposes a more complex economic and social structure." *Man Makes Himself*, C. A. Watts & Co., Ltd., London, 1951, pp. 13–14.

This is in sharp contrast to the view of Boas which he and his disciples used to combat the theory of cultural evolution. "The early attempts of Morgan to associate social organization and economic condition have proved to be fallacious.... We have simple industries and complex organization, or diverse industries and simple organization." Franz Boas, "Some Problems of Methodology in the Social Sciences," *Race, Language and Culture*, The Macmillan Company, New York, 1940, pp. 266–267. See also Franz Boas, "The Aims of Anthropological Research," reprinted from *Science*, 1932, in *ibid.*, p. 254, and Franz Boas, *The Mind of Primitive Man*, 1938, pp. 178, 197.

its social system. The influence of the technology of war is quite evident in some cultures; defense against enemies, in others. The close and necessary articulation of a social system with its associated technology may be highlighted by imagining a nomadic hunting tribe and a sedentary, agricultural tribe exchanging social systems.

The influence of technology upon social organization is expressed in two ways. First, there is the *direct* effect of technological instruments upon the behavior of human organisms. A bow and arrow, digging stick, clock, or steam engine produces certain orbits, or patterns, of behavior. Secondly, these patterns must be related to each other on the social level, in order to make a coherent, integrated social system possible. The manner in which this interrelationship of social patterns takes place is conditioned by their own structure and function, which are in turn technologically determined. Thus, a brotherhood of railroad trainmen is a grouping formed upon the basis of patterns of behavior that are formed directly by the use of locomotives, cars, etc. And society must have means to relate this brotherhood to other social groupings and so incorporate it into society as a whole. The effect of technology upon social organization is thus exercised directly through the use of tools, utensils, etc., and indirectly in the process of interrelating the social patterns formed directly by the technology.

To be sure, it may not be practically possible to account for minute differences of social system in terms of technology as a determinant. One might challenge the thesis set forth here by demanding a technological explanation of such facts as the following: two tribes have similar technologies, but one has a special reciprocal term for the relationship between mother's brother and sister's son, whereas the other does not; or, that one tribe has clans, whereas the other does not. We might not be able to supply an explanation of these or other features of social systems in technological terms. But inability to do this would not necessarily mean that our thesis is invalid. It is not always possible to observe microscopic events effectively with a macroscopic spyglass.

If social institutions are shaped by the operation of technologies, then social change will tend to follow technological change. But the institutional response to technological change may not be immediate. Institutions come to have an inertia of their own. The articulation of one institution within a social structure may tend to preserve the institution intact, also. Thus a dislocation between institution and technology may arise; the lag between institutional change and cultural change is notorious. To explain the minutiae of social structure in terms of technological influence, therefore, we would have to know the history of every detail of a cultural system. Secondly, as we have seen, a social phenomenon is the resultant not merely of *one* technological factor, but of many. The denotation of the avuncular relationship by a single reciprocal term is, we may say, a minute and particular expression of the cooperation, integration, and solidarity required by the group in order to make life secure. But to break this down into all its technological determinants, such as all the tools, weapons, utensils used by a tribe, might prove to be an impossible task, even with more adequate means of analysis than we now possess. Thirdly, as we have already pointed out, a social element may serve to interrelate and integrate other social elements that have been formed directly by the technological factor, and is consequently the indirect rather than direct result of technological influence. This would, of course, make correlation between the social and the technological even more difficult. Finally, we would reply to the demand that we interpret details of kinship systems and other social forms in terms of technological influence by asking, "If they are not determined technologically, either directly or indirectly, how then are they determined?" Alternative explanations would seem to be instinct, ideas, and free will.

Instinct can probably be dismissed at the outset; no one, we dare say, would want to argue that any cultural form is determined by genes and chromosomes. If ideas determine social forms, what determines the ideas? We have touched upon this point before. To argue that a people determines its social organization by its own free will and choice [25] really explains nothing and shuts the door to further inquiry as well. Macroscopically, the effect of hunting, fishing, mining, gathering, fighting, farming, herding, and manufacturing upon social organization is easily demonstrated. We can go further and show how technological processes influence customs of marriage, residence, and descent; how lineages, clans, occupational groups, castes, special mechanisms for social regulation and integration, and so on, are powerfully conditioned, if not determined, by technology. The theory of technological determination, direct or indirect, of social organization is thus effective and fruitful; it will carry us far. The difficulties that we encounter in its application to minutiae are technical in nature rather than fundamental. They are the practical difficulties of actual measurement and correlation among numerous and specific variables; they are not due to inadequacies of our premises or to shortcomings of our theory. They are to be compared, let us say, with the difficulties of tracing the trajectory of a raindrop in

<hr>

[25] Ruth Benedict appears clearly to take this view. "The great arc along which all the possible human behaviours are distributed is far too immense and too full of contradictions for any one culture to utilize even any considerable portion of it. Selection is the first requirement ... any society selects some segment of the arc of possible human behaviour" which they then "capitalize in their traditional institutions. ..." *Patterns of Culture*, Houghton Mifflin Company, Boston, 1934, pp. 237, 254.

a windstorm rather than those involved in constructing a perpetual-motion machine.

A close correlation between types of philosophy and types of technology can be established. Here again fishing, hunting, fighting, farming, herding, and manufacturing, as technological processes, have their philosophic counterparts. Fishing implies a certain body of knowledge, belief, lore, and understanding; farming, herding, or manufacturing implies another. And in each one of these fields, the philosophic component varies as the technological factor varies. Large-scale farming as a capitalist venture, made possible today by machinery and tractors, carries with it a philosophy quite different from that of farming with mules or oxen in 1850 as a way of life. The same may be said for the other ways of making life secure: the medical, military, and industrial arts.

The philosophy, or ideological component, of every culture thus far is made up of naturalistic and supernaturalistic elements. The role of each in any given situation is determined by the underlying technology. Supernaturalism flourishes best where man's control over his relations with the external world, with the realm outside his own ego, is least, and this control is exercised and expressed in materialist, mechanical, physical, and chemical—i.e., technological—terms. Thus, where the ceramic art is well developed, a minimum of magic is employed. In occupations in preliterate cultures like hunting, fishing, combating illness, warfare, and in dealing with the weather, where control over things and events is relatively slight, supernaturalism luxuriates. In the course of cultural development, as control has increased, supernaturalism has waned. Knowledge and understanding increase as the material, mechanical, physico-chemical means of adjustment and control are improved and extended. Witness, for example, the great effect wrought upon knowledge, belief, and outlook—i.e., upon philosophy—by the telescope and microscope; by such advances in agriculture as irrigation, draining, use of artificial fertilizers, and plant breeding; by technological explorations in the physical, chemical, biological, geological, meteorological, and astronomical realms. Astronomy and mathematics—geometry especially—may be regarded to a great extent as by-products of agriculture.

An explanation of a philosophy requires more than an appeal to technological determinants alone. A philosophy is an expression, in verbal form, of experience. Much of the experience of man *as an animal* is determined by his organism in its interaction with its environmental setting. But the experience of man *as a human being*, i.e., as a "culture-bearing animal," is determined at bottom by the technological means with which he is articulated with his natural habitat. This means that as the technological structuring of experience changes, the philosophic expressions of experience will change.

But there is more to a full and adequate explanation of a philosophy than this. All human experience takes place within a social system. The experience of the human organism in interaction with its environment may be structured technologically, but it is filtered through a network of social relations before it receives expression in traditional, verbal form. The expression of experience arising from technological sources is conditioned by passing through the medium of a social system, and this medium may refract the expression in one way or another. A primitive tribe, a feudal order, an industrialized capitalist society will each have its philosophy conditioned by its respective social, political, and economic institutions. Furthermore, much of human experience is of institutions themselves directly. The social system of a culture is always an important factor in the philosophic expression of experience.

The importance of social systems in shaping philosophies and affecting their content in no way invalidates our theory of technological determination; it merely qualifies and amplifies it. If social systems affect philosophies, the social systems themselves are determined by technologies. We may say, then, that philosophies are determined by technologies (1) directly and (2) indirectly, through social systems.

Our theory of technological determination does not enable us to deal with microscopic details in philosophy any more than in the realm of social organization. We cannot explain in terms of technology why, for example, in one culture there is a belief in three souls per person whereas in another there is a belief in only one. But it must be remembered that our theory specifies generic kinds of belief rather than specific beliefs. Philosophically, there is no difference in kind between a belief in one soul and a belief in three. The difference between a belief in soul or souls and a belief in protoplasm can, however, be accounted for technologically. We can distinguish various types of philosophy and correlate them with types of technology. Thus, any cultural anthropologist could tell in advance what type of philosophy would be correlated with an upper Paleolithic type of technology, for example. Hunting, fishing, farming, etc., each has its philosophic reflexes and emphases. As a theoretical principle, the proposition that in the system that is culture, philosophy is determined by technology in its type, emphasis, orientation, and generic content is illuminating and fruitful.

The application of the theory of technological determination to the category *sentiments* in culture is less significant than its use in the social and philosophic spheres. This is not because the theory is less valid here than elsewhere. It is because sentiments themselves are less significant in an explanation of cultural systems than social institutions and systems of belief. To a considerable extent, sentiments are merely an emotional accompaniment of technological, social, and philosophic elements of culture. There is no event in the culture process that does not have its feeling tone. But we do not claim that we can explain each expression of sentiment or attitude in terms of technology. We may not be able to explain in terms of technology why one people regards bats with fear and loathing whereas another is indifferent to them, nor why the Navajo have an attitude of fear and dread toward the dead whereas their neighbors, the Hopi, do not. We do believe, however, that the theory of technological determination will help to explain many sentiments that would remain unintelligible without it. Thus, the attitude toward mothers-in-law that has become crystallized in many cultures as a formal rule of avoidance has been "explained" psychologically in terms of mother images, the Oedipus complex, identification of self with daughter on the part of the mother, and so on. What these psychological explanations leave unanswered is, why do we find the mother-in-law taboo in some cultures and not in others? The materialist, technological theory is useful here. The presence or absence of the taboo may be correlated with certain social forms, such as customs of residence in relation to marriage, division of labor between the sexes, mode of subsistence, offensive-defensive relations with neighboring tribes, etc., all of which can be correlated with the technological foundation upon which the cultural system rests.

Ideals of beauty in women may in some instances be correlated rather closely with the mode of subsistence as technologically determined. In cultures where technological control over food supply is slight and food is frequently scarce as a consequence, a fat woman is often regarded as beautiful. In cultures where food is abundant and women work little, obesity is likely to be regarded as unsightly. In some societies, a sun-browned skin in women was a mark of the lower class of peasants, for example. Ladies, on the other hand, took great pains to preserve a fair skin. In other cultures, e.g., our own today, the pallid skin is a mark of the urban working girl who sees little of the sun, whereas the well-tanned girl is one who can afford to spend much time on golf courses or bathing beaches. The attitude toward sun-browned skins is here reversed. The social systems involved are of course obviously shaped by their respective technologies.

Sentiments pertaining to the distinction between "we" and "they" groups on the tribal, national, and international levels are of course tremendously powerful and significant in social intercourse. Size of social unit is especially relevant here. In some situations we find small groups, each with its independence, integrity, and solidarity. Individuals within these groups owe allegiance to them, respectively, and regard all groups save their own as inferior or hostile. In the course of social evolution, however, a number of these separate and sovereign groups may become united into a single political entity. A synthesis of a number of rival loyalties into a common allegiance follows. What produces this change of sentiment? The answer is, of course, the forces that made small political units obsolete and their amalgamation inevitable. And these forces were those of technology, specifically those exercised in production, commerce, communication, transportation, and warfare. Evolution toward larger political units is at bottom a technological affair. Those who think a world state can be brought about by playing upon the sentiments of citizens directly have the cart before the horse. It is not a changing sentiment that turns the wheels of social evolution. Rather, it is the alteration of social and political groupings by the operation of technological forces that determines the direction and scope of the sentiment.[26]

Many other sentiments could no doubt be rendered intelligible, or more intelligible, by the use of this theory. We might suggest such things as attitudes toward chastity, euthanasia, slavery, divorce, industry, frugality or waste, specific rules of warfare, and a thousand others. It seems likely that many sentiments which are now either not fully understood or are dismissed as irrational vagaries could be made more intelligible through the application of our theory of technological determination.

Thus we may say, in summary of our discussion of the interrelationship of technological, social, philosophic, and sentimental sectors of culture, that technology is the basis upon which the cultural system as a whole rests. Secondly, it is the technology of a culture that determines in a general way the form and content of social systems, philosophies, and sentiments. In the system that is culture, technology is the independent variable, the other sectors the dependent variables. All human life, and consequently culture itself, depends upon the material, physical, chemical means of adjustment of man as an animal species, as living material systems, to the surface of the earth and to the surrounding cosmos. This fact is so obvious that to emphasize it would be quite superfluous were it not for the prevalence of theories which rest upon other premises. Society, philosophy, and sentiment are, in effect, nontechnological forms of expression of the basic technological process.

A word of caution is in order here, however. In emphasizing the dominant and determining role of technology one should not lose sight

[26] "... If, as often happens, one sees in the organization of the family the logically necessary expression of human sentiments inherent in every mind, the true order of facts is reversed. On the contrary, it is the social organization of the relationships of kinship which has determined the respective sentiments of parents and children.... Every time that a social [i.e., cultural] phenomenon is directly explained by a psychological phenomenon, we may be sure that the explanation is false." Émile Durkheim, *De la Division du travail social* (our translation), 1893, p. 390, and *The Rules of Sociological Method*, 1938, p. 104. See also Leslie A. White, "Culturological vs. Psychological Interpretations of Human Behavior," *The Science of Culture*, 1949.

of the influence exerted upon technology by social, philosophic, and sentimental factors. To assert the preeminence or dominance of technology is not to deny all power and influence to other factors. We insisted at the very outset upon the interaction and interrelationship of all aspects of culture, even though the roles played by each were not equal in magnitude of influence. Having demonstrated the dominance of the technological factor in the culture process, it would be well to cite a few examples of influence exerted upon technology by other kinds of factors.

Technologies exist and function within social systems and are consequently conditioned by them. A social system may stimulate the technology it embraces, encourage full and free exercise of its functions, and promote its growth and development. Or it may restrict free technological exercise and expression and impose curbs upon its growth. There is room for much variation between these two extremes. Some of our Indian pueblos have refused to adopt machinery from their white neighbors or to accept it from the Federal government. The Luddite movement in England, 1811 to 1816, in which bands of handicraftsmen destroyed the newly introduced textile machinery, was a dramatic expression of the attempt of a social factor to oppose an advance in technology. Corporations producing goods for sale at a profit occasionally buy patents in order to keep them from being put into use and by so doing rendering obsolete much technological equipment. Monopolies frequently hold technological progress back in one way or another.

Much the same observations can be made with regard to philosophies or sentiments. They, too, may aid or oppose free expression or growth of the technologies which, respectively, they embrace. A set of beliefs may oppose medical technology, for example. Certain attitudes or sentiments might do likewise.

We are confronted by no theoretical problem when social systems, philosophies, and sentiments promote the free and full expression of the technological process. But what becomes of our theory of technological determinism if social or philosophic factors may successfully oppose the technology?

Culture in general, or *a* culture in particular, is a system, a whole made up of moving interrelated parts. A cultural system, like any other, tends to establish and maintain an equilibrium, even though this be a moving equilibrium. In cultural systems a balance is struck between the technological, social, philosophic, and sentimental factors. The technology is the basis of all other sectors of culture. It is technological change or development that produces change or growth in the other cultural sectors. The motive power of a culture, so to speak, lies in its technology, for here it is that energy is harnessed and put to work. But the magnitude of this motive power is always finite, however great it may be. Now when a technology of a given magnitude of strength or power is opposed by nontechnological cultural elements, be they social, ideational, or emotional, what happens? The answer is obvious. The technology overcomes this opposition if it is strong enough to do so; if it is not strong enough, then it must submit. If a technology is powerful enough to break up a social system that thwarts it, it does so and brings a new system into existence. If it is not sufficiently powerful, then it must submit to the restrictions. The same remarks will apply to philosophies and sentiments also as curbs upon technology.

It is important to recognize the fact that these observations are not concessions made to an opponent of our theory of technological determinism. This theory states merely that of the various classes of forces within a cultural system, technology is the basis and the motive power of the system. It does not assert that it is omnipotent, independent of conditions and subject to no limitations.

The Science of Culture

We have gone to some pains to distinguish a suprabiological, suprapsychological class of phenomena, i.e., a class of things and events which consist of or depend upon the exercise of man's unique ability to symbol, but which are considered in their extrasomatic aspect. We call this class of phenomena *culture*. It constitutes a distinct order of reality in our conceptual scheme of analysis and interpretation. As a distinct order of phenomena, culture requires a special science for its study and interpretation.[27] This science is most properly and precisely labeled *culturology*.[28]

We have shown that cultural phenomena behave in accordance with their own principles and laws. This means, as we have already indicated, that cultural phenomena as such must be studied and interpreted in terms of culture;[29] i.e., the interpretations must be in culturological rather than psychological, physiological, chemical, or physical terms.[30] We now wish to note briefly the kinds of behavior manifested by cultural phenomena and to distinguish emphases or aspects within the science of culture.

[27] "During the last hundred years it has become increasingly clear that culture ... represents ... a distinct domain. We have [in culture] a thing *sui generis* that demands for its investigation a distinct science." R. H. Lowie, "Cultural Anthropology: A Science," *American Journal of Sociology*, vol. 42, p. 301, 1936, and *Culture and Ethnology*, 1917, p. 17.

[28] See L. A. White, *The Science of Culture*, 1949, pp. 115-117, 409-415, for a discussion of the term culturology.

[29] "Culture ... can be explained only in terms of itself," says Lowie in *Culture and Ethnology*, p. 66.

[30] See L. A. White, "The Expansion of the Scope of Science," "Culturological vs. Psychological Interpretations of Human Behavior," and "The Science of Culture," in *The Science of Culture*, 1949, for extensive discussion of this point.

We have already noted that culture is composed of units which we call *elements*, or *traits*. These traits are not all alike, like so many atoms of hydrogen, but are of different kinds. In our scheme of analysis (there can be, and are, others), we distinguish objects, acts, ideas, and sentiments or attitudes, as convenient and useful categories. Culture traits do not move about singly and in haphazard fashion like the molecules of a gas; they are attached, or related, to one another in configurations of various kinds, and these configurations are interrelated, forming an integrated whole. Thus, we have clusters of traits such as those involved in grinding grain, taking an oath of office, riding a horse, making a pun, honoring one's parents, suing for divorce, throwing dice, calculating the area of a field, treating an illness, worshiping a god, uttering a magical spell, tying one's shoe, drinking coffee, and so on. Every culture trait is a component of a system whether of a model of culture in general or of a particular and actual culture. Particular cultures vary among themselves in specific form and content, but all are alike in general respects; i.e., all have tools, language, customs, beliefs, music, etc. And every cultural system functions as a means of relating man to the earth and cosmos, and as a means of relating man to man. The science of culture will therefore concern itself with the structure and function of cultural systems.

Diffusion of culture. Although culture traits always exist as components of a system, some, at least, may propagate themselves from one system to another. Thus, *tapu* (taboo), a Polynesian word, becomes incorporated into the English language; the use of tobacco has entered one system after another until it is virtually world-wide; the horse, and firearms, were incorporated into cultures of Plains Indian tribes. The transmission of culture traits from one system to another is called *diffusion*. It is a process that takes place readily and is a phenomenon of widespread occurrence. As someone has said, culture is contagious. Culture may diffuse as single traits, such as the incorporation of *tapu* into the English language; as clusters, or *complexes*, as they are frequently called, of traits, such as baseball, Christianity, or agriculture; or the transfer might take place on such an extensive scale as virtually to swamp or obliterate the receiving system, as, for example, the adoption of European culture by certain aboriginal tribes of North America, Africa, or Polynesia. The science of culture will deal, therefore, with these migrations of culture from system to system and from place to place, and with the changes taking place in systems as a result of these diffusions.

Evolution of culture. Culture undergoes another kind of change, also: a developmental or evolutionist process of change. Evolution may be defined as a temporal sequence of forms: one form grows out of another; culture advances from one stage to another. In this process time is as integral a factor as change of form. The evolutionist process is irreversible and nonrepetitive. Only systems can evolve; a mere aggregation of things without organic unity cannot undergo evolution. Culture may diffuse piecemeal, as we have seen, but only a systematic organization of cultural elements can evolve.

The concept, or theory, of evolution is applicable to any cultural system, whether it be our model of the culture of mankind as a whole, or the culture of any people, group of people, or area *in so far as it can properly be regarded as a system*, or to those portions of the total cultural system that can be treated as subsystems, such as technology, social organization, or philosophy, or to even finer subdivisions such as writing, currency, the plow, Gothic architecture, geometry, or the theory of reincarnation.

The evolutionist process is like the historical, or diffusionist, process in that both are temporal, and therefore irreversible and nonrepetitive. But they differ in that the former is nomothetic in character, whereas the latter is idiographic. The historic process is particularizing; the evolutionist process, generalizing. History is concerned with particular events, unique in time and place. Evolution is concerned with classes of things and events, regardless of particular time and place. To be sure, the evolutionist process always takes place somewhere and in a temporal continuum, but the particular time and the particular place are not significant. It is the temporal sequence of forms that counts. The battle of Waterloo or the assassination of Lincoln are defined and delimited by temporal and spatial coordinates. This is not the case with such developmental sequences as picture, rebus, and alphabetic writing, or stone, copper, bronze, and iron. Here it is the sequence of forms, the one growing out of another, irrespective of particular time and place, that is significant.[31]

It follows from the foregoing that culture may be regarded as a one or as a many, as an all-inclusive system—the culture of mankind as a whole —or as an indefinite number of subsystems of two different kinds: (1) the cultures of peoples or regions, and (2) subdivisions such as writing, mathematics, currency, metallurgy, social organization, etc. Mathematics, language, writing, architecture, social organization, etc., may each be considered as a one or a many, also; one may work out the evolution of mathematics as a whole, or a number of lines of development

---

[31] Many anthropologists have confused these two processes, but they are fundamentally different. See the author's essay "History, Evolutionism and Functionalism: Three Types of Interpretation of Culture," *Southwestern Journal of Anthropology*, vol. 1, pp. 221-248, 1945, and A. L. Kroeber's reply, "History and Evolution," *ibid.*, vol. 2, pp. 1-15, 1946.

may be distinguished.[32] Evolutionist interpretations of culture will there-fore be both unilinear and multilinear. One type of interpretation is as valid as the other; each implies the other.

Nontemporal, formal-functionalist studies. The culturologist may con-cern himself with the way a cultural system is organized and with the way it behaves without reference to time, either to history or to evolution. In this case his concern is with the structure and functions of a cultural system. This is to say, he will be interested in the component parts—technological, social, and ideological—of a system, and how they are related to each other structurally and functionally. And his point of view will be nontemporal, or synchronic, rather than diachronic, i.e., historical or evolutionist. Anthropologists who have been identified with this point of view have been termed "functionalists"; A. R. Radcliffe-Brown and Bronislaw Malinowski have been outstanding exponents of this type of interpretation of culture.[33]

Thus we see that the science of culture includes three distinct types of interpretation: evolutionist, formal-functional, and temporal.[34] In this respect culturology is like science everywhere, on the physical and bi-ological levels as well as upon the cultural. Whether one engages in ev-olutionist, formal-functional, or historical studies of culture will, of course, depend upon his objective or inclination; they are all equally valid kinds of inquiry and interpretation.

Plan of this work. A complete and adequate account of the evolution of culture would embrace it in its entirety, from anthropoid levels to the present time. This would indeed be a tremendous task, and we shall not undertake it in this volume. Instead, we shall carry our story only as far as the collapse of the Roman state, i.e., to the end of the era of the great Bronze and Iron Age cultures. In a subsequent work we shall trace the development of modern civilization from the fall of Rome to the present time.

[32] This analysis presents the courses that are logically possible. It does not follow, however, that the application of the theory of evolution will be equally fruitful or meaningful in all cases. As a matter of fact, it might not be possible to work out a meaningful evolutionist interpretation in some instances. We have as yet no acceptable unilinear theory of the evolution of language, or of the human family. But this does not mean that the theory of evolution itself is invalid. It means merely that certain scopes and organizations of phenomena do not lend themselves to meaningful inter-pretation in terms of this theory.

[33] Raymond Firth, Meyer Fortes, Daryll Forde, and others of the British school of "social anthropology" of the 1950s also exemplify this point of view.

[34] See the author's essay "Science is *Sciencing*," in *The Science of Culture*, and "His-tory, Evolutionism, and Functionalism: Three Types of Interpretation of Culture," already cited, for a more extensive treatment of this subject.

We shall divide the present work into two parts, the first, Primitive Culture, and the second, The Agricultural Revolution and Its Consequences. The first part will deal with that vast era in which cultural systems were activated almost exclusively by human energy and were dependent upon wild foods. The second part will treat of the cultivation of plants and the domestication of animals, and of the institutional changes brought about by the development of agriculture and animal husbandry. In a subsequent volume we shall deal with the Fuel Revolution and its institutional consequences.

Culture is a many-sided phenomenon, and although one can envisage its evolution as a whole, it is necessary in any detailed treatment to trace its course of development in its several aspects, one by one. This shall be our procedure in both Parts One and Two. First we shall sketch the evolution of culture from the standpoint of technological development. Our reasons for giving this aspect priority over others have been set forth in what we have had to say of the relationships obtaining between one sector of culture and the others: the technological sector is the basis upon which all others rest, and it is here that the motive power that activates cultural systems is generated and applied. Next, we shall trace the development of culture in its social, political, economic, and philosophic aspects, respectively. At the end of each era, however, we shall try to form a picture of the process of cultural development as a whole.

Chapter 2   ENERGY AND TOOLS

Everything in the universe may be described in terms of matter and energy, or, more precisely, in terms of energy. Whether we are dealing with galaxies with their millions of blazing suns, a tiny atom with its tightly packed nucleus and darting electrons, a single living cell or a complex multicellular organism, or with a society of ants, apes, or men, we are confronted with a dynamic material system, one that can be described and made intelligible in terms of energy magnitudes and transformations. Energy is the basic and universal concept of science. "Through the various ideas of phlogiston, imponderable fluids, attractions, repulsions, affinities, and forces, science has ended with the simple universal conception of energy," as the eminent British physicist Frederick Soddy observed many years ago.[1]

According to the second law of thermodynamics,[2] the universe is breaking down structurally and running down dynamically; i.e., it is moving in the direction of lesser degrees of order and toward a more uniform distribution of energy. The logical conclusion of this trend is a uniform, random state, or chaos.

In a tiny sector of the cosmos, however, we find a movement in the opposite direction. In the evolution of living material systems, matter becomes more highly organized and energy is raised from lower to higher levels of concentration. This does not mean that living beings constitute

[1] Frederick Soddy, *Matter and Energy*, Home University Series, Oxford University Press, London, 1912, p. 245.
[2] The principles of thermodynamics were first formulated in their modern form by the German physicist R. J. E. Clausius (1822–1888), in 1850. The first law is the so-called law of conservation of energy, which says, in effect, that the total amount of energy in the cosmos is a constant. Clausius' formulations of the first and second laws are as follows: "Die Energie der Welt ist constant. Die Entropie der Welt strebt einem Maximum zu" [The energy of the world, or cosmos, is constant. The entropy (a mathematical factor which is a measure of the *un*available energy in a thermodynamic system) of the world, or cosmos, tends, or strives, toward a maximum]. Quoted from Clausius' *Mechanische Wärmetheorie*, Abhand. ix, S. 44, by J. Willard Gibbs in his famous monograph, "On the Equilibrium of Heterogeneous Substances," *Transactions of the Connecticut Academy of Arts and Sciences*, vol. 3, p. 108, 1874–1878.

an exception to the second law. Animate organisms are able to move in a direction opposite to that specified by the law of entropy only because they are able to draw upon free energy outside themselves and incorporate it within their own systems. All life, as the Austrian physicist Ludwig Boltzmann (1844-1906) pointed out long ago, is a struggle for free energy.[3] All living beings—on our planet at least—are dependent upon energy derived from the sun. Plants obtain energy directly from the sun through radiation and transform it into organic compounds by the process of photosynthesis. All animals live directly or indirectly upon solar energy stored up by plants. Thus, all living organisms are thermodynamic systems which are both expressions and results of a movement toward higher concentrations of energy and greater organization of matter. The process that is life is sustained, perpetuated, and in some instances developed, by energy from the sun.[4]

But, to be precise, the life process, in its maintenance in the individual organism and in its development in orders, phyla, genera, and species, is not merely a matter of capturing quantities of energy and of incorporating them within living systems to take the place of like quantities that have been expended in the process of living. In an adult organism the energy content is a constant, and since one calorie is worth as much as another, a mere exchange would bring no advantage.[5] What is it, then, that sustains the life process and makes possible its evolutionary development?

Schrödinger gives us the answer: by drawing negative entropy from its environment. "A living organism continually increases its entropy," he says, "and thus tends to approach the dangerous state of maximum entropy, which is death. It can only keep aloof from it, i.e., alive, by

[3] Ludwig Boltzmann, "Der zweite Haupsatz der mechanischen Wärmetheorie," in *Populäre Schriften*, 1905, pp. 39-40. And today: "The whole web of life is...a struggle for free energy, whether it be between shrub and tree for a place in the sun, between a locust and a rabbit for the energy-yielding compounds of leaves, or between lion and tiger for the flesh of an antelope. Free energy all living things must have...." Ralph W. Gerard, *Unresting Cells*, Harper & Brothers, New York, 1940, p. 209.

[4] "Anthropogeny likewise borrows from chemistry, physics and physiology the very basic principles that man, like other organisms, is a sort of solar engine that runs by means of the energy stored up in plant and animal food. It follows that this potential energy forms a hidden prize of great worth, to obtain which all animal life struggles unceasingly. Hence the drama of terrestrial evolution is motivated by the complexly ramifying competition and strife for food and for reproductive mates; this principle operates as strongly in the latest stages of life as it did in the earliest." William K. Gregory, "The New Anthropogeny: Twenty-five Stages of Vertebrate Evolution, from Silurian Chordate to Man," *Science*, vol. 77, p. 30, 1933.

[5] We are following here the argument of Erwin Schrödinger as set forth in *What is Life?* Cambridge University Press, New York, 1944, pp. 71-72.

continually drawing from its environment negative entropy.... What an organism feeds upon is negative entropy"; it continually "sucks orderliness from its environment ... in the case of higher animals we know the kind of orderliness they feed upon well enough, viz., the extremely well-ordered state of matter in more or less complicated organic compounds, which serve them as foodstuffs. After utilizing it they return it in a very much degraded form—not entirely degraded, however, for plants can still make use of it. (These, of course, have their most powerful supply of 'negative entropy' in the sunlight.)" [6]

Schrödinger's emphasis is upon order, upon greater or lesser degrees of orderliness. But the process of life can be described in terms of energy, also. A living organism is a structure through which energy flows, entering the system at higher potentials and leaving it at lower potentials.[7] A living organism is thus a mechanism that is operated by a downward flow of energy, much as a water wheel is turned by a stream flowing downhill.

Living systems are means of arresting, and even of reversing, the cosmic drift toward maximum entropy. Maintenance of life is achieved by offsetting the entropy produced by the very process of living with negative entropy obtained from the environment—by "sucking orderliness from the environment." By obtaining more negative entropy from the environment than the positive entropy produced by the process of living, i.e., by utilizing increasing amounts of energy as it flows through living systems to build more complicated structures, rather than merely to maintain the vital process, living species may evolve.

Thus life and death alike receive their most profound and illuminating definitions in terms of thermodynamics. The maintenance of life is a continuous balancing of positive entropy with negative entropy. The evolution of life is the ascendance of negative entropy. Dying is the losing battle to overcome positive entropy. Death is the state of maximum entropy, of thermodynamical equilibrium.

Living material bodies, like inanimate ones, tend to persevere in the motions proper to them indefinitely; their motions will be terminated only by opposition of one kind or another. Opposition to vital processes may come from the external world, from the habitat of the organism; or it may originate within the organism itself. The articulation of living organism with natural habitat involves a certain amount of wear and tear upon

[6] *Ibid.*, pp. 72, 75.

[7] "...Energies flow through their bodies ... this can take place only in such a way that the living organism takes up energy of a higher potential and gives it off at a lower potential." Wilhelm Ostwald, "The Relations of Biology and the Neighboring Sciences," *University of California Publications in Physiology*, vol. I, no. 4, p. 24, 1903.

the organism as well as some transformation of habitat. The life process thus encounters opposition or resistance at every point of contact with the external world. And, of course, some outside force may kill an organism instantly, as well as overcome it gradually. In certain habitats, however, some species will continue their vital processes indefinitely. Some organisms perpetuate themselves endlessly by fission. Trees, and even fish, we are told, tend to live forever; they are overcome only by outside forces. Some animal tissues will live indefinitely in certain kinds of solution. But in other sectors of the animate world, the vital motions are gradually overcome by resistances arising within the organisms themselves. In some species, the moving parts of the organism become materially transformed with age; especially, it would appear, do they become less elastic, thus overcoming, eventually, the momentum of the vital process. Thus, the life process is marked by "immortality"—i.e., indefinite continuation—in some areas, and by the death of individuals and the extinction of species, in other sectors.

It is interesting to note that living organisms are organized and structured as energy-capturing systems. The "correlating apparatus [of an organism]," says Lotka, "is primarily an energy-capturing device—its other functions are undoubtedly secondary. Evidence of this is manifold. The close association of the principal sense organs, eyes, ears, nose, taste buds, tacticle papillae of the finger tips, with the anterior (head) end of the body, the *mouth* end, all point the same lesson, which is further confirmed by the absence of any well developed sense organs in plants." [8] The second law of thermodynamics thus throws light upon the *structure* of living systems as well as upon the nature of the process called life.

The life process tends to augment itself. The ability to take the first step—the transformation of matter and energy from inanimate to living systems—is also the ability to take the next step, and the next. Once the mechanism of transforming energy from the sun into living material systems was effected, the way was opened for an almost unlimited expansion of the life process; the only limit is that of the earth's capacity to accommodate living beings, for the amount of available solar energy is virtually boundless.

The life process extends itself in two ways: (1) by the mere multiplication of numbers through reproduction; and, (2) by the development of higher forms of life. In some species the rate of reproduction is enormous, thousands of offspring per pair. Here we have an example of the extension of the life process in its merely quantitative aspect: the tendency to transform as much of the external world as possible into organisms of the

---

[8] Alfred J. Lotka, *Elements of Physical Biology*, The Williams & Wilkins Company, Baltimore, 1925, p. 354.

ENERGY AND TOOLS   37

species in question. "Every living being," observes Bertrand Russell, "is a sort of imperialist, seeking to transform as much as possible of the environment into itself and its seed."[9] In other sectors of the biological world, however, we find a development of higher forms of life, i.e., greater structural organization and higher concentrations of energy. Biological evolution might be defined as the progress of energy organization moving in a direction opposite to that specified for the cosmos by the second law of thermodynamics. Animals are more highly developed thermodynamic systems than plants; mammals, more highly developed than reptiles. "A change that seems often to be involved in progress [in biological evolution]," says Simpson, "is increase in the general energy or maintained level of vital processes.... The metabolic system of reptiles has a low vital minimum.... The mammalian system (typically) has a higher vital minimum.... With regard to energy level, mammals as a whole stand near but not quite at the top among animals; among vertebrates, the birds exceed them...."[10]

Thus we see that the self-augmentation of the process that is life finds expression in two ways: (1) in the multiplication of organisms, a merely quantitative change; and (2) in the development of higher forms, a qualitative change. Considering the animate world as a whole, there appears to be an inverse functional relationship between these two ways in which the life process extends itself: the lower the form of life, the greater the tendency toward self-extension in a quantitative manner, by mere reproduction of numbers. Conversely, the more highly developed the form of life, the less is the tendency toward numerous offspring.

The struggle for existence and survival has two aspects: (1) the adjustment of the organism to its habitat in terms of temperature, humidity, radiation, subsistence, etc.; and (2) the struggle with other living beings for subsistence and favorable habitats. In this struggle, in both its aspects, "the advantage must go to those organisms whose energy-capturing devices are most efficient."[11] Any gains won are kept. The tendency of the life process is always to achieve a maximum of matter-and-energy transformation.[12] This is true regardless of whether the energy is expended

[9] Bertrand Russell, *Philosophy*, W. W. Norton & Company, Inc., 1927, p. 27.

[10] G. G. Simpson, *The Meaning of Evolution*, Yale University Press, New Haven, Conn., 1949, pp. 256-257.

[11] Alfred J. Lotka, "The Law of Evolution as a Maximal Principle," *Human Biology*, vol. 17, p. 185, 1945.

[12] "...Natural selection will so operate as to increase the total mass of the organic system, to increase the rate of circulation of matter through the system, and to increase the total energy flux through the system, so long as there is presented an unutilized residue of matter and available energy." Alfred J. Lotka, "Contribution to the Energetics of Evolution," *Proceedings of the National Academy of Sciences*, vol. 8, p. 148, 1922.

quantitatively in mere reproduction of numbers of organisms or in the development of higher forms of living systems.

To understand man in particular we must understand living material systems in general. As we have just seen, the second law of thermo-dynamics contributes greatly to the understanding of the process that we call life: it illuminates its structure, its functions, and its development. And this law will help us to understand culture also; the fundamental significance of culture cannot be grasped or appreciated without recourse to this great generalization of physics.

Man, like all other living beings, is confronted with the problem of adjustment to habitat in terms of subsistence, protection from the elements, and defense from enemies. In order to effect these adjustments and to perpetuate his kind, man, like all other creatures, must capture and utilize energy. Self-extension, self-augmentation of the life process, finds expression in the human species as well as in others. In short, man is occupied with adjustment to and control over his environment, and with competition with other species for the means of existence, survival, and expansion. This means is energy.

Man employs the organs of his body in the process of adjustment to and control over his environment, as do other animals. But in addition to these somatological mechanisms, man, and man alone, possesses an elaborate extrasomatic mechanism which he employs in the process of living. This extrasomatic mechanism, this traditional organization of tools, customs, language, beliefs, etc., we have called *culture*.

A culture, or sociocultural system,[13] is a material, and therefore a thermodynamic, system. Culture is an organization of things in motion, a process of energy transformations. Whether it be chipping an arrowhead, catching a fish, hoeing a hill of beans, avoiding your mother-in-law, calling your father's sister's son "father," performing a ritual, playing a game, regarding a churinga with awe, or breathing a silent prayer, the event is an expression of energy expended.[14] "Culture" is but the name of the form in which the life forces of man as a human being find expression. It is an organization of energy transformations that is dependent upon symboling.

The principles and laws of thermodynamics are applicable to cultural systems as they are to other material systems. The "laws expressing the relations between energy and matter are not solely of importance in pure

[13] We define *sociocultural system* as the culture possessed by any distinguishable group of people.

[14] David Burns, Grieve Lecturer on Physiological Chemistry at the University of Glasgow, reports on experiments in which the amounts of energy required to give lectures were measured, the measurements being expressed in mathematical terms. See *An Introduction to Biophysics*, 1921, p. 329.

science [i.e., physics]," says Soddy, "they necessarily come *first in order*
... *in the whole record of human experience*, and *they control*, in the
last resort, *the rise and fall of political systems, the freedom or bondage
of nations, the movements of commerce and industry, the origin of wealth
and poverty, and the general physical welfare of the race* [italics sup-
plied]." [15] Schrödinger, like Soddy a Nobel-Prize–winning physicist, is
"convinced that this Law [i.e., the second law of thermodynamics] gov-
erns all physical and chemical processes, even if they result in the most
intricate and tangled phenomena, such as organic life, the genesis of a
complicated world of organisms from primitive beginnings, [and] the
rise and growth of human cultures." [16] Other physicists and chemists,
like Joseph Henry in the United States and Wilhelm Ostwald in Germany,
have contributed to the development of the energy theory of cultural
development.[17]

As we noted in the preceding chapter, culture is produced by man and
therefore derives its generic nature from its source. Since the fundamental
process of man as an organism is the capture and utilization of free energy,
it follows that this must be the basic function of culture also: the harnessing of energy and putting it to work in the service of man. And since
culture, as an extrasomatic [18] tradition, may be treated logically as a
distinct and autonomous kind of system, we may interpret the evolution
of culture in terms of the same principles of thermodynamics that are
applicable to biological systems.

Cultural systems, like biological organisms, expend the energy that is
captured and harnessed in self-extension as well as self-maintenance. Like biological organisms, cultural systems extend themselves both quantitatively
and qualitatively. Cultural systems extend themselves quantitatively by multiplication or reduplication; i.e., peoples multiply, tribes divide, forming
new tribes and therefore new sociocultural systems. Cultural systems
expand qualitatively by developing higher forms of organization and
greater concentrations of energy.[19] Degree of organization in any material

[15] Soddy, *op. cit.*, pp. 10–11.

[16] Erwin Schrödinger, *Science and the Human Temperament*, George Allen &
Unwin, Ltd., London, 1935, p. 39.

[17] See Leslie A. White, "The Energy Theory of Cultural Development," in *Professor Ghurye Felicitation Volume*, K. M. Kapadia (ed.), 1954, pp. 1–8, for a brief
history of this theory.

[18] Alfred J. Lotka uses the term "exosomatic"—he speaks of "exosomatic evolution." "The Law of Evolution as a Maximal Principle," *Human Biology*, vol. 17, p.
188, 1945.

[19] If, however, the process of cultural development moves in a direction opposite
to that specified for the cosmos as a whole by the second law of thermodynamics,
the operation of culture within the system of nature is in perfect accord with the
cosmic process. In the process of utilizing the energy that it harnesses, culture re-

system is proportional to the amount of energy incorporated in it. As the amount of energy harnessed by sociocultural systems increases per capita per year, the systems not only increase in size, but become more highly evolved; i.e., they become more differentiated structurally and more specialized functionally. We shall see this principle abundantly illustrated as we survey the evolution of culture in general.

Culture, as a thermodynamic system, may be analyzed into the following factors: energy, tools, and product. As we have seen, culture is a mechanism for serving the needs of man. And to do this it must harness energy and put it to work. The use of energy requires technological apparatus, and we may extend the use of the term *tools* to cover all the material means with which energy is harnessed, transformed, and expended. We shall designate all goods and services capable of serving the needs of man that have been produced or formed by the cultural use of energy, the *product*. Thus, catching fish, shooting game, making pottery, cutting hair, piercing ears for pendants, filing teeth for beauty's sake, weaving cloth, and a thousand and one other cultural processes are examples of the control and expenditure of energy by instrumental means in order to serve some need of man. We may, then, think of the culture process in terms of motive power, means of expression, and satisfaction of need. This conception can be expressed by a simple formula, $E \times T \rightarrow P$, in which E represents the energy involved, T the technological means of utilizing it, and P, the product or result which serves a need of man.

By *energy* we mean "the ability to do work." "... Energy and work are interchangeable terms," says Soddy; [20] one is defined in terms of the other. Thus, a stone is moved from here to there, or its shape is changed by chipping or grinding. Energy is expended; work is done. Energy has both quantitative and qualitative, or formal, aspects. Quantitatively, energy is measurable in terms of definite and standard units, such as ergs, calories, British thermal units, etc. One magnitude of energy may therefore be compared with another. Qualitatively, energy is manifested in a

---

duces it from higher to lower levels of concentration, contributing to a more diffuse distribution of energy in the cosmos. Thus food is transformed and diffused as heat and work and reduced to lower levels of organization, i.e., to inorganic matter. In the burning of coal and oil, energy is transformed from compact, concentrated forms to loose and more diffuse forms. And in harnessing the energy of atomic nuclei, energy in even more concentrated form is released and diffused. Thus, *within* the system that is culture, we find a movement and a direction opposite to that specified for the cosmos by the second law. But in relation to the rest of the cosmos, culture is but a means of furthering the trend described by this law. The cultural process is therefore but an infinitesimally tiny eddy in the vast cosmic flow of things.

[20] Soddy, *op. cit.*, p. 25.

great variety of forms: atomic, molecular, stellar, galactic, cellular, and metazoan, as well as cultural. From the standpoint of cultural systems, solar radiation, plants, animals, wind, water in motion, fuels of various kinds, molecules, and atoms are significant forms of energy, significant because it is in these forms that they are, or may be, incorporated into cultural systems. It is understood, of course, that energy is neither created nor destroyed; it is merely transformed. Cultural systems operate, therefore, only by harnessing energy in one form or another, and by transforming it in the production of human need-serving goods and services.

Cultural systems vary as means of harnessing energy; some are more effective than others. They may be compared in terms of coefficients derived by relating amount of energy harnessed and expended in a given period of time to the number of human beings embraced by the system. Thus one cultural system may harness and use x units of energy per capita per year,[21] another, $3x$, or $10x$. The significance of this coefficient lies, of course, in the relationship between amount of energy harnessed, on the one hand, and the number of human beings whose needs are to be served, on the other. The individual human being thus constitutes the unit in terms of which human need is measured and serves, therefore, as the constant against which varying quantities of energy are measured. Thus, we can compare cultures in terms of amount of energy harnessed and expended per capita per year. Or we can make our comparisons in terms of *power*, the rate of doing work, and classify cultures in terms of horsepower per capita.

The source of energy with which cultural systems were activated at the very beginning of man-and-culture history was, of course, the human organism. The energy with which tools, beliefs, customs, rituals, and sentiments were first organized into a functioning system was derived from man himself; he was, so to speak, the power plant that supplied the first cultural systems with their motive power. The amount of energy derivable by a cultural system from this source is of course small. An average adult man is capable of generating about one-tenth of one horsepower, or 75 watts. But the power coefficient of a cultural system deriving all its energy from human organisms would not be 0.1 horsepower per capita, by any means. When everyone is considered, males and females of all ages from helpless infants to the old and feeble, the sick and crippled, the average would be much less, possibly no more than 0.05 horsepower

[21] When we deal with cultures in terms of magnitudes of energy harnessed and put to work we must specify the period of time during which this takes place, since magnitude varies with length of time. We select a year as our unit of time because, in addition to being convenient and easy to work with, it embraces a complete cycle of the seasons, and hence the whole gamut of the routine activities of any cultural system. If, however, we deal with cultures in terms of horsepower, no time period need be specified since horsepower is the rate of doing work.

per capita.[22] Since the amount of human need-serving goods and services produced is proportional to the amount of energy harnessed, or horsepower generated, per capita, other factors remaining constant, a cultural system activated by energy derived from the human organism alone would represent the minimum in the range of capacities of cultural systems. From the standpoint, then, both of energy, or power, per capita and amount of human need-serving goods and services produced per capita, cultures that have the energy of human organisms only, under their control and at their disposal for use in the service of human needs, are at the bottom of the scale.

There is room for variation among cultural systems activated by human energy alone. In our formula $E \times T \rightarrow P$, E, the energy factor, may vary with daily calorie consumption. T, the tool factor, varies with degrees of efficiency. Quite apart from natural habitat, therefore, which varies from tribe to tribe and from place to place, we are confronted with variation of cultural systems. Amount of energy harnessed per capita per year is the basic factor in this situation; the other two are meaningless or nonexistent without it. Without energy, tools would be meaningless, no work would be done, no product brought forth. The energy factor provides us, therefore, with an objective and meaningful yardstick with which to measure these, and all other, cultures. A culture is high or low depending upon the amount of energy harnessed per capita per year. At bottom, then, cultural development is the process of increasing the amount of energy harnessed and put to work per capita per year, together with all the consequences attendant upon this increase.

In order to form a conception of primordial cultural systems based upon and activated by energy drawn from the human organism alone, one

[22] The amount of energy that the human organism is capable of producing will depend largely upon the food-energy intake. Naturally we do not have figures for the diet of primordial man, nor even adequate data for present-day preliterate peoples. We do, however, have statistics for modern nations. The range within which the amount of food energy consumed per capita per diem varies is interesting and significant, especially with respect to animal proteins:

Daily Food Supply per Capita

	All foods (calories)	Percentage of United States	Animal proteins (ounces)	Percentage of United States
United States	3,098	100	1.8	100
Sweden	3,171	100.2	2.2	122
Japan	2,230	72	0.4	22
China	2,234	72	0.2	11
India	1,976	64	0.3	17
Mexico	1,855	60	0.7	40

Source: *Point Four*, a mimeographed publication of the U.S. Department of State, 1949, p. 109.

could examine some of the cultures of modern times having generically similar technological foundations, such as those of the Tasmanians, the Ona, various pygmy groups, and so on.[23] To be sure, technological and environmental factors both operate to produce cultural differences quite apart from source and magnitude of energy harnessed, but we shall deal with these factors later. But however much modern cultures, based upon human energy alone, may vary in specific detail, all are alike in one respect and that a fundamental one: all are extremely limited in their ability to exercise control over the external world, in their ability to produce human need-serving goods per unit of human labor. Sociologically they are all simple, i.e., relatively undifferentiated structurally. And their philosophies —their systems of knowledge and belief—are likewise simple and undeveloped. We have every reason to believe that the earliest cultures of mankind were of the same general type as the cultures of modern times that have had only the energy of human bodies at their disposal, although the latter might be more highly developed technologically. And we may be equally sure that cultural development would never have gone beyond a certain level, and that a low one, had not some way been found to harness additional amounts of energy per capita per year. Mankind would have remained in a condition of savagery indefinitely had not an increase of his available energy resources been made possible. Cultural systems are not developed by intelligence, high ideals, and earnest endeavor alone, as faith is supposed to move mountains; they must have energy—as, we suspect, mountain moving must have also.

Some qualification of our statements regarding the source of energy for the earliest of cultures should be made. The human organism was the principal source for all the earliest systems and the only source for many. There was, however, another source open to some, namely, flowing water. Even the most primitive peoples could float materials downstream instead of carrying them. But water power is insignificant in the course of cultural development until the Iron Age or even later. It is relatively insignificant even today.

Winds were available also to the most primitive peoples, but they had no means to harness them and use their energies. On higher cultural levels winds become significant as a source of energy in watercraft equipped with sails. Mechanical power derived by means of windmills comes very late in culture history, and it has never, in any culture, been of much importance.

Many discussions of harnessing energy begin with a discussion—or rhapsody—of fire. They often degenerate quickly, however, into musings

[23] The reader may be referred to George P. Murdock's excellent book *Our Primitive Contemporaries*, 1934, for descriptions of cultural systems activated by human energy alone, as well as systems of a higher order.

about fire as a symbol of the home, the family fireside, vestal virgins, and what not. Man unquestionably learned to use, and even to make, fire very early in his career. But he did not use it extensively as a form of energy —or more precisely, as a means of doing work—until the recent invention of the steam engine. Fire may be useful in keeping ferocious beasts away from human habitations at night (although it would be easy to exaggerate its value in this respect), and it may constitute a precious symbol in family life and religious ritual. But these uses of fire do not fall within the thermodynamic context *energy*. Even the use of fire in cooking can hardly be put into an energy context because the cooking is not a substitute for something that can be done by an expenditure of muscular energy; fire in this instance cannot be equated with muscular energy or energy in general.

On moderately advanced cultural levels fire assumes considerable importance in the ceramic art, in the firing of pottery. And on still higher levels, fire acquires great importance in the metallurgical arts, in the smelting of ores and in the processing of metals. But in neither of these contexts does fire function as *energy* in the sense in which we are using the term. In pottery making and in metallurgy fire has an *instrumental* significance, as it does in cooking. It is a means of transforming materials. But it cannot be replaced by an expenditure of muscular energy. Since, therefore, we cannot equate fire in the ceramic and metallurgical arts with muscle power, we do not consider it significant as a form of mechanical energy.

There is, however, a very practical use to which fire may be put as a form of energy by very primitive peoples. They may use it to hollow out tree trunks in the manufacture of canoes. Here fire is substituted for, and hence equated with, muscular energy. There is no known cultural system, however, in which energy so derived and used constitutes more than a tiny fraction of the total amount employed. Fire is used also as a form of energy by some peoples to clear land for planting. But when the agricultural level has been reached we are already far advanced culturally and have in agriculture itself a method of harnessing energy compared with which this accessory use of fire is utterly insignificant.

We may distinguish, then, as the first stage of cultural development an era in which the human organism itself was the principal source of energy used by cultural systems, an era in which wind, water, and fire, as sources of energy, were very insignificant indeed. This stage began with the origin of man himself; it ends with the domestication of animals (ruminants), or the cultivation of plants, or both. In duration of time absolutely, and relatively in proportion to the lengths of other periods in culture history, this "human-energy" era is very impressive. If we assume, as many authorities do, that culture began one million years ago, and if we date the beginning of agriculture at about 10,000 years ago,[24] then the human-energy stage of cultural development comprises some 99 per cent of culture history thus far. This fact is as significant as it is remarkable.

The era in which cultural systems derive all but a very little of their energy from the human organism is characterized by another feature, namely, subsistence wholly upon wild food. This gives us another convenient and significant index of cultural development, and a category for the classification of cultures.

When man subsisted wholly upon wild foods he differed but little from the lower animals, who of course did likewise. True enough, he could cook his food, and this was unquestionably an important consideration in his survival. It would be possible to exaggerate the importance of cooking, however, as has been done in the case of fire. While man subsisted wholly upon wild foods he might be considered a wild animal, at least in a sense. He is now a domesticated animal, and it was the agricultural arts primarily that brought about the transition; domesticated man is a by-product of agriculture. Here again we are impressed with the tremendous duration of the wild-food stage as compared with subsequent eras.

The amount of energy per capita per year obtainable by cultural systems from human organisms is of course both small and limited. Unless cultural systems could add to this amount by tapping other sources, they could never have developed beyond a certain level, and that a very low one. And as we have just seen, water, wind, and fire have proved insignificant as sources of usable energy on the lower levels of technological development. Culture could not, and for ages on end did not, develop beyond the limit thus set by the $\frac{1}{20}$ horsepower, more or less, per capita. Eventually, however, an effective way of augmenting energy resources for culture building was found, namely, in the domestication of animals and the cultivation of plants; in short, by harnessing solar energy in nonhuman biological forms.

Plants and animals are, of course, forms and magnitudes of energy. Plants receive, transform, and store up energy received directly from the sun. Animals subsist, directly or indirectly, on plants; all life depends, in the last analysis, on the process of photosynthesis performed by plants.

[24] V. Gordon Childe sets the date at about 8000 B.C., in *What Happened in History*, 1946, p. 17; *History*, 1947, p. 7; Robert J. Braidwood at 7000 B.C., plus or minus 1,000 years, in *Prehistoric Men*, 1948, p. 89. The tendency has been, during the last two decades, to shorten the era of food production by bringing the date of its origin closer to our own times.

But are not wild plants and animals forms and magnitudes of energy just as cultivated and domestic ones are? Yes, they are indeed. But here we must recall the fact that energy is not created or produced; it is merely transformed or controlled. Man is exploiting the energy resources of nature when he appropriates and eats a wild plant or animal, and we may properly say that he is exercising control over these natural forces. But hunting, fishing, and gathering are not forms of *harnessing* plant and animal energies; they are merely acts of appropriation and consumption. To *harness* a force is to lay hold of it, to direct and control it, so that it is not merely introduced into the cultural system but made an integral part of it. A flowing stream is a form and magnitude of energy. But apart from floating materials downstream, this energy does not become significant culturally until it has been harnessed by means of water mills and incorporated into a cultural system. So it is with plants and animals. The domestication of plants and animals was a way of laying hold of them as forces of nature, of directing and controlling them, of incorporating them into cultural systems. This innovation was of tremendous significance, for it tapped new sources of energy and thus freed culture from the limitations imposed by dependence upon man's body for motive power.

The advantages of animal husbandry over hunting wild game are of course numerous. Herds and flocks are within man's grasp and of easy access as contrasted with the difficulty of finding game. Domestication gives man more assurance that he will have food and hides; hunters often return empty-handed. Food supply may be increased as a consequence of domestication. Hunting carried on beyond a certain point will actually decrease man's food supply; game can be killed off faster than it can reproduce. But protection of herds and flocks against attack by wild beasts fosters an increase of numbers under domestication, and hence an increase in food supply. New and valuable materials are made available as a result of domestication. The use of milk, a food whose importance in some cultures it would be hard to exaggerate, is made possible by domestication. Furs and hair were, of course, available to hunters, but the extensive use of wool for textiles was made possible by the domestication and breeding of sheep;[25] the wild varieties did not have wool suitable for such use, apparently.[26]

A tremendous advantage of domestication over hunting lies in the

[25] Wool of the domesticated llama and vicuña was used in the Andean highlands in pre-Spanish times, and some Indian tribes of the Northwest Coast of North America used the hair or wool of the domestic dog for textile purposes.

[26] "The dense, curly wool of sheep is wholly a product of genetic change and selection under domestication." A. L. Kroeber, *Anthropology*, rev. ed., Harcourt, Brace and Company, Inc., New York, 1948, p. 692; see also E. Cecil Curwen, *Plough and Pasture*, 1946, p. 31, and R. H. Lowie, *An Introduction to Cultural Anthropology*, rev. ed., 1940, p. 52.

continuous use of animals in the living form instead of the consumption of dead ones. Milk, eggs, and wool can be obtained again and again from animals without killing them. At certain levels of cultural development domestic animals may be used as forms of mechanical power, to pull sledges or travois, to carry burdens including human beings, to draw plows and carts. And through selective breeding, domesticated animals may be greatly improved as food- or wool-producing machines and as forms of mechanical power.

Thus, the domestication of animals is a way of harnessing, controlling, and using solar energy in a variety of forms to produce food, clothing, and mechanical power. All the advantages that we have cited for domestication as compared with hunting can, however, be reduced to a single and simple statement: it is a means of producing more human need-serving goods and services per unit of human labor, and hence, per capita. Culture has advanced as a consequence of increase in the amount of energy harnessed per capita per year.

Much the same observations may be made concerning the advantages of agriculture as compared with gathering wild plants for food and other uses. Horticulture renders the food supply more certain and more abundant. Reducing the competition with weeds gives cultivated plants more chance to grow and yield abundantly. Hoeing, plowing, fertilizing, irrigating, rotation of crops, and selective breeding are also means of increasing yields. Here, as in animal husbandry, agriculture produces more human need-serving goods per unit of human labor than the gathering of wild plants. And this is a consequence of the greater control exercised over the forces of nature by the agricultural arts.

We may express the significance of both animal husbandry and agriculture from the standpoint of cultural development with a simple formula. Instead of $E \times T \to P$, energy times technology producing a quantity of human need-serving goods and services, let us write $E (H \times N) \times T \to P$, in which H and N are the human and nonhuman components of the energy factor, respectively. If we hold the tool factor constant, we can rewrite our formula simply thus: $H \times N \to P$. This expresses the relationship between the amount of energy derived from the human organism and that from other sources. This ratio is an important one in all cultures above the level of 100 per cent subsistence upon wild food and becomes more important as culture advances. As a matter of fact, cultural advance is well expressed in terms of this ratio: *culture advances as the proportion of nonhuman energy to human energy increases.* Or we may define cultural advance in terms of the ratio between the *product* and human labor: *culture advances as the amount of human need-serving goods and services produced per unit of human labor increases.*

Animal husbandry and agriculture are alike, therefore, in being means of extending control over the forces of nature and of advancing culture as a consequence. But these arts are not equal in their potential capacities for culture building; agriculture has a much greater capacity for culture building than has animal husbandry. The difference in their respective capacities rests upon a simple zoological fact: herds and flocks must feed upon plants; cultivated plants harness solar energy directly. A pastoral system, for all its control over animals, still rests upon a wild-food basis in the last analysis: the plants upon which the herds or flocks feed. The growth and abundance of these plants lie outside cultural control. If pasturage fails, the herds diminish or die. Control over forces of nature is greater and more immediate in agriculture. Plants harness solar energy directly. Fields may be fertilized, excess water drawn off, crops irrigated, advantages derived from use of hotbeds, and so on. It goes without saying that the control exercised through agriculture, though greater than that in animal husbandry, is never complete and perfect; the farmer is of course never wholly immune from natural disaster. But the extent to which culture can develop on a pastoral basis is limited, theoretically and practically. It cannot develop beyond the limit set by the natural production of pasturage. Attempts to increase herds beyond this point merely produce the opposite effect: a diminution of herds as a result of deterioration of pasture caused by overgrazing. In the agricultural arts, on the other hand, there may be a limit to the extent to which human need-serving goods can be produced per unit of human labor, but this limit has not been reached even to this day. Indeed, we seem not to be close enough to it yet even to foresee it and to distinguish its characteristics.

If an agricultural system is superior to a pastoral system in its capacity to harness energy for culture building, a system combining agriculture and animal husbandry is superior to agriculture by itself. In such a system, the production of crops is facilitated by the use of animals as beasts of burden and motive power—to draw plows and other agricultural implements, to transport crops, to "tread out grain," to operate machines for grinding grain, irrigating fields, etc.—and as producers of manure for fertilizer. Agriculture aids animal husbandry, not only in making the food supply of herds and flocks more secure and abundant, but in making it easier and more advantageous to keep certain types of animals such as pigs and fowls. In no culture without agriculture are these kinds of animals domesticated and kept in large numbers. In systems with agriculture, however, they may become of considerable importance. Agriculture and animal husbandry have combined and cooperated to produce the greatest cultures of history prior to the Age of Fuels, except in those regions like Mexico and Middle America where domesticable animals were absent.

It should be kept in mind that in our discussion of hunting, fishing, gathering, animal husbandry, and agriculture, thus far, we have been concerned with only one aspect of these processes, namely, the energy factor. We have not dealt with the tool factor at all so far, and we have ignored environment completely. It is obvious that every culture is determined by instrumental and environmental factors as well as by that of energy, but it is convenient and desirable to treat each one singly while disregarding the other two. In considering the culture process, we may think of any two of these factors as constants while we vary the third. Culture will vary, therefore, as the variable determinant varies. Thus, in the formula $E \times T \times V \to P$, in which E, T, and P have values as before and V stands for environment, we may hold any two of the three determining factors constant and vary the third. P, the total product, or degree of cultural development, will then vary accordingly. The status, or degree of development, of any actual cultural system will, however, be determined by all three factors working together.

These observations are made at this point to supplement our discussion of cultural development in terms of energy alone. It might be pointed out, for example, that a certain pastoral, or even a hunting or fishing, culture is more advanced, more highly developed as measured in terms of our own standard, the amount of human need-serving goods and services produced per unit of human labor, than a certain culture in which agriculture is practiced. This is quite possible, but it does not affect the validity of our generalizations concerning these modes of life as ways of harnessing energy. An exceptionally favorable environment, or a highly efficient set of tools for the use of energy, or both, might offset an inferior means of harnessing energy. Some hunting or fishing cultures might produce more food per unit of human labor than some primitive horticultural systems. An abundance of game, such as bison in the Plains, especially after the introduction of the horse, or of fish such as salmon in the Northwest Coast area, plus effective means for appropriating such resources, might produce a higher culture than a crude agricultural technique in an unfavorable environment. There are even cases of peoples abandoning horticulture and reverting wholly to hunting. But these facts do not affect the validity of our generalizations concerning the harnessing of energy. They merely illustrate the fact that every cultural system is determined by instrumental and environmental factors as well as by that of energy. We may note, however, that all the lowest cultures have neither agriculture nor herds or flocks; all the highest have agriculture, and in no case has a pastoral system produced a culture as advanced as the highest produced by the cultivation of plants. Our generalizations regarding the relative merits of hunting, fishing, gathering, pastoral, and agricultural systems, as types of control over the forces of nature, are thus supported by culture history in world outline. Subsistence upon wild foods is the most inferior of these methods of control; agriculture, the best.

This does not mean, however, that a people must "pass through these three stages of development" in succession. A *people* may go directly from a wild-food economy to agriculture without ever having flocks or herds at all, as of course many American Indian tribes have done. A *people* may even give up their gardens and return wholly to a wild-food economy as some North American tribes did, living in or near the Great Plains with its swarming herds of bison, after the introduction of the horse and the beginning of a westward migration of white men. Neither is it necessary for a pastoral stage to precede an agricultural stage in the cultural-evolutionary process. It would be superfluous to mention this, so obvious is it, were it not for the tradition, still extant, that early evolutionists insisted upon a pastoral stage as a prerequisite to an agricultural stage. We know of no reputable anthropologist, however, who ever held such a view.

We are not concerned here with the *history* of the domestication of animals or the cultivation of plants. We might merely mention in passing that it has been animals who live in flocks and herds, like sheep, cattle, and horses, that have played prominent roles in culture building by providing food, hides and fibers, and motive power. Among cultivated plants the cereals are of greatest importance. They have been, as Tylor put it, "the great moving power of civilization"; [27] all the great cultures of history have been developed and sustained by the cultivation of cereals.

We may remark also that the domestication of animals was the work of men, principally, as the origin of cultivation of plants was the achievement of women. The male hunter became a pastoralist; the female collector of wild plant foods, a horticulturalist. This division of labor between the sexes has had great import for social organization, in domestic food economies as well as in wild-food cultures.

Environment. We propose to deal at length with the instrumental factor in cultural development later. We may, however, dispose of the environmental factor now, once and for all, so far as evolutionist theory is concerned. Every cultural system exists and functions in a natural habitat, a collocation of flora, fauna, topography, altitude, meteorologic conditions and forces, and so on. And every culture is of course affected by these environmental factors. But the relationship between culture and environment is not a one-to-one correlation by any means. Environment does not "determine" culture in the sense that "given the environment,

---

[27] E. B. Tylor, *Anthropology*, 1881, p. 215.

we can predict the culture."[28] Environments vary, and their influence and effect upon cultures vary likewise. Some habitats are suitable for agriculture, a pastoral economy, or fishing, manufacturing, etc.; others are not; they may even render certain types of cultural adjustment to nature impossible. But the relationship of culture to environment is determined to a very great extent by the degree of cultural development. The region now known as Kansas was not suitable for agriculture for a people with a culture like that of the Dakota Indians in A.D. 1800. The same region is not suited to a hunting economy now. Whether the coal and iron deposits, or the water-power resources, of a region will be exploited or not depends upon the degree of development of the culture of that region. This observation helps to make explicit and apparent an important generalization about the relationship between culture and environment: features of the natural habitat become significant only when and as they are introduced into cultural systems and become incorporated in them as cultural elements. The coal and iron of western Europe, or the water power of England, become significant only at certain levels of cultural development. The flowing streams of England were relatively insignificant culturally in A.D. 1200; they became tremendously important as sources of power for industry in the seventeenth and eighteenth centuries; with the development of the steam engine and the exploitation of coal resources, they became relatively insignificant again. Thus we see that although natural habitat exerts an influence upon culture, we can learn more about this influence from a consideration of the culture and its degree of development than by a mere inventory of environmental features.

But a consideration of environmental influence is relevant only to studies of particular cultures; it is not pertinent to a general study of culture as such. If we are concerned with the culture of Egypt in 3000 B.C., of England in A.D. 900, of British Columbia or Kansas in 1850, etc., then one must take the natural habitat into account. But if one is concerned with culture as a distinct class of phenomena, if one wishes to discover how cultural systems are structured and how they function as cultural systems, then one does not need to consider the natural habitat at all. If one wishes to ascertain the relationship between technological instruments and social organization, how and why social systems change,

[28] "While it is true that cultures are rooted in nature, and can therefore never be completely understood except with reference to that piece of nature in which they occur, they are no more produced by that nature than a plant is produced or caused by the soil in which it is rooted. The immediate causes of cultural phenomena are other cultural phenomena...." A. L. Kroeber, "Cultural and Natural Areas of North America," *University of California Publications in American Archaeology and Ethnology*, 1939, p. 1.

the role of art in social life, the relationship between mode of subsistence and the status of woman, how and why the culture of mankind taken as a whole has grown and developed through the ages, he does not need to consider the environment. The culturologist wants to work out the laws of behavior of cultural systems as such, just as the physicist has worked out laws for falling bodies. To be sure, the natural habitat is always there, and it exerts an influence upon culture at all times and places, just as the nature of the falling body and the density of the atmosphere always affect its fall. An autumn leaf falls in one way, a hailstone in another. A bullet falls one way in the atmosphere, another way in a vacuum. But the law of falling bodies is valuable *precisely because* it ignores the influence of atmosphere and the composition and structure of the falling body. In exactly the same way, the culturologist is trying to formulate laws of behavior of cultural systems in general. Like the physicist, he wants valid universals. If one wishes to deal with particulars, with particular cultures or particular falling bodies, then allowance must of course be made for particular conditions in each instance.

The significance of the origin and development of the agricultural arts, alone or in conjunction with animal husbandry, for the growth of culture was tremendous. For some 990,000 years culture had been developing and accumulating. But at the end of the Paleolithic era it was still on a very low level, comparatively speaking. Man had advanced considerably beyond other animal species, thanks to his use of tools and symbols. But he still subsisted upon wild food as did other animals, lived in small groups, and had neither metals nor writing. In a few thousand years, however, after agriculture got under way, the entire system had undergone a profound transformation. Technologically, the change was from a cultural system based almost wholly upon human energy alone, to one based primarily upon solar energy harnessed in cultivated plants and domesticated animals. There were profound social changes, also. Populations increased greatly in numbers and densities, which in turn found expression in new forms of social organization. Small villages grew into towns, and eventually large cities. Nations and empires took the place of tribe and clan organization. The industrial, aesthetic, and philosophic arts flourished. Metallurgy was developed; writing, mathematics, the calendar, and currency came into use. In short, in a relatively brief time,[29] only

[29] "...Finds in the Near East seem to indicate that the domestication of plants and animals in that region was followed by an extraordinary flowering of culture." Ralph Linton, "The Present Status of Anthropology," *Science*, vol. 87, p. 245, 1938.

"For a very long time no significant progress was made [in the New World], but eventually there came the discovery of agriculture; and with it increase of population and rapid development of higher culture." A. V. Kidder, "Looking Backward," *Proceedings of the American Philosophical Society*, vol. 83, p. 532, 1940.

a few thousand years, after agriculture had become established as a means of control over forces of nature, the great civilizations of Egypt, Mesopotamia, India, China, and, in the New World, of Mexico, Middle America, and Peru, came into being. The origin and development of agriculture brought about a revolution in culture. The Agricultural Revolution will be the subject of Part Two of this work.

The role of tools. The technological process may be analyzed, as we have noted earlier, into two components or aspects. On the one hand, we have energy, harnessed and expended, and on the other, the mechanical means with which this is accomplished. A woman digs edible roots with a stick; a man shoots a deer with an arrow; corn is ground with a metate or a water mill; an ox draws a plow. Having sketched the course of technological development from the standpoint of energy, we now turn to the aspect of tool, or instrumental, means.

As Ostwald has pointed out, the structure, use, and development of tools may be illuminated by thinking of them in their relationship to energy. "When a man took a staff in his hand," he says, "he increased the radius of his muscular energy ... and was therefore able to apply it more usefully. By the use of a club he could accumulate his muscular energy in the form of kinetic energy and bring it into play with sudden force when the club alighted. By this means it was possible to perform work which could not have been accomplished by the unaided activity of his muscular energy in the form of pressure...." [30]

In the bow and arrow, muscular energy is transformed into form energy of the drawn bow, from which it may be released instantaneously and with great intensity. In the crossbow, muscular energy can be stored up indefinitely.

"Another kind of transformation," says Ostwald, "relates to the concentration of energy in small surfaces, as edges and points; both bring it about that muscular work by virtue of the diminution of resistance in the surface, is able to exercise so much greater an intensity of pressure.... Sword and spear unite the increased length of the arm-radius with the concentrated effectiveness of edge and point." [31] Other mechanical devices, such as levers, wheels, ball bearings, etc., have their significance in relation to the most effective or economical expenditure of energy.

The result obtained from an expenditure of energy within a cultural system is of course conditioned by the mechanical means with which the energy is controlled. Means vary; some are more efficient than

---

[30] Wilhelm Ostwald, "The Modern Theory of Energetics," *The Monist,* vol. 17, p. 511, 1907.
[31] *Ibid.,* p. 512.

others. One ax, for example, may be better than another. This is to say, more wood can be chopped per unit of energy expended with one ax than another. We may speak of the quality of the ax, or of instrumental means in general, as its degree of efficiency, or briefly, its efficiency. The efficiency of a tool may vary from none at all—or even less than nothing —to a maximum. We may express this range in terms of percentages: efficiency may range from 0 per cent, or less, to 100 per cent, but not more.

Consider a canoe paddle in a given situation. It might be so long, so slender, or so heavy as to be worthless or even to have a negative value. Its efficiency is then 0 per cent or less. But we can imagine and actually construct a paddle which is of such dimensions and proportions that any change would decrease its efficiency. Its efficiency is now 100 per cent of its capacity, practically as well as theoretically. What is true for a paddle is true for every other mechanical device for harnessing and expending energy, whether it be a needle, a bow, or type of locomotive, or airplane. Each has a point of maximum efficiency beyond which it cannot be improved. Gains in the efficiency of an instrument may be made by the substitution of one material for another in the composition and manufacture of the instrument, as well as by improvement in design. Thus, an aluminum or plastic paddle might be superior to one of wood; certain alloys might yield greater efficiency in axes or engines than iron or steel. In other words, one type of instrument may be substituted for another type, but each type has a maximum of efficiency. And the number of types made possible through the use of combinations of materials is finite in practice, if not in theory. In final analysis, therefore, improvements in the efficiency of instrumental means must always be confined within certain limits. Practically, as we know from observation, actual limits often fall short of those theoretically possible.

There is an aspect of economy as well as of mechanical efficiency to be considered in evaluating the role of instrumental means of controlling energy. One type of tool may be more economical though no more efficient, or even less efficient, than another. *Economy* is here measured in units of energy required for the production of the tool. Early copper axes or knives were little, if any more, efficient than the stone implements they replaced, according to Childe.[32] But if a stone ax were broken, it would be difficult, if not impossible, to repair it so that another would have to be manufactured to replace it. The copper ax, on the other hand, could be repaired with relative ease. The cost in labor of the stone implement was much greater than that of metal, and so the latter would be preferred at equal degrees of efficiency. The same principle will apply to higher levels of technological development.

[32] V. Gordon Childe, *What Happened in History*, 1946, p. 69.

It is no doubt often possible to make a machine more efficient than one of its type in use, but at a cost, either in energy or money, that would make it less economical to use. Thus considerations of economy may limit the efficiency of tools and machines in many instances. But whether we consider the use of tools from the standpoint of mechanical efficiency or of cost of production, the end result is the same: the tool or instrument that makes possible the greater product per unit of energy expended will tend to replace one yielding the lesser product in processes where the efficient and economical production of goods is the primary consideration.

We need not concern ourselves here with the varying skills with which a tool is used by craftsmen, since they may be reduced to an average, and thus considered a constant.

The social organization of the use of tools and machines is an important aspect of the technological process. Such things as division of labor, specialization, cooperation, systematization, and rationalization may affect the operation of the technological process very considerably, and with it the magnitude of result produced. But we need merely to recognize these facts here; we do not need to take them into account in our consideration of the nature and function of the instruments themselves.

Returning to our formula $E \times T \rightarrow P$, we may formulate another law of cultural growth: *culture develops as the efficiency or economy of the means of controlling energy increases, other factors remaining constant.* This means, also, that the status, "height," or degree of development of a cultural system is proportional to the efficiency and economy of the mechanical means with which energy is harnessed and expended.[33]

A review of culture history brings out the following: Progress in cultural development, during the long era when cultural systems derived the overwhelming proportion of their motive power from the human organism, was accomplished almost exclusively in the realm of tools. Progress of this sort consisted in adding new tools to the cultural tradition and in the improvement of ones in use.

Mechanical progress was continued during the Agricultural Age also. But here we are confronted by a special situation. In cultivated plants and domestic animals we have both *energy* in definite magnitudes and *means* of harnessing and expending energy, and the two are inseparable. A plant of *Zea mays*, or Indian corn, is not only a certain amount of energy; it is also a means of controlling energy. A cow may be regarded as a means of producing milk, a milk-producing machine, that may be

[33] "The degree of efficiency is a very good measure of culture ... for we call every machine and every process better which yields a larger amount of useful energy for an equal amount of raw energy, that is, which works with less waste." Wilhelm Ostwald, "Efficiency," *The Independent*, vol. 71, p. 870, 1911.

considered from the standpoint of efficiency and economy. Some cows, as machines, are more efficient than others; i.e., they produce more milk and butterfat per unit of diet than others. The same kind of observations could be made about hogs, sheep, and hens as meat-, wool-, and egg-producing machines, respectively. In some cases, such as milk cows, egg producers, etc., it is relatively easy to distinguish the means aspect from the energy aspect. But efficiency as a means, and energy in definite amounts, are virtually one and the same thing in cases such as the cultivation of cereals. A more efficient means of harnessing energy is also a greater magnitude of energy—larger ears of corn, for example.

We may distinguish, therefore, two classes of means of harnessing and expending energy: biological and mechanical. In the latter, instrumental means and energy are easily distinguished. The quality of the ax does not affect the amount of energy offered by the woodsman; the engine neither adds to nor subtracts from the amount of coal burned by it. But as plants or animals become more efficient means of controlling energy, the amount of energy varies also. We may distinguish the two aspects in logical analysis of course, but in actuality they are inseparable.

We may summarize our discussion of energy and tools in the following law of cultural development: *culture advances as the amount of energy harnessed per capita per year increases, or as the efficiency or economy of the means of controlling energy is increased, or both*.[34] Progress was due almost wholly to increase of efficiency or economy of mechanical means in the first stage of cultural development. In subsequent eras development has come from both sources.

It must not be assumed, however, that these two factors, energy and mechanical means, are equally significant merely because both play a part in cultural evolution and progress. The energy factor is much more fundamental and important. The fact that energy is of no significance as a culture builder without mechanical means of expression in no way invalidates this evaluation. If energy is useless without mechanical contrivances, the latter are dead without energy. Furthermore, no amount of addition to, or improvement of, mechanical means can advance culture beyond a certain point so long as the energy factor remains unchanged. Culture would retrogress, even if its tools and machines were

---

[34] "... Progress of technical science is characterized by the fact: first, that more and more energy is utilized for human purposes, and secondly, that the transformation of the raw energies into useful forms of energy is attended by ever-increasing efficiency." *Ibid.* Ostwald is here speaking of technical science. But if cultural development as a whole rests upon and is determined by technological advance, what he says here would apply to the evolution of culture in its entirety.

perfect—and precisely because they were perfect—if the amount of energy harnessed per capita per year were diminished. On the other hand, an increase in amount of energy harnessed will not only carry culture forward because of this increase but will foster mechanical improvement as well. Mechanical instruments are indeed essential. But they are merely the vehicle, the means, the scaffolding, the skeleton; energy is the dynamic, living force that animates cultural systems and develops them to higher levels and forms.

Chapter 3 THE NATURE OF
SOCIAL ORGANIZATION

Social organization is but a particular form of organization in general. Organization is an attribute of reality wherever it confronts us. It is the task of science to render the world intelligible to us. This means explaining how things are arranged or put together, how events are related to one another, and how they behave. In other words, it is the business of science to describe and explain the structure and function of things and events whatever they may be. Structure and function are, of course, closely related; they are merely complementary aspects, static and dynamic, of a single phenomenon. The word "organization" embraces both of these aspects, although it emphasizes structure perhaps more than function. But since we cannot fully understand a formal arrangement of parts without knowing how they are related to each other functionally, the term organization may be taken to include both. One might say, therefore, that the subject matter of science is organization.

There are, of course, various kinds of organization: cosmic, galactic, stellar, planetary, molecular, atomic, protozoan (unicellular organisms), metazoan (multicellular organisms), and social (systems composed of a number of living organisms). Or we might put the matter in another way and say that there are physical, biological, and social types of organization. The first category would embrace all forms of organization of non-living matter; the second, the various organizations of matter into living beings; and the third, the social, would contain the arrangement and relationships of living beings to one another. The study of social organization is therefore merely a portion of scientific inquiry taken as a whole; it is that portion of science which is concerned with the interrelationship of living beings.

Social organization is the general category of which *human* social organization is but a particular manifestation. If we are to understand the particular, we must also understand the universal; we must discover principles common to all social systems. When we have done this we shall be in a position to see how these principles operate in human social systems.

58

One living being is related to another. We can think of all these relationships, past, present, and future, as constituting a single system. We actually do this in the theory of biologic evolution in which all individuals and all species are considered as being related to one another in a single web of life. This unity of relationship is, it must be noted, social as well as biological. A science of social organization comprehensive enough to include all living beings (on this planet, at least) would, however, be so general as to have relatively little value. But it is well to take this view of social organization occasionally, for the sake of perspective.

A practical, as distinguished from a purely theoretical, interest in interrelationships between living beings would, however, go far beyond the scope of a single species. We are often confronted by a social system which includes a number of species, genera, or families. There are many such systems in the lower-animal and plant worlds in which one species is related to another as enemy, host, food, means of propagation, and so on. The so-called food chains, in which species A feeds on species B, which in turn is dependent upon species C for existence, and so on, are examples of multiple-species social systems. Man is always and everywhere a member of a social system embracing other species, for whether he is a hunter, fisher, gatherer of wild plants, pastoralist, agriculturalist, or urban industrialist, he has relations with other species that are socially significant. Man's exploitation of plant and animal resources of nature has often been quite as significant for these various species as for himself. Since Paleolithic times he has been a powerful factor of selection and development, on the one hand, and of destruction, on the other; the pastoral and agricultural arts are the specific forms assumed by these relationships. To give a concrete example: a pastoral tribe, their sheep, the plants they feed upon, the beasts of prey who attack the flocks, domestic dogs as auxiliary defense, not to mention the lice on the shepherds, the fleas on the dogs, and ticks on the sheep, constitute a social system in which each species plays a part. An agricultural people having draft animals to draw plows, plant food for both man and beast, food and clothing supplied from livestock and fields fertilized with their dung, is another commonplace but important form of multiple-species social system.

Turning to social systems located within the boundaries of a single species, we note that there may be only one kind of system within a species, or there may be several. A social system may be fairly rigid and constant, or it may be flexible and given to change. Social relations may be frequent, intimate, and intense, or they may be occasional and feeble. They may be perpetuated by the mechanisms of biologic heredity, or they may be continued by the neurosensory process of conditioning or by verbal tradition. The specific forms of social systems among plants, fish, reptiles, insects, birds, carnivores, primates, and so on, are of course exceedingly numerous and almost infinitely varied. Yet all constitute a single and distinct class: systems of relationships among living beings. We should therefore be able to discover principles common to all forms within this class.

This we can readily do. *Organization* is a network of things and the relationships obtaining among them. *Social* organization is the subclass of organization that is concerned with living beings in particular; in short, it is simply a network of relations obtaining between living material bodies.

Social organization will therefore be distinguished from other forms of organization by the same characteristics that distinguish living systems from nonliving material bodies. We discover the nature of social organization in the properties peculiar to living beings. What factors, then, distinguish, at one and the same time, the living from the inanimate, and *social* organization from all other forms?

A living material body must do certain things if it is to maintain itself *as* a living thing. It must obtain and digest food; it must have a certain amount of protection from the elements; and it must defend itself from its enemies. And if the species is to be perpetuated, there must be reproduction of individuals. These, then, are the distinctive characteristics of living material bodies: nutrition, reproduction, and protection. Social organization, therefore, is a network of relations between living material bodies the function of which is to maintain and perpetuate their status *as* living beings through the processes of nutrition, protection, and reproduction. Any social system is determined by these three coordinates: the way in which its constituent members nourish themselves; the way in which they protect themselves from the elements and defend themselves from their enemies; and the way in which they perpetuate their kind. These are the determinants of social organization. Let us consider a few examples.

Let us return to the shepherds–herds–plants–beasts-of-prey–dogs–lice–ticks social system that we alluded to earlier. What are the determinants of this system? They are not hard to discover. The shepherds subsist on their herds; the herds feed upon grass; the wild beasts attack the herds; the shepherds and the dogs defend them; the lice and ticks feed upon their hosts; etc. Thus they are all related to each other in terms of subsistence or of offense-defense. Being composed of various kinds of animals, the social system is of course perpetuated by the reproductive processes in each of the several species.

In contrast with the above example, there are social systems composed of members of more than one species in which the mode of reproduction, rather than mode of subsistence, is the most significant determinant. The eggs of the hookworm hatch, the larvae develop, in the bodies of men. The life cycle of cluster flies requires the participation of earthworms. Here we have instances of social systems in which the mode of reproduction is the most significant of the three determinants. Some birds lay their eggs in the nests of other birds, allowing the latter to hatch and feed the young. Reproduction and nutrition are most significant here.

We come, therefore, to the following generalization: *any social system is determined by the three determinants of nutrition, protection or defense, and reproduction: $N \times D \times R \rightarrow S$.* These factors are not always of equal magnitude and influence. On the contrary, they may and do vary widely. In one system, the factor of nutrition may be the most significant or powerful determinant; in another, it may be protection or reproduction. Or there may be other kinds of combinations. As it is with systems embracing two or more species, so with systems within a single species. Let us illustrate with a few examples.

The social organization of wild ducks is different from that of eagles. The eagle, being a predatory bird, must live a rather solitary life. The nature and distribution of its food does not make group life possible. Ducks live in flocks because of the nature of their food supply and for mutual aid, each bird finding some safety and protection in the flock. So it is with tigers and bison. The beast of prey lives alone or in small groups, the bison is gregarious like the grass upon which he feeds, and the herd provides protection for its members.

The operation of the factors of nutrition and reproduction as determinants of social organization is well exemplified in the case of birds:

"Some birds are solitary in their mode of life, others tolerant, and others more or less sociable. With many species sociability is at its lowest ebb during the breeding season, when the flocks or parties break up and settle in pairs, dispersed over the country. But with others, particularly sea-birds, the reverse holds good; their scattered members rally from all directions to particular points where they breed in massed colonies, often so dense that they hardly leave room to tread. These are not simply manifestations of a communist or an individualist temperament; they are solutions of the economic problem which, in one form or another, every species has to meet. This is well illustrated by the case of finches which live on seeds themselves, but feed their young entirely upon insects. In winter they are sociable, living in mixed flocks; in spring a revolution takes place, and they are found everywhere in pairs, occupying compact territories from which all others of their kind are jealously excluded. Their character has not changed its mould, but the new economic problem of rearing a delicate brood consuming its own weight in small insects every day has temporarily imposed upon the species a different manner of life.

"Once this pressure is relaxed the social instincts reassert themselves, and the family parties, renouncing a fixed territory, begin to drift together into flocks again. . . .

"The bird population and the manner in which it is distributed at various seasons are therefore controlled within fairly narrow limits by the *amount of suitable food available* and the *periodic demand for nesting sites*" [italics supplied].[1]

Among the so-called social insects the anatomy of sex and reproduction comes to the fore. Males, females, and neuters constitute *social*, as well as *sex*, classes. These classes are also related to subsistence and defense. The social life of a species may have two quite different forms of organization, depending upon the exercise or quiescence of the sexual functions. Some species live in herds for the greater part of the year. But during the breeding season, the herd breaks up into family groups. This is the case with the northern fur seal, for example:

"During a great part of the year these seals lead a pelagic existence, their attention given over to the capture of fish. Sexual activities at sea are impossible, as mating can not take place in the water. In May and early June the males . . . arrive at the Pribyloff Islands, where each individual takes up a position on the breeding grounds and fiercely defends it against his rivals, there to await the coming of the females. About the middle of June the females begin to appear." [2]

The males fight fiercely among themselves, first for the most suitable breeding grounds, and later for the cows themselves. Naturally the most powerful and aggressive males secure the best sites and the most mates. Some males win as many as fifty mates, though the average is fifteen to twenty. Others are able to secure only one or two, and some, no doubt, are unable to obtain a mate at all.

This is an extremely interesting example in which the role of each of the three determinants of social organization is revealed with singular clarity. First we have the herd form in which the factors of nutrition and mutual protection are dominant, the sexual factor being quiescent. The awakening and upsurge of the sexual force transforms their social life: the herd breaks up into family groups. Sexual activity draws male and female together, repels male from male. Aggression and defense inject a selective factor into the reproductive process; the more powerful and aggressive males beget the most offspring. The family groups are polygynous rather than polyandrous because the male is more powerful than the female and therefore dominates the process of mate selection.

[1] E. M. Nicholson, "Birds," *Encyclopaedia Britannica*, 14th ed., vol. 3, 1929, pp. 631–632. By permission of Encyclopaedia Britannica, Inc., Chicago.
[2] Gerrit S. Miller, Jr., "The Primate Basis of Human Sexual Behavior," *The Quarterly Review of Biology*, vol. 6, p. 382, December, 1931.

As the sexual factor was dormant in the herd, so is the nutritional factor negligible during the breeding season. The abstinence and endurance of the bulls are truly remarkable:

"[They] abstain entirely from food of any kind, or water, for three months at least; and a few of them actually stay out four months, in total abstinence, before going back into the water for the first time after 'hauling up' in May; they then return as so many bony shadows of what they were only a few months anteriorly; covered with wounds, abject and spiritless, they laboriously crawl back to the sea to renew a fresh lease of life." [3]

Thus the social life of this species varies as the coordinates of social organization vary. The herd form of organization is the expression of the subsistence factor primarily, supplemented by mutual protection; the sexual factor is insignificant. The periodic ascendancy and dominance of sex produces family organization, with fighting and male dominance determining the size and composition of the family. With the ascendance of the sexual factor, that of nutrition subsides.

As it is with other animals, so it is with man. But before we discuss the social organization of this species, let us consider plant life for a moment. It is not customary, perhaps, to think of trees, grass, and shrubs as having social life.[4] But if by social organization we mean relations between living beings—and if we do not include *all* living species, where and with what justification shall we draw the line?—then we must include plant life.

We find that our theory applies equally well to plants: the form of social organization will be determined by the way in which plants nourish, protect, and reproduce themselves. Some plants reproduce in one way, some in another. In some species new plants are formed by the division of bulbs underground. In others, seeds are carried far afield by the winds or by other methods. The social relations between plants thus vary from species to species. The sexual structure and behavior of plants, the methods of pollination, etc., may also be significant in determining social relations. The mode of subsistence, too, is sometimes noteworthy. Some plants get their food from the ground, others from the water, and still others are parasitic on other plants. Most plants are

[3] *Ibid.*, quoting from Elliott, *The Habits of the Fur-seal*, 1884.
[4] See, however, George D. Fuller and Henry S. Conard (trans. and eds.), *Plant Sociology: The Study of Plant Communities*, 1932, a translation of *Pflanzensoziologie*, by Josias Braun-Blanquet. Frederic E. Clements discusses plant communities in such terms as "cooperation," "competition," "integration," "domination," "subordination," "families," and even "clans." "Social Origins and Processes among Plants," chap. 2, *A Handbook of Social Psychology*, Carl A. Murchison (ed.), 1935. See also Theodor Just, *Plant and Animal Communities*, 1939, and John E. Weaver and Frederic E. Clements, *Plant Ecology*, 2d ed., 1938.

sedentary, but some are nomadic, wandering about as currents of the water in which they live carry them. And plants may provide each other protection and shelter by certain forms of association. Thus our theory of social organization is as applicable to plant forms of life as to animal forms. Let us now return to man, or more properly, the order of Primates.

Primates are distinguished among mammals by the absence of a rutting season.[5] Among other placental mammals, there are seasons or periods of heat during which the sexual forces become active; at other times they are quiescent. Among monkeys, apes, and men, however, the sexual forces are continuously active, although not with uniform intensity. This variation in sexual function among mammals produces a corresponding variation in social organization. Among species having a rutting season, or periods of heat, there is a close attachment between male and female only during the season or period; at other times association is indifferent to sex. Pairing, or family groups, among nonprimate mammals is therefore only occasional; most of the time this type of organization is lacking, and the herd, pack, or other type of grouping prevails. We have a good example of this in the seals previously noted. The same situation is found, too, among cattle, deer, and other species.

Among primates, however, the situation is different. Since the sexual forces are continuously operative, the two sexes are drawn and held together. The family group becomes a permanent social form among primates.[6] The form of the family may vary; a male may have only one mate, or he may have several. Or he may have none if he is unable to win and keep one in competition with his fellows, in which case he constitutes a distinct element in the social configuration: the celibate male, an animal with desire but without the means of gratifying it. He becomes, therefore, a hanger-on of one family group or another, a sexual satellite, ever ready to seize an opportunity for surreptitious gratification or to challenge the monopoly of a mated male. He thus constitutes an ever-present threat to the solidarity of a specific family group, though not to family organization itself.

While variations of social organization among primates exist, it is pos-

[5] Cf. S. Zuckerman, *The Social Life of Monkeys and Apes*, 1932, pp. 51, 146-147.

[6] Freud has some keen observations on sex and social organization in *Civilization and Its Discontents*, Jonathan Cape, Ltd., London, 1930, pp. 65-66: "Even earlier, in his ape-like prehistory, man had adopted the habit of forming families.... One may suppose that the founding of families was in some way connected with the period when the need for genital satisfaction, no longer appearing like an occasional guest who turns up suddenly and then vanishes without letting one hear anything of him for long intervals, had settled down with each man like a permanent lodger. When this happened, the male acquired a motive for keeping the female, or rather, his sexual objects, near him; while the female, who wanted not to be separated from her helpless young, in their interests, too, had to stay by the stronger male."

sible to generalize as follows: Primates live in groups, each of which has its own territory through which it habitually roams and forages and which it endeavors to defend against aggressors and trespassers. The size of the local group varies, tending to be larger among the monkeys, smaller among the apes. Differentiation of social structure can be discerned within the local group: it is composed of family groups and unattached males. The family consists of one adult male, his mate or mates, and their off-spring. We can explain all features of their social organization in terms of the three determinants of social organization: nutrition, protection (offense-defense), and reproduction.

A group of primates confines itself to a certain locality instead of ever exploring new territory. "Territoriality, or the residence of a primate group within well-defined territorial limits," writes Hooton, "has been established for howler monkeys, red spider monkeys, various baboons, gibbons, and, in all probability, orang-utans. The list is restricted by the number of field studies made. It is quite possible that nearly all primate genera share this habit of remaining within a certain area which they regard as their own and from which they attempt to expel trespassers, especially those belonging to their own species."[7] The reasons for this are fairly clear: Familiarity with one's surroundings breeds confidence and a sense of security. Strange terrain makes one apprehensive; no one knows what dangers might lurk there. Furthermore, one can forage more efficiently in familiar surroundings; not only is the actual task of food getting rendered more efficient by an acquaintance with the details of the locality, but one needs to spend less time on the lookout for danger.[8] Hence the local-group character of primate society.

The number of individuals in the local group will be determined by the mode of subsistence and by activities of offense and defense. If the food supply is abundant and is concentrated in space, the local group will tend to be large. If, however, the food supply is meager and is thinly distributed in space, the group will tend to be small. Other factors remaining constant, a group cannot increase in numbers beyond a certain point without reducing the amount of food per capita per unit of distance traveled in foraging. In short, density of population is a function of concentration of food supply. The size of the animal also is a factor of some significance. A small animal naturally requires less food than a

[7] E. A. Hooton, *Man's Poor Relations*, Garden City Books, New York, 1942, p. 331. See also C. R. Carpenter, who concludes that "territorialism of groups would seem to be a primitive basic characteristic of non-human primate groupings...." "Societies of Monkeys and Apes," in *Levels of Integration in Biological and Social Systems*, Robert Redfield (ed.), Biological Symposia, vol. 8, Lancaster, Pa., 1942, p. 190.

[8] When a "clan" of howler monkeys gets "out to the edge of its territory [while wandering about, foraging], it becomes slowed up by unfamiliarity with the roads, and a good deal of milling about and frustration results, so that it eventually turns back to the known pathways and haunts." Hooton, *op. cit.*, p. 239.

large one. Other factors being constant, a given food supply will nourish a greater number of small animals than large ones. Size of local groups will tend,[9] therefore, to vary inversely with the size of the individual member of the species; troops of monkeys tend to contain more members than groups of anthropoid apes.

The size of the local group is conditioned, too, by factors of defense and offense. An individual's safety and security are dependent to a certain extent upon the other members of his group who may observe signs of danger, utter cries of warning, or attack or repel an enemy. The security of individuals and the survival of groups in the struggle for existence will depend, therefore, upon the size of the group, and to the extent that other factors permit, the group will tend to assume that size which will provide the greatest chance of survival. Since offense and defense are conditioned by the size and fighting abilities of the species and by their mode of life in the trees or on the ground, these factors also affect the size of the local group. Thus we see that the size of the local group is a natural phenomenon and is regulated by natural forces which can be evaluated. In this respect it is no different from a hailstone.

Turning now to the *internal structure* of the local group, we shall show how this, too, in every detail, is determined by the factors of nutrition, reproduction, and offense-defense.

The local group of subhuman primates is composed, as we have seen, of families, and perhaps some adult males without mates. The permanent family form is the result of continuous attraction between the sexes. The intimate social relation between mother and offspring is initiated by the factor of reproduction and continued by those of nutrition and protection. The social relation between father and offspring is relatively insignificant, but such a tie does exist; it is merely incidental to his sexual relationship to their mother. The number of mates possessed by a male and, correspondingly, the number of celibate males are determined by their respective aggressive-defensive abilities: the more powerful males get the most mates; the weaker, one or none at all. Whether the family group tends toward polygyny or monogamy depends upon the relative size, strength, and aggressiveness of the sexes. If the male is more powerful and fierce than the female, as in the case of the baboon, he will dominate the mating process and the family group will tend toward polygyny. If, however, the sexes are about equal in size and aggressive-

---

[9] The reader will please note that we say "other factors being constant," "will tend," etc. "Other factors" are not always constant; the "tendency" of factor p to produce effect q may be offset by another factor or factors. But this does not mean that we cannot, by means of evidence and logical analysis, isolate factors and evaluate them singly, with the full realization that in most, if not all, actual situations, more than one factor is operative.

ness, as they appear to be in the gibbon, they would play approximately equal roles in the selection and acquisition of mates and the family would tend to be monogamous. If the female were the dominant sex, the family would tend to be polyandrous. We know of no primate species where this exists, but our theory enables us to say what the family organization of such a species would be like if it did exist.

Thus we see that primate social organization in all its variations and details, from the size and function of the local, territorial group to the structure and composition of the family group, is determined by the factors of subsistence, offense-defense, and reproduction and is to be explained in these terms.

We turn now to a particular primate species, *Homo sapiens*.[10] If our theory is sound so far, we must begin our survey of human social organization with the premise that all forms of human society are determined by the factors of subsistence, reproduction, and protection; obviously, what is true of all primate species must be true of each one. Secondly, we must assume that any characteristics of social organization that are distinctively human and peculiar to *Homo sapiens* are due to distinctive and peculiar ways in which the human primate carries on the activities of subsistence, reproduction, and offense-defense. This assumption is merely a corollary of our major premise.

Before turning to behavior peculiar to man, we should note that the biological factor of reproduction is a constant in the human species, and therefore it may be eliminated from our consideration of differences of social organization within this species. This does not mean that the factor of reproduction is not one of the determinants of human social organization in general. It is a determinant, and an important one in this species as in all other forms of life. The continuous and mutual attraction between the sexes, which is the initial stage of the process of reproduction, results in a continuous union between male and female, and consequently establishes a permanent family form. This fact alone, as we shall see in the next chapter, is sufficient to negate the theory, once widely held, that man began his career as a human being in a condition of promiscuity, or the hypothesis that in an early stage of human social evolution the ties between mothers and children were the only significant social relationships.

Anatomically, physiologically, and psychologically (using this term to designate innate, biologically determined qualities or processes), all peoples are alike sexually. Therefore we cannot account for differences

[10] We are not interested here in the question of genera or species of man other than *Homo sapiens*, because what we have to say about one species would be applicable to all.

of social organization among the various groups of mankind in terms of this constant. Contraception, abortion, infanticide, castration, infibulation, and celibacy are practiced by one people or another. But these practices are culture traits and should not be confused with the biological process of reproduction. Customs such as these condition the operation of this biological process and affect the results, but they do not alter its nature. There are no differences of social organization within the human species that we can attribute to differences in the biological process, or mode, of reproduction. We have therefore but two determinants, rather than three, to reckon with in accounting for different forms of human social organization. These factors are subsistence and offense-defense.

The concept of subsistence may be expanded to include materials for clothing, ornaments, tools, utensils, etc., as well as food; in short, all materials appropriated from nature to satisfy human needs. "Mode of subsistence" may well embrace magical means employed to secure food; magic and ritual constitute a pseudo technology. Offense and defense includes intrasocietal enemies, such as witches and traitors, as well as foreign foes. And here too, supernatural means of offense and defense should be included.

Environment, or natural habitat, plays the same role with regard to social organization as it does to culture in general: particular social systems are influenced by particular habitats; but in a consideration of human social systems in general, the factor of habitat may be reduced to a constant.

In a consideration of variations of human social systems in general, therefore, we need to consider only two variables: subsistence and offense-defense. When dealing with particular social systems we must take habitats into account also. But in any problem involving merely variations of human social organization, the biological factor of reproduction is irrelevant, being a constant.

As in our previous discussion of the role of technology in cultural systems (Chapter 1, "Man and Culture"), we may not be able in every instance to explain every detail of any given human social system in terms of subsistence, offense-defense, and habitat. Each of these factors is a complex variable. A social system as we observe it may show the effects of influences no longer operative, and we may have no history of the culture. We may not know what cultural influences it has been exposed to in the past, and so on. In a given situation, therefore, we may not be able to explain every feature of social organization in terms of these three determinants. But these factors, plus that of historical-cultural influence, will take us as far as it is possible for us to go in the direction of scientific explanation.

Chapter 4 THE TRANSITION FROM ANTHROPOID SOCIETY TO HUMAN SOCIETY

With the decline of Christian theology with its drama of the creation, science undertook to provide its own account of the origin and evolution of man and human society. Several outstanding men of the latter half of the nineteenth century made contributions toward this end. In the field of social evolution, J. J. Bachofen and John F. McLennan developed independently theories of social evolution in which mankind was assumed to have begun its career in a condition of promiscuity, out of which emerged the institutions of mother right, followed eventually by father right and monogamy.

Herbert Spencer did not "think that even in prehistoric times, promiscuity was checked by the establishment of individual connections, prompted by men's likings and maintained against other men by force.".[1] With regard to the family in particular, however, he wrote: [2]

"We have thus to begin with a state in which the family, as we understand it, can scarcely be said to exist. In the loose groups of men first formed, there is no established order of any kind: everything is indefinite, unsettled. In either case there are no guides save the passions of the moment, checked only by fears of consequences."

In the United States, Lewis H. Morgan developed a rather elaborate theory of social evolution in which mankind was supposed to have begun its career in a condition of virtual chaos and promiscuity, and subsequently to have developed through various stages of group marriage until monogamy was achieved.

The theory of primordial promiscuity had considerable vogue in the latter decades of the nineteenth century, but it did not meet with universal approval by any means. Darwin was willing to admit that "almost

[1] Herbert Spencer, "Promiscuity," *Principles of Sociology*, vol. 1, D. Appleton & Co., New York, 1885, pp. 662, 665.
[2] *Ibid.*, p. 632.

promiscuous or very loose intercourse was once extremely common throughout the world." But considering "what we know of the jealousy of all male quadrupeds," he felt "that [completely] promiscuous intercourse in a state of nature is extremely improbable." Turning to man in particular, he concluded:

"Therefore, looking far enough back in the stream of time, and judging from the social habits of man as he now exists, the most probable view is that he aboriginally lived in small communities, each with a single wife, or if powerful with several, whom he jealously guarded against all other men." [3]

The English anthropologist Tylor took a similar view in 1881:

"Mankind can never have lived as a mere struggling crowd, each for himself. Society is always made up of families or households bound together by kindly ties, controlled by rules of marriage and the duties of parent and child." [4]

Thus, as the nineteenth century drew to a close, there were three theories of social evolution in the field: (1) from promiscuity through group marriage to monogamy, of which Morgan was the principal champion; (2) the family from the very beginning, espoused by Darwin and Tylor; and (3) the "matriarchate," of Bachofen and McLennan, revived in 1927 by Robert Briffault in *The Mothers*. No one theory was able to win out over the others because the facts necessary to establish one and eliminate the others were not available.

Before one of these theories could be established—or a new one formulated—an important turn of events took place in anthropological circles: a vigorous reaction against evolutionist theory set in. In America, this movement was led by Franz Boas. He and his students came to the conclusion that it was futile and senseless to try to discover the original condition of human society—or, in fact, to concern one's self with the general problem of cultural origins at all.[5]

Margaret Mead has expressed the point of view of the Boas school on the question of human social origins in a positive statement in the *Encyclopaedia of the Social Sciences:* [6]

---

[3] Charles Darwin, *The Descent of Man*, 2d ed., vol. 2, J. A. Hill and Co., New York, 1904, p. 295.

[4] E. B. Tylor, *Anthropology*, 1881, p. 402.

[5] M. J. Herskovits has been perhaps the most articulate spokesman of this point of view. "Modern anthropology," he says, "has given over the search for 'origins' since the time when it became recognized that, except as archaeological materials can be dug out of the ground, the beginnings of any phase of human activity cannot be scientifically established." *The Economic Life of Primitive Peoples*, Alfred A. Knopf, Inc., New York, 1940, p. 34. See also his "Man, the Speaking Animal," *Sigma Xi Quarterly*, vol. 21, pp. 73, 75, 1933.

[6] Margaret Mead, "Family, Primitive," in *Encyclopaedia of the Social Sciences*, The Macmillan Company, New York, 1931.

"All of these attempts to reconstruct the earlier forms of organization of the family remain at best only elaborate hypotheses. Contemporary refutations of these hypotheses rest upon criticisms of the evolutionary position with its arbitrary postulation of stages and upon a methodological refusal to admit the discussion of a question upon which *there is not and cannot be any valid evidence* [italics supplied]."

The Functionalist schools likewise have repudiated the quest of origins. Thus, Radcliffe-Brown asserts that "if we are to make it [i.e., comparative sociology] the science it should be, we must reject resolutely all attempts to conjecture the origin of any institution or element of culture ...the newer anthropology rejects...all the theories of origins...." [7] He has expressed this point of view repeatedly.[8] Similarly, Malinowski and some of his students have spoken disparagingly of a search for cultural origins, using such phrases as "conjectural reconstructions" and "the limbo of untrammeled conjecture." [9]

This is a rather curious position for any science—or any organized endeavor calling itself a science—to take. Science claims for itself a free and a full field, as far as its eyes can see and as far as its hands can reach. But where, except in certain schools of cultural anthropology, has science attempted to cut itself off from such an endeavor? Certainly not in astronomy, geology, or biology. Scientists unhesitatingly tackle such problems as the origin of galaxies, stars, planetary systems, and life in general and in its many orders, genera, and species. If the origin of the earth some two billion years ago, or the origin of life untold millions of years ago, can be and is a proper problem for science, why not the origin of culture a mere million years ago?

The answer to this question by members of the Boas and the Functionalist schools is that this particular search for origins is futile; they cannot ever be found. As Margaret Mead has said flatly, it is a question "upon which there is not and cannot be any valid evidence." But we recall the wise words of Darwin on this point:

"It has often and confidently been asserted that man's origin can never be known; but ignorance more frequently begets confidence than does knowledge: it is those who know little, and not those who know much, who so positively assert that this or that problem will never be solved by science." [10]

---

[7] A. R. Radcliffe-Brown, "The Present Position of Anthropological Studies," *Proceedings of the British Association for the Advancement of Science*, 1931, pp. 153-154.

[8] Cf. A. R. Radcliffe-Brown, "The Methods of Ethnology and Social Anthropology," *South African Journal of Science*, vol. 20, pp. 124-147, 1923, especially pp. 137-139, and "The Study of Kinship Systems," *Journal of the Royal Anthropological Institute*, vol. 71, p. 1, 1941.

[9] Cf. B. Malinowski, "Social Anthropology," in *Encyclopaedia Britannica*, 14th ed., 1929, p. 864; also Raymond Firth, "Economics, Primitive," in *ibid*.

[10] Introduction to the second edition of *The Descent of Man*, 1904.

We unhesitatingly elect to follow Darwin here rather than the "positive assertions" of Mead and others of the schools of Boas, Radcliffe-Brown, and Malinowski. We shall therefore take up again the task of formulating a scientifically adequate theory that will describe the original social condition of man.

The opponents of the quest-for-culture origins use such terms as "conjecture," "unverifiable," and "sheer speculation." They might—but we recall no instance at the moment—have used the term *inference* also. An inference is a judgment based upon an observation—or another judgment. Thus, I excavate chipped-stone implements but no potsherds, and infer a type of culture; or I know that a people subsisted wholly upon wild foods, and infer a type of society. Hypotheses are built up with inferences. Hypotheses are checked—verified, modified, or rejected—by further observations. If a hypothesis can accommodate a given body of data and is not incompatible with any known fact, and if, moreover, it illuminates the data in question and renders them intelligible, it does about all that science requires.

In anthropology we have an enormous amount of data—real things and events and accurate observations and records of them—to work with. We have a paleontological record of the evolution of primates which, though incomplete, is substantial and informative. We know a great deal about the comparative embryology, anatomy, and physiology of monkeys, apes, and men. We have an archaeological record of cultural evolution which, though partial and incomplete, can serve as a sound basis for many valid inferences. Finally, we have numerous ethnographic accounts of exceedingly simple cultures whose societies are so primitive that they can have advanced but little beyond the earliest stage of human social evolution. We thus have a great amount of data from four sources—paleontology, comparative biology, archaeology, and ethnology—which will provide a solid foundation for valid inference and fruitful theory.

We can construct a theory of the origin of human society—or more specifically, of the transformation of anthropoid society, the society of man's immediate prehuman ancestors, into human social organization—in the following way and in these steps: (1) We know what the social organization of subhuman primates is like; the general pattern of this organization was set forth in the preceding chapter, "The Nature of Social Organization." (2) We are justified in believing that man's immediate prehuman ancestors conformed to this general primate pattern because of the fundamental similarity—anatomical and physiological—between man and other primates. Therefore we have a valid conception of what the social organization of man's prehuman ancestors was like. (3) We know what it is that distinguishes man from other primates from the standpoint of behavior: the use of symbols and the symbol-based use of tools. (4) Therefore the transition from anthropoid society to human society, the transformation of the social organization of man's prehuman forebears into human social organization, was effected by the operation of symbols and tools upon anthropoid social organization. We can trace this transformation in considerable detail by deducing the consequences of symboling and tool using upon social organization.

The general pattern of prehuman primate social organization may be summarized briefly as follows: It consisted of (1) local, territorial groups which were, in turn, composed of (2) family groups, i.e., an adult male who has one or more mates and their immature offspring. In species where the male is the dominant sex—and this will include the human species—some adult males have more than one mate while others have none, being unable to obtain and keep one in the physical struggle for mates. Now let us see what effect the use of symbols and tools will have upon this type of social organization.

The first effect will be a pronounced trend toward monogamy.

The social organization of man's immediate prehuman ancestors was marked by polygyny because, as we have already seen (p. 66), the male was the dominant sex. The mating process was therefore dominated by males. In the mating process, i.e., in the struggle among males for mates, the stronger and more aggressive males would obtain more than one mate, leaving some of the weaker males with none at all.

The desire for mates, for sexual satisfaction, is, however, felt by all males alike. But in a society and in a mating process based upon brute force, the desires of the weaker males are denied. The introjection of symbols—articulate speech—and tools into this process transforms it and makes possible an equal distribution of mates. This is the way it came about.

Why did not two or three celibate males cooperate in opposing one of their polygynous fellows? They could overpower him and divide his mates among themselves. Nothing of this sort took place in baboon society, according to Zuckerman. "There is no evidence," he says, that a fight "begins as a concerted attack of unmated males upon the harem" of a powerful and aggressive male; as a matter of fact, "there is no concerted action or strategy about their" activities at all.[11]

The reason for lack of cooperation is plain: lack of a suitable means to communicate the requisite idea. Cooperation among subhuman primates is possible upon an elementary conceptual level and to a limited extent. One ape can communicate a simple idea to another by means of ges-

[11] S. Zuckerman, *The Social Life of Monkeys and Apes*, K. Paul, Trench, Trubner & Co., Ltd., London, 1932, pp. 253–254.

tures, or signs, but anything more complicated than this is impossible for them. Even such simple ideas as "You go around the hill that way while I go around this way and we will meet on the other side," or "Tomorrow morning when the keeper comes through the gate you fall down and pretend you are sick," are far beyond the possibilities of any subhuman primate.

With the emergence of the ability to symbol and the development of articulate speech and language, however, the ability to communicate ideas becomes almost unlimited. When certain anthropoids had become human and had acquired speech, the weaker, celibate males could form a plan, communicate it to one another, and execute it cooperatively. Together they could overpower the powerful, polgynous male in a single struggle, or, one by one, they could stand watch over him until he fell asleep and then despatch him. In any event, articulate speech made versatile and extensive cooperation possible, and cooperation led toward a uniform distribution of mates.

It might be argued that the stronger males could cooperate with one another too, and thus maintain their advantage, but this reasoning is unsound. They would derive no advantage from such cooperation because they are, by the very nature of the situation, rivals. They do not have common interests; on the contrary, each wants as many mates as he can get at the expense of his fellows. Consequently there could be only competition among the strong. But with the weak it would be different. They have interests in common. All want mates; they have a common foe. By united opposition to the aggressor they could all gain their ends.

The human use of tools, i.e., tools, symbols, and concepts integrated into a single mind-body process,[12] also tended to break up polgynous families and to bring about an equal distribution of mates.

Apes, as we have noted earlier, use tools, but the process of their use is sporadic and occasional. The tool does not enter the psychic life of the ape as deeply as it does with man. To the ape the tool is never more than an accessory, a foreign object. Man, on the other hand, so incorporates tools into his life, psychically as well as mechanically, that they become *inner* realities to him as well as things in the external world. Now the significant thing about tools in our present discussion is that a weapon can make a small and weak individual the equal of a large and powerful one. Among tool-using men, therefore, mere brute force loses much of its advantage: little David can lay low the big Goliath. So in the competition for mates the little man derives an advantage from weapons that the anthropoid cannot secure.[13] By arming himself

---

[12] See our previous discussion of this point in Chapter 1, "Man and Culture," p. 7.
[13] Apes use tools with skill and versatility, but not in fighting. As Kroeber puts it: "Sticks are brandished threateningly in play combat. But let a chimpanzee lose his

the little man can actually "add cubits to his stature." The strong can arm themselves, too, but when one fights with slings, spears, blowguns and poisoned darts, bows and arrows and pistols, superiority of size and strength loses much, if not all, of its advantage. The little fellow can kill the strongest man with a knife, sling, or poisoned dart. The weapon tends to make all men equal.[14]

One of the objections raised against the theory of the original promiscuous horde, out of which various forms of the family evolved, until finally the stage of monogamy was attained, was that many of the most primitive peoples of the world are monogamous and that polygamy flourishes only in more advanced cultures. According to the theory of primordial promiscuity the reverse should be true: "group marriage" or polygamy should prevail on lower cultural levels, with monogamous tendencies appearing late and growing slowly as culture advanced. But as Darwin pointed out long ago, "there are tribes standing almost at the bottom of the scale, which are strictly monogamous." [15] This observation has been confirmed by subsequent ethnographic investigation; it has been well established that many of the most primitive tribes known, such as the Veddas, the Andamanese, various groups of pygmies, etc., are monogamous.[16] This, however, is precisely what our theory calls for. Before man acquired culture in sufficient degree to influence his behavior, his sex unions tended to be polygynous. But after the faculty of speech had developed sufficiently to permit versatile communication of ideas, and consequently, cooperation, and after the use of tools had become traditional and effective, sexual unions became increasingly monogamous. It was only later, in higher stages of cultural development, that this equitable distribution of mates could be disturbed and polygamy established. Our theory, therefore, not only agrees with the evidence from the most primitive cultures known; it explains why they have monogamy rather than some other form of marriage.

We turn now to another extremely interesting and important aspect of the transformation of prehuman primate social organization into hu-

---

temper, and he drops his stick and plunges into attack with hands and teeth." A. L. Kroeber, "Sub-human Cultural Beginnings," *The Quarterly Review of Biology*, vol. 3, p. 336.

[14] A revolver or "six-shooter" is often called colloquially "the old equalizer" in certain strata in our society today.

[15] *The Descent of Man*, 2d ed., chap. 20, 1904.

[16] Cf. R. H. Lowie, "Anthropology and Law," in *The Social Sciences and Their Interrelations*, William F. Ogburn and A. Goldenweiser (eds.), p. 52; John M. Cooper, "The Early History of the Family," *Primitive Man*, vol. 3, pp. 58–59, 1930; M. J. Herskovits, "Man, the Speaking Animal," *Sigma Xi Quarterly*, vol. 21, p. 69, 1933.

man society. The subhuman primate family is a sex grouping; it was formed to provide sexual satisfaction and is maintained for this purpose, and this purpose alone. It has no economic functions. To be sure, the mother suckles her young and on occasion gives them food which she has foraged. But this is not a function of the *family*, but of the mother-child relationship. The male in the monkey or ape family has no economic functions. He does not provide either his mate or her offspring with food. On the contrary, he not infrequently deprives them of it, even snatching it out of the hands of a baby.

Neither does the simian family as such have any protective functions to speak of. A troop will defend itself against enemies upon occasion, but this is not done on a family basis. The male head of a family group might attack an intruder who threatened him and his mate, but he would do so as an act of self-defense, not as the head of a family. As a matter of fact, the male is sometimes aggressive and abusive toward his mate and her offspring, and the mother may be obliged to defend herself and her children against the aggressions of the father. There is defense against enemies, to be sure, among the lower primates, but it is a function of the individual or the local group rather than of the family.

Thus we see that of the three functions of social organization in general—food, sex, protection—the simian family has only one: that of sex. The family among the lower primates is a group formed by sexual attraction; its sole function is the gratification of the sexual appetite. In short, the prehuman family is a sex group.

When man acquired articulate speech and language a new way of life was made possible, namely, one of almost unlimited cooperation in all sorts of activities. We have already seen that the weaker males in simian society could not unite in opposition to the stronger in the competitive struggle for mates because they could not communicate the idea of concerted attack to one another. In most cases, no advantage could accrue from cooperative endeavor in foraging for food among the lower primates because of the nature of the mode of subsistence; it was as efficient for each to forage for himself as to work together even if they could. But even if there had been situations in which cooperation would have been advantageous, they could not have availed themselves of it save in the simplest of situations. Without speech, therefore, the lower primates were debarred from progress in the social organization of food getting; social evolution was rendered impossible in this sector.

With regard to protection and defense the situation among the subhuman primates is much the same: a minimum amount of cooperation within the local group, but an inability to advance beyond that minimum. One individual warns others of danger by uttering appropriate cries. Whether this is "true cooperation" or not depends, of course, upon one's definition; certainly it is no more than a most rudimentary form of the process. In attack and defense against enemies there is no plan, no working together. The stories of baboons posting some of their number as sentinels to warn others who are raiding a maize field of danger imply cooperation. But the observed facts—one or two baboons on the watch while the others feed—are susceptible to another, and more plausible, interpretation. Not all baboons are equally mature, experienced, prudent, or hungry. Some go readily to the fields to forage, while others lag warily behind, looking over the situation carefully before venturing farther. These are the so-called sentinels. There is further objection to the "sentinel" interpretation. How could baboons select and designate certain individuals to serve as sentinels? How could the will of the group be made known to the individuals? How could agreement be reached in this matter? Do individuals serve in rotation as sentinels? Are the sentinels fed by others in return for their services? How could an arrangement of this sort be effected without articulate speech?

Cooperation among the lower primates in food getting and offense and defense is of the simplest kind and extremely limited in extent. Furthermore, without speech it is impossible for them to advance beyond this elementary form. This is why social evolution is impossible for monkeys and apes. With man, however, the situation is different. Given articulate speech and language, the potentialities for cooperation are tremendously enlarged; in fact, they are virtually unlimited. We shall see how primordial man realized these potentialities.

Again let us recall that man is an animal and, like all other animals, is engaged in a life-and-death struggle for survival. The situation in which the first human beings found themselves was peculiar, if not unique. Compared with other animals, they were weak and defenseless. At almost every point they were inferior to many of their competitors in the Darwinian struggle. They had lost their coat of hair and their facility in climbing trees. They were not possessed of great strength. They were not fleet of foot. They could not fly, nor were they at home in the water. They had a thin skin and no protective armor. In the senses of sight, smell, and hearing they were not outstanding; in fact, they were definitely inferior to many of their neighbors in this respect. They had no potent venom like the snake, no sting like the hornet. They did not even have an especially offensive odor to protect them.

We may assume, on the basis of evidence from very primitive cultures directly known to us, that primordial man did not regard himself as the lord of creation, or even as the being for whom creation was performed. On the contrary, he had a realistic appreciation of his own weaknesses and shortcomings. He realized and frankly admitted that birds and snakes and beasts were his superiors in many respects. In fact, he commonly made gods of them and besought their help and "power." So weak and defenseless were early men that one wonders how they managed to survive at all. What evidence we have indicates that early man was numerically insignificant when compared with his brute neighbors. It might possibly be that had man been more numerous in primordial times so that some powerful carnivore might have formed the habit of hunting and eating him, he would have been exterminated entirely. But like the ugly duckling, or Cinderella, in the folk tale, the weak little man won out in spite of everything, eventually rising to mastery and dominance over all other species. This is the story of man's adventure on this planet. It is the oldest and greatest of success stories. It is little wonder that stories of this sort have always appealed to man. The popularity of the Christian epic, in which the weak and lowly are destined for triumph and everlasting glory and in which the meek shall inherit the earth, is without doubt due in large part to the appeal of this folk theme. But if man has won for himself a place of dominance, it has been because of his cultural equipment rather than his physical prowess. And culture is a cooperative enterprise which has been made possible by symbols.

Culture is, as we have noted repeatedly, a mechanism whose function is to make life secure and continuous for groups and individuals of the human species. Just as biological organisms behave in a manner the consequences of which tend to be security of existence and continuity of life, so do cultural systems behave in such a manner as to protect and sustain the human organisms within their embrace. And just as biological organisms develop means of greater control over their life process, so do cultural systems tend to develop more effective means of making life secure and perpetual for groups of human beings. At bottom, the function of culture is zoological, the maintenance of life of the human species.

The possibility of extensive and varied cooperation having been introduced into primate social organization by the maturation of the symbolic faculty, expressed in articulate speech, and since cooperation in subsistence and defense-offense is a way of making life more secure, we may expect to see cultural systems develop in the direction of more extensive and effective cooperation. Let us see how this was effected in the earliest stages of human social evolution.

Primordial man inherited the local territorial group and family organization from his prehuman ancestors. But it was the family primarily that was to provide the foundation for social evolution; this was the organization that was to be transformed by means of symbolic communication into human society.

We have emphasized the fact that the family group among anthropoids was formed and held together by sexual attraction. The function of the prehuman family was sexual, the gratification of the sexual appetite. It must be pointed out, however, that this anthropoid family was more than a mere physical and physiological affair. Union between the sexes is more than a biochemical reaction; it is a social relationship as well. Similarly, the relationship between mother and child was social as well as parturitive and nutritive. The relationship between the "father," i.e., the mate of the mother, and the offspring, too, was social in character. We see, then, that the subhuman primate family, although at bottom an organization of biological processes, is also a cluster of social—but noncultural—relationships.

With the emergence of man, a new factor was introduced into this constellation of primate family relationships, namely, symboling expressed in articulate speech. This new factor transformed the anthropoid family in both form and function in the process of humanizing it. It diminished polygyny and fostered monogamy, as we have already seen. And as a consequence of the possibility of extensive and versatile cooperation in the human species, and of the advantages to be derived therefrom, *the family acquired two new functions, namely, mutual aid in subsistence and in defense and offense.*

The effect was revolutionary. The sole function of the prehuman family was the gratification of sex needs. This was a constant, which means that there was no possibility of social evolution. When, in the transition from anthropoid to man, the family acquired the ability and the means to behave cooperatively in the life-sustaining activity of subsistence and the life-preserving activity of defense and offense, the door was opened to virtually unlimited social evolution because of the almost limitless possibilities of the development, of the expansion and extension, of cooperation.

The formula for the prehuman, anthropoid family is $F = f$ (sex)—the family organization is a function of sex. The formula for the human family is $F = f$ (sex) $\times C$ (subsistence and defense-offense)—the family is a function of sex times cooperative endeavor in subsistence and in defense-offense. We say *times* rather than *plus* to indicate the relationship between the sex factor and the cooperative factor in this formula because the relationship between them is one of inverse ratio: as the mutual-aid factor increases in magnitude and significance, the sexual factor decreases correspondingly. Thus we shall see that as social evolution progresses, the biological factor of sex diminishes in importance, whereas the cultural factor of mutual aid increases. Or to put the matter in terms of cause and effect: it is the expansion of the factor of mutual aid, in the cultural contexts of subsistence and defense-offense, that brings about the development of culture. But we are getting ahead of our story; we shall return to this point later.

Any species will tend to make full use of any means that it possesses to make life secure and also to expand and extend itself. This generalization, arrived at inductively, we believe to be a valid one; we know of no facts that tend to contradict it. It is also a corollary of one of the principles formulated in Chapter 2, "Energy and Tools," as a consequence of the application of the second law of thermodynamics to living material systems: the life process is self-expanding, self-augmenting (see p. 36).

We may apply the above generalization specifically to cooperation: cooperation being a way and a means of making life secure, any species possessing the ability to behave cooperatively will not only avail itself of this ability but will extend and develop it as far as possible. We shall now undertake to trace the course of this extension and this development in the human species, which means within sociocultural systems since cooperation is organized and expressed within that extrasomatic tradition that we call culture.

The family was the basic social unit of primordial human society as it was of its antecedent, anthropoid society. It was here that the first effects of speech and tools were felt in the shift toward monogamy. And it was here that cooperation as a human way of life made its first appearance.[17]

The family in prehuman society was not, as we have already seen, a mutual-aid group. With the exception of the mother's care of immature offspring, each one looked out for his, or her, own interests. With the advent of speech, however, it became possible for husband and wife to help each other in all sorts of ways, for children to help each other, and for children to assist, or take care of, their parents as the latter came to need aid and the former became able to provide it. There were innumerable occasions upon which mutual aid would be a decided asset in the business of daily living, and we may assume that, given the capacity and the means of cooperation, this mutual aid would be forthcoming. Did men and women have some recognition of the value of cooperation, some appreciation of the advantages of mutual aid, conscious or unconscious, at the very outset of their career as human beings? It seems reasonable to

---

[17] It might be suggested that with the appearance of an ability to behave in a new way an organization would be formed *ad hoc* with which to express it. The suggestion is logical but not realistic. Nature is economical; she builds the new upon the old. The primate family was firmly established before the ability to cooperate appeared. And the family was of vital importance in the process of life and survival. The new ability of mutual aid was therefore adapted to this already existing and fundamentally important structure.

suppose that they did; an appreciation of cooperation would go hand in hand with the capacity for it. After the achievement of monogamy, therefore, the next consequence of speech was the transformation of the primate family into a mutual-aid group.

If mutual aid within the nuclear family, i.e., husband, wife, and their offspring, is desirable, why not extend it beyond the family's boundaries? Biological relationships among anthropoids, as well as all other living beings, extend beyond the family group. One has parents, and they too have parents, and so on indefinitely. One's parents have siblings, and these have descendants; the children of one's own siblings provide other branches of the genealogical tree. One's mate has parents, siblings, and other relatives. A species is thus a continuous web of ties of consanguinity and affinity. And as we have previously noted, all these biological relationships—of mates, parents and offspring, and siblings—are also *social* relationships as well.

In prehuman primate society the relationship between an individual and someone outside his family group, but within his local, territorial group, was simple and relatively insignificant. Members of different family groups were potential sex partners or rivals to each other. They were also "comrades" in the sense that they belonged to the same band, foraged in the same territory, faced the same dangers, and enjoyed life, together. But this was all. Between individuals in different family groups a simple and general social relationship alone prevailed. They were not relatives in the sense of father, cousin, aunt, etc., to each other. One was simply "another-individual-who-does-not-belong-to-my-family-group-but-is-a-member-of-my-local-group" to another. Thus the local, territorial groups, or bands, in anthropoid society were merely loose associations or aggregations of families. The families were in association with one another like marbles in a sack; they were not knit together by specific and particular ties between their respective constituent members. Specific genealogical relationships could not be defined, recognized, or expressed in the absence of articulate speech. How, for example, could "cousin" be distinguished from "uncle" or "sibling" without language?

In human society, however, it became possible easily to distinguish all manner of relationships, extrafamilial as well as familial, and relationships of affinity as well as those of consanguinity. In the earliest stages of human society these extrafamilial relationships became important since they provided the raw material and a framework for cooperative organization. But these extrafamilial relationships became significant in their social aspect only. Primordial man was quite ignorant of the physiology of reproduction,[18] and therefore his social systems were incapable of

---

[18] This question has been debated and may perhaps still be debatable with reference to present-day aborigines, despite the fact that reputable ethnographers have claimed

taking account of biological relationships. Furthermore, for the purpose of cooperative endeavor in food getting and defense-offense, actual blood relationships were irrelevant. Ignorance of the biological nature of reproduction was therefore no bar to the development of an effective social system on the basis of cooperation.

What the primordial culture system did, therefore, was to go outside the family group and organize and incorporate extrafamilial consanguine relatives into a cooperative system along with the members of the nuclear family. This is simply and briefly stated, but the process of its accomplishment was undoubtedly a long and difficult one. These extrafamilial relationships had first to be defined and made explicit. Immediate *family* relationships are of course apparent, in anthropoid as well as in human societies; you see and have dealings with your mate, your immature offspring, and, while you are still a child, with your parents. But this is not the case where extrafamilial relatives are concerned in simian society. Here one cannot recognize his parents' parents and their siblings, for the simple reason that his parents have severed the *specific* social relationship which formerly existed between them and their parents and their parents' siblings. Consequently, on the anthropoid level, one cannot recognize and distinguish his grandparents, uncles, aunts, cousins, and so on. By the time one is old enough to mate he has lost track of his own siblings, and so cannot reckon with nephews and nieces. In short, without language one cannot keep track of extrafamilial relatives at all.

It was articulate speech, language, that made it possible to recognize and distinguish these extrafamilial relationships, to organize them into a socially effective system. The first step was the *naming* of the various kinds of relationship. We may assume that this process began with the immediate family and was subsequently extended to extra- and interfamily areas. As a matter of fact, the process of designating these relationships may well have originated in the social intercourse between parent and child. It is impressive to note how widely spread relationship terms like

---

that evidence discovered and weighed by them proves that some peoples even today remain in such ignorance. The issue has been confused by the fact that some tribes believe that copulation is a *prerequisite* to childbearing, but deny that semen *causes* conception. In any event, it seems safe to attribute an ignorance of the physiology of reproduction to primordial man. Why should it be assumed that he knew more than his anthropoid forebears? Furthermore, the "facts of life" are not so obvious and self-evident by any means. Once a fact is known it may seem self-evident. But to connect pregnancy with an act of copulation weeks or even months before rather than relate it from a mystical or magical point of view with one of a thousand and one other events is to expect sophisticated techniques of correlation of primitive man—particularly when pregnancy does not always follow copulation by any means. An understanding of "the facts of life" is indeed a mark of a fairly high degree of sophistication.

mama, papa, dada, nana, etc., are. They are found all over the world among the most diverse languages and cultures. It is tempting to ascribe this uniformity to the similarity of "baby words" the world over, but there may be a better explanation.

To name a relationship is to make it explicit, apparent, something which can be reckoned with. But naming does more: it specifies, tells what kind of a thing it is. *Coal* is one thing; *copper*, another. An *uncle* is one kind of relationship; a *cousin*, a different kind. Finally, naming things classifies them: these animals we shall call *mammals;* those, *reptiles.* Similarly, we may group a number of specific relationships into a class and call them *cousin.* Thus, relatives can be named, beginning with members of the immediate family group and extending outward from this group along genealogical lines indefinitely. Relationships depending upon the marriage tie can be included as well as those resting upon the parent-child and sibling relationship. It should be noted also that it is the *relationship* which is named rather than the person occupying it. The two things may amount to the same in the end, but it makes for greater clarity and understanding to look at it in this way. Thus we have a social relationship which we call "brother." An indefinite number of individuals may occupy this relationship. A person is called "brother," and indeed *is* my brother, because he stands in a certain social relationship to me, not the other way around.

We must now state specifically what we mean by relationship. We have already made it clear that we mean *social* rather than *biological* relationship. But what *is* a social relationship? In a word, it is the way in which two or more persons behave toward one another, what they do, say, feel and think; and *how* they do these things. A social relationship is a group of reciprocal or correlative duties, rights, obligations, prerogatives. One person has certain duties and obligations toward another. In return he may legitimately make certain demands upon the other which may not be refused. These duties, rights, privileges, and prerogatives may be defined minutely and specifically in a social system, or they may be expressed in general terms only. Thus I might have a general obligation to contribute food to a certain relative at unspecified times or in times of need. Or I might be obliged to supply him with fish, or plant food only, and then only upon certain specified occasions. I might be required to treat a certain relative with general respect, or I might have to show this respect in a definite and particular way with some gesture or ritual observance.

But whether the requirements are indefinite and general or specific and particular, they are always real, concrete, and significant in the lives of all concerned. In other words, they are always expressed in overt behavior of one kind or another, whether it be feeding, dressing, training, teaching, defending, nursing, loving, admonishing, punishing, respecting, joking, or burying.

To get back to primordial human society. A cooperative organization for the purpose of making life more secure was formed in this way: (1) The social aspect of intrafamily relationships was recognized and made significant in its own right; they had been merely incidental to their respective biological connections in prehuman primate society. (2) This was made possible by language, which not only made cooperation within the family possible, but organized and regulated it so that it could be carried on effectively. (3) What was done first within the family was next undertaken and effected outside the family. This, too, was accomplished by defining and classifying these relationships by means of kinship terms.

Thus a cooperative organization of relatives was formed about the family as a nucleus. It consisted of the husband, the wife,[19] and their children, together with the parents of husband and wife, the parents' siblings and their children, and so on. It was a group in which each was bound to all the others by social ties. Each one had duties toward the others, depending upon the kind of relationship, and in turn enjoyed rights and privileges from them. They helped each other in the food quest, in providing shelter from the elements and defense from their enemies; they loved, respected, taught, disciplined, punished, praised, nursed, and buried one another. It was, in fact, a mutual-aid society, a community of human beings carrying on the struggle of life together.

Our discussion so far has taken the family as its point of departure. We have shown how the biologically determined social relationships of the anthropoid family became social relationships with mutual-aid functions in human society. This transformation meant that whereas social relations within the anthropoid family arose out of the needs of the individual organism and were directed toward the satisfaction of those needs—gratification of the sexual appetite, maternal care of offspring--social relations in the human family came to have a different source and objective: the welfare of the group through mutual aid in subsistence, shelter, and defense. In short, in the anthropoid family social relations were functions of the individual organism; in the human family they became increasingly functions of the family group. In the anthropoid family social relations were subordinate to sexual requirements; in the human family sexual needs became increasingly subordinated to social requirements. Social evolution among primates above and beyond the anthropoid level was made possible by the emancipation of the family as a social unit from the limitations

[19] We are not here concerned with the question of monogamy versus polygamy; we wish only to present the family in its simplest form.

of the needs of individual biological organisms. Biological union between the sexes was retained as the basis of the new social organization and the point about which it revolved. But human society was now free to develop on a new plane, and free to extend itself indefinitely.

To establish a kinship tie, i.e., a sociocultural relationship, with an individual outside one's own family is, of course, to relate two family groups by a common bond, since the person who is outside the one group will be a member of the other. Thus, the process of establishing kinship ties with individuals outside the family group and of incorporating them within the mutual-aid organization, being an activity carried on by each family, is therefore a process of relating one family group to another, of forming a mutual-aid organization of which *families* are the units.

The first kind of union between families to become socially significant would undoubtedly be that between the family group in which one is a child and the family group in which he is a parent. In other words, the social relationships established biologically in the anthropoid family would be the first to become socially significant on the human level. Thus, the social relations with my parents, established in infancy, would tend to persist after I had grown up, married, and had children; and in turn my relations with my children would tend to persist beyond the time of their marriage and be extended to their children. Similarly, the relationships established between myself and my brothers and sisters during infancy and childhood would be continued after we had grown up, married, and had children of our own; and the relationships between siblings would be extended to the children of these siblings. In this way human social relationships would be established and extended, up and down the genealogical tree (with myself as a starting point), and collaterally to my parents' siblings and their descendants, to my siblings and their descendants, and so on.

So far we have been concerned only with relationships established and extended along lineal and collateral lines of consanguinity. We now turn to marriage as a means of establishing relationships along affinal lines. Families can be brought into relationship with each other for purposes of mutual aid upon an affinal as well as a consanguine basis. And of course, an interfamily tie may be both consanguine and affinal: I may marry my cousin. A double tie, such as this, may be stronger than either one alone, and as we shall see, in the early stages of human social evolution, when it was imperative that the tie between cooperating units be intimate and strong, more than one tie was almost always used.

But there were serious obstacles to be overcome before families could be customarily bound to each other by marriage in order to form a two-family cooperative group. The prehuman primate family was compact, autonomous, and independent. It was marked by strong endogamous tendencies: attraction between father and daughter, between mother and son, and between brother and sister; the only exogamous feature arose from rivalry between father and son as the latter matured sexually. Moreover, the male heads of the anthropoid families were rivals of one another in the competitive struggle for mates. The earliest of human families must have inherited many of these features from their anthropoid ancestors. If, therefore, families were to be united by marriage in order to form a larger cooperative group, social-cultural systems would have to find some way to overcome these resistances. This way was found in the "invention" of incest and the institution of rules to prohibit it.

Incest may be defined as the union, in sexual intercourse or in marriage, of two individuals of the opposite sex who stand in too close a relationship to each other. "Relationship" here means *social* relationship, regardless of biological considerations. "Too close" means any relationship that is deemed by society to be too close, and this conception will vary from one society or time to another; it may be between parallel cousins, first cousins, or persons belonging to the same clan or having the same surname. Each society provides its own definition, in specific terms, of incest. "Too close" means, also, that incest is always prohibited; there is no such thing as "permissive incest" among the ancient Hawaiians, Egyptians, Incas, or any other people. Incest is by definition a crime.[20]

The concept of incest has meaning with reference to the human species only; the lower species, lacking the ability to symbol and to express themselves with articulate speech, can have no such concept, or behavior proper to this term. Among the lower animals, adults may, indeed, drive their offspring away either at the time of weaning, as in the case of cows, or later, when they begin to mature sexually, as among baboons. This might well have the effect of preventing or diminishing inbreeding, but it can hardly be maintained that this is the motive for their action. Furthermore, incest and inbreeding are not synonymous by any means; there can be inbreeding without incest and incest without inbreeding. Finally, incest is not simply a union between relatives, but between relatives who are too close to each other. And the lower animals, without language, have no means of classifying relatives or distinguishing degrees of relationship. Incest and its prohibition is not a factor, therefore, in the social life of the lower animals.

But in the human species the situation is different. Every people on earth, so far as our knowledge goes, has both a conception of incest and

---

[20] It is remarkable to note how many writers on incest speak of "permissive incest." Even *Notes and Queries on Anthropology* (edited for the British Association for the Advancement of Science by a Committee of Section H, 6th ed., London, 1951), which defines incest as "sexual intercourse between prohibited degrees of kindred," on p. 113, has on the very next page a heading "Legalized Incestuous Marriages."

customs or laws to prohibit and punish it. What is more, it is precisely among the most primitive peoples that the concept is most sharply defined and violations most drastically punished.[21] This indicates clearly that the concept, together with rules pertaining to it, is not a recent development in social evolution, but is very primitive and remote in origin. The problem for the social scientist is: Why and how did the concept of incest originate in human society and what is the nature of the social rules pertaining to it?

The problem of incest has occupied social scientists for a very long time, and the literature on the subject is vast indeed. Since we have dealt with this problem at some length in "The Definition and Prohibition of Incest," [22] we shall merely summarize the thesis and argument here.

The theories that have attempted to explain the origin of incest taboos can be grouped into four categories: (1) instinctive, (2) physical deterioration, (3) psychological, and (4) sociocultural theories.

The theory that incest taboos were instinctive was held by Hobhouse, although he had a rather elastic conception of instinct.[23] Lowie subscribed to this theory at one time,[24] although he later abandoned it.[25] And Rose speaks of an "instinctive dread of inbreeding" and "exogamous instincts." [26]

Little need be said about the instinct theory. If the dread were instinctive, explicit rules would be unnecessary. Secondly, this theory is incapable of accounting for the great variation of specific taboos.

Among anthropologists Morgan stands out as a proponent of the theory that incest taboos were instituted in order to prevent biological deterioration brought about by inbreeding.[27] This theory has been widely held by others, also. The theory is invalid because, first of all, inbreeding per se does not cause physical or biological deterioration. Secondly, very primitive peoples, without an understanding of the biology of reproduction, could not have attributed deterioration to inbreeding if such had been its consequence. And given an understanding of paternity, how could primitive peoples have established inbreeding as the cause of deterioration without objective means of measurement and statistical tech-

[21] Cf. Reo Fortune, "Incest," in *Encyclopaedia of the Social Sciences*, vol. 7, 1932, p. 620.

[22] *American Anthropologist*, vol. 50, pp. 416–435, 1948, reprinted in *The Science of Culture*, 1949.

[23] L. T. Hobhouse, *Morals in Evolution*, 3d ed., 1915, pp. 145–146.

[24] R. H. Lowie, *Primitive Society*, 1947, p. 15.

[25] R. H. Lowie, "The Family as a Social Unit," *Papers, Michigan Academy of Sciences, Arts and Letters*, vol. 18, p. 67.

[26] Horace A. Rose, "India," in *Encyclopaedia Britannica*, 14th ed., vol. 12, 1929, p. 159.

[27] Lewis H. Morgan, *Ancient Society*, 1877, pp. 69, 378, 424.

niques of correlation? Finally, the theory cannot explain why, for example, marriage with a parallel cousin is regarded as incest whereas marriage with a cross-cousin is permitted or even required.

The psychological theories of Freud,[28] Durkheim,[29] Westermarck,[30] and others are, one and all, incapable of explaining the enormous range of variation among the incest taboos of the world.

Because of the failure of theories such as the foregoing to explain the origin of incest taboos, many scholars virtually gave up in despair, believing that the problem was insoluble. Freud concluded that "we do not know the origin of incest dread and do not even know how to guess at it." [31] And the anthropologist Wissler confessed that after years of search for an explanation, "we are no nearer a solution than before." [32]

The reason for the failure of biological and psychological theories to solve the problem is fairly plain: the problem is not a biological or a psychological one. It is a culturological problem, and the solution must be culturological; i.e., incest taboos are cultural phenomena and must be explained in terms of other cultural phenomena. When the problem is approached culturologically it yields readily to solution. The key to an understanding of the origin of incest taboos was provided by E. B. Tylor many years ago: [33]

"Exogamy, enabling a growing tribe to keep itself compact by constant unions between its spreading clans, enables it to overmatch any number of small intermarrying groups, isolated and helpless. Again and again in the world's history, savage tribes must have had plainly before their minds the simple practical alternative between marrying-out and being killed out."

The word "clan" in this passage should be interpreted merely as "a group of kindred" rather than as an exogamous, unilateral kinship group, since incest prohibitions and exogamy preceded clan organization, as we now use the term, exogamy being a prerequisite to clan structure.

Thus, Tylor made it clear that it was a *social*, rather than a psycho-

[28] Sigmund Freud, *Totem and Taboo*, New Republic, Inc., New York, 1931.

[29] É. Durkheim, "La Prohibition de l'inceste et ses origines," *L'Année Sociologique*, vol. 1, 1898.

[30] E. A. Westermarck, *The History of Human Marriage*, 3 vols., chap. 20, 1921.

[31] Freud, *op. cit.*, p. 217.

[32] Clark Wissler, *An Introduction to Social Anthropology*, Henry Holt and Company, Inc., New York, 1929, p. 145.

[33] In his significant essay "On a Method of Investigating the Development of Institutions, Applied to the Laws of Marriage and Descent," *Journal of the Royal Anthropological Institute*, vol. 18, p. 267, 1888.

Fifteen hundred years earlier St. Augustine had a very clear conception of the sociocultural nature of rules of exogamy; see quotations from *The City of God*, book 15, in the author's aforementioned essay, "The Definition and Prohibition of Incest."

logical, process that brought about the origin of incest taboos and rules of exogamy: society required individuals to marry outside their respective families, or other groups of kindred, so that life could, through the cooperation thus effected, be made more secure for all. Prohibitions against incest and customs of exogamy were the products of sociocultural systems rather than of neuro-sensory-glandular-etcetera organisms; the problem was culturological rather than psychological.

Since Tylor's day, a number of anthropologists, working from a culturological point of view, have come to an understanding of incest taboos and exogamy. Malinowski stresses the disruptive influence of endogamous unions rather than the advantages of cooperation fostered by exogamy. Fortune, Seligman, Thomas, Gillin, Murdock, Firth,[34] and others, have likewise grasped the sociogenesis and function of incest prohibitions. And Freud, despite his fancies about the killing of the primal father, has a very fair appreciation of the cultural significance of incest and exogamy. "The incest prohibition," he observes in *Totem and Taboo*, "had . . . a strong practical foundation. Sexual need does not unite men; it separates them. . . . Thus there was nothing left for the brothers [after they had killed their father], if they wanted to live together, but to erect the incest prohibition."[35] And in another work he writes: "The observance of this [incest] barrier is above all a demand of cultural society, which must guard against the absorption by the family of those interests which it needs for the production of higher social units. Society, therefore, uses all means to loosen those family ties in every individual. . . ."[36] Let us return now to our sketch of human social evolution.

As we have seen, when man became a human being his newly acquired faculty of speech transformed his social life, which up to now had been determined by biological factors alone, into a form of social organization in which extrasomatic cultural factors also were significant. Cooperation became a new means to an old end: security and survival. Mutual aid was introduced into family organization. Individuals were organized into cooperating groups along lines of consanguinity. Family groups, or larger

[34] Reo Fortune, "Incest," in *Encyclopaedia of the Social Sciences*, vol. 7, 1932, pp. 620–622; B. Z. Seligman, "Incest and Descent: Their Influence on Social Organization," *Journal of the Royal Anthropological Institute*, vol. 59, pp. 231–272, 1929; William I. Thomas, *Primitive Behavior*, 1937, p. 197; John Gillin, "The Barama River Caribs," *Papers, Peabody Museum*, vol. 14, no. 2, p. 93, 1936; George P. Murdock, *Social Structure*, chap. 10, 1949; Raymond Firth, *We, the Tikopia*, 1936, p. 324.

[35] Sigmund Freud, *Totem and Taboo*, New Republic, Inc., New York, 1931, pp. 250–251.

[36] Sigmund Freud, "Three Contributions to the Theory of Sex," *The Basic Writings of Sigmund Freud*, A. A. Brill (ed.), The Modern Library, Random House, Inc., New York, 1938, pp. 616–617.

consanguineal groups, were bound to each other by marriage, as a consequence of incest prohibitions, thus extending and multiplying ties of mutual aid and obligation. At the same time, these groups of kindred, organized for mutual aid, were rendered more effective in their activities of subsistence and defense by eliminating sexual rivalries among members of the group through the operation of incest taboos and rules of exogamy. Thus, by the definition and prohibition of incest, cooperation was furthered, on the one hand, and the possibilities of disruption and conflict lessened, on the other. In this way human society embarked upon a course of evolutionary development which it will be our task to trace in the pages that follow.

Having noted the positive aspect of incest regulations, namely, their purpose and achievement, we now turn to the negative side and inquire what human society would have been like without these prohibitions. Granting a universal and powerful desire to effect sexual unions with close associates—an assumption which is supported by ethnologic and psychologic evidence—we discover that human social evolution could not have progressed very far without definitions and prohibitions of incest. As a matter of fact, it could have advanced but little beyond the level of the anthropoids, for without a concept of incest and compulsory exogamy, social organization would have been confined to the family line, with sexual attraction operating as a centripetal force to keep each family line intact and discrete. It was incest and exogamy that effected the next step in social evolution: the union of each family line with other family lines. Once this step was taken it could be extended indefinitely and along other lines than kinship, as we shall see later. Once the cooperative process had leaped the barrier of intrafamilial sexual attraction and had, furthermore, relegated sex to a subordinate position, there was no limit to the extent to which it might extend and develop itself. This situation has its parallel in biological evolution. Had no way been found to unite unicellular organisms into multicellular systems, evolution would have been unable to advance beyond this point. Once means were devised for uniting single-celled organisms into larger, multiple-celled systems, the way was wide open for almost unlimited and infinitely varied development.

Having shown that rules of exogamy were instituted to compel individuals to marry outside the group of their immediate relatives instead of within it, let us now see if we can trace the course of exogamy from its inception.

We shall begin with the family groups of man's immediate prehuman ancestors. These groups, we recall, consisted of one adult male, his mate or mates, and their immature offspring. According to psychological theory, each member of this group would be drawn to other members of the opposite sex. Thus father and daughter, mother and son, and brother and sister would be attracted toward each other.[37] The relationship between mother and children was, no doubt, more intimate and intense than that between father and offspring: in addition to suckling the young, the mother fondled and protected them as monkey and ape mothers do today. We might assume, therefore, that the tendency of mother and son to unite sexually would be greater than the tendency of father and daughter. But there is another important factor to be considered also, namely, male dominance. In the prehuman primate family, the dominant male might appropriate his female offspring for sexual purposes. But he would not permit his male offspring to have sexual access to their mother. He would also discourage or prohibit sexual relations between his sons and his daughters. Thus we may assume that before the anthropoid family had reached the human level, a form of exogamy had already been established by the brute force of the dominant male. This must have been the situation when man became a human being. Our task now is to see how formal rules of exogamy were instituted in human social life and how the scope of these rules was extended.

When man became possessed of articulate speech he formulated explicit rules for the regulation of his social life. Since sexual unions between mother and son had already been prohibited in the prehuman family, this practice was given formal sanction and definition in the first incest prohibition to be formulated.[38] There are two reasons for assuming that sexual relations between mother and son were banned as incestuous before relations between father and daughter, and between brother and sister, were so defined and prohibited. In the first place, there was the dominance of the husband-father who would not allow his male offspring to have access to either their mother or their sisters because he wished to monopolize them himself. And in the second place, a union between son and mother would be less effective socially (economically) than a union between father and daughter, or one between brother and sister.

Since exogamous rules were instituted in order to obtain the benefits of cooperation brought about by intergroup marriage, those unions be-

[37] Not *because* they were "father" and "daughter," "mother" and "son," but because they were opposite in sex and in intimate association. Sexual attraction tends to vary inversely with the distance—social distance—between individuals.

[38] The origin of the concept of incest and the origin of ethics are inseparable, according to Freudian theory (cf. Freud, *Totem and Taboo*, pp. 249, 250). This seems perfectly sound to us, although we come to this conclusion from somewhat different premises—or at least by a different course of reasoning. The first instance in human history, of which we have evidence, of the subordination of individual desire to general welfare is in the definition of incest and the inauguration of rules of exogamy. If the first moral act was the observance of the prohibition of incest, was not violation thereof the "original sin"?

tween close relatives which contributed least to the formation of an effective social organization for food getting, protection, and defense would be prohibited first. To put the matter in another way, society would gain more from the prohibition of a union between two close relatives that was relatively ineffective in food getting and defense than from the prohibition of a union between two close relatives who could form a relatively effective unit for food getting and self-defense. For example, a mother-son union would be less effective as an organization for self-defense, food getting, and reproduction than a father-daughter union. In the one union there would be an immature male and a female past her prime. In the other, there would be a mature, experienced male and a female approaching the prime of life. A union between brother and sister, both in or approaching the prime of life, would be more effective as an organization for nutrition, defense, and reproduction than either mother-son or father-daughter unions. Thus we see that society would lose the least and gain the most by prohibiting marriage between mother and son. Added to this consideration is the factor of male dominance, which would prohibit union between son and mother. We may conclude, therefore, that this relationship would be the first to fall under the ban. Unions between father and daughter would be prohibited next, before those between brother and sister, *if* the effectiveness of the unions as food getting, self-defense, and reproduction units were the only things to be considered. But as we have seen, the dominance of the father over the son might outweigh the superiority of brother-sister marriages from the standpoint of social welfare. These two forms of marriage might therefore have been prohibited as incestuous at about the same time.

Regardless of which of these two unions was prohibited first, we have discovered an important principle which has been operative in the extension of exogamy: *other factors being constant, that union which contributes least to the advantages derived from cooperation will be prohibited as incestuous first.*

If two individuals are already closely related by ties of social consanguinity—such as parent and child, or brother and sister—little, if any, further social advantage could be derived from a marriage between them. Society could gain considerably, however, by compelling two such individuals to marry others more distantly related rather than each other. The already existing ties would not be severed by exogamy: brother and sister would still remain brother and sister even though each married someone else. And new ties, relations of mutual aid, obligation, and privilege would be established by the brother and sister with other individuals and their respective groups. It is clear, then, that society would gain but little by reinforcing an already existing social relationship between brother and sister with a marriage between them. But the group at large would gain much by compelling the brother and sister to establish new and strong ties with other individuals, with other family groups. The operation of the exogamous principle is now clear. The tendency is to unite individual family groups, to form an organization of individual families, so that through cooperation and mutual aid the welfare of all can be promoted. Unions between relatives will be permitted, required, or prohibited in terms of their relationship to the welfare of society, as defined in terms of security and subsistence. Marriages between relatives will be declared incestuous in the same order in which their prohibition would contribute the most to the general welfare.

In accordance with this principle, marriage between full brother and sister would be prohibited before unions between half brother and sister, since the social relationship between children having the same mother [39] and father [39] is closer and more intense than between children who have only one parent in common. Society would lose less and gain more by prohibiting full brother and sister marriage than by banning unions between half brother and sister. Brother-sister marriage would therefore be proscribed before matings between half-siblings.

Similarly, marriage between parallel cousins would be prohibited before the ban fell upon the cross-cousin [40] unions. The social relationship between parallel cousins is often much closer than between cross-cousins. With patrilocal [41] residence, I would be in closer association with my father's brothers' children than with my father's sisters' children; I *might* have close contact with my mother's sisters' children, but my mother's brothers' children would already live elsewhere. With matrilocal residence, I would be in closer relationship to my mother's sisters' children than to my mother's brothers' children—all my life, if a female; if a male, until marriage. I *might* have close contact with the children of my father's brother (if he should marry into my mother's household or locality); but my mother's brothers' children would always live elsewhere. Consequently, unions between parallel cousins would come to be regarded as incestuous, and therefore prohibited, before marriage between cross-cousins comes to be so regarded.[42]

[39] Defined sociologically, not biologically, of course.

[40] My parallel cousins are the children of my father's brothers and of my mother's sisters; my cross-cousins are the children of my father's sisters and of my mother's brothers.

[41] Patrilocal residence is the name of the custom in which a married couple lives with the family or group of the husband; in matrilocal residence, they live with the group of the wife.

[42] There are peoples who require, or prefer, marriage with parallel cousins rather than with cross-cousins, but this has another explanation, which will be given later.

Carrying the principle of exogamy further, marriage between first cousins would be prohibited before unions between second cousins are banned.

Such is the social process of exogamy. It extends its scope by branding first one and then another kind of marriage union incestuous. And as we have noted, it always proceeds outward from its center, the family. It expresses a centrifugal force, so to speak, in society. But there is also an opposite, or centripetal, force or process. This is endogamy: the custom or requirement of marrying within a specified group. We shall treat endogamy and exogamy at some length in our next chapter. It remains now to point out how the introduction of cooperation within the human family, and the establishment of cooperative ties between families, have affected the institutions of marriage and the family.

Marriage

The institution of marriage is a socially sanctioned relationship, usually but not always between persons of the opposite sex, which, in the case of union between man and woman, permits and sanctions sexual intercourse and the begetting of children. Marriage is the humanization, the institutionalization, the sociocultural expression of the relatively durable union between the sexes in subhuman primate society. In the transformation of anthropoid society into human society *mating* became *marriage.*

Among nonprimate mammals sexual intercourse has reproductive significance primarily; the sex act is performed only during a breeding season or when the female is in heat. Among primates sex acquires a nonreproductive function; sexual activity is carried on for its own sake as well as for reproductive purposes. But even in subhuman primate society sex may acquire a nonsexual function. According to Zuckerman, a female baboon would endeavor to obtain food in the possession of her mate by exciting him sexually so that his attention would be diverted from the food.[43] Or she might try to avoid corporal punishment by her overlord, or to avert his wrath, by the same means. Thus we note that among subhuman primates—and therefore, presumably, among man's immediate prehuman ancestors—sex had (1) reproductive, (2) sexual, and (3) nonsexual, socioeconomic functions. These same functions were carried over into human society with the advent of speech.

A naïve notion exists in certain quarters that marriage was instituted to provide men and women with a means of sexual satisfaction. It is true that marriage, as a human institution, grew out of relatively permanent sexual unions among subhuman primates. But in human society the institution of marriage is not founded upon sexual need and satisfaction.

---

[43] S. Zuckerman, *The Social Life of Monkeys and Apes,* 1932, pp. 238ff.

Quite the contrary. In no society is sexual activity limited to the marriage union. It is true that virginity tests are imposed upon brides, and measures are taken to ensure the fidelity of wives, in some cultures. On the other hand, there are cultures in which the greatest sexual freedom is allowed before marriage and in which pregnancy may frequently precede marriage. Prostitution, which flourishes in many of the higher cultures, is a way of institutionalizing sexual activity outside of marriage. As a matter of fact, marriage may tend seriously to circumscribe and to limit sexual activity in some societies: monogamy ideally considered is the next thing to celibacy. And there are some forms of marriage in which sexual intercourse plays no part whatever, as we shall see later.

The function of marriage in human society is to establish a mutual-aid group to carry on the processes of nutrition, protection, and defense. According to R. H. Lowie: [44]

"Marriage, as we cannot too often or too vehemently insist, is only to a limited extent based on sexual considerations. The primary motive, so far as the individual mates are concerned, is precisely the founding of a self-sufficient economic aggregate. A Kai [New Guinea] does not marry because of desires he can readily gratify outside of wedlock without assuming any responsibilities; he marries because he needs a woman to make pots and to cook his meals, to manufacture nets and weed his plantations, in return for which he provides the household with game and fish and builds the dwelling."

A similar view is expressed by A. R. Radcliffe-Brown: [45]

"The important function of the family is that it provides for the feeding and bringing up of the children. It is based on the cooperation of man and wife, the former providing the flesh food and the latter the vegetable food, so that quite apart from the question of children ... this economic aspect of the family is a most important one. ... I believe that in the minds of the natives themselves this aspect of marriage, i.e., its relation to subsistence, is of greatly more importance than the fact that man and wife are sexual partners."

The economic basis and functions of the family are universal in human society; they are as conspicuous upon high levels of cultural development as upon the lower levels. In colonial times in America, says Ogburn: [46]

"... The family was a very important economic organization. Not in-

---

[44] *Primitive Society*, rev. ed., Liveright Publishing Corporation, Black and Gold Library, New York, 1947, pp. 65–66.

[45] "The Social Organization of Australian Tribes," *Oceania*, vol. 1, p. 435, January–March, 1931.

[46] William F. Ogburn, assisted by Clark Tibbitts, "The Family and Its Functions," in *Recent Social Trends in the United States* (Report of the President's Research Committee on Social Trends), McGraw-Hill Book Company, Inc., New York, 1933, pp. 661–662.

frequently it produced substantially all that it consumed, with the exception of such things as metal tools, utensils, salt and certain luxuries. The home was, in short, a factory. Civilization was based on a domestic system of production of which the family was the center.

"The economic power of the family produced certain corresponding social conditions. In marrying, a man sought not only a mate and companion but a business partner. Husband and wife each had specialized skills and contributed definite services to the partnership. Children were regarded, as the laws of the time showed, not only as objects of affection but as productive agents. The age of marriage, the birth rate and the attitude toward divorce were all affected by the fact that the home was an economic institution. Divorce or separation not only broke a personal relationship but a business one as well."

The economic character of marriage is revealed in such legal and judicial procedures as suits for breach of promise, alienation of affection, separation and maintenance, and alimony. With regard to breach of promise, Ruling Case Law discusses marriage as follows:[47] "The law generally takes the rather worldly view that marriage is a 'valuable' consideration; a thing not only possessing value, but one the value of which may be estimated in money, and therefore, in a sense, marriage engagements are regarded as business transactions, entered into with a view, in part, at least, to pecuniary advantage." Suits for alienation of affections involve "the loss of consortium": "This is a property right growing out of the marriage relation," according to the Supreme Court of Connecticut.[48] Eleven out of twelve items in a "Personal" advertisement column selected at random in a newspaper of a large city expressed a refusal to accept responsibility for debts contracted by the wife. Marriage has a definite occupational aspect in some cultures; it may serve as an alternative to working for wages as a means of support. In the United States in recent decades marriage offers many young women, especially in the middle, or upper-middle, class a greater economic return than could be obtained by unskilled labor. And "homemaker," i.e., a housewife, has come to be recognized—on radio and television programs, at least—as an occupation in the contemporary United States.

The reasons for the economic, rather than sexual, or erotic, basis of the family in human society are fairly plain: (1) the family is the fundamental and universal unit in human society in which the essential processes of nutrition and other human need-serving activities are carried on; these processes are primarily economic in character; (2) sexual attraction, or love, cannot provide marriage and the family with a secure and enduring

[47] William McKenney and Burdette A. Rich (eds.), *Ruling Case Law*, vol. 4, Rochester, N.Y., 1914, p. 143.

[48] *Cases Argued and Determined in the Supreme Court of Errors of the State of Connecticut*, vol. 117, May, 1933, to January, 1934, Hartford, Conn., 1934, p. 208.

foundation. It is too uncertain, ephemeral, fickle, unpredictable, and therefore undependable. Love may be strong today, but gone tomorrow. Economic needs we have with us always.

It is interesting to note that Freud has much the same view of the human family and society, of sex and economics, that we hold. "The motivating force of human society is fundamentally economic," [49] he says—an observation, by the way, that is hardly in accord with a notion widely held that Freud "explains everything in terms of sex." He postulates a conflict of interest and goal between sex and subsistence and asserts that the development of culture requires that sex be curbed, contained, and limited so that human energies can be used for culture building. "It is impossible to ignore the extent to which civilization is built up on renunciation of instinctual gratifications ... [human] energies [must be] diverted from sexual activity to labor." [50]

That Freud, starting from quite different premises, and following different courses of reasoning, should nevertheless come to the same conclusions as ourselves seems significant—and encouraging.

Marriage: an alliance between groups. The role of marriage as a means of establishing ties of mutual aid, as distinguished from the satisfaction of sexual desire, is further indicated by the fact that everywhere in human society marriage is an alliance between groups. In some cultures marriages are initiated and carried through wholly by groups of kindred rather than by the individuals who will be thus united. In some societies young men and women have virtually no voice in their marriage arrangements; they may not even see each other before the wedding. A girl may be betrothed in childhood, or even infancy, in some cultures. Marriage arrangements are sometimes made between two families even before the bride-to-be is born; e.g., in aboriginal Australia, one family may have a son, another a daughter. They form a marriage pact. But the boy will not marry the girl, but her daughter, after the girl has grown up, married, and borne a female child. We do not say that no one in primitive society has a voice in the selection of his or her spouse. In some cultures one does, but it is always a matter of degree. Even where marriage arrangements are made by the parents of the prospective bride and groom, the latter may be consulted regarding their wishes and choice.

Bride price and dowry. Since a family is, to a great extent, an organization for carrying on economic activities, marriage may become an

[49] Sigmund Freud, *A General Introduction to Psychoanalysis,* Liveright Publishing Corporation, New York, 1920, p. 269.

[50] Sigmund Freud, *Civilization and Its Discontents,* Jonathan Cape, Ltd., London, 1930, p. 63; see also pp. 72–74 and *A General Introduction to Psychoanalysis,* 1920, p. 269.

economic transaction. In many cultures gifts are exchanged between the families of bride and groom at marriage. This may be no more than a social ritual. But in some instances the family of the bride or the groom will give a quantity of goods to the family of the other spouse. The amount of wealth may be very considerable, and thus be important from an economic standpoint. "Since a girl in ruder societies represents economic value," says Lowie, "her family surrenders her only for an equivalent." [51] The institution of bride price is rather widespread in primitive society. The terms "price" and "purchase" do not mean that the wife thus obtained becomes a chattel or suffers an inferior status as a consequence of "purchase." The property given to the bride's family, or larger group of relatives, is a means of cementing the marriage union, of making it more binding and durable. Since, in some societies, the wife's relatives would be obliged to return the bride price, or its equivalent, in the event of divorce or separation, the wife's relatives might do everything they could to keep the marriage from breaking up.

The dowry is the counterpart of bride price. It is relatively rare or insignificant among preliterate peoples, but has been common among the upper, i.e., propertied, classes in ancient Greece and Rome and in western European culture in more modern times. The custom of dowry has a number of aspects: it tends to encourage marriage—a large dowry makes a girl more desirable as a mate; it may encourage marriage, or make it possible, by providing the means of establishing a household or of setting up the husband in business; [52] it helps to protect the wife against abuse or maltreatment from her husband and to enhance her status; it tends to perpetuate the marriage, since the dowry had to be returned in the case of divorce; and it was a means of providing widows with some economic security.

Levirate and sororate. Some marriage rituals in our society today require the contracting parties to pledge themselves to perpetuate the union "until death do us part." But in many preliterate cultures even death is not permitted to terminate the alliance formed between families or groups of kindred by marriage. If the husband dies, his brother is obligated to marry the widow. This is the levirate [53] (L. *levir,* husband's

---

[51] R. H. Lowie, "Marriage," in *Encyclopaedia of the Social Sciences,* vol. 10, The Macmillan Company, 1933, p. 148.

[52] Benjamin Franklin tells us in his *Autobiography* that he proposed marriage to a girl and her parents, but on condition that said parents put up enough money to pay off the debt on Franklin's printing shop. The parents replied that they could not put up that much money, whereupon Franklin suggested that they "mortgage their house in the loan-office." The parents declined to do this, saying that they did not approve of the match: "...Therefore I was forbidden the house, and the daughter shut up," says Franklin.

[53] We find a good example of the levirate in the Bible, including an account of the

brother). If the wife dies, her family, or group of kindred, must, if it can, supply a woman to take her place (the sororate). The sororate is frequently associated with the custom of bride price; if the husband's kindred have "bought" a wife for him and she dies, her family or kindred are obligated to replace her. The institutions of levirate and sororate are very widespread in primitive society, and in many instances a tribe will observe both customs. The levirate and sororate give significant support to the theories advanced here: (1) marriage is, or may be, primarily an alliance between groups of kindred; and (2) so important is this mutual-aid compact in the conduct of life that society cannot afford to allow it to be terminated even by death. Certain religious groups, notably the Roman Catholic Church in our own culture, strive to preserve the ties established by marriage by refusing to sanction divorce.

Enduring sexual unions among subhuman primates have become sociocultural mechanisms in human society. Sometimes they have legal significance almost exclusively, e.g., as a means of acquiring title or claim to property, or as a vehicle of inheritance. Cases of adventuresses marrying Indians who had suddenly become rich through the discovery of oil come to mind here. In the cultures of the Northwest Coast of America, where titles and rank play such an important role in social life, a man may marry another man's leg or arm as a means of acquiring a title which he may pass on to his son.[54] In west Africa a woman may marry another woman or women, i.e., perform the same ritual—including payment of bride price—that would take place in marriage between a man and a woman; she becomes the father of children born to this union.[55] In India a person may marry a tree or even an inanimate object. Marriage may serve as a means of political integration within a nation. The king of Buganda, for example, marries a woman from each clan or territory in his domain as a means of establishing close ties with his subjects. And finally, marriage may serve as a means of international alliance. In ancient Egypt, Amenophis III asked the King of Mitanni for a bride for his son. In modern Europe marriages between royal households of different countries have been frequent. Louis XIII of France married Anne of Austria, who in turn was the daughter of Philip III, King of Spain. One of the provisions of the Treaty of the Pyrenees (1659), which concluded a war between Spain and France, was that Maria Theresa, daughter of the Spanish Hapsburg king, Philip IV, should

---

punishment of a man who refused to marry his brother's widow (Deut. 25:5–12). Genesis 38:6–11, too, tells of how Onan married his brother's widow but took measures to prevent pregnancy, whereupon the Lord killed him in anger.

[54] Franz Boas, "The Social Organization and Secret Societies of the Kwakiutl Indians," *United States National Museum Report*, 1895, p. 359.

[55] M. J. Herskovits, "A Note on 'Woman Marriage' in Dahomey," *Africa*, vol. 10, pp. 335–341, 1937.

marry the French Bourbon king, Louis XIV. Napoleon I married Maria Louisa, daughter of the Austrian emperor, Francis II. The way in which human culture took over the relatively permanent sexual union among anthropoids, transformed it into a sociocultural mechanism, and has used it for social and political purposes for a million years, from the primordial human family to alliances among nations in the nineteenth century, is truly remarkable.

The transition from anthropoid society to human social organization was made possible by the emergence of the faculty of symboling expressed in articulate speech. Language opened the door to cooperation to a virtually unlimited extent. Cooperation made life more secure. Consequently, social evolution moved in the direction of more extensive cooperation. The family became a mutual-aid group. The formation of larger cooperative groups by the intermarriage of families was brought about by the definition of incest and the institution of laws of exogamy. Kinship became a sociological rather than a biological affair. Marriage and the family acquired a pronounced economic character. As human society evolved, the sexual factor diminished in significance as the economic factor grew in importance. The union between the sexes became a legal device in acquiring or transferring property rights or titles. And in marriage the simple union between the sexes eventually became an instrument of international intercourse and alliance.

Chapter 5   *EXOGAMY AND ENDOGAMY*

The subject of exogamy has enjoyed a prominent place in the history of ethnological theory. We have had books and articles almost without end dealing with "the problem of exogamy." With regard to endogamy, however, the situation is different; interest in endogamy appears to be slight, and the literature meager. And we find little discussion of the relationship between exogamy and endogamy. Many authors never take note of any relationship at all between them—except, perhaps, to state that in the one case you marry out, in the other you marry in. Still fewer appreciate the fact that exogamy and endogamy are inseparable; that they always go together. Lowie, for example, observes that "exogamy and endogamy are not mutually exclusive except with regard to the same unit." [1] This means that a clan, or any other kind of social unit, cannot be both exogamous and endogamous at the same time, which is self-evident, but that a people may have an exogamous rule with reference to one kind of unit and an endogamous rule for another type of unit. For example, a caste might be endogamous but at the same time be composed of exogamous clans. Another anthropologist, Camilla H. Wedgwood, remarks that "exogamy and endogamy are by no means mutually exclusive ... [they] are often found together...." [2] All this is, of course, true. But to say that endogamy and exogamy are not mutually exclusive, that they are "often found together," is confusing and misleading. It implies that if a tribe has exogamy, it is not likely to have endogamy also, although it *could* have both. This view is unwarranted: every society has both exogamous and endogamous characteristics. Exogamy and endogamy are complementary aspects of the same social phenomenon; they are, like the poles of a magnet, opposite but inseparable.

Some authors speak as if endogamy and exogamy were traits which a people or culture might or might not possess. Thus Lowie has remarked

---

[1] R. H. Lowie, *Primitive Society*, rev. ed., Liveright Publishing Corporation, New York, 1947, p. 17.
[2] Camilla H. Wedgwood, "Endogamy," in *Encyclopaedia Britannica*, 14th ed., vol. 8, 1929, p. 436.

that "the Andean region lacks both exogamy . . . etc." [3] Brenda Z. Seligman speaks of "cultures . . . where there is no trace of the custom [exogamy]." [4] And Wedgwood declares that "among primitive peoples it [endogamy] is rare." [5] What Lowie and Seligman mean, probably, is that certain exogamous social units or, more specifically, clans, are lacking in the Andean region—although Lowie has defined exogamy as "the rule which prescribes that an individual must find a mate outside of his own group, whether that group be the family, the village, or *some other social unit* . . . [italics supplied]." [6] In any event, his phraseology, like that of Wedgwood, is misleading. Both authors obscure the fact that both endogamy and exogamy are found everywhere in human society. It is not definite and discrete social units that define exogamy and endogamy and reveal their nature. Exogamy and endogamy are social *processes*.

In view of the repudiation of an interest in social origins, which we noted earlier (p. 70), we should not expect to find much light thrown upon the genesis of customs of exogamy and endogamy in human society by contemporary anthropologists. And in this expectation we are fully justified; they have virtually nothing to say on the subject. These customs exist and function; but how they arose and developed is today, as it was to Frazer in 1910, "a problem nearly as dark as ever." [7] This is perhaps understandable in view of the false lead given to the problem by McLennan many years ago in *Primitive Marriage*. But we know much more about primitive society today than McLennan and his contemporaries did. We may therefore take up once again the question of the origin of exogamy and endogamy in human society.

The processes of in-mating and out-mating can be observed, as a matter of fact, in the social life of man's anthropoid ancestors. Thus there was sexual attraction, made powerful by the intimacy of social contact, between father and daughters, between mother and sons, and between brothers and sisters. If there were no other factors to be reckoned with, these classes of relatives would be more likely to mate with each other, respectively, than with more remote—remote in a social as well as a biological sense—relatives. This is an *endogamous* tendency. But there was an opposing tendency also in anthropoid society. Because of the dominance and sexual jealousy of the father, the young maturing males were not permitted

[3] R. H. Lowie, "American Culture History," *American Anthropologist*, vol. 42, p. 412, 1940.

[4] Brenda Z. Seligman, "The Problem of Incest and Exogamy: A Restatement," *American Anthropologist*, vol. 52, p. 314, 1950.

[5] Wedgwood, *op. cit.*

[6] R. H. Lowie, *Primitive Society*, 1947, p. 16.

[7] J. G. Frazer, *Totemism and Exogamy*, vol. 1, Macmillan & Co., Ltd., London, 1910, p. 165.

to mate with their mother or their sisters. They were driven out of their family group and had to seek mates elsewhere. This was an *exogamous* process.

When primate society acquired the human form, the processes of in-marrying and out-marrying were not dropped or discarded. On the contrary, they were carried over and made a vital and integral part of the new social order. But they were organized on a somewhat different basis and given a different function, as we shall see.

We have already noted how the newly formed sociocultural systems undertook to organize individuals and family groups on a cooperative basis for the business of living—food getting, shelter, protection, and defense—in order to make life more secure. This process of social development took the family as its starting point and proceeded outward from there, incorporating first close, then more distant, relatives into the co-operating organization. Definition and prohibition of incest made marriages between families compulsory. In this way, a body of relatives, consanguine and affinal, were organized into a cooperative group, a mutual-aid society so to speak, in order to make life more secure for its members.

This cooperative group was effective. Its effectiveness was not a single element, however, but a compound. It was made up of two elements or factors: size and solidarity. By *size* we mean the number of persons in the group; a group of thirty is twice the size of a group of fifteen. By *solidarity* we mean the strength and intensity of the ties, the social relations, between the individuals who compose the group. Persons may be united to each other by weak, tenuous, and ephemeral ties; or the bonds may be intimate, strong, and enduring. And of course there may be innumerable gradations between these extremes.

The effectiveness of a group, in the struggle for existence and survival, depends both upon its size and upon its solidarity. These factors are variable and stand in an inverse ratio to each other. Other factors being constant, the degree of solidarity varies inversely with the size: the larger the group the less the solidarity; an intensification of solidarity would mean a diminution of size. The relationship between size and solidarity with reference to the effectiveness of the cooperating group can be expressed with precision in the following simple formula: $E = Sz \times So$, where E stands for the *effectiveness* of the cooperating group; Sz, for *size;* and So, for *solidarity.* If the degree of solidarity remains unchanged, an increase in size of the cooperating group would make it more effective in the struggle for existence. If, however, the group lost through diminution of solidarity as much as it gained from increase in size, the net result would be zero; it could even lose if it suffered more from a weakening of solidarity than it gained by increase in size. The desirable goal of social evolution, from the standpoint of success in the competitive struggle for existence, is therefore *increase in size without loss of solidarity*. But since the factor of solidarity may vary also, we may formulate the following generalization: *every society tends to behave in such a way as to achieve that balance between size and solidarity that will give it the maximum effectiveness in carrying on its life-sustaining activities*.

Let us return now to the earliest stage of human social evolution and, having already seen how the process of exogamy operated, let us observe the manner in which the opposite process, that of endogamy, expresses itself. We shall begin, as before, with the primordial human family in its most simple form: an adult male, his mate, and their offspring. After rules of exogamy had prohibited marriage between parents and children and between brother and sister, the youngsters were of course required, when they matured, to seek mates outside of their immediate family group. But whom should they marry? Would *any* individual of the proper sex and of suitable age, temperament, and beauty do? By no means; there is more to marriage than individual taste and preference. As noted in the previous chapter, marriage is a socioeconomic alliance between groups of kindred as well as a sexual union between individuals. It is natural, therefore, that each family, or group of kindred, should take a hand in the formation of an alliance that is to be so vital to their security and survival. In the earliest stages of social evolution, we may reasonably assume that the role of the individual decreased, the role of group of kindred increased, in importance in contracting a marriage.

Marriage within the family, a union of brothers with sisters, for example, would give a high degree of solidarity: the strength of the marriage tie would be added to that of brother and sister. But the cooperative group thus formed, confined within a single family line, would be small, and hence relatively weak. The conception of incest and rules of exogamy tabooed marriage within a family and compelled brothers and sisters to marry into another family line, and in this way to form a cooperative group composed of at least two family lines. *Exogamy operates to enlarge the size of cooperative groups of relatives.*

But solidarity must be considered, also, if advantage is to accrue from increase in size. The coefficient of solidarity of two families, or groups of kindred, united by marriage may vary. Under optimum circumstances it will attain a maximum, which we may designate 100. Under less favorable circumstances it will be lower. It may go to zero or even below this point: the relationship might become one of hostility and strife rather than of friendship and mutual aid. Obviously, it is to the advantage of the families forming the alliance to have as high a degree of friendliness and solidarity as possible. Therefore interfamily marriage alliances will tend to unite those family groups whose union will bring about a maximum, or rather an optimum, degree of solidarity in relation to other conditions and circumstances.

Taking any family as a starting point, it will be observed that all other family groups stand in varying degrees of relationship to it. Some are close genealogically and spatially, others are remote in one or both of these respects. To unite two families remotely related would establish little, if any, solidarity; in fact, enmity rather than cooperation might result. *Other factors being constant, the degree of solidarity achieved by the union of families by marriage is directly proportional to the closeness of the social relationship before marriage.*

We are now in a position to observe the simultaneous operation of the processes of exogamy and endogamy. The unit which in protohuman society is carrying on the struggle for existence is the family. It is a small group and correspondingly weak. The inauguration of rules of exogamy compels marriage outside the family, thus uniting families into larger cooperating groups, making life more secure. But "marriage with another family" is not all there is to it. As we have seen, not all families are equal in the kind or degree of relationship which they bear to any given family. Some are related in one way, some in another; the relationship may be close in one case, remote in another. The selection of the family to become allied to yours through marriage is therefore an important matter. If your family forms a marriage alliance with a family having only a weak and tenuous relationship to your own, or none at all, a larger group will be formed, but it will have so little solidarity as to make the alliance of little or no value to either family in the struggle for existence. It may even have a negative value if the marriage should instigate a feud rather than cooperation. It would be desirable, therefore, for your family to ally itself through marriage to a family which already stands close enough to yours in social relationship to guarantee a high degree of solidarity and mutual aid.[8]

[8] Just as St. Augustine had a sound insight into the nature of exogamy, which we noted in an earlier chapter, so did he have more than a superficial understanding of endogamy. This is natural, of course; anyone who really understands the one must understand the other, for they are but centrifugal and centripetal aspects of the same phenomenon. After discussing the reasons for exogamy, Augustine proceeds to treat of endogamy as follows:

"But the ancient fathers, fearing that near relationships might gradually in the course of generations diverge, and become distant relationships, or cease to be relationship at all, religiously endeavored to limit it by the bond of marriage before it became distant, and thus, as it were, to call it back when it was escaping them. And on this account, even when the world was full of people [inbreeding was

Thus we see how and why the processes of exogamy and endogamy operate. The rules of exogamy say, in effect: "Do not marry close in; marry out so as to increase the size of the cooperating group thus formed." The rules of endogamy say: "Do not marry too far out, for by doing so the effectiveness of your alliance will suffer through weakened solidarity. Marry close in so as to achieve a high degree of solidarity." In short, the rules of exogamy and endogamy say, "Marry out but not too far; marry in, but not too close." The processes of exogamy and endogamy are simply ways of securing maximum effectiveness of group effort in the struggle for existence by achieving a balance between size and solidarity that will produce this maximum.

Appreciation of exogamy and endogamy as correlative social processes, and understanding of their functions, objectives, and consequences, have not been too plentiful in the course of ethnology's history and development. Herbert Spencer thought of exogamy and endogamy as "correlative results of the same differentiating process," [9] but limited as he was by McLennan's theories, he was not able to grasp the actual working of these processes in societies. Tylor, too, held to McLennan's thesis that some tribes were exogamous, others endogamous. He seems, therefore, to contrast these two principles without realizing that they are both complementary and universal.[10]

Among anthropologists of the present day we have noted but one instance—we may have overlooked others—of what may be appreciation of the complementary nature of exogamy and endogamy—although these terms are not used in this instance, and we are not sure that we know what the author means by "expansion" and "contraction" of "social solidarity." Radcliffe-Brown generalizes as follows: [11]

"In any society there are normally present a certain number of factors tending towards an expansion of social solidarity [i.e., an increase in size of social group?], and other factors tending in the opposite direction towards a contraction [intensification?] of social solidarity. These two sets of opposing factors may be in a state of equilibrium, or they may not."

---

necessary when there were only a few people, the children of Adam, etc.], though they did not choose wives from among their sisters or half-sisters, yet they preferred them to be of the same stock as themselves." Marcus Dods (ed. and trans.), *The City of God*, vol. 2, book 15, Hafner Publishing Company, New York, 1948, p. 80.

[9] Herbert Spencer, *Principles of Sociology*, vol. I, pt. 3, chap. 4, "Exogamy and Endogamy," 1885, p. 657.

[10] E. B. Tylor, "On a Method of Investigating the Development of Institutions," *Journal of the Anthropological Institute*, vol. 18, pp. 267–268, 1888.

[11] A. R. Radcliffe-Brown, "The Social Organization of Australian Tribes," *Oceania*, vol. 1, no. 4, p. 445, 1931.

We may now undertake to sketch the probable course of development of human society in its earliest stages from the standpoint of endogamy.

In the earliest period of human history there was, as we have seen, a tendency for parent to mate with child, brother to mate with sister. When these unions had been prohibited we may assume that union between half brother and half sister was preferred, since these individuals were already related through the possession of one parent in common, and consequently a high degree of social solidarity was brought about by marriages of this sort. In time, such unions became incompatible with maximum effectiveness of the cooperating group, and the laws of exogamy were extended to include marriage between half-siblings. The endogamous tendency, ever striving to foster solidarity, would then place marriage between parallel cousins at the top of the list of preferred unions because, among the kinds of unions possible, this would provide the highest degree of solidarity. Marriage between parallel cousins would, in many if not most instances, achieve a higher degree of solidarity than marriage between cross-cousins because, with matrilocal or patrilocal residence, which is very common in primitive society, the social relationship between parallel cousins prior to marriage is closer and stronger than is the relationship between cross-cousins.

In time, as technological progress advanced culture as a whole, marriage between parallel cousins would become incompatible with the maximum size and effectiveness of the mutual-aid organization formed by marriage, and consequently the rules of exogamy would be extended to prohibit marriage between parallel cousins. Marriage between cross-cousins would now become the preferred type, since union between these relatives would foster the highest degree of solidarity compatible with the maximum size and effectiveness of the cooperative group.

We see, then, how the processes of exogamy and endogamy work. As enlargement of cooperating group becomes possible in the course of social evolution, the processes of exogamy and endogamy work hand in hand, the one to increase size of group by extending the radius of the group of persons within which one may marry; the other, endogamy, operates to foster solidarity by preventing this radius from becoming too great. In the instance just considered, the rule of exogamy says that one must marry at the genealogical and social distance of first cross-cousin at least; the rule of endogamy says that one cannot marry at a greater distance.

Up to this point our sketch is inferential. Inference is, however, a legitimate and an essential process in all science. The question is not, "Is our account inferential?"—or "conjectural history?" as some would express it

—for inference is everywhere in science. The questions, rather, are, "Are our premises sound?" and "Is our reasoning valid?" If these questions can be answered in the affirmative, then our conclusions must be accepted.

Cross-cousin marriage is exceedingly widespread among primitive peoples. Some groups however, such as the modern Arabs and Mohammedans generally, prefer marriage between parallel cousins. The reason for this is to keep property within the patrilineal lineage instead of allowing it to pass outside. Since the influence of the inheritance of accumulated property upon the selection of mates is a characteristic of more advanced cultures rather than of the less developed, we may regard these instances of parallel-cousin marriage as a comparatively recent development. Our sequence of preferred types of marriage, running from unions between siblings and half-siblings to parallel-cousin marriage and then to cross-cousins, is unaffected, therefore, by the Arabian instance of parallel-cousin unions. As a matter of fact, our theory helps to make Arabian marriage institutions intelligible. Parallel-cousin marriage and certain rules of inheritance of property are devices for forming and keeping intact a certain grouping of kindred, a patrilineal lineage, which under the conditions in which they live—plus cultural background—make this grouping highly effective in the struggle for existence. Here we find solidarity emphasized at the expense of size of cooperative group.

Similarly, the instances of brother-sister marriage in the royal families of ancient Egypt, Peru, and Hawaii are examples of an intensification of solidarity at the expense of size of cooperating group. In these royal families a large cooperating group is not an advantage; they hold the power and authority of rulers, and hence do not need the help of many relatives. On the other hand, a small compact group is a decided advantage as it keeps the royal power from becoming diffuse and weak. Brother-sister marriage is an effective device for keeping kingship in a single family line. In Egypt, for example, the right to the throne was transmitted in the female line. But since a woman could not, legally or customarily, become king, the son of a pharaoh married his sister, giving him a double claim to the throne and also making it possible for his son to succeed him. In ancient Hawaii, brother-sister marriage was a way of intensifying rank and status among the ruling class. The occurrence of brother-sister marriage on advanced cultural levels does not therefore invalidate our theory of exogamy and endogamy. On the contrary, our theory helps us to understand this form of marriage.

In tracing the course of social evolution from the standpoint of endogamy, we witness the same steps and the same stages that we observed in following the extension of the rules of exogamy. This is, of course, natural; it could not have been otherwise. What we have is a process of development which contains two opposite but inseparable tendencies, a tendency to marry out and a tendency to marry in, the one to increase the size of the mutual-aid group, the other to foster its solidarity. These tendencies are balanced against each other in such a way as to achieve a maximum of effectiveness of the cooperating group. As conditions change so as to make possible an increase in size of group without diminution of effectiveness due to impaired solidarity, the rules of exogamy are extended and the frontiers of endogamy recede. It is inevitable, therefore, that our history of endogamy and of exogamy should present the same stages of development. With regard to the "conditions" whose change brings about a shift in the balance between the tendencies of exogamy and endogamy, these are the technological means of subsistence in relation to habitat and of defense and offense in relation to neighboring groups.

What happened when marriage between first cross-cousins became incompatible with maximum size and effectiveness of the mutual-aid group formed by marriage? First of all, the endogamous rule requiring marriage between first cousins would be relaxed and marriage between more distantly related individuals would be permitted. Secondly, solidarity would be fostered and maintained either by requiring marriage with a second cousin or by other means. We have a particularly fine example of what happened when marriage between first cross-cousins became excessively endogamous in certain tribes in Australia, an example that illustrates admirably the significance of rules of exogamy and endogamy and the way they work together.

According to Radcliffe-Brown, one of the foremost students of Australian social organization, the kinship systems of Australia can be grouped roughly into two main types, the Kariera and the Arunta types.[12] In the Kariera type, a person must marry his first cross-cousin. In other words, the rules of exogamy prohibit unions between parent and child, between siblings and half-siblings, and between parallel cousins. But the rules of endogamy require one to marry his first cross-cousin. In the Arunta type, one is not permitted to marry a first cross-cousin but is required to wed a second cross-cousin.[13] In contrast with the Kariera system, the Arunta rule of exogamy has been extended to prohibit marriage with

[12] Cf. A. R. Radcliffe-Brown, *ibid.*, vol. 1, no. 1, p. 46, 1930.
[13] It may be asked why marriage with second parallel cousin was not the first step beyond the point of first cross-cousin, in the extension of the rules of exogamy and the corresponding retreat of endogamous requirements. The answer is that since the tribes in question are patrilineal and patrilocal, one half of your parallel cousins, those belonging to your father's patrilineal lineage, would necessarily reside in your own locality; some of the other half, those belonging to your mother's patrilineal lineage, might. Your cross-cousins, however, of the second degree, as well as the first, would have to live in another locality and consequently be more remotely related to you—both socially and geographically—than parallel cousins residing in your own territory.

first cross-cousins, but the rule of endogamy, after retreating from the frontier of first-cousin marriage, stops and entrenches itself at its new boundary, that of second-cousin marriage. The Arunta type of kinship system has therefore grown out of the Kariera type; [14] the Kariera system was transformed into the Arunta system by the simple device of changing the rule of marriage, which meant changing the rules of both exogamy and endogamy.

The transition from the Kariera type of organization to the Arunta type brought about the formation, through marriage, of a larger group of kindred. In the former, two families were united: ego's and that of his mother's brother. In the latter, the Arunta type, four families were involved, namely, ego's own, or that formed by the marriage of his mother and father, his mother's mother's family, that of his mother's mother's brother, and that of his mother's mother's brother's daughter. The number of "hordes," or local territorial groups, that were brought into relationship with one another was doubled, also. The simultaneous changes in the rules of exogamy and endogamy have therefore produced a larger mutual-aid group formed by marriage.

The transformation of the Kariera type of organization into the Arunta type was brought about by changes in the adaptation of the socio-cultural system to its natural habitat and to neighboring societies, i.e., changes in the mode of subsistence and of relations of offense and defense. We do not know what these changes were, specifically. But the goal of the process of change is clear: the formation of a larger mutual-aid group of kindred in order to make life more secure. In Chapter 7, in our discussion of segments in Australian tribes, the transition from Kariera to Arunta types of organization will be described in some detail, and the reader is advised to consult that discussion, which will further illuminate the point just treated.

Theoretically, the size of the cooperating group, determined by the rules of exogamy, on the one hand, and by the rules of endogamy, on the other, could be enlarged indefinitely by requiring marriage with progressively more remote cousins. But this would place too great a burden upon genealogical reckoning; as a matter of fact, the Arunta system is rare, being virtually unknown outside of Australia. When a certain point is reached in social evolution, the expression of the processes of exogamy and endogamy assumes a new form. In addition to specific prohibitions reckoned genealogically, the rules of exogamy come to be formulated with reference to *groups* whose members need not know

---

[14] "We are thus justified, I think, in regarding the Kariera and the Aranda [Arunta] systems as two terms in an evolutionary process. . . ." Radcliffe-Brown, *op. cit.*, vol. 1, no. 4, p. 452, 1931.

their genealogical connections with one another. In other words, in addition to saying, "You may not marry your parents, siblings, cousins, etc.," the rules of exogamy will say, "You are prohibited from marrying anyone in such and such a group (e.g., clan), regardless of the genealogical tie between you and the members of this group." Similarly, the rules of endogamy will cease to specify, in terms of genealogical connection, those individuals whom you must marry; they will now merely indicate and define the group within which you must marry, regardless of genealogical tie. Such groups vary. The exogamous social unit may be a family, local group, clan, moiety, or some other grouping. Endogamous groups vary even more widely. They may be moieties, tribes, classes, castes, nations, races, religious faiths, or other kinds of groups.

In view of the fact that exogamy is frequently identified with clan organization, and therefore that discussions of exogamy often begin at this point, it is significant that we have been able to set forth and explain all the principles and essential characteristics of exogamy without reference to clan organization at all. Exogamy began with the origin of human society, or even earlier among the lower primates; its nature and operation were fully revealed and expressed long before clan organization came into being. Equally significant is the fact that, far from treating exogamy and endogamy as separate phenomena, or as "not mutually exclusive," we have shown that these processes are inseparable and universal and that one cannot be understood apart from the other.

We shall discuss exogamy and endogamy with reference to clans, moieties, castes, or other kinds of groups later. We now understand these processes, why they operate, the ends served, and results achieved. The exogamous or endogamous features of social groupings on levels of cultural development considerably above the most primitive are merely further manifestations of these two processes. We shall now turn to a few other institutions that may be illuminated by the application of our theory of endogamy and exogamy.

Although the institutions of levirate and sororate are not usually discussed in terms of endogamy, they are nevertheless manifestations of this process. The obligation of a man to marry the widow of his deceased brother is, of course, an instance of endogamy. Likewise, the obligation of a group of kindred to supply a woman to take the place of a deceased wife in order to keep intact the alliance formed by marriage is endogamous in effect. The institutions of bride price and dowry may, though not necessarily, support the endogamous effect of levirate or sororate by encouraging or permitting the replacement of a deceased spouse as an alternative to the return of bride price or dowry, as the case may be. The endogamy fostered by levirate and sororate and by bride price and dowry is incidental to the perpetuation of the ties of mutual aid and obligation established between two family groups by marriage; but it is still endogamy.

Sororal polygyny and fraternal polyandry are likewise expressions of the endogamous process. A custom requiring, encouraging, or permitting a man to marry his brother's wife, or a woman to marry her sister's husband, is endogamous in effect. It is a way of promoting solidarity through establishing and multiplying intimate, and therefore powerful, ties by marriage.

Likewise, rules of avoidance, restrictions upon freedom of social intercourse between individuals closely related by ties of consanguinity or affinity, on the one hand, and customs designed to promote and foster intimacy between individuals, such as those commonly listed under the heading "joking relationship," on the other, are further examples of exogamous and endogamous processes, respectively, in society. Rules of avoidance minimize intimacy or ban social intercourse completely; they thus tend to keep individuals apart and to prevent sexual or marital liaisons from taking place. Customs requiring or encouraging familiarity, on the other hand, promote intimacy, privilege, and solidarity even in instances where marital unions do not follow as a consequence.

Our discussion of exogamy and endogamy thus far has dealt with the very origin of human society and with the earliest stages of its development. We shall take cognizance of these processes from time to time in subsequent chapters where our concern will be with higher levels of cultural development. Before leaving this subject, however, we may make a rapid survey of endogamy and exogamy in advanced cultures.

The processes of endogamy and exogamy operate on all levels of cultural development. Preliterate and literate societies present somewhat different aspects in this respect, however. In preliterate societies it is the rules of exogamy that attract attention by their ubiquity and severity, whereas endogamy appears to be relatively insignificant—as we noted earlier (p. 102), Wedgwood finds that endogamy is "rare" among primitive peoples. In literate cultures, on the other hand, it is endogamy that attracts attention and exogamy seems to be less significant relatively, if not absolutely. A certain amount of optical illusion is involved here. In preliterate societies, the local group, or band, or the tribe may be the only sharply defined endogamous group. As a consequence, the operation of the endogamous process in marriage may escape notice. In advanced literate cultures, on the other hand, one frequently finds a considerable number of kinds of endogamous groupings, whereas exogamy seems actually to be less important than in preliterate cultures, if one may judge by the degrees of severity with which the two types of cultures punish persons guilty of incest. Actually, of course, endogamy and exogamy are important social processes on all cultural levels, although their manifestations may differ in degree of conspicuousness in the two types of society that we have distinguished.

The scope of rules of exogamy tends to be less extensive in literate than in preliterate societies. In preliterate cultures we find rules of exogamy referring to members of a group, such as a clan, as well as to individuals whose genealogical connection is known and reckoned with. Thus, a person may be prohibited from marrying another merely because both belong to the same group (clan or moiety). He is forbidden also to marry certain individuals because of their specific genealogical connection. In literate cultures, the group specification of exogamic rules tends to disappear, leaving only genealogical ties to be considered. In China, however, even today, one Li is not supposed to marry another as a general rule, which is without doubt a persistence of clan exogamy. But in the United States and most, if not all, European countries, genealogical ties alone need be considered.[15] In so far as rules of exogamy exist in literate cultures they are much the same as in preliterate societies.

In advanced, literate cultures one finds many kinds of endogamous groupings.[16] In some societies, occupational groups, or guilds of specialized artisans, tend to be endogamous, or at least to perpetuate the group by inheritance in the male line. Slaves and nobles frequently constitute endogamous classes. In our own society, religious denominations, especially certain ones, make a great effort to achieve and maintain endogamy, either marrying only those of their own faith or by attempting to incorporate the outsider into their own group. Many states of the Union have laws prohibiting interracial marriages of one sort or another.[17] These prohibitions of exogamy have the effect, of course, of laws of endogamy. Nationalities in the United States—communities of Italians, Germans, Poles, etc.—also tend toward endogamy. We have an unwritten and ill-defined caste system based upon wealth and culture which tends to prohibit members of distinguished or wealthy families from marrying common people without "family" or fortune. There is even

[15] We offer the following example from the Compiled Laws of the State of Michigan: "(12692) Sec. 3. No man shall marry his mother, grandmother, daughter, granddaughter, stepmother, grandfather's wife, grandson's wife, wife's mother, wife's grandmother, wife's daughter, wife's granddaughter, nor his sister, brother's daughter, sister's daughter, father's sister, or mother's sister, or cousin of the first degree."

[16] "Endogamy flourishes in stratified societies...." R. H. Lowie, "Marriage," in *Encyclopaedia of the Social Sciences*, vol. 10, The Macmillan Company, New York, 1933, p. 146.

[17] That these laws are not to be taken lightly is indicated by a story circulated by the Associated Press in the fall of 1948: A young man from a small town in Mississippi served as a white man in the United States Navy in World War II. Upon returning home he married a white woman. But since he was believed to be a Negro, at least to the extent of one-eighth blood, he was tried on a charge of miscegenation, convicted, and sentenced to five years in the penitentiary.

a tendency for political parties to exercise endogamous restrictions; many a rock-ribbed Republican would be loath to have his daughter marry a Communist—or even a Democrat.

The purpose of endogamous rules and customs in advanced cultures is clear. Their objective is the same as in preliterate society: solidarity. And, of course, solidarity is not an end in itself. It is valued and striven for because solidarity means effective group effort, efficiency in the conduct of life, success in competition, perpetuation, and survival. Thus, for example, the Jews favor endogamy because it promotes solidarity and effectiveness in group competition. Southern whites oppose marriage with Negroes because marriage would dissolve caste lines and thus remove the economic and political advantages they now enjoy over Negroes as a subject class. There is some indication that Negroes, too, especially those in the North, are showing some inclination toward endogamy, probably as a means of strengthening their solidarity in competition with the whites. For an heiress to marry a poor nobody is to expose her own fortune and, through laws of inheritance, the fortunes of her close relatives, to claims of numerous "poor relations." It is significant to note, in this connection, that the ancient Greeks made an exception to the rule of clan exogamy in the case of heiresses. And as we have already seen, the custom of parallel-cousin marriage among the Arabs was due to the desire to keep property within the patrilineal lineage.

Since incest is merely illegal endogamy, we may add a word or two upon this subject here. In the first place, we may note that whereas incest is a most heinous crime, often punishable by death and disgrace in primitive society, it is a relatively insignificant offense in modern civilized cultures. The Punishment of Incest Act, passed by the British Parliament in 1908, for example, makes this offense a relatively minor one, punishable by a moderate fine or term of imprisonment. It is an offense of approximately the same magnitude in the United States. The punishment of incest in England or America today is less severe than that for theft of food to the amount of $10 in some instances.[18]

The reason for the difference in the evaluation of incest as an offense in these two types of culture is fairly plain. In primitive society cooperation between families, between groups of kindred, is of the utmost importance. In the struggle for survival cooperation must be had at all costs. And incest prohibitions were means of establishing and enforcing cooperation. Incest was a blow struck at the very foundation of the social order. This is why it was punished so drastically. It is significant to note also that incest is one of the few offenses against the gods in

[18] According to the law of the state of Michigan, incest is "a felony, punishable by imprisonment in the state prison for not more than ten years." *Michigan Statutes Annotated*, vol. 25, 28.565, Incest, Sec. 333.

preliterate society; homicide, lying, stealing, etc., are seldom set in a supernaturalistic context. Primitive peoples regarded most ethical rules and their violations as merely human, nonreligious affairs that they were able to cope with without aid from the gods. But so urgent was the need to prevent incest in order to promote cooperation and solidarity that its violation was punished by the gods as well as by men. In modern literate cultures, however, the situation is different. Here, society is based upon property relations and territorial distinctions. Civil organization replaces that of kinship. State and church, police, prisons, and courts organize and regulate social intercourse. Economic organization, occupational groups, guilds of specialized artisans, and the professions also organize and conduct much of social life. Society does not need to lean so heavily upon exogamy because it has so many other structures to support it. Consequently, the crime of incest diminishes from one of the most heinous of all crimes to the category of a relatively minor offense.

It might seem farfetched, at first glance, to interpret the celibacy of a social class in terms of the processes of endogamy and exogamy, since they have to do with marriage, and celibacy is the negation of marriage. But it is precisely the "negation" that makes endogamy and exogamy relevant to celibacy. If rest is but a form of motion, as Whitehead says,[19] then we may regard celibacy as a form of marriage. Celibacy is a form of marriage in which there is no spouse, just as rest is a form of motion in which the velocity is zero. It is a condition reached by extending the rules of exogamy to infinity, or rather, to a point where no one is marriageably eligible. Conversely, celibacy is endogamy carried to its furthest extreme, because the solidarity of the group is not diluted by the admission of spouses.[20] Thus, endogamy and exogamy find their extreme and final form of expression in celibacy.

Applying these principles to the Roman Catholic clergy as a class, their celibacy becomes intelligible. The wealth of the Church is not consumed by wives and children nor dissipated by heirs. Having no wives or children to claim their allegiance, the priests are free to devote themselves wholly to the service of the Church. Celibacy is a means of fostering the integrity, of promoting the solidarity, of the clergy, in order to make the group as a whole a more effective and efficient organization. The Roman clergy, as we know, has not always observed or

[19] "Rest is merely a particular case of such motion, merely when the velocity is and remains zero." A. N. Whitehead, *Introduction to Mathematics*, Oxford University Press, New York, 1948, p. 29.

[20] No earthly spouse, that is. In some monastic orders, women become brides of Jesus. Thus, marriage and celibacy—like parallel lines in a non-Euclidean geometry —meet and intersect in the infinity of Christian theology.

enforced celibacy upon its members. It seems more than probable that the prohibition upon marriage has grown up and become institutionalized for the reasons given above.

To summarize briefly the central thesis of this chapter: Exogamy and endogamy are two opposite but universal processes in human society. They are means of regulating the size and solidarity of cooperative groups, the rules of exogamy tending to increase the size, and therefore the strength, of the group, the rules of endogamy fostering solidarity and integrity. These rules vary specifically with the situation as determined by habitat, technology, conditions of subsistence and defense—in short, the mode of life.

Exogamy appears to be more conspicuous, and even important, in preliterate societies than in literate cultures, whereas the reverse is the case with endogamy. Prohibitions of incest are less important in a society based upon property relations, one having occupational groups, the political state, and a police force, than in a society based upon kinship. Conversely, in a highly structurally differentiated society like our own, endogamy finds more frequent expression in castes and other in-groups than in the more structurally homogeneous societies on primitive levels.

Chapter 6 KINSHIP

In our account of the origin and early stages of evolution of human society we discussed such matters as the organization of the family, incest taboos, the distinction between parallel cousins and cross-cousins, the operation of rules of exogamy and endogamy, and so on. But we had little to say about the means with which such organization was effected and such processes carried on. We did indicate that the means were kinship terms, and we showed how they were used to organize and to regulate family life in the earliest stages of human social evolution. But the subject of kinship terms, or more broadly, kinship systems, is of great significance; it deserves particular and extensive consideration.

A kinship term is a word that designates a social relationship arising out of the husband-wife, parent-child, or intersibling relationship (or a relationship which is equated with such a tie of consanguinity or affinity; we shall return to such relationships later on). Since a kinship term designates a relationship between one person, or class of persons, and another, each term presupposes and requires a correlative or a reciprocal term.[1] Thus, *father* requires the correlative term *son* or *daughter; cousin* requires the reciprocal *cousin*, and so on. The overt behavior and the attitudes of persons designated by kinship terms toward one another, and in terms of the relationships designated by these terms, constitute a *kinship system.*

A kinship term designates a relationship between individuals, or classes of individuals, rather than the actual individuals themselves. Thus, Mary is my aunt because she stands in a certain relationship to me; she may stand in another relationship to you, and consequently be your sister or your mother. A relative is therefore a person who stands in a certain relationship to you. And any relationship, such as cousin, brother-in-law, aunt, etc., may contain an indefinite number of individuals; mother is

[1] It is interesting to note that Lewis H. Morgan, the founder of the science of kinship, distinguished between correlative and reciprocal terms, whereas most students today are content with *reciprocal* only. See Morgan's *Systems of Consanguinity and Affinity of the Human Family*, Smithsonian Contributions to Knowledge, vol. 17, 1871.

the name of a class of relationships, or relatives, even though the kinship system may admit of only one mother; some classes may have only one member.

A kinship system must have a point with reference to which kinship terms have meaning. To say that John is a son tells us nothing definite; it is like saying that Toledo is east. The fixed point of reference in a kinship system is the person speaking, conventionally called *ego*. Every individual is the center of a kinship system; the various relationships radiate out in all directions, lineally and collaterally, from this point.

We have already emphasized the fact that the relationships with which incest taboos and the rules of exogamy and endogamy are concerned are *social*, rather than biological, relationships, and we have given reasons why this must be so. In addition to ignorance of the biological nature of reproduction, which must have characterized human society during the earliest stages of its evolution, there is the impossibility of knowing with certainty who the father of a child is; in some cases a woman might not know which of a few men is her child's father. All kinship systems must, therefore, be based upon and consist of social, rather than biological, relationships. The culture of the United States disposes many persons to believe, or to feel, that our kinship system rests upon a biological basis, but this error is easily exposed. The mother of a child is a woman who stands in a certain socially defined and accepted relationship to that child regardless of who brought the child into the world. Our laws with regard to adoption illustrate this. And again, how can a husband be sure of the paternity of his wife's children? No society has ever been able to prove paternity. The Code Napoleon has come as close to it as any society can: "The father of the child is the husband of the mother." If the mother has no husband, the child has no father, i.e., no one standing in a certain socially sanctioned and legally prescribed relationship to him.

The sociological character of kinship systems is demonstrated also by the use of such terms as mother and father in some systems: a person may have several fathers and as many mothers; or he may have a "father" who is in the same generation as his grandchild. And in some cultures, "mother" may designate a male: among the Akamba of East Africa mother's brother is a "male mother." Conversely, among the Zulus father's sister is called "father."

The purpose, or function, of a kinship system is to relate persons to one another, to organize them into a group or aggregation, and to direct, regulate, and control their behavior toward one another in a great and varied number of contexts and situations. In the preceding chapters we have discussed the organization of individuals for cooperative activity, the formation of mutual-aid groups. These groups were kinship groups; they were organized, regulated, and controlled by kinship systems.

A kinship tie is a compound made up of concept, attitude, and overt behavior: I have a concept of *father*, I have a certain attitude toward anyone who stands in this relationship to me, and I must behave toward him in a certain manner. Correlatively, my father will have a certain attitude and will behave in a certain way toward me. A kinship tie is conceptually defined, oriented by attitude, and expressed in overt behavior. Concept, attitude, and behavior are, of course, matters of sociocultural determination. A kinship system is therefore a means of organizing a number of individuals upon the basis of ties of consanguinity and affinity and of directing, regulating, and controlling their interkin behavior in various contexts. What are these contexts?

In a word, the goal of a kinship system is the security of life. It functions in contexts of subsistence, offense, and defense and protection in general. It focuses upon certain times in a person's life when assistance is especially needed: birth, naming, puberty, marriage, sickness, and death. Teaching and training children to carry on life-sustaining activities in subsistence, offense and defense, and medicine—to hunt, fish, grow crops, tend herds, fight, cure sickness, to acquire proficiency in the arts and crafts—are functions of a kinship system.

But a kinship system does more than help a relative cope with the external world, at least directly. It relates person to person in order to promote social solidarity, as well as to obtain the benefits of mutual aid in activities in which the external world is directly concerned. But solidarity is not an end in itself; it is a way of making a group more effective in the conduct of life, and hence a way of making life more secure. Instruction of the young in ethics and etiquette, i.e., in proper ways to behave toward others, is an important function of kinship systems. And there are numerous rituals which have as their function the intensification of a kinship tie, or a reaffirmation of its importance. The ritual of gashing one's self with a knife upon the death of a relative is a case in point.

We thus see that the cooperative organization discussed in the previous chapters and the kinship system of this are one and the same thing. They are organizations of individuals upon the basis of kinship ties that have as their function making life more secure in man-to-nature aspects (subsistence, protection) and in man-to-man aspects (solidarity).

Fison and Howitt have given us a very interesting example of the way in which economic and social life may be regulated by the rules of kinship in a very primitive tribe.[2] Among the Kurnai of Australia

[2] Lorimer Fison and A. W. Howitt, *Kamilaroi and Kurnai*, 1880, p. 265.

during the 1870s, food was divided and distributed in the following way: A hunter returns to camp with a wombat (a kangaroolike animal). It is cooked, then cut up and distributed. The hunter keeps the head. His father gets the ribs on the right side, his mother the ribs on the left side plus the backbone. The elder brothers receive the right, the younger brothers the left, shoulder. The right hind leg goes to the elder sister, the left hind leg to the younger sister. The rump and liver are sent to the camp of the young unmarried men. But the distribution, on the basis of kinship, goes even farther. When the father has received his portion he must share it with his parents, giving them the skin. Similarly, the mother of the hunter must share her portion with her parents: she gives the backbone to her father, some of the skin to her mother.

At first glance this distribution would seem to have reference to the man-to-nature relationship only, since it is ostensibly concerned with food supply; it might be interpreted merely as a means of mutual security through sharing. But every family would contain at least one hunter and possibly more, and game was not so scarce that each animal captured would have to be widely distributed. We may reasonably conclude, therefore, that much of this distribution was done for the sake of promoting social solidarity. The rules of distribution made people dependent upon one another, and therefore intensified the ties that related them to one another. An ostensibly economic device thus serves also as a means of fostering solidarity by creating and exercising a set of reciprocal duties and rights.

The origin and development of kinship systems were identical with the origin and development of the cooperative organization in the earliest stages of human social evolution. The cooperative group, organized upon the basis of kinship, had its origin in the family that man inherited from his anthropoid ancestors, as we have already seen. Kinship relations were first defined and designated within the family; later they were extended beyond the nuclear family along lines of consanguinity, both lineal and collateral. They were also established between families by marriage and extended among affinal relatives both lineally and collaterally. Thus, kinship as a sociocultural phenomenon had its origin within the primordial, nuclear family, and then extended outward in all directions along genealogical lines to embrace an ever-widening circle of people. And the kinship system, being an organization of attitudes and acts, of duties and rights, became a powerful and effective means of directing and regulating social life.

As kinship ties are extended outward from one family, so are they extended by all families, and as a consequence an indefinite number of family groups become interrelated through mutual bonds of kinship.

This process can continue until the entire tribe becomes a continuous web of kinship, a political structure erected upon the foundation of consanguinity and affinity. Everyone becomes a relative of everyone else and consequently knows how to behave toward him and what response to expect in return. The tribe will then become the over-all cooperative group. In fundamental respects the social life of the tribe, interpersonal behavior in the basic activities of subsistence and offense-defense, is organized and carried on in terms of kinship.

Kinship may be extended to intertribal relations also. "In a typical Australian tribe," says Radcliffe-Brown, "it is found that a man can define his relation to every person with whom he has any social dealings whatever, whether of his own or of another tribe, by means of the terms of relationship." [3] In some instances, friendly social intercourse is impossible except on a basis of kinship. Radcliffe-Brown tells of a journey that he made among native tribes in Australia accompanied by a black-fellow.[4] When they arrived at a camp where his companion was not known the natives began at once to look for a bond of kinship between the stranger and themselves, the inquiry proceeding along genealogical lines. When a kinship connection had been discovered, the stranger was "admitted to the camp and the different men and women were pointed out to him and their relationship to him defined." Then and only then did friendly social intercourse with him become possible. On one occasion, all attempts to discover a bond of kinship with the stranger failed. "That night," says Radcliffe-Brown, "my 'boy' refused to sleep in the native camp, as was his usual custom and on talking to him I found that he was frightened. These men were not his relatives and they were therefore his enemies. This represents the real feeling of the natives on the matter. If I am a blackfellow and meet another black-fellow, that other must be either my relative or my enemy. If he is my enemy I shall take the first opportunity of killing him for fear he will kill me."

We have been speaking of extending kinship relations along genealogical lines.[5] To do this requires both precise information and memory: one must know, and be able to remember, who married and who begat whom. Without written records, genealogical reckoning breaks down

[3] A. R. Radcliffe-Brown, "The Social Organization of Australian Tribes," *Oceania*, vol. 1, no. 1, pp. 44–45, 1930.

[4] A. R. Radcliffe-Brown, "Three Tribes of Western Australia," *Journal of the Royal Anthropological Institute*, vol. 43, pp. 150–151, 1913.

[5] By genealogical reckoning we mean tracing a relationship between two persons in terms of the actual and particular connections, affinal and consanguine. Examples: my mother's mother's brother's daughter's daughter; my father-in-law's brother's son's wife.

sooner or later. The writer found among the Southwestern Pueblos that few, if any, informants could name their mother's mother's mother's siblings, and many could not be sure of the siblings of mother's mother. Then, too, genealogical reckoning tends to fail as the size of the tribe increases. In an endogamous tribe of only two or three hundred, one might be able to know precisely how he is related to everyone else. But suppose the tribe contains a few or several thousand. Generations of endogamy would of course relate each person to everyone else. But lacking written records, it would be impossible for one to know how he was related to thousands of other individuals, specifically and genealogically. In short, the kinship system, expressing genealogical relationships in terms of consanguinity and affinity, has limits beyond which it cannot function effectively. This means, therefore, that the size of the sociopolitical unit, i.e., the tribe, that can be organized on the basis of genealogical reckoning alone is limited, and that social evolution on this basis could not go beyond these limits unless new means of dealing with kinship were devised. New means were developed, however, and it then became possible further to extend the radius of kinship organization by supplementing genealogical reckoning with nongenealogical reckoning.

A kinship system based upon genealogical reckoning alone is specific and particular. The person speaking is always the focal point of the system, which means that the significance of the terms of designation and classification is always relative, rather than absolute. "Uncle" has meaning only with reference to a particular person or class of persons; to say that a certain person is my "uncle" is to say nothing about his relationship to you. Hence each person is obliged to remember a great number of specific and particular genealogical connections, and memory has limits. If, however, a system of classification could be devised that would be general instead of particular, absolute instead of relative, in which everyone in the tribe would find himself in one or another of a few or several groups into which the tribe was divided, and in which membership in a group, rather than genealogical connection between individuals, was the basis of reckoning, the scope of the kinship system could be much extended.

Clans, lineages, and moieties are groups of this kind. A clan is a body of kindred; everyone in it is related to everyone else. But it is often impossible for a person to determine his genealogical connection with many of his clansmen. This is not necessary, however; mere membership in the clan is sufficient to provide a basis for an adequate social relationship. The significance of the clan as a device for classifying relatives is now disclosed. A clan system is a general system of classification rather than a particular one. A man is "uncle" only to certain individuals; a Corn clansman is Corn clansman to all the world. The individual is no longer the sole basis upon which kinship is reckoned; tribal subdivisions, clans, have been added. Now a person need no longer depend upon genealogical reckoning alone. He need not know whether his mother's mother's mother was the uterine or collateral sister of my mother's mother's father or not; if both belonged to the same clan they may be assumed to have been brother and sister. When the limits of genealogical reckoning have been reached, the clan system comes to his service. Instead of being obliged to know whether a person is his mother's mother's mother's brother's daughter's daughter's son or not, he can rely upon clan membership as a guide to kinship and behavior. And, moreover, he does not need to memorize the clan affiliation of everyone with whom he may have social intercourse; he can ascertain this readily by inquiry.[6]

Thus clan organization serves as an effective device for classifying relatives and determining relationships on a metagenealogical basis. Instead of being faced with the necessity of determining one's genealogical connection with each of a few thousand individuals, one can now establish his relationship to them on the basis of clan membership. Each individual will be personally connected with a number, perhaps all, of the clans of his tribe by genealogical ties known to him. Thus his father belongs to clan A, his mother to B. His parents' parents might involve two other clans, C and D. His children and grandchildren might bring him into relationship with other clans. He would be related to clans also through marriage: his own, those of his siblings, his uncles and aunts, his children, and so on. Thus each individual would be closely related genealogically to members of several clans. Then, through this genealogical connection, a relationship with the entire clan is established. In some kinship systems, any male member of my father's clan is my "father" and his children will be my "brothers" and "sisters." Female members of another clan would be my "aunts," "sisters," or "mothers," because of my genealogical connection with a member of that clan. The clan thus provides a means of establishing significant and specific relationships between myself and an indefinite number of persons with whom I can trace no exact genealogical connection.

What we have said here about the clan would apply also to moieties as kinship groups (i.e., excluding moieties not based upon kinship; see p. 158). In tribes divided into two exogamous lineages or moieties, kinship is reckoned upon the basis of affiliation with the moiety as well as upon genealogical reckoning. My parallel cousins, for example, will belong to

[6] The difference between a particularistic, relativistic genealogical mode of reckoning kinship ties and a general, absolutistic method such as clan organization provides is analogous to the difference between a system which locates one point on the earth's surface as northeast by east of another point and a system which locates any and all points in terms of latitude and longitude.

my moiety; my cross-cousins, to the opposite moiety. I do not need to know the exact genealogical connection between myself and others in order to establish kinship relations as a basis of behavior; I need only to know their moiety affiliation, and this I can easily ascertain by asking someone if I do not already know it.

We have now considered two ways of reckoning kinship: (1) by actual genealogical connection, and (2) by means of group affiliation. But the latter may be called an assumed genealogical basis, because the clan or moiety is in fact a kinship group. There is an actual genealogical connection between me and other members of my clan, even though I cannot determine what it is for lack of information. When, therefore, I call a man "father" or "brother" because he is a member of my clan, I am justified in assuming a real genealogical connection, even though I do not know what it is.

But in addition to actual genealogical relationships, whether they be known or not, many cultures create kinship ties and equate them with genealogical relationships when it is known full well that this is not the case. There is a variety of ways of creating kinship ties.

One very common device by means of which genealogical relationships may be created is the ritual of providing an infant with another set of parents. These may be called by our own term, "godparents." The ritual is usually performed when the child is named. The man and woman who become the godparents may of course be related to the infant prior to the ritual. In a small tribe they certainly would be, since in relatively small endogamous groups each person is related to everyone else. But in any event, they would almost certainly not be "father" and "mother" to the baby prior to the ritual. The godparents are chosen as a rule by the parents of the infant. The principles of endogamy and exogamy would operate in their selection. They would not choose persons already intimately related to the baby because very little in the way of solidarity would be gained thereby. Nor would they select persons very remotely related because the tie of godparent would then be too tenuous and weak to be of much use. The parents would try to pick a man and woman who were at the optimum distance—not too close, not too far—from the baby in order to derive the maximum benefit in the form of solidarity from the selection. The ritual device of godparents gives the baby another father and mother who are bound intimately to him by powerful ties. But the ritual may, and usually does, do more than provide the baby with *parents;* it gives him uncles and aunts, brothers and sisters, etc., as well. A whole new set of reciprocal or correlative rights and obligations is thus established by the ritual of godparents, and social solidarity and mutual aid are much promoted thereby. The survival of godparents in our own culture today is an interesting example of the vitality of kinship as a mechanism of social organization.

The ritual of godparents might be called a form of adoption. There are other forms of ritual adoption. Clan adoption is widespread among primitive peoples, although induction into a clan is almost always, if not universally, effected by adoption into a particular family, one member of which is also a member of the clan in question.[7] When a person has been cured of an illness by a medicine man he may be adopted by the doctor as his "son." This is quite common among the Pueblos of the Southwest. Here again a person acquires a whole new set of relatives as a consequence of a ritual. In some tribes a youth has a sponsor who attends him during his progress through an initiation ritual. This sponsor may become the youth's "father." It is significant that the initiate is said to be "born again" in many such instances of initiation and ritual adoption. Then there are rituals of establishing brotherhood, often by mixing the blood [8] of the contracting parties.

The reason for multiplying kinship ties by artificially creating them should be fairly plain by now: it is done to increase the number of people to whom one is bound by powerful ties of mutual aid; the more relatives to help you the better.

The extension of kinship ties goes even farther in primitive society than we have described so far. Special groups such as secret societies or other ceremonial organizations are frequently, if not usually, cast in the form of a body of kindred, with the members being "brothers" or "sisters" to one another, the leaders being "fathers" or "mothers." Thus, the members of a medicine society among the Keres are "brothers" to one another, while the head of the organization is the "father." The same is true of their hunters' and warriors' societies. Tribal officers, too, are frequently designated by kinship terms, "father" ("sire" in civil society) being the most usual, but "mother" may be the designation of the male head of a political system, as is actually the case among the Keres.[9] One of the titles of the principal wife of the Inca emperor was *Mamancik*, "Our Mother." [10] The principle of kinship may be applied to clan and moiety organization, also, the clans in each moiety being brother clans to one

[7] See, for example, L. A. White, "The Pueblo of Santa Ana, New Mexico," *American Anthropological Association, Memoir*, 60, pp. 149–152, 1942; also William I. Thomas, *Primitive Behavior*, 1937, pp. 140–150.

[8] "Blood brotherhood" has been an enormously widespread and important way of creating kinship ties; see, for example, Thomas, *op. cit.*, pp. 150–171, for a survey of this custom among preliterate peoples.

[9] Cf. White, *op. cit.*, p. 296, footnote 6.

[10] J. H. Rowe, "Inca Culture at the Time of the Spanish Conquest," *Handbook of South American Indians*, J. H. Steward (ed.), 1946, p. 258.

another, the clans in the opposite moiety being parents, children, or cousins.

Thus, the principle of kinship may permeate the whole structure of a tribe and operate on all levels from the individual tribesman to the chief of the tribe. The kinship organization forms a network which encloses each individual in a web of multiple ties; it operates along genealogical lines, being established by consanguinity and affinity; it is established also by a variety of ritual devices; it is the basis of clans and moieties; it is the form assumed by secret societies and other associations; and it gives a particular status to the officers of the tribe. Thus, from top to bottom, and throughout its extent laterally, tribal organization tends to assume the form and spirit of kinship. This is, of course, both logical and natural; it is but the development of the principle upon which human social organization was founded in the first instance: cooperation on the basis of kinship.

Kinship systems, or more particularly kinship nomenclatures, vary enormously. These variations can be grouped together into classes or types. Classification presupposes a principle of classification, of course, and therefore the number of classes or types distinguished will depend upon the principle employed, and there are a number of principles, or criteria, that may be used. But we shall return to the problem of classification later. We wish here merely to indicate something of the range and variation of types of kinship nomenclature, using the term *type* merely to designate an indefinite number of nomenclatures that resemble one another in some significant respect. There is no generally accepted classification of nomenclatures and but little uniformity of names of types. But we can display something of the variation among them, nevertheless.

In the Hawaiian type of nomenclature (Figure 6–1) there are really only five terms: grandparent, parent, sibling, child, and grandchild, with, however, qualifiers to indicate sex. This means that parents' siblings are called "parent," or "father" and "mother." One's cousins are called "sibling," or "brother" and "sister." Nephews and nieces are called "child," or "son" and "daughter." Similarly, in the grandparent and grandchild generations all relatives are called "grandparent" and "grandchild," respectively. In short, there is a terminological merging of collateral and lineal kin in each generation. This interesting system was discovered by Lewis H. Morgan, who called it Malayan rather than Hawaiian. It was this system that played such a prominent part in his formulation of the theory of group marriage and primordial promiscuity: if brothers and sisters married each other, then all would be equally "mothers" and "fathers" to their offspring, and all one's cousins would be "brothers" and "sisters."

In the Iroquois type (Figure 6–2), father's brother is "father," mother's sister is "mother," and their children are "siblings." Cross-cousins are

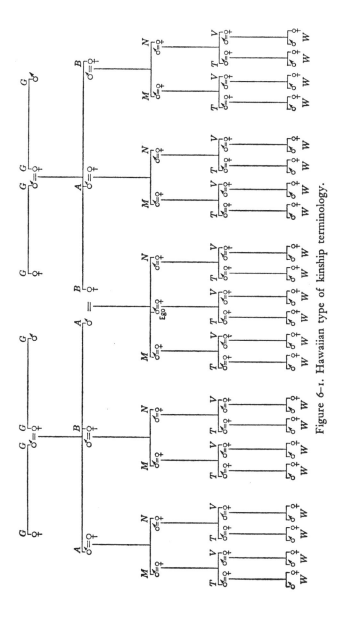

Figure 6-1. Hawaiian type of kinship terminology.

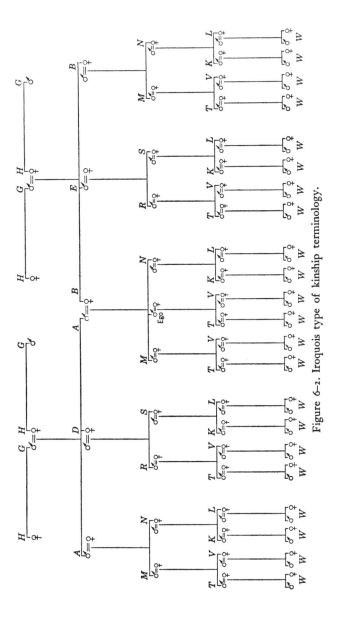

Figure 6–2. Iroquois type of kinship terminology.

"cousins." The Salish system distinguishes parents' siblings from parents, but father's siblings are not distinguished from those of mother. All cousins are "siblings," and the children of cousins are "nephew" and "niece," as distinguished from "son" and "daughter." In the Mackenzie type, parents' siblings are distinguished from parents, and father's siblings from those of the mother. All cousins are "siblings," and their children are "nephew" and "niece." The distinguishing characteristic of the Crow and Omaha types is the disregard of generation in the designation of relatives in certain lineages. Thus, in the Crow system (Figure 6–3), all males in ego's (a male) father's matrilineal lineage are "fathers"; in the Omaha system, all females in ego's (a male) mother's patrilineal lineage are "mothers." In the Eskimo system there is very little merging of lineal and collateral kin. Parents' siblings are differentiated from parents, cousins from siblings, and nephews and nieces from children. But in the second descending generation, all persons, collateral and lineal, are called "grandchildren."

Finally, we might cite such systems as our own in which there is no merging of collateral and lineal kin, but in which parents' male siblings are designated by a single term; their female siblings, by another; and all cousins are grouped together under one term. Or we might cite the Arabic nomenclature, which is much more specific and particularizing in the designation of relatives than our own. In this system, for example, father's father's brother is actually called father's father's brother; and father's sister's son is called father's sister's son.

The problem of classifying the numerous and varied patterns of kinship nomenclature is a difficult one, and a completely satisfactory solution has not yet been worked out. The principal difficulty seems to be that of determining what criterion or principle should be used. To use one thing only, e.g., the way in which cross-cousins are designated, does not seem to be sufficient, but what combination of traits would provide the basis for an adequate classification remains to be determined.

Morgan distinguished two major types of terminology, the classificatory and the descriptive. The former he subdivided into Malayan (Hawaiian) and Turano-Ganowanian. He recognized, but did not name, further subdivisions within the Ganowanian, or American Indian, group of nomenclatures. Rivers distinguished three types of nomenclature: (1) the "family system," brought into being by the nuclear family organization such as our own; (2) the "kindred system," arising from the extended family, in which father's siblings are distinguished from mother's siblings, father's brother from father and mother's sister from mother; and (3) the clan system, in which lineal and collateral relatives are merged terminologically at certain points (Morgan's classificatory system).[11]

[11] W. H. R. Rivers, *Kinship and Social Organization*, 1914, pp. 76–82.

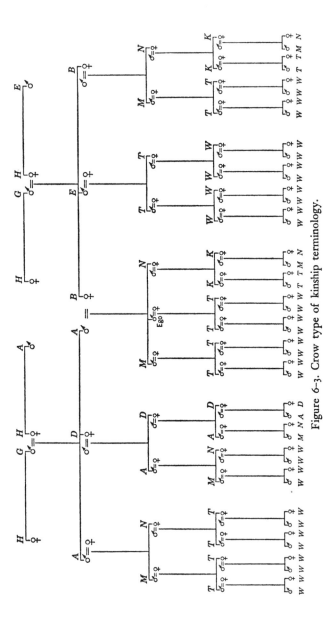

Figure 6-3. Crow type of kinship terminology.

Spier distinguished eight types of nomenclature in aboriginal North America, but they do not all rest upon the same basis, or principle of classification.[12] Radcliffe-Brown has distinguished an indefinite number of types of kinship nomenclature in his various papers, but nowhere has he undertaken a comprehensive classification of systems. Murdock has six types: Eskimo, Hawaiian, Iroquois, Sudanese, Omaha, and Crow. His classification rests upon the way in which cross-cousins are designated.[13]

Perhaps the most adequate over-all classification, one that embraces descriptive as well as classificatory systems, is one that has been devised independently by Lowie [14] and Kirchhoff,[15] at least according to Murdock.[16] In this classification there are four types of terminology: (1) *bifurcate merging,* in which father and father's brother, mother and mother's sister, are merged; (2) *bifurcate collateral:* father's siblings are distinguished from mother's siblings, father is distinguished from his brother, and mother is distinguished from her sister; (3) *lineal:* father is distinguished from his brother, mother is distinguished from her sister, but father's brother and mother's brother are called by the same term, and mother's sister and father's sister are designated by the same term; and (4) *generation:* father, father's brother, and mother's brother are designated by one term; mother, mother's sister, and father's sister by one term also.

How is this great variety of kinship nomenclature to be explained?

Free will and caprice may be dismissed at the very outset. A people, or sociocultural system, does not designate relationships among kindred in accordance with whim or fancy. On the contrary, each people believes its own nomenclature to be a natural institution. And the ethnologist, too, as a scientist, must regard kinship nomenclatures as natural phenomena among which the principle of cause and effect operates, and which therefore constitute a realm pervaded by order.

Morgan was the first to attempt an explanation of the various types of kinship nomenclature. They were created, he reasoned, by different forms of marriage and the family, and consequently they expressed "systems of consanguinity and affinity." According to his theory, mankind began its career in a condition of promiscuity. The evolution of society proceeded

[12] Leslie Spier, "The Distribution of Kinship Systems in North America," *University of Washington Publications in Anthropology,* vol. 7, 1925.

[13] George P. Murdock, *Social Structure,* The Macmillan Company, New York, 1949, pp. 223–224.

[14] R. H. Lowie, "Relationship Terms," in *Encyclopaedia Britannica,* 14th ed., 1929.

[15] Paul Kirchhoff, "Verwandtschaftsbezeichnungen und Verwandtenheirat," *Zeitschrift für Ethnologie,* vol. 64, pp. 46–49, 1932.

[16] Murdock, *op. cit.,* p. 141. The author has discussed this point with Professor Lowie, who concurs in this interpretation.

through the various forms of group marriage until monogamy was reached. As a new form of marriage and the family was evolved, it produced a new system of consanguinity and affinity, and consequently a new type of kinship nomenclature. Roughly, the communal family produced the Malayan (Hawaiian) system; clan organization, the Turanian-Ganowanian system; and the modern, monogamian family instituted the descriptive system. Thus we find Morgan formulating a sociological theory of kinship terms: nomenclatures are expressions of social organization in general, but particularly of forms of marriage and the family.

Morgan's theory was attacked by the Scottish jurist and ethnologist John F. McLennan, who branded *Systems of Consanguinity* as "utterly unscientific" in character.[17] The classificatory nomenclature was "a system of mutual salutations merely," McLennan insisted, "and not a system of blood-ties." [18] In 1909 Kroeber opposed Morgan's sociological theory with a psychological theory: [19] kinship terms were conceptual devices for classifying people and relationships on the basis of similarities and differences such as age, sex, generation, etc. "Terms of relationship reflect psychology, not sociology," Kroeber argued. "They are determined primarily by language. . . ." [20]

Kroeber's psychological theory has found few adherents. It was subjected to telling criticism by W. H. R. Rivers,[21] in which Morgan's sociological theory was given effective support. In 1934 Kroeber again opposed the sociological interpretation of kinship terms.[22] But this was virtually the last significant instance of opposition; the sociological theory has now become firmly established and almost universally accepted.

General acceptance of the theory that kinship nomenclatures are functions of social systems does not mean, however, that correlations of terminologies with various forms of social organization are easily made; were this the case the sociological theory would undoubtedly have been established long before it was. At the outset, as we have already seen, Morgan thought that it was variation in the form of marriage and the family that produced the different kinds of terminologies that he had discovered and collected. Rivers, too, placed great emphasis upon marriage as a determinant, but recognized that social structures such as lineages, clans, and

[17] John F. McLennan, *Studies in Ancient History*, 1876.

[18] *Ibid.*, xxvii of analytical table of contents, new ed., 1886.

[19] A. L. Kroeber, "Classificatory Systems of Relationship," *Journal of the Royal Anthropological Institute*, vol. 39, pp. 77–84, 1909.

[20] *Ibid.*, p. 84.

[21] *Kinship and Social Organization*, 1914.

[22] A. L. Kroeber, "Yurok and Neighboring Kin Term Systems," *University of California Publications in American Archaeology and Ethnology*, vol. 35, pp. 15–22, 1934.

moieties have an effect upon kinship nomenclatures also.[23] Lowie did much to demonstrate a close correlation between clan organization and nomenclatures of the Dakota-Iroquois type.[24] This was followed by the author's thesis that nomenclatures of the Crow and Omaha types have evolved out of Dakota-Iroquois systems, and that the transformation was effected by increased influence of clan organization upon the designation of relatives as compared with the influence of the family.[25]

The relationship between kinship nomenclatures and the underlying social life and institutions is a much more complicated affair than it was formerly thought to be, both by the proponents and the opponents of the theory of sociological determination. Just as some believed that form of marriage, or clan organization, or both, were sufficient to explain a kinship terminology, so others believed that they had dealt the sociological theory a mortal blow when they showed that correlation between clan organization and the Dakota-Iroquois system was lacking in some instances. Any kinship nomenclature is the resultant of a considerable number of factors, each of which is a variable. In addition to rules of marriage and forms of the family, and in addition to such formal structures as lineages, clans, and moieties, there are customs of residence and inheritance that may affect the designation of relatives. Division of labor between the sexes and the roles of men and women with reference to dominance and subordination within a grouping of kindred, as well as in society at large, may be significant as determinants. Then there are innumerable patterns of behavior, together with their respective attitudes, among relatives that must be taken into account. And on top of all this, the problem of correlation is made more difficult by a time lag: a social force may be operative, but it may not have had sufficient time to find expression in a kinship terminological usage; or, contrariwise, a terminological usage may persist after the social condition that produced it has ceased to exist. The problem of correlation is therefore not as simple as it was once thought to be; on the contrary, it is enormously complicated, and the wonder is that so many correlations have already been made. Only competent and sophisticated statistical techniques are capable of coping with the problem. Murdock has made a notable contribution in this respect,[26] and further studies of this sort will undoubtedly be made in the future.

[23] Rivers, *op. cit.*, pp. 76–83.

[24] R. H. Lowie, "Exogamy and the Classificatory System of Relationship," *American Anthropologist*, vol. 17, pp. 223–239, 1915.

[25] Leslie A. White, "A Problem in Kinship Terminology," *American Anthropologist*, vol. 41, pp. 566–573, 1939.

[26] Murdock, *op. cit.*, especially chap. 7.

Some students believe that kinship systems diffuse readily from one tribe to another. If this were the case, still one more difficulty would be added to those already enumerated with regard to correlations. In some instances there is evidence to indicate that the kinship system of one tribe has been influenced or affected by that of a neighboring tribe; in some cases actual kinship terms have been borrowed. But the theory of diffusion of kinship systems, in general, encounters many difficulties. Why would a tribe wish to borrow the kinship system of a neighbor? Or precisely how can the kinship system of one tribe "exert influence" upon that of another? Could a tribe borrow a system of nomenclature that was incompatible with its own social system? If compatibility is essential, could it not develop its own system? If there were no rhyme or reason to the borrowing, then of course correlations between terminologies and social organization would be impossible. But the "no-rhyme-or-reason" view is incompatible with a scientific view of natural phenomena. The diffusion of kinship systems has often been postulated as an easy way of explaining distributions. But distributions may be explainable in other terms, e.g., ecological. Until the theory of diffusion is supported by more and better evidence than it has had in the past, it must be regarded as a highly tentative, not to say dubious, hypothesis.

Effective support of the sociological theory has come from studies of changes that have taken place in kinship systems since Morgan's *Systems* was published in 1871. Eggan has shown, for example, that the kinship terminology of the Choctaws has undergone a number of changes since Morgan's day, and he has been able to explain why these changes have taken place in terms of changing social conditions occasioned primarily by the influence of the United States government and the conditions of reservation life.[27] Spoehr and others have made similar studies.[28]

Evolution of kinship systems. The science of kinship was established upon an evolutionist basis at the very outset by its founder, Morgan. According to his theory, kinship systems evolved as concomitants and as functions of evolving forms of the family. Rivers accepted Morgan's evolutionary hypothesis, but suggested that the sequence of systems be changed. Then came the wholesale rejection of evolutionist theories as applied to culture, and this of course did away with the theory that kinship systems have evolved. In a relatively recent work, Murdock states that his exhaustive study of 250 societies tends to show that "there is no

[27] Fred Eggan, "Historical Changes in the Choctaw Kinship System," *American Anthropologist*, vol. 39, 1937.
[28] Alexander Spoehr, "Changing Kinship Systems," Chicago Natural History Museum, *Anthropological Series*, vol. 33, no. 4, 1947. Other studies, too numerous to cite here, have been made in more recent years.

inevitable sequence of social forms nor any necessary association between particular rules of residence or descent or particular types of kin groups or kinship terms and levels of culture, types of economy, or forms of government or class structure." [29] This statement is made, incidentally, in a chapter entitled "Evolution of Social Organization."

Morgan's theory of the evolution of the various forms of the family and their concomitant systems of kinship has been obsolete for decades. And no one since his day has been able to work out and establish a valid theory of the evolution of kinship systems. But this does not mean that no evolution has taken place in this sector of culture. Certainly, if culture as a whole has evolved, kinship systems have partaken of this development. Or if kinship nomenclatures are functions of social systems, and if social systems have evolved, then kinship systems must have evolved along with them. In short, if evolutionist theory is applicable to culture as a whole, it certainly is relevant to kinship systems.

The difficulty here is probably like the difficulty encountered in establishing the sociological theory of kinship terms: the problem is too complicated to be solved by a simple one-to-one correlation as Morgan supposed, i.e., between a form of the family and a type of terminology. As a matter of fact, experience with Morgan's theories has made it fairly clear that one cannot properly speak of the evolution of the human family at all, for the simple reason that the family cannot be treated as an independent and autonomous system; it is an integral part of a larger unit, the society, and must be treated as such. We should not, therefore, try to correlate sequences of kinship systems with forms of the family, but with the evolution of societies as wholes. No one in recent years has undertaken to do this, as far as we know, except for one student, Gertrude Evelyn Dole.[30] Miss Dole correlated six types of terminology with a like number of types of kinship structure; three other types of terminology were produced by unusual conditions affecting some of her six types of kinship structure. She concluded that "patterns of kinship nomenclature were . . . correlated in a general way with the development of subsistence techniques and with levels of complexity in social organization." [31]

Dole's study is a thorough and painstaking one. It has been published thus far (1957) only in microfilm for the Library of Congress. Considered judgment of her findings will have to wait upon a critical examination of her monograph by competent scholars, and this will take time. We believe, however, that even though some of her conclusions should prove to be untenable in detail, her over-all thesis is sound, and that it is along

[29] Murdock, *op. cit.*, p. 200.
[30] Her doctoral dissertation, *The Development of Patterns of Kinship Nomenclature*, embraces some 450 nomenclatures.
[31] *Ibid.*, abstract, p. 2.

the general lines that she has indicated that a valid and illuminating theory of development will eventually be worked out.

The classificatory system of relationship. As we have already seen, Morgan classified all kinship systems into two major groups: *classificatory* and *descriptive* systems (Figures 6–4 and 6–5). These terms have been much criticized and widely misunderstood. With regard to the latter, it has been argued that our system, which Morgan placed in the descriptive

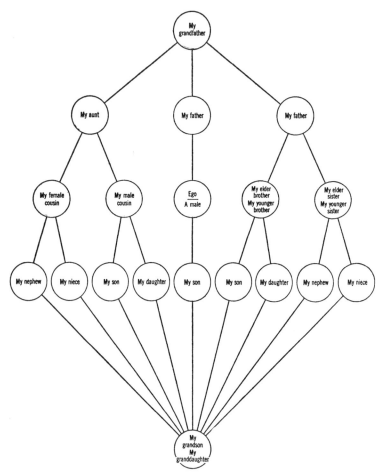

Figure 6–4. The classificatory system (Seneca-Iroquois).

category, is really classificatory, because words like "cousin" embrace more than one kind of relationship. Needless to say, Morgan was aware of this, but this is not what he meant by classificatory. He makes it perfectly clear in *Systems* that only those terms that include more than one kind of genealogical relationship are classificatory. For example, when father, father's sister's son, and father's sister's daughter's son are called "father," then the term is classificatory. But "cousin" designates but one kind of genealogical relationship, namely, parent's sibling's child, and is

Figure 6–5. The descriptive system (English).

therefore a descriptive term. With regard to criticism of the term "classificatory" itself, Radcliffe-Brown has remarked: "Doubtless it is not the ideal word; but it has long been in use and no better one has been suggested, though others have been put forward." [32]

Just as Morgan classified all systems of relationship into two categories, so did he classify social systems into two major types: primitive society organized upon the basis of kinship, which he called *societas*, and civil society founded upon property relations and territorial distinctions, which he called *civitas*.[33] Finally, he correlated classificatory systems of relationships with primitive society and the descriptive systems with modern civil society. This correlation is not wholly valid, although in the main it is. Some primitive peoples have kinship systems that are not classificatory at all or are so only to a limited extent. All systems among civil societies are descriptive, however, and certainly classificatory systems are characteristic of the majority of primitive societies. The transition from classificatory systems to descriptive systems was a concomitant and a function of the transition from primitive, tribal society to civil society and was therefore an evolutionary sequence. But it is not this evolutionary aspect of kinship systems that interests us here. It is the classificatory system itself. The classificatory system of relationship was closely correlated with the social organization and life of most primitive peoples, and an understanding of it will illuminate and make more intelligible the basic processes of primitive society, namely, those of kinship.

The classificatory system of relationship is characterized by two basic features: (1) it merges collateral and lineal kindred terminologically at certain points; and (2) it contains only primary terms. With regard to the first, we have such examples as calling father's brother, father's sister's son, and father's sister's daughter's son "father," or designating parallel cousins by sibling terms. It is this characteristic that Morgan called *classificatory:* a number of different kinds of genealogical relationships were classed together. With regard to the second characteristic, there are no terms like our "second cousin" or "great grandfather" in the classificatory systems. Every relative, i.e., every person designated by a kinship term, is therefore a close relative, a relative of the first degree, from the standpoint of behavior and attitude in social intercourse, even though, genealogically speaking, he may be a sixteenth cousin.

The classificatory system of relationship expresses in an eloquent way the kinship nature and basis of primitive society. It is a wonderfully ingenious mechanism. It is at once both a self-expanding and a self-enclosing system. On the one hand, it operates so as to increase the size of

---

[32] A. R. Radcliffe-Brown, "The Study of Kinship Systems," *Journal of the Royal Anthropological Institute*, vol. 71, p. 7, 1941.

[33] Lewis H. Morgan, *Ancient Society*, 1877, pp. 6-7.

the mutual-aid group, and on the other, it effectively promotes solidarity among the members of the group. In short, it is a means of serving the exogamous and endogamous processes of society at the same time. Let us see specifically how this is accomplished.

My father's brothers are my "fathers," and their children are my "brothers" and "sisters." But my father will call his male parallel cousins "brother," which means that they are also my "fathers" and their children are my "brothers" and "sisters." My father's parallel cousins extend indefinitely from his own line of descent in degrees which we can designate with cardinal numbers, 1, 2, 3, etc., and all these male cousins are my "fathers," and their children my "brothers" and "sisters." The same reasoning will apply to my mother, to her sister, her female parallel cousins, whom she will call "sister" and I will call "mother," and to their respective children, all of whom I will call "brother" and "sister." Thus I will have "fathers" and "siblings," extending outward indefinitely on one side of my own line of descent, and "mothers" and "siblings," on the other. The extent to which they may be recognized and become significant in social life depends, of course, upon various conditions and circumstances, such as size of band or local group, size of tribe, place of residence, mode of life, and so on. The *tendency*, however, in primitive societies with the classificatory system of nomenclature is to extend the bonds of relationship until the boundaries of the tribe are reached. In this way every individual will become related, in a way that is significant in the social life, to every other individual in the tribe. In short, the operation of the classificatory system tends to organize all individuals in the tribe into a single network of relatives. "The use of the terms of relationship," says Radcliffe-Brown, "is so extended as to embrace all persons who come into social contact with one another. If we take any single member of the tribe, then every person with whom he has any social dealings whatever stands to him in one or other of the relations denoted by the terms in use and may be addressed by that term. *In this way the whole society forms a body of relatives* [italics supplied]." [34]

The classificatory system thus operates to produce the maximum size of cooperating group possible within the tribe, namely, the entire tribe itself. If cooperation is an advantage in the struggle for survival, and if size of group is an advantage in this competitive struggle, then the classificatory system of kinship and nomenclature admirably serves both these ends. It organizes individuals for cooperative endeavor, and it tends to increase the size of the group until it reaches the limits of tribal boundaries.

But if, on the one hand, the classificatory system serves the process of

[34] A. R. Radcliffe-Brown, "Three Tribes of Western Australia," *Journal of the Anthropological Institute*, vol. 43, p. 150, 1913.

exogamy by extending the ties of kinship indefinitely on all sides, it serves the endogamous process, on the other, by establishing close and powerful social bonds between relatives genealogically remote. Although the classificatory system is a device for extending kinship ties indefinitely and to great distances measured genealogically, it is also a way of making the *social* ties thus established close and intense. Thus, the classificatory system reaches out to my father's parallel cousin's parallel cousin's parallel cousin—all males, in this instance. But when it has finally reached him it brings him very close to me: it makes him *my father*. There are no terms such as "second" or "third" cousin in classificatory systems. As the system operates, no one, no matter how remote genealogically he may be, can be more remote sociologically than a "cousin," "uncle," "niece," or "grandparent." [35] Thus the classificatory system not only operates to provide one with an indefinite number of relatives; it makes each one of them a *close* relative. Solidarity of the group is promoted as the size is increased.

But kinship may go beyond the boundaries of a tribe; it may serve as the basis of intertribal relations as well. All five of the Iroquoian tribes composing the famous League had three clans in common, and other clans were shared by two or more tribes. Members of the Bear, Wolf, and Turtle clans in the Seneca tribe had fellow clansmen in the Cayuga, Onondaga, Oneida, and Mohawk tribes. All Iroquoian tribes were regarded, therefore, as related to one another.

The League of the Iroquois itself, an intertribal political organization, was based upon kinship ties. The confederacy was governed by a council of fifty chiefs chosen from the several tribes. But each chieftainship belonged not merely to a tribe, nor even to a moiety or clan of the tribe; it belonged to a certain matrilineal lineage. When a League chief died, the matron of his lineage would select, with the advice or consent of other members of the lineage, his successor from the male members of the lineage. In practice, the successor was usually a younger brother of the deceased chief or a son of one of his sisters. The candidate selected by the matron and other members of the lineage was then subject to the approval or disapproval of the clan, moiety, and tribe, in succession, before being presented for installation by the League council. Thus we have the remarkable example of a supertribal political structure whose roots extended down into the subsoil of intimate kinship ties. They ran from the League council down through the tribe, the moiety, the clan, and lineage to family fireside.

The concept of kinship in primitive culture may extend even beyond the boundaries of human society: it can embrace plant and animal species, and even inanimate phenomena. In totemic systems in aboriginal Aus-

[35] Cf. Morgan, *Systems of Consanguinity and Affinity of the Human Family*, 1871, pp. 147, 160.

tralia certain plants, birds, and animals are totemic ancestors, and certain topographic features are intimately associated with the totemic system. Among North American Indian tribes, the bear may be "father" or "grandfather"; the spider, "grandmother." The sun is commonly "father" or "sun youth," and the earth is usually "our mother." Just as persons with whom one has friendly social relations are, or must be, one's relatives, so plants and animals and inanimate natural phenomena are incorporated into the social systems of primitive peoples. It would hardly be an exaggeration to say that kinship is the connective tissue of the world that preliterate peoples live in.

The Agricultural Revolution transformed primitive society, based upon kinship, into civil society, founded upon property relations and territorial organization. Class structure and class division replace lineage and clan; competition and conflict take the place of mutual aid. From the standpoint of the needs and satisfactions of human beings, this transformation meant a great loss: the loss of kinship, which, as Tylor pointed out, means "kindliness" and mutual aid. This transformation of social organization finds expression in kinship terminology, namely, in a change from classificatory systems to descriptive systems. The new type of terminology does not seek to keep and contain relatives within a fixed and definite boundary as the old classificatory systems did (Figures 6–4 and 6–5), but, on the contrary, deliberately allows them to become dispersed and lost sight of.

But with the advent of civil society, the memory of primitive kinship was preserved,[36] and the new sociocultural systems often cast their various organizations into the image of kinship, if not its substance. Members of medieval guilds were "brothers" to one another. The church was organized in terms of kinship: the pope, il papa, at the head, with "fathers," "mothers," "brothers," and "sisters" among the clergy and congregations. Even the gods were organized into a Holy Family. Secret societies and lodges multiply and proliferate as "fraternal" orders. Labor unions think of themselves as fraternal organizations; there are "brotherhoods" of railway trainmen. Universities become "our mothers," and one's nation is always a mother country or a fatherland.

Kinship was both pervasive and precious in primitive society. When it was lost, as a basis of social organization, in the cultures produced by the Agricultural Revolution, an attempt was made to create as much of society as possible in the image of kinship.

[36] Legends of the "Golden Age" might conceivably be ethnic memories of a time and of a society when all men were brothers.

Chapter 7 STRUCTURE, FUNCTIONS, AND EVOLUTION OF HUMAN SOCIAL SYSTEMS

All societies of living beings are *systems*, organic wholes composed of inter-related parts. They thus present themselves to our observation under two aspects, structural and functional. On the one hand, we may study social systems from the standpoint of the kind or kinds of parts of which the whole is composed, and on the other, we may focus our attention upon the interrelationship of these parts, upon the relationship of one part to another and to the whole. Structure and function are therefore merely two ways of looking at a single phenomenon, namely, a system, or organism.

The problems of the social scientist in general and of the culturologist in particular do not differ in nature from those of scientists in the physical and biological realms. The basic problems of all science are those of structure and function, of differentiation and integration. The astronomer's objective is to discover the structure of the cosmos, galaxies, star clusters, and the stars and to interpret their behavior. The physicist is concerned with the structure of the atom and the interrelationship of its parts. The biologist wants to know how living beings are constructed and how they behave. Like his fellow scientists in other fields, the culturologist analyzes the structures of cultures in general and of social systems in particular and interprets their behavior. Our immediate interest now is in the structure and function of human social systems. We want to know how they are constructed, of what kind or kinds of parts they are composed, and how these parts are put together and held together to form an integrated whole. In short, we shall view social systems from the standpoint of differentiation of structure and specialization of function, on the one hand, and of integration on the other; as *parts* and as *wholes*.

By *social system* we mean the whole network of relationships among the individuals of a distinguishable group. We shall analyze human social systems in three kinds of structures: segments, classes, and special mechanisms. By *segment* we mean one of an indefinite number of parts comprising a whole in which one part is like another in structure, or composition, and function. A family is thus a segment. Society as a whole is divisible into families, and one family is generically like another, in any given system, in structure and function. Lineages, clans, and moieties also are segments. The process of segmentation may express itself in other forms also, as we shall see later. A *class*, as we shall use this term, is one of an indefinite number of parts into which a society as a whole is divided, in which one class differs from another in composition, or structure, and function. Thus, men and women, or males and females, constitute social classes. Society as a whole may be divided into two classes according to sex, male and female, and the classes differ in their composition and function. The married, unmarried, and widowed constitute so many classes. So also do adults and children.

All human societies are thus composed of, or divisible into, both segments and classes. Classes and segments are alike in that each is a subdivision of the system as a whole; all of a given society is subdivided into an indefinite but aliquot number of parts, in the one case segments, in the other, classes. To put this statement in reverse, the sum of the segments or classes is precisely equal to the system as a whole. Classes and segments differ from each other as kinds of structures in that one segment is like another, but each class is unlike all others.

By the term *special mechanism* [1] in our consideration of social morphology, we mean a structure distinguishable within the system as a whole but which is not one of a class of structures into which the entire society may be subdivided. A chief, shaman, or secret society is such a structure. We do not think of society as a whole being subdivided into special mechanisms, as we do segments or classes. Rather, we see a special mechanism merely as a distinguishable structure with a specialized function within a social system. As a matter of fact, a society may have no special mechanisms at all, as we define this term. Some primitive societies, such as the Tasmanians, certain pygmy and Eskimo groups, and others, come very close to being without internal structures sufficiently differentiated to warrant the use of this term. They are virtually without political chiefs or specialized shamans; they have only classes and segments. A special mechanism, therefore, is a different kind of a *part* of the social whole from a segment or a class. The latter are *general* structures; their sum is totality of social system. Special mechanisms are always less than

---

[1] We are not satisfied with this term but can think of none better. By "mechanism" we mean a structure that does something as a heart that pumps blood. By "special" we mean not general, or coextensive with social system. Thus, a system of ethics is a general mechanism of social control; it is structurally coextensive with social system. A chief, however, is a special social mechanism of integration and control.

the whole. A class or a segment is a part *of* a whole; an organ is a part distinguished *within* the whole. A society may, as we have just noted, have no specialized structures, or mechanisms, at all; or it may have a number of kinds of such structures, and it may have more than one of each kind. Chiefs, shamans, priests, police, secret societies, and so on, are so many kinds of special mechanisms.

Our tasks are therefore (1) to distinguish, define, and classify types of social structures; (2) to discover the way in which each part is related to others and how all are integrated into a coherent whole; and (3) to trace the course of social evolution in both its aspects, structural and functional.

The first human social systems were, as we have seen earlier, local territorial groups, each of which was composed of families. These two forms of social organization, local group and family, were inherited from man's subhuman ancestors. At the very outset of human history, therefore, we distinguish but one kind of segment, namely, families within the local group or band. Male and female, mature and immature, mated and unmated, are distinguishable social classes. No special mechanisms are to be distinguished at all unless an outstanding individual, a leader, of the local group or band may be so distinguished and designated. We now wish to trace the development of human society from the standpoint of structure and function and from its starting point on the anthropoid level.

We have seen in an earlier chapter how anthropoid society was transformed into human society. Families were organized into a network of ties of consanguinity and affinity. This network, or kinship system, was defined by relationship terms and regulated by a set of rules and sanctions. We have seen how the processes of exogamy and endogamy operated as means of relating part to part and of integrating parts into a coherent whole. We now wish to inquire further into the process of structural differentiation and functional specialization as culture evolves as a consequence of increased control over the forces of nature by technological means.

In Chapter 2, "Energy and Tools," we noted that a close relationship obtains between degree of organization and concentration of energy. As matter becomes less organized as energy becomes more diffuse, so conversely, the degree of organization of a system increases as the concentration of energy within the system increases. Social systems are but the social form of expression of technological control over the forces of nature. Social evolution is therefore a function of technological development. Social systems evolve as the amount of energy harnessed per capita per year increases, other factors remaining constant. This is to say, they become more differentiated structurally, more specialized functionally, and as a consequence of differentiation and specialization, special mechanisms of integration and regulation are developed. Thus human social evolution becomes intelligible in terms of entropy, in terms of a corollary of the second law of thermodynamics: *the degree of organization of a system is proportional to the concentration of energy within the system.* We may thus view social evolution against the background of a principle fundamental in nature and cosmic in scope.

Segments

The phenomenon of segmentation is closely related to another, namely, integration. A segment is, in fact, a mechanism of integration; a segment is a part, and *part* implies a *whole*. Segmentation, as a process, is a means of increasing the size of systems while preserving at the same time a high degree of inner cohesion or solidarity. As we noted in our discussion of endogamy and exogamy, the solidarity of a social group tends to diminish as the size of the group increases. If advantage is to continue to accrue from increase in size, a way must be found to maintain solidarity at a high level. We saw how the laws of endogamy and exogamy operate to balance size and solidarity of group in such a way as to achieve maximum effectiveness of group endeavor. We now see how the process of segmentation operates to do the same thing. It makes possible an increase in size; no system, physical, biological, or social, can increase its size beyond a certain point without resort to segmentation. By means of the segmentive process any type of system may be enlarged, for not only is an increase made possible by the integration of one class of segments on one level, but the segments of one level may become integrated into units that constitute segments of a higher level of organization, and so on indefinitely. But at the same time that the process of segmentation operates to increase the size of the system, it functions to maintain its inner cohesion or solidarity. The segments remain small even though the system grows large, and within the segment a high degree of cohesion or solidarity may be preserved. Secondly, integration takes place between segments just as among the elements comprising the segments; the segmentive process is intersegmental as well as intrasegmental. The process of segmentation is thus a marvelously ingenious way of uniting two opposite principles or tendencies into a harmonious and balanced synthesis: unity and plurality, discreteness and synthesis, size and solidarity.

From the foregoing it is obvious that the segmentive process is closely related to that of evolution. Evolution is made possible or brought about by establishing new bases of integration on successively higher levels.[2]

---

[2] "The growth of segmentary structures is a constant feature of social development, and it seems that certain forms of structure can only reach stability and permanence by that means." A. R. Radcliffe-Brown, "The Social Organization of Australian Tribes," *Oceania*, vol. 1, pt. 4, p. 440, 1931.

This is not the only way in which evolution can take place, of course. It may occur also as a consequence of differentiation of structure and specialization of function, but we shall deal with this later. Our concern now is with the relation of segmentation to evolution.

The process of segmentation is observable everywhere and on all levels of organization, physical, biological, and social. A galaxy is a segment of the cosmos; a star is a segment of a galaxy. An atom is a segment of a molecule, as the latter is of larger material systems. A segment may be composed of a number of parts, just as it is one of a number of parts of a larger system. We now come face to face with a very interesting and apparently fundamental principle: any system, whether it be a segment itself or an organization of segments, has a maximum limit of size. Thus a molecule is a segmented system, as the chemist pictures it, the segments being atoms. But the size of a molecule of a given element, i.e., the number of its component atoms, cannot be increased beyond a certain point. A molecule of oxygen usually contains two atoms. It may have three, but apparently no more than this. On a higher level of integration we may consider a drop of mercury. It is not a mere aggregation of molecules, but an organized, segmented system in which the molecules are segments. But this system, too, like the molecule of oxygen, cannot be increased in size beyond a certain point. Thus we observe two aspects of material systems of this sort: (1) units tend to combine and form integrated systems, but (2) the integrative process cannot form larger and larger systems indefinitely; there is a maximum size and limit for each kind of system. These aspects of systems are observable elsewhere also. We may suppose that a galaxy is a grouping of stars that tend to unite to form a system. But the size of a star grouping is limited, just as is the size of the drop of mercury. When this limit is reached, a new galaxy is formed. We do not find, therefore, one organization of stars of in-definite—or infinite—size in the cosmos, but many systems, like so many droplets of water.

In biological systems also we may observe the limits of the integrative process on the basis of segments of a given order. A metazoan system can-not be increased in size indefinitely on the basis of segmentation and in-tegration alone; sooner or later it reaches a point beyond which it would fall apart, just as in the case of a molecule of oxygen or a drop of mercury. The same is true of a colony of unicellular organisms—a segmented sys-tem in which each single-celled organism is a segment.

Thus, we see that any given system based upon the integration of seg-ments cannot be increased in size beyond a certain point. But, and here we come to a most important point, systems can be formed by integrat-ing these original maximum-sized systems into a still larger system in which the original systems become segments. A molecule of mercury cannot contain more than a certain number of atoms, but a larger multi-molecular system can be formed in which the molecules become segments. A galaxy has a limit of maximum size, but galaxies themselves become segments of a supergalactic system. Thus we note two important principles: (1) on a given level, the number of units that can be integrated into a segment is limited, and therefore the size of systems on this level cannot be increased beyond a certain point; but (2) *systems* on one level may be integrated *as segments* of a larger system on a higher level. In this way the process of evolution may proceed indefinitely by organizing the systems of one level into larger systems on a higher level.

We shall now apply these principles to human social organization and evolution. A society of human beings is a material system. If, therefore, there be principles applicable to material systems in general, as science is obliged to assume, they must be applicable to human social systems in particular. And an interpretation of human social organization and evolution in terms of principles cosmic in scope must be more fundamental and significant than an interpretation limited to human society itself. We may demonstrate the relationship of segmentation to integration, and the roles of both in social evolution, with the example of military organization.

An army is a highly developed form of a segmented social system. It is, in fact, a pyramid composed of strata of segments, the units of one level becoming segments of the units on the next higher level. On the lowest level of organization are the individual soldiers, or units. They become segments of units called squads, which in turn become segments of units called platoons, which in turn become segments of companies, and so on through battalions, regiments, and divisions, to armies. A number of armies may then be integrated into a superarmy, or fighting force, of a nation under a single command. And the military forces of a number of allied nations may be integrated under a joint staff.

Why is an army organized in this way? Why not have just one large aggregation of men, a horde without differentiation of internal structure? The answer is, of course, obvious. An unorganized group of this size would fall apart of its own weight, just as a drop of mercury cannot exceed the limit of size set by the cohesive power of its molecules. The basic units of an army are living material particles called *soldiers*, or *men*. They attract each other and form groups. They do this because mutual aid and security are served thereby. But the force of attraction between one man and another in a group tends to vary inversely with the number of men in the group; the more numerous the members, the weaker the force of attraction between them. The solidarity of a group, and with it its effectiveness for concerted action, diminishes as the number of its component individuals increases. A point will eventually be reached, if the size continues to increase, where the group will tend to fall apart of its own weight; its solidarity and effectiveness will reach a vanishing point. The number of individuals in a group must be small enough to provide a high degree of solidarity if effectiveness of concerted action is to be achieved.

The smallest grouping of an army, therefore, cannot exceed a certain size. It must be small enough so that the attraction between the component elements, the men, will be strong enough to make the group militarily effective as well as a mere integrated unit. If the military organization is to become larger, the men must be further integrated, not on the level of individuals, but upon a higher level, that of squads, platoons, or companies.[3] Further increases in size of the military organization are accomplished by successive integrations on higher and higher levels.

We are, of course, describing an army structurally and functionally, not genetically. We are not saying that in the course of the evolution of armies you first had squads, which were put together to form platoons, and these in turn combined to form companies, battalions, regiments, etc., as a child might build a pyramid of blocks. Segmentation is a process of a *system*, or *organism*, and an organism is always a whole, a one. Segmentation is a process that goes on *within* a system; it is not a process out of which systems are built by addition and accretion. Military organization has evolved with segmentation and increase in size going hand in hand. Our description of an army as an organism integrated through segmentation is not, therefore, an account of how it came into being, but of how it maintains its being. An army can hold thousands of men together because they are first of all organized into small, highly cohesive groups; then these groups, *as groups*, are organized into larger groups on a higher level. The number of segments of a given class decreases as the number of men contained by each segment increases; so that although the force of attraction between *individuals* decreases as we go up the pyramid of stratified segments, this is compensated for by the integration and reintegration of *segments* as we ascend. For example, two men in different army divisions may be closely related to each other through the relationship between divisions since each man is integrated and reintegrated with his division many times by his membership in a succession of segments: company, battalion, brigade, and regiment. The two soldiers may thus face each other directly as members of divisions.

Ecclesiastical organization also offers an interesting and instructive example of integration through segmentation. On the lowest stratum we have congregations, unless one distinguishes segments within this grouping. Congregations are organized into parishes, and these into

---

[3] Whether the smallest significant unit is the squad, platoon, or company is a matter of particular fact rather than of general theory, and therefore is not germane to our discussion here.

bishoprics, archbishoprics, and so on up to the Church, which contains them all.

In military and ecclesiastical organizations we see processes at work which have played an important role in social evolution: evolution through segmentation and integration. We shall now turn to human society and observe the operation of these processes in the course of social evolution.

Let us again consider the social organization of anthropoids. It exhibits two types of units, the family and the local group. Families are segments of the local groups. Here as in physical and chemical systems, we do not find our units distributed at random, i.e., anthropoids scattered at random over the landscape; they tend to group themselves together. We may be able to give no better answer to the question, "Why do atoms of oxygen tend to form molecules?" than to say, "It's their nature to do so." But we can say more than this about the social organization of anthropoids: they come together to satisfy sexual hunger, because group life affords some protection to the individual, and because the nature and distribution of their food permit and encourage group organization. We may not know why an atom of a given element has five electrons rather than four or six, but we know what determines the size of the anthropoid family. We know also what determines the size of the local group (Chapter 3). Thus we may observe and understand the phenomena of segmentation and integration in the society of man's immediate subhuman ancestors.

In our discussion of the definition and prohibition of incest and of the operation of the processes of exogamy and endogamy, we saw how primate social organization was affected, and human social evolution initiated, by the emergence and operation of a new mechanism of integration, namely, articulate speech. Kinship systems were formed by the integration of families as segments. But here also we noted that a kinship system based upon genealogical reckoning alone cannot increase in size indefinitely and remain effective; eventually a point will be reached when it will tend to fall to pieces. It is here that the process of segmentation again becomes significant: the formation of new kinds of segments made integration on higher levels possible. We have already seen how clans, as segments of society, served as mechanisms of integration in the operation of kinship systems. We now wish to consider them in another context, namely, that of the evolution of social structure. We wish specifically to see how clans are formed by the segmentive process, how they become segmented in turn, and how clans function as mechanisms of integration.

In the previous chapter we noted that kinship was extended outward from the family laterally and lineally. Recognition of, and emphasis upon, kinship ties along the lines of ascent and descent result in the formation of socially significant groupings that we call *lineages*. We may distinguish two main types of lineages, bilateral, or ambilateral, and unilateral. In groupings of the former type, descent is reckoned in either or both lines, the father's and the mother's. In unilateral groupings, descent is reckoned in one line only, the father's, or male, *or* the mother's, or female, line. We thus have two kinds of unilateral lineages, patrilineal and matrilineal. To illustrate these types of groupings we may cite the Maori as an example of the ambilateral, the Iroquois of the matrilineal, and the Omaha as an example of the patrilineal, type of lineage. In some sociocultural systems lineal ascent and descent are not sufficiently emphasized to produce significant lineage groupings.

Lineages are segments, vertical segments so to speak, as distinguished from families, which at any given time are distributed on a horizontal plane. Whether a social system has lineages or not, and whether the lineage is ambilineal, patrilineal, or matrilineal, is a matter that is determined by the mode of life of the people, specifically by the way in which they nourish themselves, defend themselves from their enemies, and protect themselves from the elements. In other words, it is the specific technological means of adjustment and control in the life-sustaining activities of nutrition, defense, and shelter that determine the social organization of a people in this respect as in others. Let us consider unilateral lineages first.

A patrilineal lineage is a unilateral grouping of relatives composed of a man, his children, and other descendants in the male line only. A matrilineal lineage is composed of a woman, her children, and other descendants in the female line only. A society may have an indefinite number of unilateral lineages, but if it recognizes any, it must have at least two: one unilateral lineage implies or requires another since it includes descendants in one sex line only and excludes descendants in the other. Some societies recognize only two, in which case we call them *moieties*. This is a special kind of unilateral organization, which we shall discuss later.

The factors that tend to produce unilateral lineages are specifically numerous and varied. Generically, however, they may be reduced to three: division of labor between the sexes, exogamy, and place of residence of a couple after marriage. Obviously, this is not to say that wherever these factors are found unilateral lineages will be present also, for a division of labor between the sexes, exogamy, and a place of residence are universal, whereas unilateral lineages are very far from such a distribution. What we wish to say is that unilateral lineages have been formed by the operation of these factors and that they have not come into being as a consequence of other primary factors; but they are not *always* a consequence of division of labor, exogamy, and place of residence. It is only under certain conditions that these factors produce unilateral lineages.

As a general proposition we may say that prominence or predominance of men in the mode of life of the society will tend to produce patrilineal lineages; prominence or predominance of women will tend to form matrilineal lineages. Thus a culture in which warfare, hunting, or herding is an activity of paramount importance will tend toward patrilineal lineages because these occupations tend to be masculine pursuits. In systems where woman's role in subsistence, house building, and ownership, or in some handicraft, puts her in a position of considerable importance as compared with men in the mode of life, there will be a tendency toward matrilineal lineages. These general statements are sound enough, but they could easily be misleading because they tend to obscure, by the very generality of their nature, the complex organization of numerous and diverse factors at work in specific situations. Thus men and women both may be food providers. As such their roles may be equal in importance, or one may be more significant than another in degrees, varying from a small amount to a very great extent. In some cultural systems one factor may tend to counterbalance another. In some societies, such as some of the Apache tribes, men may derive social importance from frequent and critical participation in warfare, but women may be quite important in gathering and processing wild plant food and in the manufacture of buckskin and other articles. Among the Eskimo the man is the principal food getter, but the woman is essential in the manufacture of skin clothing and other important household duties. Among the Iroquois, the men were the hunters and warriors, but the women cultivated the gardens and had charge of the houses and custody of stored crops. Magical considerations are sometimes important as well as rational, technological factors—magic in this respect as in others may be regarded as a pseudo technology. In some Australian tribes only men may have custody of certain sacred spots and of objects stored at those places; and only men may perform ceremonies believed to be essential to the group's welfare and which are associated with these sacred places. Thus, if there is to be unilateral organization, this factor will operate powerfully to cast it into the patrilineal mold.

We see, then, that the factors relevant to the formation or absence of lineages are numerous and varied. We have various activities of men in subsistence, M $(S_1, S_2, S_3, \ldots)$; and of women, also, W $(S_1, S_2, S_3, \ldots)$. Similarly, we have their roles in offense and defense, in shelter—housebuilding and upkeep, the manufacture and repair of clothing—in the arts and crafts, such as the ceramic, textile, metallurgical, magical arts, and so on. In any cultural situation a great number of factors relative to lineage formation will thus be operative. Some will *tend* to produce patrilineal lineages, others matrilineal lineages. Whether a society will have distinct lineage groupings or not, and whether the lineages will be ambilateral or unilateral, patrilineal or matrilineal, will depend upon the integrated summation of all these factors.

The discovery of correlations between lineage grouping and the roles of men and women in basic technologic activities is further complicated by this fact: a group whose social system was shaped by one set of technological and occupational factors may change its mode of life but preserve its former type of social organization, at least for a time. A people can change its mode of life quickly and abruptly; social systems tend to change more slowly. The Crow Indians of 1880 were a war-like, equestrian, hunting people; these characteristics emphasize the role of the man and tend to elevate him above the woman in social importance. We would expect, therefore, to find the Crow with patrilineal lineages if they had unilateral groupings of kindred at all. But they did not; they had *matrilineal* lineages and clans. A case of this sort appears, therefore, to contradict and refute our theory that predominance of the male in the basic life-sustaining activities tends to produce patrilineal groupings. But as it happens, we know something about the history of the Crow. They formerly lived with the Hidatsa and other agricultural village tribes on the upper Missouri River. Under such conditions of life matrilineal lineages were probably formed as a consequence of prominence of women in horticulture and custody or ownership of houses: the Hidatsa were matrilineal and matrilocal. Then, after the introduction of the horse and firearms and with increased pressure of white settlers ever pushing westward, the Crow left their settled habitations and their cornfields and moved out into the Great Plains to become roving hunters and warriors. The roles of the sexes in the mode of life of the tribe were profoundly changed. But the social organization did not change at once and overnight. The older matrilineal organization was preserved and adapted to the new way of life. They have, however, "shifted to patri-local residence though they still retain their matri-sibs." [4]

The formation of social systems under technological and occupational influence is a complicated process, one in which many factors are at work and exerting their influence in opposite or divergent, as well as parallel or convergent, directions. And added to this is the lag of institutional change following technological change. Only the superficial or naïve will therefore expect or demand easy, simple, one-to-one correlations.

But division of labor between the sexes is only one of the significant

[4] G. P. Murdock, *Social Structure*, The Macmillan Company, New York, 1949, p. 206.

factors that produce unilateral lineages; we still have to consider exogamy and place of residence. All three factors work together.

Incest was invented, so to speak, defined, and prohibited in order to make cooperation between family groups compulsory by prohibiting marriage within the family. But incest and exogamy involve place of residence as well as consanguinity. A family has a place of residence, and therefore if marriage within the family is prohibited, someone, either the bride or groom, or both, must change his place of residence at marriage. Custom may require a newly married couple to reside with the family of the groom (patrilocal residence) or with the family of the bride (matrilocal residence). Or it may require them to live with the parents of either the bride or the groom as they please (ambilocal residence). Or bride and groom may establish their residence apart from the homes of the parents of either one (neolocal residence). The last alternative is relatively rare in primitive society; the newly married couple usually lives with the family either of the bride or of the groom. This is done for reasons of economy of housing facilities or of mutual aid or both.

We may distinguish two kinds of *place* exogamy, household and district exogamy. Thus, a person may merely leave his or her household group upon marriage and go to the household of his or her spouse in the same village or locality, such as is the case among the Iroquois or the Pueblo Indians. Or one may leave his village or district at marriage and go to live in the village or district of his spouse, as in the case of the patrilocal Arunta or the matrilocal Chiricahua Apache. The factors that determine place of residence are essentially the same as those which determine descent in lineages, namely, division of labor between the sexes and the relative importance of the roles of men and women in the fundamental activities of the group. If the woman plays the lesser role in activities closely correlated with residence, she will tend to leave home at marriage and go to live with her husband at his parents' home. If, however, she has a relatively important role, she will tend to remain in her own home after marriage and her husband will leave his home and come to live with her. Nomadic herding or prominence of hunting or warfare in the life of a people tends toward patrilocal residence, whereas horticulture, or even a considerable dependence upon wild seeds or other plant food, gathered by the women, will incline the society toward matrilocal residence.

In aboriginal Australia the man has a prominent role in food getting. It is highly desirable for the male hunter to be intimately acquainted with the terrain over which he hunts. "A boy begins to acquire this knowledge about the country of his own horde from a very early age," says Radcliffe-Brown. "If he left his own country, say at marriage, this knowledge would be lost and he would have to start over again to learn all that he would be required to know about the country to which he moved." [5] The woman, too, should know where plant food can be found, but detailed topographic knowledge is less important in this occupation than in hunting. Therefore it is more desirable from the standpoint of group efficiency for the man to remain in familiar territory than the woman. But more important perhaps than food getting in Australian culture is male supremacy in the pseudo technology of totemism. As Phyllis Kaberry has pointed out, only men can take care of sacred objects stored in fixed holy places and perform the necessary ceremonies associated with them.[6] It is necessary, therefore, for them to remain in their own districts, whereas the women are in this respect quite free to leave. Thus, exogamy plus division of labor between the sexes in Australian culture operates rather strongly to bring about patrilocal residence and local patrilineal lineages.

Among the Iroquois the situation is different. Here the men hunt, fish, and fight; the women till the gardens and fields and have important household duties. A woman and her daughters own the house which their respective families occupy together. They have custody of the crops stored in the houses. They prepare the food and have charge of its distribution. They thus play a prominent role in subsistence. It would be a great inconvenience for a woman to leave at marriage the house and its stores that are part hers. It would also tend to disrupt the economic organization of the household. But it would be quite easy for the man to leave; all he would need to do would be to pack up his few personal belongings and move. Here again, exogamy and division of labor along sex lines produce unilateral groupings of kindred, this time, however, in the female line.

Thus we find three important factors, division of labor along sex lines, exogamy, and place of residence, that tend, in certain cultural systems, to produce a particular kind of segment: a unilateral grouping of kindred. As we have pointed out earlier, these factors alone and by themselves are not sufficient to form distinct and socially significant unilateral lineages; it is only when they are operative in certain contexts, under certain circumstances, and to a degree which we have described and illustrated that this result is produced. Secondly, in cultural systems where these factors tend to produce unilateral lineages their influence and effect vary in degree. We may observe merely a slight tendency toward unilateral grouping, or it may be very pronounced. Lineages may or may not be exogamous. They may or may not have names. In short, we observe lineages in varying degrees of development. In their incipient stages

[5] Radcliffe-Brown, *op. cit.*, p. 439.
[6] Phyllis Kaberry, *Aboriginal Woman*, 1939, pp. 136–138.

they are relatively indistinct and insignificant. As they grow they become more distinct structurally and more significant functionally. When a unilateral grouping has become a distinct unit, set apart from other like groupings by the customs of exogamy, and distinguished from them by a name, then we call it a *clan*. A clan is therefore a crystallization, so to speak, of the social process of segmentation in which exogamy and division of labor between the sexes are the significant determining factors.

Until this crystallization has taken place, i.e., until the lineage has become an exogamous group distinguished from other like groups by a name, its organization and cohesion depend upon genealogical reckoning alone. A person belongs to a lineage and has a definite place in it because of the specific genealogical connections between himself and other members of the lineage. After the lineage has become crystallized into a clan with a name, however, a knowledge of specific genealogical connections is no longer essential to the integrity and inner structure of the group; one may now reckon in terms of group affiliation rather than genealogical connection. Thus, there may be so many persons in a clan that no one may know how a given individual is connected genealogically with everyone else in the clan. But this does not matter; common clan membership is sufficient to determine the relationships between them. According to theory, ethnologic as well as native, all members of a clan constitute a single lineage. But the clan may be so large that no one can know, exactly and with certainty, the genealogical connection between the several sublineages. In the absence of complete and precise genealogical data—a lack due to the absence of written records and to the limitations of man's memory—the sublineages of a clan appear as genealogically independent groups. The clan name and the laws of incest and exogamy, however, hold these lineages together and unite them into a coherent whole. Thus the clan is a mechanism that makes, in effect, a multilineage group possible.

We have now seen how certain factors and processes segregate one group of kindred from another, one unilateral lineage from others. This process develops by degrees until the lineage becomes a distinct and significant structure. It is then distinguished from other lineages by a name and by the laws of exogamy. But the evolutionary process which brought the distinct, named, exogamous lineage into existence does not stop at this point. Thanks to the name—and insignia that often go with the name—the process of segmentation can go farther. The clan is the culmination of one process of social evolution, but the beginning of another. Instead of unilateral groups of one lineage each, we may now have a unit, the clan, composed of a number of lineages, among which genealogical connections are not distinguishable. A new level of segmentation and integration has been reached. Heretofore, lineages have been segments of society as a whole; after the level of named clans has been reached, lineages become segments of clans, and clans in turn become segments of the social whole. This process of segmentation by means of unilateral reckoning of descent can go even farther. Among the Hopi Pueblos, for example, the tribe is divided into a number of exogamous, matrilineal kinship groups. Each, or most, of these groups are composed of a number—two, three, four, or so—of *named* groups that are also matrilineal and of course exogamous. At Oraibi, one of the larger exogamous groups is made up of Sand, Snake, and Lizard subgroups, another is composed of Rabbit, Kachina, Parrot, and Crow subgroups, and so on. The larger group itself has no name of its own; it may be, and commonly is, referred to by the name of one or another of the named subgroups of which it is composed.[7] But these named subgroups may be so large as to have lineages whose genealogical connections with one another are not distinguishable. We have here three levels of segmentation: lineages based upon specific genealogical connection, named groups composed of these lineages, and, thirdly, exogamous groupings of these named groups.

Whether, among these Hopi tribes, one calls the named exogamous groups clans, and the exogamous groupings of them phratries, or whether the largest exogamous group be called a clan and the named groups subclans, or lineages, is a terminological problem to a certain extent, but not wholly; the question of developmental sequence is involved also. Some students have held that a grouping such as Sand-Snake-Lizard was formed by the subdivision or segmentation of an exogamous group (clan), in which case the lineages of Sand, Snake, and Lizard would be subclans. Others,[8] however, believe that Sand, Snake, and Lizard were once independent clans that combined to form a phratry. We would hold that Sand, Snake, and Lizard are subclans formed by the process of segmentation; we would not know how to explain why independent clans would combine to form a phratry.

Clan organization is a means of enlarging the size of the cooperative group and of fostering solidarity at one and the same time. It achieves the former by extending the range of genealogical reckoning by supplementing known genealogical connections with those merely assumed; i.e., a person is a "father" or a "brother" to me not because of genealogical connections which I can trace, but because he is a member of the same named exogamous group—the same clan—that I belong to. The cooperative group is now composed of persons whose genealogical relations

---

[7] Author's field notes, 1932. See also R. H. Lowie, "Notes on Hopi Clans," *American Museum of Natural History, Anthropological Papers,* vol. 30, pt. 6, pp. 331ff., 1929.

[8] R. H. Lowie, for example, "Social Organization," in *Encyclopaedia of the Social Sciences,* vol. 14, 1934, p. 143.

with one another need be merely assumed, not definitely known. Clan organization promotes solidarity by treating individuals who are so remotely related to me that I do not know the genealogical connection as if they were so close that the genealogical relationship would be known. Clan organization, like the classificatory system of terminology, extends the radius, or scope, of kinship, on the one hand, and intensifies social relationships among individuals on the other.

Clans often employ nonkinship devices to implement their function as integrative mechanisms. Each clan may have certain articles of sacred paraphernalia such as fetishes, altars, or other instruments or utensils. These, together with rituals, establish and reinforce common sentiments among clan members. Insignia, face paintings, house and property marks also serve the same end. A clan may have an ancestral house or spot as a point of integration. Clans may own a set of names for the exclusive use of its members. They may also own fields or other real property such as burial grounds. A clan is thus more than a mere kinship group; it may be a ceremonial and economic group as well. Or perhaps it would be more accurate to say that clans promote solidarity indirectly through ceremonial and economic contexts, as well as directly in the context of kinship.

So effective and important have clans been as means of fostering social solidarity that we have come to call a people or a group *clannish* if they have a high degree of social integration and cohesion: "Mine host is a Dorsetshire man; and with a pardonable clannishness, has imported a little colony from his country"; or, "The clannish spirit of provincial literature" (Coleridge).[9]

Clans do more than integrate a number of lineages and individuals into a compact, close-knit group; they serve also as a means and a basis of tribal integration. In a tribe of five hundred persons there might be one hundred families, twenty-five genealogically distinguishable lineages, and five named, exogamous clans. Tribal solidarity may therefore be fostered on a supraindividual, suprafamilial, supralineage, i.e., upon a clan, level: the tribe is composed of five compact, closely knit groups instead of numerous lineages and still more numerous families. Clan organization provides a basis for intertribal solidarity also: the five tribes of the Iroquoian confederacy shared clans in common and were therefore bound together by these kinship ties.

Clans serve as mechanisms of tribal integration in still another way. Each clan may acquire a special function, ceremonial or otherwise, the exercise of which is regarded as essential to the common welfare. Each clan thus becomes necessary to all the rest, and all are bound together in

[9] Cf. "clan," "clannish," in *A New English Dictionary on Historical Principles*, James A. H. Murray (ed.), Oxford, 1893.

an organization of interdependence. Tribal solidarity is powerfully promoted in this way. Among the Hopi, the Bear clan provides the chief of the pueblo and has charge of the important Soyal ceremony; the Badger clan has the Powamu ritual; the Coyote clan provides the war chief, the Reed clan the town crier; to the Spider clan belong the Blue Flute and Antelope societies; and so on. Among the Ganda we find a similar division of tribal labor among clans. The Leopard clan has custody of the temple of the first king; the Monkey clan supplies the king with his chief butler, the Otter with bark cloth, the Elephant clan his chief herdsman. The Lungfish clan is related to fishing and canoe making, and so on. Division of labor and cooperation are of course but two sides, obverse and reverse, of but one social process. In the division of tribal labor among the several clans, each is bound to all the others by ties of dependence and necessity. The clan thus becomes an effective mechanism in the integrative process.

In some societies, such as the Ganda of Uganda, tribal or national solidarity is promoted clanwise by the marriage of the king to a woman from each clan in the realm.

Moieties, or dual organization. Many tribes are divided into two equal parts, or *moieties* (Fr. *moitié,* half). We may distinguish two kinds of moieties, those based upon kinship ties and those not so organized. Kinship moieties are unilateral, exogamous groups of kindred. They are thus *lineages* and, consequently, *segments.* A moiety based upon kinship is like a clan, except that the number of clans composing a tribe may vary, whereas of moieties there are always two, no more, no less. One might say that if there were only two clans in a tribe we would not call them clans but moieties. Since kinship moieties are exogamous and unilateral, husband and wife may not belong to the same moiety, and their children will belong to the moiety of one parent only. If they belong to the moiety of the mother, the moieties are matrilineal; if to the group of the father, they are patrilineal. Moieties may or may not be designated by a name. We see, then, that moieties based upon kinship are simply a special kind of lineage organization, a particular form in which the process of segmentation expresses itself. We may expect to find, therefore, that the premises, principles, and reasoning that we have already applied to segmentation and lineages in general will be applicable to moieties in particular, as they have been to clans.

Moieties based upon kinship ties are for this reason an integral part of the basic social structure of the tribe. But some tribes, as we have just noted, have moieties of a different sort. They are not basically kinship organizations, although membership may be determined by marriage or by descent. These nonkinship moieties are simply halves of a social whole, distinguished for the purpose of performing reciprocal or complementary functions; any connection with kinship is merely incidental. In some tribes, a person may belong to his father's moiety but the moieties may have nothing to do with marriage; i.e., they are not exogamous. Or membership might be determined by marriage: a woman may be required to join the moiety of her husband if she does not already belong to it prior to marriage. One's membership in the "social-function" type of moiety may therefore change from one to the other, which is of course impossible in the case of "kinship" moieties. Sometimes membership in a ritual moiety is merely a matter of personal choice. In some instances it is determined by place of residence. In some of the Keresan Pueblos, for example, residents in one part of the village belong to the Squash kiva group; residents of the other half, to the Turquoise moiety. Among the Central Eskimo the season of one's birth determines whether he will belong to the Summer or the Winter moiety. "Ritual" moieties are thus fundamentally different from kinship moieties with respect to the *basis* of organization. All moieties, however, are alike in that they are coequal parts of a tribal whole and as such have certain functions to perform. We shall return to the nonkinship type of moiety and its functions later. We wish now to consider the organization of moieties upon the basis of kinship.

Since kinship moieties are lineages, segments of a social whole, and since we have analyzed the segmentive process and have demonstrated its operation, we have already dealt with the general category, of which moieties are but a particular example. Consequently, we already know a great deal about moieties, not merely as segments but also as *lineage* segments. But moieties are a particular form of expression of the process of segmentation, and for an explanation of this we must have a special theory. The question that confronts us at this point is, therefore, why has the general process of segmentation expressed itself in some societies in the formation of two and only two exogamous, unilateral kinship groups, *moieties,* whereas in other cultural systems an indefinite and varying number of such groups, *clans,* has been the result?

In discussing the process of segmentation earlier, it will be recalled, we observed its operation in astronomical, physical, chemical, and biological sectors as well as in the social field. We may now observe a similar scope and extent of the bilateral form of the segmentive process.

Unity in the form of two parts is a fairly common phenomenon in nature. The positive and negative poles of a magnet constitute a unity. Electricity is manifested in positive and negative forms. Binary stars constitute unity of a sort. Bilateral symmetry is a characteristic of many living organisms. The division of a species into two sexes is an instance of unity in dual form. Mitosis, or cell division into halves, is a characteristic biological process. And in human society, moieties may constitute a single whole. Thus we see that moiety organization is not a unique phenomenon but a particular expression of a principle that may be cosmic in its scope; [10] bilateral unity, like multiple segmentation, appears to be a characteristic of many kinds of systems, social, biological, and physical.

In some cases of bilateral unity one part is like the other qualitatively, structurally, and functionally. Thus, one moiety is like its counterpart, and binary stars may be alike. In other instances we may simply have opposite aspects of a single phenomenon, such as the poles of a magnet, or positive and negative charges of electricity. And in still other cases, we may have a qualitative difference between the two parts, e.g., the two sexes of a species. All forms of bilateral unity have one thing in common, however: the parts are inseparable. One magnetic pole, one sex, or one moiety cannot exist without its counterpart, whether the parts be alike, opposite, or merely qualitatively different.

A consideration of a certain form of bilateral unity may be instructive here, namely, the division of a species into two sexes, male and female. Here we have a form of dual organization that presents two significant aspects, biological and sociological. The species, as a system, has been divided into two opposite, or complementary, and inseparable parts. Male and female form a biological unity. But the relationship between males and females is *social* as well as biological. Copulation is a social relationship as well as a biological one, and among primates, social relations between the sexes have other forms of expression also, such as grooming, courting, playing, fighting, etc. Thus, in the course of biological evolution we find that dual, or moiety, organization has been developed in certain sectors. If we can discover the reason for this, or to express ourselves more precisely, if we can discover the function of this type of organization in general, perhaps some light will be thrown on our problem of moieties in human society.

The differentiation of a species into two distinct sexual forms is of course the result of ages of evolutionary development. But between the levels of asexual and bisexual reproduction, we find some interesting intermediate forms. In certain hermaphroditic species, such as snails, copulation between individuals nevertheless takes place. Each snail has the elements necessary for reproduction, both male and female. Yet instead of reproduction by a single individual, two snails come together and exchange services and substances. This is very interesting and may prove instructive. Why do these organisms, each of which is capable of the act of reproduction, cooperate instead of functioning singly?

[10] It has recently been suggested by physicists that to the world of matter there corresponds a world of nonmatter, or of antimatter.

We suggest that the answer is that life is made more secure by co-operative reproduction, that reproduction is more likely to occur and offspring will tend to be more numerous, if the snails cooperate, mix their sperm and egg cells—pool their resources, so to speak—than if each went its way by itself. In other words, *differentiation of structure, specialization of function, and cooperation are three aspects of a way to make life more secure.* In snails we find differentiation of structure and specialization of function, male and female, even though both are housed in one body. But we find division of labor and cooperation on the social plane, between individuals. As biological evolution progresses, sexual structure and function become further differentiated, and eventually, somatically separate and distinct structures are produced. Division of labor and cooperation on the social plane now become a biological necessity. It might seem paradoxical that the life of a species could be made more secure by differentiating two sexes and making one dependent upon the other, or by making reproduction and survival of the species dependent upon the mutual dependence of the sexes. But mutual dependence is not a thing by itself. It is merely the obverse of a process of which cooperation is the reverse side. And cooperation, the formation of larger and better integrated systems, is a most effective way of making life secure. In social as well as biological evolution interdependence increases as structural differentiation and functional specialization increase. Farmer, physician, miner, telegrapher, etc., are dependent upon one another.[11] But together they form a system that is much more effective in the struggle for survival than the relatively undifferentiated and atomistically self-sufficient societies of early stages of social evolution.

We are now in a position to understand moieties in the process of social evolution. They are means of making life more secure in the struggle for survival. Moiety organization is a way of increasing size of the cooperative group, on the one hand, and of promoting solidarity, on the other. It accomplishes the former by extending the radius of kinship organization by supplementing known genealogical reckoning with assumed genealogical relations: any member of my moiety becomes my

[11] Dependence of one upon another may sometimes make life less secure for particular individuals. Thus, a diamond cutter or a die maker in a highly developed culture may actually have less control over his means of life than a hunter or farmer in tribal society. But in a consideration of social evolution it is the sociocultural system that is of primary importance. The security of *systems* rather than of *individuals* comes first, for without systems there is no security for *any* individuals; the individual derives his security from social systems. If, therefore, some individuals are made less secure, or even extinguished in the course of social evolution, this does not negate or minimize the advance made. The individual may be and often is sacrificed for the security and survival of the society.

relative because of assumed genealogical ties. Moiety organization fosters solidarity by the same means: by treating a relative too remote to be identified genealogically as if he were a close, genealogically identifiable relative.

Dual organization, like that of clans, provides a means and a basis of tribal integration upon a suprafamilial, supragenealogically distinguishable lineage level. Instead of a tribe achieving solidarity through the integration of several clans, it now accomplishes it through the integration of two moieties.

Tribal integration is promoted by having each moiety perform some function necessary to the welfare of the other, such as burying the dead. Here again, mutual dependence, reciprocal functions, make for tribal integration. Rivalry between the moieties in games, dances, and ceremonies also is a way of fostering tribal solidarity and of nourishing a healthy *esprit de corps*.

Having examined certain forces and characteristics of systems in general that tend to produce bilateral unity, we now turn to other processes that might produce the same effect in human society. Let us go back to our discussion of incest and the processes of exogamy and endogamy. It will be recalled that we traced the extension of the taboo against inbreeding from within the family outward through a succession of degrees of relationship. Prohibition of marriage with a half brother or half sister would follow the prohibition of marriage with a full brother or sister. Marriage with parallel cousins would be the next to fall under the ban. But owing to the operation of endogamy as a process complementary to exogamy, marriage with a cross-cousin would be required at the same time that marriage with parallel cousins was prohibited. And it so happens, as we have noted earlier, that the institution of cross-cousin marriage is quite widespread in primitive society. We now come to a significant point: *cross-cousin marriage as an established custom or institution would tend to produce dual organization.*

A social system that practiced cross-cousin marriage would reckon descent unilaterally since it would distinguish cross-cousins from parallel cousins. Thus, I would distinguish my father's brother's children from my father's sister's children and my mother's sister's children from my mother's brother's children. But with cross-cousin marriage, my mother's brother's children may also be my father's sister's children and my mother's sister's children may be my father's brother's children. But whether my mother's brother's wife is my father's sister or not, their children will be terminologically equal: they will be my classificatory siblings. Thus, I will distinguish two, and only two, lineages, a paternal and a maternal. If descent is reckoned matrilineally, the significant lineages will be my father's matrilineal lineage and my mother's matrilineal lineage; if descent is reckoned patrilineally, the significant lineages will be my father's and my mother's patrilineal lineages, respectively. Now if the social system is small and well integrated, everyone in the society will be related to everyone else, and that relationship will be known. In terms of the classificatory system of relationship, all persons in the tribe will be my immediate relatives. Outside my own family, all men in my parents' generation will be my "fathers" (my father's brothers) or my "uncles" (my mother's brothers). Persons on my own generation level will be my "siblings" (my parallel cousins) or my "cousins" (my cross-cousins). From my standpoint, the whole tribe is divided into two great lineages, my father's and my mother's, patrilineal and matrilineal, as the case may be. Now what is true from *my* standpoint is true for any other person, of course. Everyone, therefore, finds the society divided into two equal parts, his father's exogamous, unilateral group and that of his mother. These two groups are, in effect, moieties.

But let us carry this process of social evolution farther. The dual organization of a society that we have just described is based upon genealogical reckoning: I marry a woman because she is my mother's brother's daughter, or my father's sister's daughter. She is my first cross-cousin genealogically, not a more distant "classificatory" cross-cousin. At a certain stage of social evolution the requirements of social solidarity and integrity would oblige me to marry, not *any* person in the class "my female cross-cousin," but a particular one, namely, the daughter of a sibling of my own parents. At a higher stage of social development, however, this particular endogamous requirement may be relaxed, and I may be permitted to marry *any* of my female cross-cousins. Let us see how this might be brought about, and also what specifically we mean by "higher stage of social development."

Cross-cousin marriage belongs, according to our theory, to a relatively early stage of social evolution, to a stage where marriage is determined by genealogical relationship rather than by general group membership. As culture evolves, as technological control over nature, particularly over the food supply, increases, the population will increase. The social system will tend to incorporate this increase in numbers within itself, if circumstances permit, instead of letting some split off and form a new social system, for the reason that larger social groups have a better chance of survival, other factors being constant, in the competitive struggle for existence than smaller groups. But as the size of the group increases, a number of interesting consequences follow: (1) It becomes increasingly difficult, and eventually impossible, to organize and integrate a society on the basis of genealogical reckoning alone; one simply cannot remember genealogy beyond a certain point. (2) The need for close endogamous marriage decreases; the need for integration with a larger group increases. Cross-cousin marriage is, of course, restrictive; its immediate effect is to unite but two families into a mutual-aid group. If marriage can unite an individual with a larger group without a loss of solidarity as great as or greater than the gain from union with a larger group, then such a marriage is advantageous. (3) Integration on a level higher than genealogical reckoning is fostered.

We can now see what type of social system would succeed cross-cousin marriage. As the population increased and the tribe became larger, the rule of marriage would change, which is to say, the specifications of exogamy and endogamy would be redefined. Marriage would no longer be determined by genealogical reckoning alone; instead of being required to marry a particular cross-cousin, I could now marry *any* cross-cousin, i.e., any member of a *group*. The two lineages of the tribe have now become moieties. A lineage is a grouping of kindred based upon known genealogical relationships; a moiety is a group of relatives among whom genealogical connections are assumed. Marriage is now determined by moiety affiliation rather than by genealogical reckoning; one must marry into the opposite moiety from his own, but within that moiety he may marry as he pleases.

The shift from genealogical reckoning and lineage organization to marriage by group membership and moiety organization brings with it new alignments in the process of integration. With cross-cousin marriage I am united to a family and to a lineage as far as genealogical knowledge can reach. But this is a relatively small group. When cross-cousin marriage and genealogical reckoning have been superseded by moiety organization, I become united in marriage not merely with my bride's lineage, but with an entire half of the tribe. To each member of my wife's moiety I assume obligations and acquire rights by virtue of moiety membership alone. The scope of marriage as an integrative mechanism is increased greatly by passing from cross-cousin marriage and genealogical lineages to moieties.

And finally, as we have noted earlier, the moieties themselves provide a new basis for tribal integration. They assume reciprocal or complementary functions and by this means foster tribal solidarity. Integration is now achieved on a supralineage level.

In view of the extensive discussion in anthropological literature of the relationship between the custom, or institution, of cross-cousin marriage and dual organization, it might be well to summarize our position on this point. According to our theory, cross-cousin marriage tends to divide a society into two, and only two, lineages, into two unilateral, exogamous kinship groups. When marriage in accordance with genealogical connection gives way to marriage by group membership—as it does when population and size of group are increased by an advance of techno-logical control—these lineages become crystallized into moieties with names. Thus, moiety organization is regarded as a higher stage of de-velopment than that of mere cross-cousin marriage, or as a culmination or consequence of this form of marriage.

A relationship between dual organization and cross-cousin marriage has been recognized for a long time, but explanations of this connection have varied considerably. Tylor felt that " 'cross-cousin marriage' ... must be the direct result of the simplest form of exogamy, where a population is divided into two classes or sections." [12] At one time, Rivers believed that cross-cousin marriage "has probably arisen in most, if not in all, cases out of this form [dual] of social organization." [13] Further-more, Rivers and others have held that the custom of cross-cousin mar-riage may outlive the dual organization that produced it. Therefore the mere presence of cross-cousin marriage proves the former existence of dual organization.[14] But there is serious objection to this theory. In cross-cousin marriage, one marries his *own* mother's brother's daughter or father's sister's daughter, not merely a classificatory cousin. Dual or-ganization and exogamy would require merely that one marry into the opposite moiety, i.e., with *any* cross-cousin. How dual organization could bring about marriage with one's own first cross-cousin was not explained. Rivers himself noted this difficulty.[15] Westermarck and Lowie have made the same objection to this theory.[16] Our theory shows how cross-cousin marriage could produce a dual organization of society. And we have ex-plained cross-cousin marriage also.

With regard to the relationship between cross-cousin marriage and dual organization, it has been pointed out that many tribes have one in-stitution but not the other. As Lowie has observed: "Further, Dr. Rivers has shown that in Melanesia it is precisely the tribes lacking such an organ-ization which practice cross-cousin marriage, while this institution is absent where the dual organization is in full swing." [17] But this, too, is

[12] E. B. Tylor, "On a Method of Investigating the Development of Institutions, &c.," *Journal of the Anthropological Institute,* vol. 18, p. 263, 1888.

[13] W. H. R. Rivers, "Marriage," in *Encyclopaedia of Religion and Ethics,* J. Hastings (ed.), 1915, p. 426.

[14] W. H. R. Rivers, "The Marriage of Cross Cousins in India," *Journal of the Royal Asiatic Society,* art. xxv, pp. 611–640, 1907; Govind S. Ghurye, "Dual Organiza-tion in India," *Journal of the Royal Anthropological Institute,* vol. 53, pp. 79–91, 1923; R. L. Olson, "Clan and Moiety in Native America," *University of California Publications in American Archaeology and Ethnology,* vol. 33, p. 359, footnote, 1933.

[15] W. H. R. Rivers, *The History of Melanesian Society,* vol. 2, pp. 121–122, 1914.

[16] Edward Westermarck, *History of Human Marriage,* vol. 2, 1922, pp. 78–79; R. H. Lowie, *Primitive Society,* Liveright Publishing Corporation, New York, 1947, p. 30.

[17] Lowie, *Primitive Society,* p. 30.

to be expected on the basis of our theory. In the early stages of the cross-cousin-marriage-moiety-organization sequence, we would expect to find cross-cousin marriage but not moieties; the latter have not yet had time to become sufficiently crystallized to be distinguished, functionally significant, or named. In the latter stages of this sequence, we would expect to find moieties, but not cross-cousin marriage; the latter, marriage according to genealogical connection, has been superseded by marriage according to group membership. Midway in this sequence, we might expect to find both institutions, the end of one stage and the beginning of another overlapping. Far from interpreting a lack of coincidence of these two institutions as indicating no genetic relationship between them, our theory would lead us to expect a greater number of societies with only one of these institutions than with both.

Although our theory postulates a functional relationship between cross-cousin marriage and dual organization in many situations, it does not assert that the former must always produce the latter or that moieties are impossible without cross-cousin marriage as their efficient cause. Water does not always turn to ice at 0°C, or become steam at 100°C. It is quite possible that a society could practice cross-cousin marriage but that the two lineages formed by this type of marriage might never become crystallized into distinct exogamous moieties with names, either because the evolutionary process is not carried far enough or because of the operation of other factors. If salt is put into water, for example, it will not freeze at 0°C. On the other hand, we believe that dual organization might be produced by other factors than cross-cousin marriage. The whole class of "ritual" moieties has been formed independently of cross-cousin marriage, and it would seem unwarranted to insist that moieties of the kinship type must be produced only by cross-cousin marriage. However, cross-cousin marriage is, according to our theory, a stage of development in the normal process of evolution,[18] and the formation of moieties is a normal, logical consequence of the operation of this rule of marriage. But this does not mean that this sequence of events must occur always and everywhere.

We now turn to the question, "Why has the process of segmentation produced multiple lineage segments in some instances and but two in

---

[18] To recognize abnormalities in the evolutionary process, to admit that the normal sequence can be upset by fortuitous circumstances or accidental factors, is not to deny the existence of an evolutionist process or to negate evolutionist theory. A disease of the pituitary gland, a malady produced by extreme starvation, or a severe blow on the head might seriously disturb and distort the "normal process of growth" —or abruptly terminate it. But this does not mean that growth is not a real process or that the concept of growth is invalid.

others?" The answer seems to lie in a consideration of the mode of life of the society. If the tribe is widely distributed over the landscape and divided into a considerable number of local territorial groups, then the process of segmentation would be inclined to produce a corresponding number of local exogamous lineages. If, however, the mode of subsistence and defense kept the group intact and together, the inclination might be toward dual organization. As we have repeatedly observed, social evolution is not a process *in vacuo*. On the contrary, it is always and everywhere a function of the technological processes by which life is sustained, and these in turn are intimately related to the specific features of a particular habitat. We may not always know the answers to questions regarding different forms of social organization, but we know where to look for them: in the technological adjustment to habitat and to neighboring peoples.

With regard to multiple lineages, or clans, and dual organization, it is not to be assumed that the question is of an "either-or" nature, that a people must have the one or the other. They may, and often do, have both; tribes with moieties and clans are not at all uncommon. In societies having both moieties (of the "kinship" type) and clans, the former must be assumed to have been formed first, the latter by a subsequent process of subdivision by segmentation. We know of no process that would group full-fledged clans into two exogamous "kinship" moieties (although they might be grouped into *ceremonial* halves for the purpose of promoting tribal solidarity through rivalry and reciprocal functions). The formation of clans as subdivisions of moieties is, however, easy enough to understand: as the population increases and the moieties become larger, they would tend to become segmented as a means of maintaining their integrity—to keep them from falling apart from sheer size and weight.

Moieties originating as kinship groups may, however, and often do, acquire ritual functions. Some of these functions may be regarded merely as adjuncts of kinship organization, as ways of expressing or validating relationships between groups of kindred. But moieties may acquire ritual functions in addition to this. Tribal labor may be divided between moieties as it is in many cases among clans, and by this division of labor tribal solidarity may be promoted. Thus we see that moieties originating as kinship groups may acquire a ceremonial or ritual character. At the same time, they might lose some of their functions as kinship groups, specifically the regulation of marriage. We have seen how cross-cousin marriage may be superseded by moiety exogamy, that marriage may come to be determined by moiety affiliation rather than by genealogical connection. But if the moieties should become subdivided into clans, the former might lose their exogamous character and the regulation of marriage might be taken over by the clans entirely. According to Morgan, the moieties of the Iroquois were once exogamous, but by the early 1800s they had lost this characteristic.[19] Goldenweiser's field studies of Iroquoian culture led him to the same conclusion.[20] It may sound paradoxical to say so, but the role of moiety exogamy has an endogamous effect; it compels an individual to marry *within* a certain restricted group, although in this case it is not his own. The restriction of scope of marriage choice obtains, nevertheless. As we have already seen, the scope of marriage choice grows larger as society evolves. This is merely another way of saying that as culture advances, a larger mutual-aid group can be, and is, formed by marriage without impairment of solidarity; and this increased size is an advantage in the struggle for existence. At a certain stage of social evolution, marriage between clans of the same moiety is incompatible with optimum conditions of solidarity. As culture advances, however, it becomes not only possible, but it may become desirable, to enlarge the scope of choice of marriage in the interests of tribal integration and solidarity. As this point is approached and reached, moiety exogamy weakens and breaks down. This is not to say, however, that moieties must always lose their exogamous character or even that this is the "normal" course of evolution. We say merely that it may occur and that it has in all probability happened in many instances.

Thus, we see that moieties may originate as kinship groups, acquire ritual functions, beget clans, and eventually lose their exogamous character.

Segments in Australian society. No account of social evolution in general or of segmentation in particular would be complete without some discussion of the tribes of Australia. Let it be noted, however, that we deal with these groups at the conclusion of our discussion of unilateral kinship segmentation rather than at the beginning. Unlike some earlier writers, we do not regard the social organization of Australian tribes as representing a primordial condition out of which all other forms have subsequently developed. The social organization of aboriginal Australia is, however, extremely interesting, and an analysis of it can be very illuminating. It has certain features that are in a sense unique, and a close study of them will enrich our understanding of social organization in general. But the significant thing about Australian social organization is not that it is more elemental or primordial than other social systems, for we find even more primitive systems elsewhere, but that it presents in highly specialized form the same sort of thing that is found elsewhere in more simple form.[21] Aboriginal Australia exhibits, in magnified form so to speak, the workings of processes that we have become familiar with elsewhere, namely, endogamy, exogamy, and segmentation. Australian social organization is not, therefore, to be thought of as typical even of primitive society, much less as the primordial trunk from which all other social forms have branched or grown. Rather, it is a highly specialized form of human social structure upon a primitive and early level. As such it is not only interesting but instructive.

There is a considerable variation of social organization from tribe to tribe in Australia. However, most, if not all, forms can be assigned to one or another of two main types, according to Radcliffe-Brown: the Kariera and the Arunta types.[22] In the former, the tribe is divided into four named

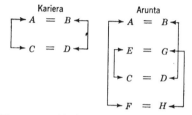

Figure 7–1. Kariera and Arunta segments.

exogamous segments; in the latter, eight. These are the so-called "marriage classes" that have become so renowned in ethnological literature. In both Kariera and Arunta types, an individual is not only forbidden to marry within his own segment, he is required to marry into a particular segment. And in both types the children belong to a segment different from that of either parent. The relationship of the segments to marriage and descent is indicated in Figure 7–1, in which letters stand for the named segments, the equals sign for the marriage union, and the broken arrows for father-child relationship.

Thus, in the Kariera type, a man in segment A marries a woman in segment B, and their children belong to segment C; a man in D marries a woman in C and their children are B. In the Arunta type, a man in segment G marries a woman in E, their children are H; a man in B marries a woman in A, their children belong to segment D, and so on.

Analysis of these two types of organization will disclose the fact that

<hr />

[21] See Radcliffe-Brown's discussion of this point in "The Present Position of Anthropological Studies," *Proceedings British Association for the Advancement of Science*, 1931, pp. 24–25.

[22] A. R. Radcliffe-Brown, "The Social Organization of Australian Tribes," *Oceania*, vol. 1, pt. 1, p. 46, 1930.

both are expressions of the processes of endogamy, exogamy, and segmentation, with which we are already familiar. We find no principle operative in Australian social organization that we are not well acquainted with elsewhere.

In both Arunta and Kariera types we have exogamous, patrilineal, and patrilocal territorial groups as a consequence of the mode of subsistence and division of labor between men and women. In both systems the laws of endogamy and exogamy are specific and concise. And in each case, there is an alternation in each patrilineal lineage between the segment of the father and the segment of his children; if the father belongs to segment A and his children to segment C, his sons' children will belong to A, and the children of his sons' sons will belong to C, and so on. Each system is the resultant of the operation of a few factors. We can define these factors precisely and observe plainly the effect produced by each.[23]

First, we may note that in both the Kariera and the Arunta types, the tribe is divided into both matrilineal and patrilineal moieties, each of which is exogamous. The Kariera tribe is divided into four exogamous sections by the intersection of matrilineal and patrilineal moieties. Thus, in Figure 7–1, segments A and C comprise one patrilineal moiety; segments B and D, another. Segments A and D form one matrilineal moiety; B and C, another. Since both kinds of moieties are exogamous, A male cannot marry a woman in segment C because it is a part of his patrilineal moiety. He cannot marry into D because that is a part of his matrilineal moiety. He can, therefore, marry into segment B only. In the Arunta system, segments $AECF$ comprise one patrilineal moiety, $BGDH$ another. Matrilineal moieties are $HADE$ and $CBFG$. A male in Segment A cannot marry into segments E, C, and F because they are in his patrilineal moiety, nor into segments H, D, and E because they are in his matrilineal moiety. This leaves segments G and B. He is not permitted to marry into G because it contains his first cross-cousins. He must therefore marry into segment B, which contains his second cross-cousins (Figure 7–2).

The foregoing presentation is, in a sense, given backward; we have used the segments to show how both patrilineal and matrilineal exogamous moieties operate. Actually the two kinds of exogamous moieties came

[23] F. Galton seems to have been the first to provide an explanation of Australian sections in "Note on Australian Marriage Systems," *Journal of the Anthropological Institute*, vol. 18, pp. 70–72, 1889. A. B. Deacon's paper, "The Regulation of Marriage in Ambrym," *Journal of the Royal Anthropological Institute*, vol. 57, pp. 325–342, 1927, threw additional light on the subject. W. E. Lawrence's "Alternating Generations in Australia," in *Studies in the Science of Society*, G. P. Murdock (ed.), 1937, and Radcliffe-Brown, *op. cit.*, pts. 1–4, 1930–1931, have further clarified the whole problem of segmentation and marriage in aboriginal Australian society. See also G. P. Murdock, *Social Structure*, 1949, pp. 51–52.

first; *the named segments have been formed by the operation of moiety exogamy.*

The question "How have Australian tribes come to have both patrilineal and matrilineal exogamous moieties?" is pertinent here, but we shall not deal with it other than to refer to our previous discussion of division of labor along sex lines, and to add that patrilineal descent and the moieties may express the monopoly by men of certain tribal religious

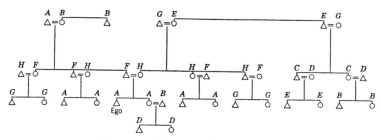

Figure 7-2. Segments: Arunta system.

functions, whereas the matrilineal moieties express an emphasis upon descent of some kind through females. Our purpose here is to explain the segments of the Kariera and Arunta types of organization, and the presence and operation of exogamous patrilineal and matrilineal moieties are two of the three factors that bring them about.

The third factor is the rule of marriage: a man must marry his first cross-cousin in the Kariera type, his second cross-cousin in the Arunta type (Figures 7-2 and 7-3).

So far, we have encountered nothing in Australian social organization with which we are not already familiar: unilateral descent, lineages, moieties, and now, exogamy and endogamy. In the Kariera type, the laws of exogamy prohibit marriage with parent, sibling, or parallel cousin, while the law of endogamy requires marriage with a first cross-cousin. In the Arunta type, one must marry out as far as a second cross-cousin, but no farther.

We now understand the Kariera system, but what about the Arunta system; how is it to be explained?

The Arunta system was developed out of the Kariera system [24] by a very simple device: a change in the rule of marriage from marriage with a first cross-cousin to marriage with a second cross-cousin. Let us see

[24] "We are justified, I think, in regarding the Kariera and the Aranda systems as two terms in an evolutionary process." Radcliffe-Brown, *op. cit.*, pt. 4, 1931, p. 452.

how this change in the rules of endogamy and exogamy affected the system as a whole.

Figure 7-3 will serve to illustrate both the Kariera and the Arunta types. For the Kariera system, however, we shall consider the letters standing for the native names of the four exogamous segments only; the numerical subscripts will be ignored. In dealing with the Arunta system, both letters and numerical subscripts will be considered. In the Kariera system, a man marries his first cross-cousin, his mother's brother's daughter: A male marries B. But suppose the rules of exogamy and endogamy

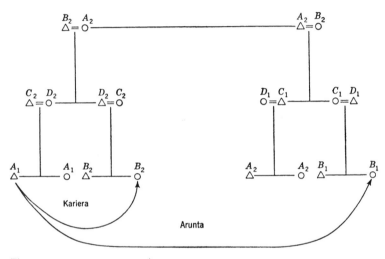

Figure 7-3. Marriage rules: Kariera system indicated by letters only; Arunta system by letters plus numerical subscripts.

are changed so that a man is prohibited from marrying his first cross-cousin but is required to marry his second cross-cousin. All his cross-cousins belong to segment B. But the new rules of exogamy and endogamy distinguish first cross-cousins from second, and more distant, cross-cousins. Segment B is therefore divided in two, one part, B_2, containing the first cross-cousins; B_1 the second and more distant cross-cousins. What is done to this segment in this particular case is, of course, done to each other segment in other cases. Thus, each of the four segments of the Kariera system is divided into two parts, and we now have A_1, A_2, B_1, B_2, C_1, C_2, and D_1, D_2, eight segments in all. The operation of the rule of marriage with reference to the segments is shown in Figure 7-4.

After each segment has been thus divided in two, one part—probably the one containing the first cross-cousins—will retain the old name of the original segment, while the newly distinguished part will receive a name of its own. Thus, A_2 will become E; C_2, F; B_2, G; and D_2 will become H (see, again, Figure 7-1 a and b). Thus, the simple device of changing the rule of marriage divides each segment of the Kariera system in two, and produces the eight-segment system of the Arunta.

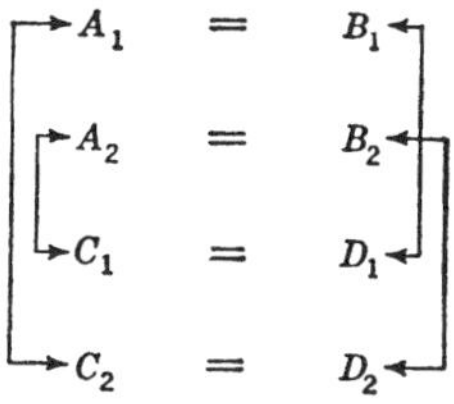

$$
\begin{array}{ccc}
A_1 & = & B_1 \\
A_2 & = & B_2 \\
C_1 & = & D_1 \\
C_2 & = & D_2
\end{array}
$$

Figure 7-4. Segments: Arunta system derived from Kariera system.

But why was the rule of marriage changed? We cannot answer this question specifically and in detail. But we can illuminate the problem by applying to it our theory of social evolution.

At a certain stage of cultural and social evolution, marriage between first cross-cousins was the form of marital union best suited to the formation of a cooperative group of relatives of maximum effectiveness. The size and solidarity of the cooperative group formed by marriage were so balanced, at a certain level of cultural development, by union between first cross-cousins as to produce the maximum of its effectiveness (see our earlier discussion of this matter on p. 107). But at a higher stage of cultural development and social evolution, the maximum effectiveness of the cooperative group formed by marriage could not be achieved by union between first cousins. A larger group could be formed by marriage between second cousins, and if the gain in size was not offset by a diminution in solidarity, the larger group would be more effective as a mutual-aid group, and there would thus be a distinct advantage accruing to each component member of the group.

At any rate, the marriage rule of the Arunta system was brought about by changing the rules of exogamy and endogamy of the Kariera system so that a man married his mother's mother's brother's daughter's daughter —his second cross-cousin—instead of his mother's brother's daughter—his first cross-cousin. And a larger group of relatives was formed by a marriage union of the Arunta type than by one of the Kariera system. In the Kariera system, two families and two local groups, or "hordes," to use Radcliffe-Brown's term, are united by my marriage: my father's family and local group and my mother's brother's family and horde. In the Arunta system, the families and local groups of my father, my mother, my mother's mother's brother, and the husband of my mother's mother's brother's daughter are all involved. Arunta marriage effects larger or more comprehensive integrations[25] than does marriage in the Kariera system, and thus constitutes a higher stage of social evolution.[26]

There are two other significant consequences of the change of marriage rule from that of the Kariera system to the rule of the Arunta system, namely, a doubling of the number of patrilineal lineages into which the tribe is divided, and corresponding changes in the kinship terminology.

Only two patrilineages are distinguished in the Kariera system: my own and that of my mother, AC and BD in Figure 7–3. In the Arunta system, four patrilineages are distinguished: my father's father's, my father's mother's brother's, my mother's father's, and my mother's mother's brother's, AF, BD, GH, and EC in Figure 7–2. Arunta-type marriage unites members of four patrilineages; Kariera marriage only two.

Changes of kinship terminology accompany the transformation of the Kariera system to one of the Arunta type. In the Kariera system, for example, there are only two terms for male grandparents, father's father and mother's father, and two for female, father's mother and mother's mother. In the Arunta system, four kinds of male relatives and four kinds of female relatives are distinguished terminologically in the second ascending generation. But only four terms are employed, not eight. "This is because the same term that is applied to a male relative is also applied to his sister."[27] Thus, father's father and father's father's sister are designated by the same term, as are mother's mother's brother and mother's mother. Thus we see that the four patrilineages of the Arunta system find expression in the kinship terminology, as the terminology of the Kariera system expresses their two patrilineages.

The Arunta system has been presented here as a higher stage of social evolution than that of the Kariera, as indeed it is. This evolutionary advance was brought about by changes in the conditions of life; of this we may be sure: the alternatives to this view are free will and caprice, which are inadmissible as explanatory concepts in science. Unfortunately, however, we do not know specifically and in detail what the "changes

[25] "In terms of hordes the marriage system of the Aranda type results in a more complex integration than the Kariera system, linking an individual to four hordes in all." Radcliffe-Brown, *op. cit.,* p. 451.

[26] "...Evolution...is a process by which stable integrations at a higher level are substituted for or replace integrations at a lower level." *Ibid.,* p. 452.

[27] *Ibid.,* pt. 1, p. 50, 1930.

in the conditions of life" were in this case. There appears to be no significant difference in technology between Kariera and Arunta sociocultural systems. But the conditions of subsistence may have been quite different. And the relations, in terms of offense and defense, with neighboring tribes may have been different also. The application of our general theory of social evolution to this particular instance would be more convincing if we could support it with technological and ecological data. But the absence of such information in no way invalidates our theory.

From the preceding discussion and analysis it is clear that Australian social organization exhibits processes and structures that are found among many other tribes. We find division of labor along sex lines, local groups ("hordes," or bands), families, unilateral residence and unilateral descent, the formation of lineages, moieties, exogamy and endogamy, the formation of segments, etc., among the Kariera, Arunta, and other Australian tribes, just as we find them in many other societies. Social evolution in Australia has proceeded along the same fundamental lines that it has followed elsewhere. The only remarkable feature of Australian social organization is the formation of a number of named, exogamous segments within the moieties. Australia is not wholly unique in the possession of segments of this sort, though nearly so. A. B. Deacon found a similarly segmented system in Ambrym,[28] and further investigation may disclose systems of this sort in other parts of Melanesia. But the segments of Australian tribes are in no sense mysterious; they have been brought about by processes that we are well acquainted with in many parts of the world. They are but a particular kind of expression of the process of segmentation.

It might be well to include in our treatment of segmentation in Australian social organization some discussion of *clans*. Many writers speak of clans in Australia, among such tribes, for example, as the Arunta. But the Arunta did not have true clans in the sense in which we have defined the term: a unilateral, exogamous group of kindred distinguished from other like groupings within the tribe by its own name. There was no grouping in Arunta society that corresponds exactly to this definition. A single one of the named segments was not a clan, because the children of a married couple did not belong to the segment of either parent. But there was a grouping that came close to being a clan, according to our usage of this term. This was the local group, or *horde*, or more precisely, all persons born into the local group.[29] All persons born into a horde

<hr>

[28] Deacon, *op. cit.*

[29] See Radcliffe-Brown's distinction between clan and horde. Radcliffe-Brown defines horde as "all men born into the horde [i.e., the local, territorial group] together with their wives and unmarried daughters." He calls "all persons born in the horde" a clan. *Op. cit.*, p. 59.

constituted an exogamous, unilateral grouping of kindred. But it was not a single, undifferentiated group; it was composed of members of two named segments.

It would have been a simple matter, however, to transform the localized patrilineages into true clans. If the distinction between the segments comprising each local lineage were obliterated, which would have meant abandoning the matrilineal moiety organization, and if each local lineage were then distinguished from all the others by a name, as the localities among the Arunta are, the localized lineages would have become true, full-fledged clans. Both of these changes could have been effected very easily by, or as a consequence of, a simple change in the rule of marriage: if still further latitude were desired than the rule requiring marriage with a second cousin permitted, the rule could have been modified to permit marriage into any localized patrilineage save one's own. The named segments would then have lost their significance and would disappear, together with the exogamous matrilineal moieties, and the named localized patrilineages would have become true clans. The changes indicated here would be rather radical, but there is no reason to suppose that they could not have been effected by further advance in social evolution.

Ambilateral lineages.[30] By *lineage*, as we have indicated previously, we mean a grouping of relatives in terms of parent-child relationships, a lineal grouping as distinguished from a collateral or other kind of segregation. Lineal groupings may be unilateral—patrilineal or matrilineal—or ambilateral. Thus, the grouping may be based upon lineal relationships through one sex only, either male or female, or it may include ascendants and descendants in both lines, male and female. A patrilineal lineage is, as we have noted earlier, composed of a man and his children and the descendants of his sons in the male line only. A matrilineal lineage is composed of a woman and her children and the descendants of her daughters in the female line only. An ambilateral [31] lineage is a lineal grouping of relatives in which one traces his relationship to some married couple as a starting

---

[30] The author is indebted to Dr. Paul Kirchhoff for an illuminating discussion, in an unpublished paper, of ambilateral lineages, and also to Mrs. Grace Fuchs, a graduate student at the University of Michigan, who made a study of ambilateral lineages under the author's direction.

[31] The author prefers ambilateral to bilateral for this type of grouping. *Uni*lateral descent is reckoned in one line, *bi*lateral in both equally, and although *ambi-* means both, ambilateral, like ambidextrous, connotes "either or both." It is in this sense that Raymond Firth—who was the first to use this term so far as we know—has used it in describing the social organization of the Maori: "Descent from either males or females—or both conjoined...the *hapu*...may be called, in fact, an *ambilateral* group...." Raymond Firth, *Primitive Economics of the New Zealand Maori*, E. P. Dutton & Co., Inc., New York, 1929, p. 98.

point through either or both lines, male and female, and to either or both members of the original married couple.

Ambilateral lineages are most easily demonstrated for Polynesia and the Northwest Coast of North America. They probably exist and are significant in other parts of the world also, but because the concept of ambilateral lineages has not been a well-defined concept in ethnology, the existence of such groupings has not been generally recognized.[32] For our demonstration of ambilateral lineages we shall select the Maori of New Zealand and the Kwakiutl of the Northwest Coast as representative tribes of these regions, respectively.

The Kwakiutl-speaking peoples consisted of a number of tribes. Each tribe was divided into septs,[33] or *numaym*, to use the Kwakiutl term. A sept was a local group, a village community. All members of a sept reckoned descent, through either sex, from a common ancestor; a sept was, therefore, an ambilateral lineage.

The sept, unless very small, was divided into a number of sublineages, ambilateral in structure, each of which reckons descent from its own ancestor, but all sublineages trace their descent from the ancestor of the sept as a whole. The Kwakiutl appear to have no name for these sublineages; we shall call them *kin groups*. The kin groups are divided into households, and these in turn into families.

The social organization of the Maori is similar to that of the Kwakiutl. The tribe is divided into local groups, or septs, called *hapu*. They are ambilateral lineages since their members trace their ancestry through either sex to a common origin. The *hapu* are divided into sublineages called *whanau*, and these in turn into household groups and families.

The Maori and the Kwakiutl differ in this respect, however: among the former, one belongs to the septs of both parents, whereas a Kwakiutl belongs to the sept of either parent, depending upon which has the higher rank and upon the order of his birth among his siblings.

---

[32] Franz Boas, a student of Kwakiutl culture for forty-odd years, never grasped the concept of ambilateral lineage structure. He recognized both matrilineal and patrilineal features in their social organization. But instead of seeing it for what it was, he interpreted the presence of both patrilineal and matrilineal features as an indication that "the allegedly patrilineal Kwakiutl ... [had] borrowed ... matrilineal inheritance from their matrilineal neighbors to the north." Murdock, *op. cit.*, p. 190.

[33] Webster's New International Dictionary defines sept as "1. In the ancient and medieval civil organization of Ireland, a division of a tribe or tuath, having one or more chiefs or lords ... possessed of a given territory, living as a more or less complete village community, and owing allegiance to the tribal king.... 3. *Anthropol.* A social group in which all are believed to have descended from a single ancestor." These definitions, with a few changes in wording, such as "tribal chief" for "king," seem to be quite applicable to the ambilateral groupings of Polynesia and the Northwest Coast.

We may represent the organization of both Maori and Kwakiutl society diagrammatically, as shown in Figure 7–5.

The principle of rank permeates the entire social structure of both Maori and Kwakiutl. Status and rank depend upon distance from the ancestor from whom descent is traced; the closer to the common ancestor the higher the rank. Lineages and individuals are alike graded according

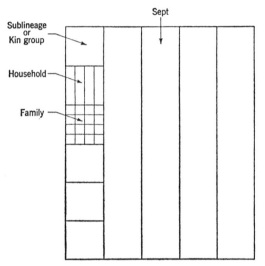

Figure 7–5. The tribe and its subdivisions.

to rank. As noted previously, a number of sublineages may be distinguished within a local group, or sept. These are graded according to the order in which they broke away from the main line of descent. The lineage in the direct line of descent from the common ancestor will have the highest rank. The first collateral line to break away and to become distinguished as a sublineage, with its own ancestor, will rank next, and so on to subsequent sublineages, as indicated in Figure 7–6.

The rank of an individual within a lineage, or sublineage, likewise depends upon nearness to, or distance from, the common ancestor: the greater the distance the lower the rank. The structure of an ambilateral lineage and the rank of individuals comprising it are shown in Figure 7–7.

Everyone in the lineage traces his ancestry, through males or females or both, to the individual, or married couple, *A*, at the peak of the pyramid. The various lines of descent, and the individuals comprising those lines, are graded. The first-born child, male or female, *B*, ranks highest among his or her siblings; the second-born, *C*, ranks second, and so on. The line of descent from a first-born child ranks above that of a second-born. But distance from the common ancestor, in terms of generations, counts also. In the line of descent of first-born children, a person in an older generation ranks above one in a younger generation: *D* ranks above *H*. But any child of the second-born child of the common ancestor, *C*,

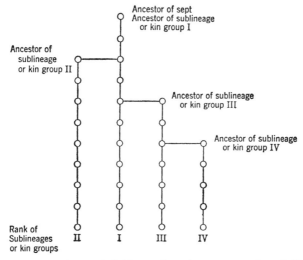

Figure 7–6. Rank of extended kin as dependent upon order of "breaking away."

would rank above the great-grandchild of the common ancestor in the line of descent through first-born children only: *F* and *G* would rank above *H*. Also, in our diagram, the line of descent *BEK* would rank above *CGO* because *B* is the first born of the common ancestor, *A*, whereas *C* is the second-born child. Similarly, *FM* ranks above *GO* because *F* is the first born of *C* whereas *G* is a younger sibling of *F*. Thus we have a conical structure of kindred in which rank is determined by two factors: (1) distance from the common ancestor in terms of generations, and (2) the divergence of the lines of descent in accordance with the relative age of siblings. The line descending through first-born children only passes perpendicularly from the apex of the cone to its base. This is the highest line; the others descend in rank as their distances from the main line increase.

As might be expected, emphasis upon order of birth is reflected in kinship terminology. Among the Kwakiutl there are special terms for eldest and youngest child; the children of mother's or father's elder siblings are distinguished from the children of their younger siblings. The Maori also make similar distinctions.

Distinctions according to rank find expression in named and graded classes in New Zealand and on the Northwest Coast. They are commonly called "nobles" and "commoners": *rangatira*, or well-born, and *tutua*, low-born for the Maori; *naxsola* and *qamola*, for noble and commoner,

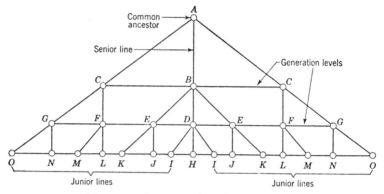

Figure 7-7. Structure of ambilateral lineage.

respectively, among the Kwakiutl. The "nobility" among the Maori consists of persons in the senior line, i.e., the line of direct descent, of each sept, plus a few persons very close to it. Among the Kwakiutl, there is but one noble in the senior line of each sept or kin group; the title is perpetuated by inheritance, but only one person may hold it at a time.

Ambilateral lineages, or "clans," as Kirchhoff proposes to call them, differ from unilateral clans—such as those of the Iroquois or the Omaha, for example—in a number of significant respects. Unilateral clans are exogamous; ambilateral groupings are neither exogamous nor endogamous by customary prescription. All members of unilateral clans have the same status; all are virtually equal. Inequality characterizes the ambilateral groupings throughout. Ambilateral lineages are cone-shaped; clans are cylindrical in structure. In both types of grouping, however, members trace their ancestry to a common point of origin. But in the ambilateral groupings the genealogy is specific, whether actual or mythical; in unilateral clan organization, the relationship to common ancestor is generic and legendary.

What is the significance of ambilateral lineages? Why, in the course of social evolution, have ambilateral lineages developed in some regions, unilateral lineages in others? We suggest the following answer:

Ambilateral lineage organization is a means of achieving or emphasizing integration on a local, community basis rather than upon an intercommunity, tribal basis. Thus, if such factors as topography, mode of subsistence, and defense-offense tended to divide a tribe into a number of relatively isolated or independent village communities, they would tend toward endogamous ambilateral lineage organization. If, however, a tribe consisted of a number of territorial bands or local communities, and if the mode of life—of subsistence and defense-offense—made interrelationships and cooperation between these groups desirable, the tendency would be toward exogamous, unilateral lineages. In short, ambilateral lineages express local community solidarity rather than intercommunity integration. The above explanation does not say, nor should it be taken to mean, that *all* relatively independent local communities *must* develop ambilateral lineages and that *all* tribes composed of spatially distinct groups *must* produce unilateral organization. Numerous factors are always operative in situations of this sort, and results will vary as the kinds and magnitudes of factors vary. What we have tried to do is to discover and isolate the factor or set of factors that *tends* to bring about an ambilateral *rather than* a unilateral type of organization.

In support of our theory we may note the following facts: Among the Maori of New Zealand, the villages were often quite isolated geographically and independent politically. Some were fortified. There was of course friendly social intercourse between villages, but each community lived pretty much to itself. As a rule, says Firth, a village was held by a single *hapu*, or ambilateral lineage. The *hapu* was a subdivision of a tribe, but, it would appear, local, village solidarity was placed above tribal solidarity. Thus we find all the inhabitants (with a few exceptions) of a village comprising a single *hapu* "as a rule." It is significant to note also that when a village contained a number of *hapu*, the sector occupied by each was marked off by "low fences or palisades." Here again, the *hapu* would seem to express a local, or spatial, solidarity rather than an intercommunity or tribal solidarity.

In the Northwest Coast, also, village organization was prominent and important. A tribe would be divided among a number of village communities, each of which was relatively isolated from the others, and virtually autonomous politically. Here, too, local solidarity was placed above tribal integration.

It might reasonably be asked, "Why, if local community solidarity rather than intercommunity integration is the principal determinant of ambilateral lineages, do the Hopi Pueblos, for example, have unilateral, rather than ambilateral, clans?" We can only suggest an answer. Every sociocultural system is three-dimensional, so to speak; it has time depth as well as length and breadth. The history of Pueblo culture, as we piece it together from archaeological evidence, indicates that the Pueblo communities of today are the result of a coalescence of a number of separate and smaller communities of former times; [34] a number of small—and no doubt interrelated—communities came together to form a larger town in order to defend themselves more effectively from attacks by their nomadic neighbors, the Utes and Apaches. The unilateral clan organization that we find today was formed, we may assume, in earlier times when a number of small, interrelated communities was the rule. The situation here may well be comparable to that of the Crow, whose matrilineal clan organization is explained by the fact that they once had a sedentary, horticultural mode of life as neighbors of the Mandan and Hidatsa.

Classes

We turn now to classes and their role in the evolution of primate social organization. By a *class*, to repeat our definition, we mean one of a number of parts into which a social whole is divided, in which one part is unlike another in structure, or composition, and function. Men and women, adults and children, married, unmarried, and widowed are examples of classes of different kinds, of sex, age, and marital classes, respectively. Noble, slave or serf, and commoner are likewise classes in the sense in which we use this term.

The social system of man's immediate prehuman ancestors had a class structure. It was divided into adult and immature individuals. There were males and females. And, we may assume, there were celibate males and mated individuals of both sexes. Each class had its own role, its own function, in the social life. The articulation of one class with another in terms of their respective functions was a means of social integration.

The classes of anthropoid society were passed on to human society. But they underwent some transformation, a redefinition, in the transition, and thereafter became part of a process of cultural evolution in general and of social evolution in particular. In anthropoid society the classes were indeed *social* groupings, but they rested upon a biological basis and were wholly determined by biological considerations. In human society, some classes rest upon a biological basis, whereas biological considerations are irrelevant to class structure at other points. And sometimes the cultural definition overrides the biological factor: an individual who is a man biologically may be a woman sociologically, as we shall see later. In some sectors of human society there may be no correlation at

---

[34] Archaeological evidence of this is supplemented by the legends, or myths, of the Hopi, which picture the formation of the pueblos of today by the coming together of various groups in the past.

all between biological differences and social class distinctions such as noble, commoner, and slave. In short, in the social organization of primates, the class structure of anthropoid society is a biological—anatomical, physiological, psychological—phenomenon; in human society it is cultural.

Age classes. Human society may distinguish more age categories than are significant in anthropoid society. Broadly speaking, there were but two age classes among anthropoids: those who were able to shift for themselves and those too young to do so. There seems to have been no class of the aged and infirm or helpless among subhuman primates. The immature young were of course cared for by adults, particularly the mother, but the aged had no one to support them and so disappeared from the scene when they could no longer care for themselves. In many human societies, too, the aged and helpless are left to die unaided or are even killed. But in other cultural systems, the aged are cared for, and in some societies enjoy a higher status and a better diet than anyone else.

Classification according to age varies from one cultural system to another. In some, the newborn child is not admitted to society as a human being until some days have elapsed. The ritual of naming or circumcision might mark the acceptance of a baby into the community. Weaning marks a new era in a child's life and becomes a significant milestone in some cultures. Puberty is almost universally a significant dividing line between child and adult, and societies without number recognize and celebrate this event with ceremonial or ritual. Many tribes have initiation ceremonies which translate the youth into an adult and full-fledged tribesman at this time. Marriage is another age threshold in some cultures. Then, after one has passed the prime of life and has become old and feeble, he may enter a new social class with its own distinctive status, high or low. In some societies, such as some of those of east Africa or the North American Plains, individuals, or perhaps males only, will pass through a series of age grades or classes as they go through life. Thus we see that societies may recognize few or many age grades or classes. Almost all regard the crises of life such as birth, naming, puberty, marriage and maturity, and old age as marking significant social categories. Some systems have other refinements.

Marital classes. In the society of man's prehuman ancestors, according to our theory set forth in an earlier chapter, some adult males had more than one mate and others therefore had none. With the advent of human society an equitable distribution of mates was instituted, but still the classes "mated" and "unmated" had significance, even though the latter might embrace only those too immature for marriage. As marriage came more and more to serve as a means of alliance between groups of kindred in order to form larger cooperative groups, new classes were formed with reference to marriage: (1) unmarried, (2) mated, (3) widowed, and (4) divorced. Each of these categories became significant in the conduct of social life. The role assumed by each varied, as may be expected, from one cultural system to another.

Sex classes. In the society of man's prehuman ancestors, and in sub-human primate society generally, it would seem fair to distinguish two, and only two, sexes, male and female. Anatomically considered, *male* and *female* are biological categories. But with regard to social behavior, so Zuckerman tells us, a dominant female baboon may assume the role of male in the pattern of sexual behavior; i.e., she may mount a less dominant female or even a passive male, as the dominant male does in the sex act. Also, there is considerable homosexuality among some, if not all, subhuman primate species. We see, then, that even among the lower primates, a social role of sex becomes distinguished from the anatomically defined sexes.

In the human species, the distinctions between the social—or, rather, sociocultural—role of sex and anatomical definition of sex are more numerous and are carried farther than among apes and monkeys. In human as well as subhuman species we have two sexes anatomically defined. But the situation is complicated by the fact that a person may be assigned to one category at birth and live as a member of that class for years, but eventually be transferred—often after surgery—to the opposite class. Cases of this sort are not infrequent in our society today, as everyone knows.

The situation is further complicated by the fact that for one reason or another—biochemical differences or circumstances of social conditioning—a person may change his sex at some time in his or her life, usually, it would appear, at or shortly after puberty. Among many primitive peoples a person grows up as a boy, but upon reaching puberty he adopts the costume and the behavior of women or the costume of a special sex category, the *berdache.* Cases in which boys abandon their sex are more frequent than those in which girls become men, apparently, at least among primitive peoples. The reason for this probably is that in many cultures the mode of life proper to men is too rigorous or too dangerous for weak and timid boys, so they become women, or berdaches, upon reaching puberty rather than assume the life and roles of men. Cases of girls becoming men are not lacking, however.

In societies such as our own, which does not recognize a third, or intermediate sex, the tendencies which among primitive peoples find expression in the institutions of berdache or transvestite are expressed in homosexuality in one way or another.

In the human species sociocultural systems have to cope with the facts of sex in all its dimensions: anatomical, biochemical and physiological, psychological, and sociological. The primary task is one of classification. Some cultural systems are content to recognize but two classes, male and female, in accordance with a normal, anatomical dichotomy. Other systems, however, faced with the discrepancies between the anatomy of sex and the psychology of sex—the adolescent boy who becomes a "woman," or a transvestite—recognize an intermediate sex in addition to male and female.

And in addition to the variations and complexities of sex already considered, some sociocultural systems create a sex artificially, a neuter sex, by castration of males.[35] Eunuchs were a significant social class in ancient oriental cultures; we shall touch upon their social roles later on. Boys in Italy were formerly castrated so that their soprano voices might be preserved for church choirs or the opera.

But however a cultural system may classify the facts of sex, the categories are always culturally defined; i.e., a man, woman, berdache, or eunuch is a person who behaves in a certain way and has a certain distinguishable role in society. These definitions may involve dress, occupation, and even speech—in some cultures the vocabulary of a woman differs from that of a man at certain points. The extent to which a sociocultural system's classification and definition correspond with the facts of anatomy, biochemistry and physiology, and psychology varies from system to system. A society that recognizes only two sexes is in close accord with anatomical distinctions but ignores biochemical or psychological factors. Cultures that have a threefold classification pay more attention to psychological factors than to anatomy.

A sociocultural system's definition of man or woman will always include nonbiological and nonpsychological criteria. "A man is an adult person who behaves thus and so" might specify whether he could wear earrings or not, what occupations he may engage in and those which he should eschew, and even his choice and use of words. None of these things has any necessary relationship to sex as a biological phenomenon: there is no biological reason why women rather than men should wear earrings, or why men rather than women should be permitted to smoke cigars. The irrelevance of items of behavior such as these to sex biologically considered is of course made clear by the fact that cultures vary in their prescriptions and prohibitions: in some societies men *may* wear earrings and women may smoke cigars.

And in some societies the cultural definition of sex may override the facts of sex biologically considered. We have already noted that in some

[35] It is only in modern cultures that females have been sterilized. In former times and in lower cultures abortion and infanticide were practiced in lieu of castration.

kinship systems a man may be called "mother" and a woman, "father." A man may marry another man's foot or a tree; a woman may marry other women and become the "father" of their offspring. The cacique, or priest-chief, among the Keresan Pueblos is a biological man, but in the socioreligious life of the pueblo he is "everyone's mother."

Division of labor and the genesis of occupational groups. The process of cultural evolution in general and of social evolution in particular is one of progressive differentiation of structure and specialization of function, and of integration on successively higher levels of development. Again we may note the parallel with the evolution of biological systems, where we find the same aspects of the evolutionary process as those listed here. This is not surprising, however, since culture is a mechanism brought into being by a biological system and used by it to perpetuate its existence.

On low levels of biological evolution, we find relatively little structural differentiation and specialization of function. Some of the lowest of animal organisms have no specialized and structurally differentiated organs of sense, locomotion, defense-offense, or subsistence. As biological systems evolve, however, specialized structures are developed to perform these various functions. Thus, eyes, nose, ears, teeth, legs, fins, and so on, are developed. Specialized structures make life more secure because they perform the vital functions more effectively. The life process here exhibits its self-expanding, self-extending characteristic. An increase in the amount of free energy captured and utilized tends to increase the organization of the structure: to effectuate further differentiation of structure and greater specialization of function. Then, as a consequence of these specialized structures, the biological system becomes a more efficient and effective mechanism for capturing and utilizing energy. Thus, each aspect of the process stimulates and nourishes the other. The result is progress as well as evolution. As a consequence of structural differentiation and specialization of function, special mechanisms of coordination and regulation must be developed to preserve the integrity of the system. The nervous system is the principal mechanism of this sort.

All the principles and characteristics of biological evolution cited above are found also in the process of cultural evolution. Here again we note the correlation between energy and the organization of a system, whether it be physical, biological, or cultural: the more the energy the greater the organization. On the lowest levels of cultural development, i.e., on levels where the human organism is the only source of energy exploited by cultural systems, we find a minimum of structural differentiation and specialization of function. By *structure* here we include both technological, or instrumental, and social structure. Thus we find few specialized tools, on the one hand, and few specialized social structures, on the other.

As culture evolves, however, specialized structures appear both in technology and in society. Life is made more secure by differentiation of structure and specialization of function in the extrasomatic system that is culture, as it is in biological organisms. Also, as in the case of the biological process, we find in the cultural process a condition of autocatalysis, so to speak, a self-stimulating self-expanding process. Technological and social differentiation and specialization are increased by additions to the amount of energy harnessed and utilized, and as a consequence of differentiation and specialization, cultural systems become more efficient and effective mechanisms for harnessing and utilizing additional amounts of energy. Evolution and progress result. Finally, to complete our comparison of the culturological process of evolution with the biological process, we note that mechanisms of coordination and control, of integration, are developed in the former as in the latter.

The development of specialized tools and weapons is easily traced on the technological level of cultural development. On the lowest levels we find the smallest number of kinds of tools, and they are the most generalized in structure and function. As we proceed to higher levels, the number of kinds increases, and they become correspondingly more specialized. The *coup de poing*, the principal tool on low cultural levels over a very wide area in the Old World, was a very generalized tool. It could be used for cutting, chopping, pounding, and scraping. In upper Paleolithic levels we find specialized tools: scrapers, choppers, knives, awls, hammers, axes, and so on. The number of kinds of tools increases as technology advances.

We find almost no division of labor in the societies of subhuman primates today, and we may assume that it was all but lacking among man's immediate prehuman ancestors. Infant offspring were nourished and cared for by the mother; the father took virtually no part in this work. Apart from this instance, which was of course biologically determined, there was no division of labor in the prehuman stage of primate social evolution.

With the advent of articulate speech, however, division of labor was introduced on a sociological basis and subsequently developed to a great extent. Division of labor and cooperation are obverse and reverse sides of the same phenomenon, as we have already noted. In our discussion of the origin and development of kinship systems we were particularly concerned with their cooperative aspect, but division of labor is equally present and significant; the cooperation is effected, one might say, by the division of labor among individuals and classes of individuals. To say, for example, that one is required by custom to behave in such and such a manner toward his uncles, in another manner toward his sisters, mothers-in-law, nephews, cousins, and so on, respectively, and that each class of relatives in turn must behave toward him in a specified manner, is to indicate a thoroughgoing system of division of labor. It should be pointed out that even instances in which the acts are identical in nature as well as reciprocal, such as a man giving meat to his brother and later receiving meat from him in return, are examples of division of labor as well as of cooperation. This example will serve also to reveal one of the important functions of division of labor, namely, the promotion of social solidarity. The exchange of goods or services of like kind between two persons, be they relatives, friends, or neighbors, whether in primitive society or our own, is an example of division of labor between them. But the function and advantage of such a type of division of labor are social rather than technological. Such an exchange does not increase the productive efficiency of the society as a whole; nor does a greater product accrue from such an expenditure of labor than if each worked for himself. But the effect upon society of such a reciprocal arrangement may be very considerable indeed. It may be a means of establishing a friendly relationship which, once formed, will express itself in acts of mutual aid in many situations. Reciprocal exchange keeps alive a friendly relationship and fosters cooperation. This simple exchange of goods or services is therefore a way of binding persons to one another by ties that may be, and often are, powerful and effective. The world-wide custom of exchanging gifts is, as we shall see in greater detail in Chapter 9, "Economic Organization," a good example of the promotion of solidarity through a reciprocal division of labor. We see, then, that a kinship system among primitive peoples is an elaborate form of division of labor that makes life more secure by making the society more effective technologically in terms of subsistence and defense-offense and by the promotion of social solidarity.

Division of labor along sex lines. We turn now to another form of division of labor found in all human societies and which must have been inaugurated at the very beginning of culture itself, namely, division along sex lines. In every cultural system, men and women are distinguished from each other as *classes,* which means that, at certain points, they are distinguished by differences of behavior. These differences are of two kinds, ritual and technological. Thus, for example, women may be permitted to wear earrings, while men are forbidden by custom to do so; this is merely a matter of social ritual. On the technological level, however, hunting may be man's work, while women gather plant food. An occupation that is assigned to men in one cultural system may be confined to women in another, or shared by both sexes in a third. Weaving, cooking, milking, hoeing, and so on, are masculine occupations in some cultures, feminine in others, and the occupation of either or both in still others. It might seem from the great variety of custom that there is no rhyme or reason to division of labor between the sexes, at least at certain points. But if we will keep in mind the *social* function of this device as well as its technological significance, we believe that all its forms can be rendered intelligible.

Let us consider, first, the question of the biological basis of the social division of labor between the sexes in human society. Nourishing the developing embryo, childbirth, and suckling infants are, as of course they must be, the work of women only. But to what extent do these factors affect the division of labor between the sexes in other respects? The obvious fact of difference of role in reproduction has apparently led some writers to assume that childbearing and suckling were the factors that have determined all divisions of functions between the sexes, at least so far as utilitarian occupation is concerned. Thus they would regard the social division of labor between men and women as being *sexually* determined, as it is between male and female in anthropoid society. But this is to take a rather superficial view of the matter. It is of course true that pregnancy and the suckling of infants render women less effective in certain occupations than men. In the interests of group efficiency, therefore, it would be advantageous to assign certain occupations to men and leave others to women. But to explain all such occupational differentiation in terms of sex and reproduction is to fail to appreciate other significant factors. Women are not pregnant or suckling children all their mature and active years. There are long periods when they are not so engaged, and some never bear children at all.

Apart from their roles in reproduction there are other biological differences between men and women which would tend to bring about a division of labor in the interest of group efficiency. Men are, on the average, stronger and fleeter of foot than women.[36] Of these two traits the latter is the more important, especially in the earliest stages of cultural development. Other factors being constant, it would be better, for the sake of group efficiency, to assign men to the tasks requiring considerable strength and leave the lighter work to women than to have each sex devoted indiscriminately to both. But fleetness is a more important factor in survival than mere strength. One can make up for a lack of strength by working a longer period of time in such occupations as chopping or carrying wood. But in certain occupations one cannot compensate for a

[36] World records, recognized by the International Amateur Athletic Federation, October, 1947, show the maximum speeds of the sexes as follows: for 100 yards, men 9.4 seconds, women 10.8; for 220 yards, men 20.3 seconds, women 24.3; for 880 yards, men 1 minute 49.2 seconds, women 2 minutes 19.7 seconds. It will be noted that women approximate the speeds of men most closely on the sprints; as the distance run increases, the inferiority of women increases. Thus, women require 15 per cent more time than men to run 100 yards, 20 per cent more for the 220, and 28 per cent more for the 880. Perhaps even more significant is the fact that the greatest distance run by women as listed among these records is 800 meters, whereas men ran up to 15 miles.

lack of speed by running a longer period of time. In hunting and in warfare a great premium is placed on speed; if you cannot run fast enough to obtain your quarry, running a longer time will do no good; and if you are not swift enough to escape your foe, you get no chance to run longer. We find, therefore, a very widespread division of labor between the sexes on very low cultural levels that has been determined to a great extent by differences in strength and fleetness, particularly the latter.

So far, then, the occupational distinctions between men and women are explainable in terms of sexual and physical differences, or in merely sexual terms if one wishes to call differences in strength and fleetness secondary sexual characteristics, as would seem justifiable. There is still another occupational context in which sexual differences are at least relevant. In many cultures women are debarred from certain occupations because they are women. The "horror" of menstrual blood is fairly widespread, and in many societies women, at least prior to the menopause, are debarred from certain occupations, usually ceremonial, on this account. Whether, however, the aversion or fear of menstrual blood is to be regarded as the *cause* of their exclusion or merely a symptom, an unconscious rationalization, of something else, is a question we are not able to answer definitely. Since the menstrual phobia is not universal, we may conclude that it is a culturological rather than a psychological phenomenon. But what the specific cultural determinants are, we cannot say. It may be merely a sociological device employed in rivalry between the sexes as social classes to win an advantage for the male sex.

But division of labor between the sexes in human society cannot be explained wholly in terms of biological differences. Men are stronger and swifter than women *on an average*. But, in any society, some women, perhaps many, will be stronger or swifter than a certain percentage of the men. If, therefore, division of labor were based wholly upon physical qualifications, we would find *some* women in occupations in which strength or fleetness is especially required and *some* men in occupations that are usually assigned to the "weaker sex." As a matter of fact, we do encounter situations such as this occasionally. Among the Keresan Pueblos of New Mexico women engage in the laborious task of plastering a house, while old men tend their small children. But instances of this kind are far from universal. As a rule, the hunters and warriors, and very often the herdsmen, are men regardless of sex differences of strength or fleetness. Furthermore, certain occupations that require neither great strength nor swiftness are exclusively masculine pursuits in certain cultures; weaving among the Pueblos, for example, was done by men almost exclusively. We must therefore look for some other determinant of the division of labor between the sexes than the purely biological ones of strength and fleetness; we must find a social, or culturological, determinant or determinants.

We have already anticipated this contingency in our general discussion of the social function of division of labor. Quite apart from technological efficiency, there is the matter of integration and solidarity. From the standpoint of technological effectiveness alone, a society would not attain its maximum effectiveness if it assigned women to certain occupations and men to others regardless of strength or fleetness. But this loss is undoubtedly more than compensated for by the gain in social efficiency fostered by the social division along sex lines. Men and women constitute distinct social classes as well as biological categories. Division of labor along sex lines is a means of distinguishing, and emphasizing the distinctness of, social classes. It is a means of promoting social solidarity by making each class necessary and complementary to the other.

As Radcliffe-Brown has remarked, in discussing marriage and the family in aboriginal Australia, "a man without a wife is in an unsatisfactory position since he has no one to supply him regularly with vegetable food, to provide his firewood and so' on." [37] Similarly, a Kai of New Guinea takes a wife, says Lowie, "because he needs a woman to make pots and to cook his meals, to manufacture nets and weed his plantations, in return for which he provides the household with game and fish and builds the dwelling." [38]

But why cannot the man provide himself with plant food and cook his own meals? He *can*, of course, but it is to society's interest and advantage to have a certain amount of interdependence among its members; interdependence means mutual aid, and cooperation means greater security.

The allocation of certain patterns of behavior, both technological and ritual, to men as a class and others to women as a class has a further and important significance in the context of social order and control, but we shall discuss this more fully later under the heading of etiquette.

Men and women constitute biological classes, distinguished from one another by anatomical and physiological differences. The social division of labor between them is based upon and determined by biological differences to a certain, but definitely limited, extent. Men and women constitute *social* classes as well as biological categories, and a purely social or culturological factor operates also to produce behavioral or occupational differences between them.

A discussion of division of labor along sex lines would not be complete without some mention of eunuchs and *castrati*, to which we have already alluded (p. 185). These are men who have been desexed by surgical means. They constitute, therefore, a distinct sex category in human

[37] A. R. Radcliffe-Brown, "The Social Organization of Australian Tribes," *Oceania*, vol. I, p. 435, 1931.

[38] R. H. Lowie, *Primitive Society*, rev. ed., Liveright Publishing Corporation, New York, 1947, pp. 65–66.

society, somewhat analogous to the neuters among some insect species. And they have special social functions, play a significant role in the social division of labor, as a consequence of their sexual—or nonsexual—character. *Eunuch* (Gr. *eunouchos*, guarding the couch) usually refers to functionaries in Oriental cultures; *castrati*, to professional "male" sopranos in Italy. The chief function of a eunuch was to take charge of the women in the harem of an Oriental potentate; castration had peculiarly fitted him for this task. But because of the intimate relationship to his master in which his duties placed him, the eunuch often became a confidant and an adviser to his lord. As a consequence, many eunuchs came to exercise considerable political influence and power. Sometimes, it appears, they served as generals and as governors of provinces. In Egypt the term eunuch came to be applied to any court official, whether a *castratus* or not.

In Italy, the practice of castrating boys in order to preserve their voices for the papal choir and other musical organizations flourished for a considerable time. The custom was condemned by Pope Benedict XIV (1740–1758). Since that time there have been no *castrati* in the service of the church, but they continued to appear on the operatic stage in Italy until the latter part of the nineteenth century.

The origin of the practice of castration is somewhat obscure. It is believed that the castration of domestic animals came first and that the de-sexing of human beings followed in imitation. Southwest Asia seems to have been the place of origin, and it must have originated at least as early as Bronze Age times. Eunuchs have been most prominent in Mesopotamian cultures—possibly the place of their origin—but they have flourished also in Persia, Greece, Muslim cultures of Africa, and Rome. The custom was introduced into China in the eighth century B.C.[39]

Specialists. The next instance of division of labor to appear in the course of social evolution occurred in the realm of ritual, namely, the emergence of the shaman as a specialist.[40]

A shaman may be defined as a person who specializes in matters super-natural by virtue of personal qualifications and initiative rather than as a consequence of being selected, trained, and delegated by society to per-form such functions. We thus distinguish a shaman from a priest, who also specializes in matters supernatural. A shaman assumes his occupation upon his own initiative and responsibilities. His qualifications and ef-fectiveness rest upon his possession of, or ability to manipulate, super-

[39] Cf. Louis H. Gray, "Eunuchs," in *Encyclopaedia of Religion and Ethics*, J. Hastings (ed.), vol. 5, 1915.

[40] Radcliffe-Brown calls shamanism "the oldest profession in the world." Preface to *African Political Systems*, Meyer Fortes and E. E. Evans-Pritchard (eds.), Oxford University Press, London, 1940, p. xxi.

natural power, with which he has been endowed in one way or another, by peculiarities of temperament or by some experience with supernatural powers. A person may or may not enter the priesthood of his own volition, but in any event he cannot become a priest unless society accepts or delegates him for this role. The priest's ability to traffick in supernatural power is acquired only by learning at the hands of socially authorized teachers; supernatural visitations and endowments play no part here. The shaman may have to learn certain techniques, too, but merely as a means of exercising his own powers. The priest, on the other hand, has no powers of his own; he is merely one trained and skilled in the performance of sacred ritual. The shaman is a free lance; the priest, a person selected and trained by society to perform certain functions. Or, to borrow a folk saying, shamans are born, not made, except by a personal supernatural experience, and then only if they have the appropriate temperament. Priests definitely are made, not born. It should be apparent that we are here making logical distinctions of function. Ethnological reality corresponds very well with this logical distinction, but not wholly and perfectly; there is overlapping at some points. In some cultures it might be difficult to say whether a certain functionary was a shaman or a priest. In most instances, however, this is rather easy. In any case, the distinctions we have drawn with regard to initiative, source of efficacy, etc., will be found valid and illuminating. It may be said further in this connection that shamans and priests characterize broadly different levels of social evolution. On lowest cultural levels we find shamans but no priests. On advanced levels, priests tend to become prominent and important; shamans, to disappear or become insignificant.[41]

We may distinguish two fundamental categories of adjustment to and control over the external world: naturalistic philosophy and technology

[41] Priests were prominent and very important in such cultures as those of ancient Egypt and Mesopotamia and apparently of the Maya and Aztecs, whereas shamans were absent or insignificant. The same is true of the Christian culture of Europe. It is significant to note that, in the early years of Christianity, free lances in religion were denounced by the priesthood as "false prophets," and effort was made to suppress or eliminate them. In recent years in the United States, however, there seems to be a resurgence of shamanism. Witness, for example, the efflorescence of cults of many kinds. Countless individuals set themselves up as free-lance adventurers, or entrepreneurs, in the field of supernaturalism—prophets, seers, healers, dispensers of revelation and salvation, and what not. As such, these individuals stand in rather sharp contrast with the professional clergy of an established church, professionals who can function only as a consequence of specialized instruction in ecclesiastical seminaries and after formal induction by the ritual of ordination. This efflorescence of shamanism today is probably to be interpreted as an indication of a weakening of the established church as a mechanism of social integration and control, of disintegration of the orthodox or traditional theologies, but unaccompanied by the development of adequate secular institutions and philosophies to take their place.

and supernaturalistic philosophy and magical ritual. All cultures employ both types of adjustment and control, but in varying proportions. The two types are related inversely to each other: the greater the amount of naturalistic, realistic knowledge, the more effective the means of technological control, the less will be the extent of supernaturalism and magical techniques, and vice versa. As culture evolves, naturalism increases in philosophy and technique; supernaturalism diminishes.

We find no supernaturalism at all among subhuman primates; it is only the advent of articulate speech that has made this kind of behavior possible. It seems reasonable to assume that in the earliest stage of cultural development there was a generalized and diffuse supernaturalism in the behavior of all members of society alike. As culture advanced, however, i.e., as language and philosophy were developed as counterparts of neuro-sensory-muscular experience, philosophy and behavior alike became differentiated. The matter-of-fact was distinguished from the mystical; the sacred from the profane. But at first this distinction was confined to the behavior of each individual. Later the distinction extended to society; i.e., certain members of the group were distinguished from others by a special concern with supernatural activities. These persons were shamans.

Shamanism as a social process, as a form of division of labor, is a matter of degree. A person may be known as a shaman, he may be distinguished from others by a specialization in magic, but at the same time engage in the occupations of his fellow tribesmen of the same sex. As a matter of fact, shamans are seldom, if ever, able to support themselves by the practice of magic alone. Usually they derive but a minor part of their subsistence from their profession. When culture has reached the point where a portion of the population can be freed from the necessity of producing their own food, the specialists in supernaturalism become priests rather than shamans.

Division of labor in the practice of magic arises from two sources: some individuals are better qualified than others; and the magical art becomes also a social function, which means interaction, complementary services, give and take. Let us turn first to the qualifications of a shaman.

Traffic with the supernatural world is by its very nature mysterious. Extraordinary abilities are therefore required or are at least an asset. Epileptic fits, trances, hallucinations, and hysteria are mysterious experiences, and hence eminently suited to communication with the supernatural world. Dreams during trances are interpreted as visits to the land of the spirits; fits and hysteria are states produced when a spirit seizes and possesses the body of the shaman. This conception is preserved in our word "epilepsy" (Gr. *epi*, upon; *lambano*, seize). Hence neurotic, abnormal, and unstable individuals are better qualified for the profession of shamanism than are normal and stable persons. As Tylor long ago observed: "... In all quarters of the world the oracle-priests and diviners by familiar spirits seem really diseased in body and mind...." [42] More recently, Lowie has commented upon the abnormal character of the shaman: "From Africa and Oceania, from Siberia and Tierra del Fuego we thus have evidence that shamans are either abnormal or at least temporarily capable of passing into abnormal mental states." [43] The advantage of abnormality in trafficking with the supernatural world is further indicated by the widespread use of drugs, liquor, fasting, self-torture, and solitude to produce temporary pathologic states as a means or a condition of supernatural experience. Thus we see that some individuals are better qualified to become shamans than others.

Some men are better qualified to hunt and to engage in warfare than others, and yet we do not find division of labor among men in these fields of activity in tribal society. Why, then, do we find it in the supernaturalistic arts? The answer to this question is threefold. In the first place, the differences of ability among men and women that set apart certain individuals as especially qualified for shamanism are greater than those relevant to hunting or warfare. Hunters and warriors differ in ability, to be sure, but only in degree; one is merely better or worse than another. But the differences of ability and temperament relevant to shamanism are, as we have just seen, very often one of kind: abnormal versus normal. Some people hear only the voices of the external world; others hear voices of intraorganismal origin. The same is true of visions. Some individuals live only in a world of real or genuine sensory experience; others live also in a world of pseudosensory experience. Thus, a distinct gap often separates individuals especially qualified for shamanism from those not so qualified, whereas one warrior or hunter differs from another merely by degree.

The second reason why division of labor appears in traffic with the supernatural world before it does in hunting or warfare is that every able-bodied person in primitive societies must engage in food production and in defense and offense; it is essential for survival. Division of labor is thus impossible in these areas. In commerce with the supernatural world, however, division of labor is quite possible.

And in the third place, the practice of the magical arts is to a very great extent a *social* function or process, which means division of labor. The shaman controls the weather, cures the sick, helps the hunter and

<hr />

[42] E. B. Tylor, *Anthropology*, 1881, p. 366.
[43] R. H. Lowie, *Introduction to Cultural Anthropology*, rev. ed., Rinehart & Company, Inc., 1940, p. 311. See also Hutton Webster's discussion of shamanism and the abnormal in *Magic: a Sociological Study*, 1938, pp. 157–159.

fisherman obtain food, aids and safeguards the warrior, and so on. Ostensibly he is exercising control over the external world. His charms, spells, rituals, and paraphernalia constitute a technology of a sort, a pseudo technology as it were. Just as a hunter, warrior, or craftsman lays hold of the external world and bends and shapes it to his will by means of tools and weapons, so does the shaman, in make-believe, do the same thing with his paraphernalia and techniques. But an ethnologist who saw no more in the shaman's art than a pseudo technology, one based upon a false premise, would be almost as naïve as the shaman himself. The chief, nay entire, significance of shamanism is social and psychological. The rain doctor has no effect upon the weather, but he does have a very real effect upon his fellow tribesmen. So it is with all his activities. Make-believe his rituals are, so far as the external world is concerned. But he has an effect, often a profound one, upon men, his foes as well as his friends and kinsmen. And this effect is real.

The characteristic situation in which appeal to magic is made is a *crisis*. A drought, a storm, an eclipse, hunger, a menacing foe, critical illness, these are the occasions in which primitive peoples turn to the gods and magic for help. A crisis situation is one of unstable social equilibrium. The security of life is threatened. The normal flow of events is disrupted. Apprehension and fear may grip the community; panic or the paralysis of apathy may ensue. The emergency calls for decisive action, but what is one to do? Disintegration stares them in the face; society is "going to pieces," leaving the individual in the stark terror of aloneness and impotence that animals other than primates feel when bereft of the herd with its reassurance and support.

Here is where the shaman comes to the fore. He steps boldly forward and confronts the crisis face to face. He uses his potent charms and spells against the danger; he subdues it with ritual, fetish, and song. The external world follows its natural course in its own sweet way, quite oblivious of the grimaces and chatter of the puny primate who utters defiance and pretends to control. But what a difference to his fellow tribesmen the little drama of the shaman makes! It releases their tensions, provides an outlet for pent-up emotions. The ritual is action, and any action is better than none. The shaman gives them assurance and courage; a sense of power returns. But most of all the shaman reunites the community in the performance of a ritual for them all and which each one may share, in spirit if not in deed. Equilibrium is restored, solidarity reestablished; each individual safe and secure again in the protective embrace of the community, the herd. This is the function par excellence of the shaman.

Division of labor is inherent in the magical practice of medicine. A man may feed himself or defend himself from his foes, but he cannot very well treat himself medically.[44] If we take magic at its face value, then a person could treat his own illness magically just as he can catch a fish for his supper or defend himself from an enemy. But we would be naïve to accept the shaman's estimate and interpretation of his profession. Besides, when one is critically ill he is in no condition to engage in magical rituals.

A person stricken with disease or severely wounded is in a crisis situation. He faces uncertainty and is full of foreboding and apprehension. His illness tends to isolate him from his fellows, from the herd; the bonds of solidarity weaken. Fear overtakes him; his helplessness oppresses him. Here also the shaman performs a valuable service. Once again he attacks the problem head on. If witches have caused the illness, he drives them away. He placates ghosts, gods, and disgruntled ancestors. Stolen souls or hearts are retrieved. With song, fetish, prayer, and ritual he restores the confidence of the sick one, gives him courage to fight his way back to health, assures him of success. The psychological effect may be tremendous and actually beneficial.

Not the least of the shaman's treatment is massage. Quite apart from any physical effect that stroking the body may have, the psychological effect may be great. Grooming is a most satisfying practice among primates, and animals of other orders love to be petted and stroked also. Bodily contact is a way of making spiritual connections, of promoting social cohesion. The "laying on of hands" is a physical form of a spiritual transaction; the hand clasp, a physical mechanism of social solidarity. In times of crisis a gentle pressure from a friend or comrade's hand can be more eloquent and expressive of compassion and assurance than any words that tongue can speak. So it is with the shaman and his massage. With this means he establishes contact with the sick one, isolated on his couch, and unites him with his fellow man once more. The potency of the medicine man or wizard is indicated by the actual efficacy of his treatments, on the one hand, and his ability to kill, on the other. Many a man has lain down and died because he knew that a powerful wizard was working magic against him.[45]

Shamanism originated in traffic with the supernatural world. But having become a distinct element of social structure, it is easy for shamans to acquire nonmagical functions. In many societies medicine men serve as integrative, directive, and regulative mechanisms. They may see to it that custom is observed and may punish offenders against it. They may take the initiative in organizing or directing community

[44] In our society a physician will frequently seek the services of another doctor rather than treat himself or even his children.

[45] Cf. W. B. Cannon, "Voodoo Death," *American Anthropologist*, vol. 44, pp. 169–181, 1942.

activities. To be sure, the supernaturalistic and the secular functions of the shaman may be, and often are, combined in a given situation. But it is important to recognize the acquisition of purely secular political functions in addition to his role in affairs supernatural. We shall see how these functions grow and become very important among the priesthoods of higher cultural levels.

Among the social functions of the shaman must be listed those of a dramatic and recreational nature also. As Durkheim observed,[46] the rituals of the shaman and the ceremonies directed by him often have dramatic and aesthetic features which are enjoyed for their own sake. Thus, natives of the arctic, in Siberia and America alike, often pass the long evenings of winter witnessing shamanistic performances. The fire and sword jugglery of the Pueblo medicine men have a dramatic quality enjoyed by spectators for its own sake. So it is with many features of the totemic ceremonies of Australia: the dramatization of episodes in mythology, the striking and elaborate costumes and face and body paintings, the songs and dances. These magical rituals, performed under the direction of the *altajuna*, the shamanistic head of the totem group, are also powerful and absorbing dramas.

Thus we see that occupational specialization appears first in the magical arts. Specialization appeared here before it entered the technological arts and crafts, first, because division of labor was fostered by temperamental differences among individuals, on the one hand, and because specialization in magic was possible before it could be effected in technology, and, secondly, because shamanism is actually, though not in native theory, wholly a social process, whereas hunting, fishing, warfare, and manufacturing are technological processes first and only secondarily sociological in character. Shamanism as a social process not only could be, but had to be, a division of labor at the very outset, whereas specialization in technologic contexts can appear only upon certain and relatively high stages of cultural development.

On higher cultural levels, particularly in civil society, we shall see the priest taking the place of the shaman, but performing all the same functions.

Occupational classes. Between the emergence of the shaman as a specialist and the origin of metallurgy we find relatively little division of labor along technological lines. To be sure, there are beginnings and even modest developments of specialized craftsmen here and there. In some societies we may find a few persons who specialize in the manufacture of arrows, bead or quill work, or some other article. In Polynesia, there

[46] E. Durkheim, *The Elementary Forms of the Religious Life*, J. Swain (trans.), 1915, pp. 379–380.

were specialists in woodcarving, canoe and house building, tattooing, and in the manufacture of adzes. These men were engaged by others who paid them for their services with a "gift" of food, apparel, or something else of value. It would appear that most of these specialists devoted but a minor fraction of their time to working for others, although a few renowned woodcarvers or tattooers might be so occupied the greater part of their time. There was a tendency in Polynesia also for specialization in a craft to be hereditary. Thus we find the beginnings of specialized crafts in societies organized on the basis of kinship, but they have developed only to a slight degree.

It is not, however, until the arts of subsistence, or more precisely, the productivity of human labor in the production of food, has reached a point where a few or a considerable portion of the able-bodied members of society can be divorced from the production of food that the formation of groups, or classes, of specialized artisans becomes possible. But when this time has arrived, society has already begun to shift from kinship to property relations as the basis of its organization, and a new type of economic organization is in the making. The metallurgist is the first of the true specialists of this era; other and older crafts, such as weaving, stone working, carving, and so on, soon become independent crafts also. In short, there was relatively little division of labor along technological lines prior to the Agricultural Revolution, prior to the development of cities. After that time, differentiation of social structure and specialization of function along technological lines were rapid and extensive. We shall return to this subject in a later chapter.

Rank. Many, if not most, societies of primitive peoples, i.e., those based upon ties of kinship, are characterized by an equality of status of their members. In some, however, inequality prevails. The societies of Polynesia and the Northwest Coast of America are perhaps the best examples of social inequality among social systems founded upon kinship. Here we have three classes, commonly called "nobles," "commoners," and "slaves." But these terms are misleading, and confusion and unwarranted conclusions have come from their use. There is a tendency to equate the so-called nobles and slaves of these cultures with the classes bearing these names in European culture. There are, to be sure, some points of similarity. But the similarities are quite superficial, whereas there is a profound and fundamental difference between the class structure of Polynesia or of the Northwest Coast, on the one hand, and that of Europe, on the other.

The class system of Polynesia and Northwest America resembled that of Europe in matters of attitude, sentiment, and social ritual. Nobles in both types of culture, primitive and modern, had high social status, were treated with deference, were distinguished by certain marks, set apart by certain observances, and so on. The so-called slaves of Polynesia and the Northwest Coast, like the true slaves of Europe or the United States, had a definitely inferior status. In short, so far as the ritual and insignia of social intercourse between noble and slave were concerned, the class system of these preliterate peoples resembles that of modern Europe. Or one might say, they resemble each other in *form*. When we turn to *content*, however, to the basis upon which the class systems rested, we find a fundamental difference.

In European culture the class system was based upon property relations. The noble was a landholder; the serf belonged to the land. The relationship between noble and serf or between master and slave was one of political power and economic exploitation backed, of course, by military might. It was an arrangement whereby one class could live by the labor of another. In Polynesia and the Northwest Coast this was not the case. Here the "slaves" were for the most part war captives. In warfare, the life of the vanquished belongs to the victor; he may be killed outright, enslaved, reduced to vassalage, or saddled with reparations and tried for "war crimes." Some primitive peoples took captives in warfare. In some instances they took them home to be put to death by protracted and ingenious torture, as was the custom of the Iroquois and other eastern Indian tribes; or they might be kept around the village indefinitely as permanent prisoners of war, put to work at menial tasks, and treated with contempt. Time and again in the literature these individuals are termed "slaves," and the conclusion has been drawn that "primitive society was not democratic but was widely characterized by the institution of slavery." [47]

It is true that slaves, in the sense of "human chattels," do exist in some preliterate cultural systems. But they are either cultures which have definitely evolved beyond kinship as the basis of tribal organization and have already developed a number of features of the political state, as in the case of some African nations; or they are societies which engage in a slave trade initiated and sustained by a higher culture, such as a few instances in the Northwest Coast, Luzon, and, again, in parts of Africa. But to call captives of war among tribes organized on the basis of kinship "slaves" is to confuse two quite different social categories.

In many instances in primitive society captives of war, if not taken for torture, were incorporated into the tribe by adoption or marriage, and consequently their children would be free. In other cultures, however, such as those of Polynesia and the Northwest Coast, captives were kept as an inferior social class with whom marriage was forbidden or looked

[47] Cf. R. H. Lowie, *Primitive Society*, rev. ed., Liveright Publishing Corporation, Black and Gold Library, New York, 1947, pp. 345ff., 389-390.

down upon. They were set to menial tasks, although they were not alone in this respect. They could be killed at will by their masters since they had forfeited their lives at the time of capture. These are the persons so often cited as demonstrating that "slavery" is widespread in primitive society.

But this slavery, so called, differs fundamentally from the ownership of human chattels in modern Western civilization. "Slavery among the Ifugao," says Barton, "was *nothing like* slavery as it has existed among our own and other peoples ... [italics supplied]." [48] Herskovits tells us that "slavery ... is widespread in primitive societies," but adds that "it was rarely the type of institution it became in the Western world in historic times." [49] Descriptions of the life of "slaves" in primitive societies make it clear that they are not at all comparable to the human chattels of modern Western culture. In general, they lived very much as their masters, the chiefs and "nobles," did. They often lived in the same house, worked at the same tasks, and ate the same foods. The "relations between ... [slaves] and their masters" among the Maori were, according to Firth, "easy and pleasant." They "did the menial work, but were well fed and housed." [50]

Among the Tlingit and the Haida, according to Goldenweiser, a student of Boas (an authority on cultures of the Northwest Coast) "the economic position and daily life of the [slave] does not greatly differ from that of his owner. The slaves live in the houses with the other people, they eat with them, work, hunt and make war on a par with the others. *It is only on occasions where social prestige and ceremonial prerogatives are involved that the disabilities of the slave become conspicuous* [italics supplied]." [51] Viola Garfield makes a similar appraisal of "slavery" among the Tsimshian.[52]

Among tribes of northern California "slaves" functioned in a context of prestige rather than of political bondage and economic exploitation. Among the Tolowa and Tututni, says Cora Du Bois, "slaves were not taken in war, but were acquired through unpaid debt." [53] But "debts

[48] R. F. Barton, "Ifugao Economics," *University of California Publications in American Archaeology and Ethnology,* vol. 15, p. 419, 1922.

[49] M. J. Herskovits, *The Economic Life of Primitive Peoples,* Alfred A. Knopf, Inc., New York, 1940, p. 91.

[50] Raymond Firth, *Primitive Economics of the New Zealand Maori,* E. P. Dutton & Co., Inc., New York, 1929, p. 95.

[51] Alexander Goldenweiser, *Early Civilization,* Alfred A. Knopf, Inc., 1922, p. 55.

[52] Viola Garfield, "Tsimshian Clan and Society," *University of Washington Publications in Anthropology,* vol. 7, no. 3, p. 271, 1939.

[53] Cora Du Bois, "The Wealth Concept as an Integrative Factor in Tolowa-Tututni Culture," in *Essays in Anthropology Presented to A. L. Kroeber,* University of California Press, Berkeley, Calif., 1936, p. 55.

could be incurred only in the realm of prestige economy," i.e., as a consequence of a ritual of social intercourse, not as the result of subjugation and exploitation. The "slave" was "not a source of income. His status was approximately that of a poor relative. In reality slavery was almost a form of adoption." In fact, says Du Bois, "to apply the term slave to such individuals...is in reality a misnomer." Again, "slavery" turns out to be *not* slavery after all.

It would be well to recall at this point that in both Polynesia and the Northwest Coast great emphasis is placed upon rank, as we have already seen in our discussion of ambilateral lineages. Those who stand closest to an exalted ancestor in the direct line of descent have the highest status or rank; those farther removed have correspondingly lower status. Captives of war thus fit easily into a pattern of social inequality. Rank is, of course, a matter of contrasts of status; no one can be a king without subjects. A mass of commoners is necessarily implied by a class of great chiefs or nobles. By the same token, a class of slaves will serve to accentuate the status of chiefs and nobles. And we find slaves performing precisely this function in Polynesia and the Northwest Coast; they serve to validate the social position of their masters. The noneconomic character of the institution of "slavery" is revealed when a Kwakiutl chief, for example, will kill a slave merely to demonstrate his high status. If these slaves were "property making machines," to use Morgan's term, and if the status of the noble depended upon the exploitation of serfs or slaves, as it did in European culture, he would lower his status by killing a slave since his wealth and power—and consequently his social position— would be diminished by so much. Lowie eliminates utilitarian and economic factors from an interpretation of rank and class in Polynesia and points to their mythological and ritual character.[54] The existence of "true economic slavery in native America is in doubt," says Steward,[55] and we would say the same for Polynesia. The social strata of the Pacific islands and of the Northwest Coast, defined in terms of descent from mythical or legendary gods or men, were parts of an elaborate social game played in these regions. "Slaves," "nobles," and "commoners" were players, or teams of players, in this game.

To speak of the social system of the Maori or the Kwakiutl as a "game" is not to say that it was devised and arranged of their own choice or free will, or to say that it was determined intraorganismically, as the rules of a game such as pinochle or football are, rather than by factors in the external world. The social systems of these tribes, like those of any

[54] R. H. Lowie, *Primitive Society*, 1947, pp. 356–357; *Introduction to Cultural Anthropology*, 1940, p. 270.

[55] Julian H. Steward, "Cultural Causality and Law," *American Anthropologist*, vol. 51, p. 21, 1949.

other, were ways of life intimately connected with their technological adjustment to their habitats and with their relations, technologically expressed, with their neighbors. In other words, social organization here as elsewhere is a function of the mode of subsistence and of defense and offense. Nevertheless, much of their social life was conducted in accordance with certain rules, like those of conventional games. We cite the following examples presented by Raymond Firth: Persons of certain rank could not feed themselves; the menial work of preparing and serving food had to be done by persons of low status. Slaves had no *tapu,* and hence were preeminently suited for this sort of work. "A chief might conceivably be surrounded by food, and yet starve if no slave were at hand." On one occasion of a tribal war, one party carried off the women and slaves of the other side. "The warriors of the latter, bereft of all who could feed them, were obliged to sue for peace." [56] In much the same spirit, or principle, we note that in some cultures of the Northwest Coast only free men and women could have artificially deformed heads; slaves were denied this mark of distinction.

Classes based upon distinctions of status, dividing society into "higher" and "lower" strata, are relatively rare in primitive society. It is not until kinship has ceased to be the basis of social systems and society has become organized upon the basis of property relations and territorial distinctions that true classes of subordination and superordination come into being. With the advent of *civil* society, classes of status become prominent and of prime importance in the conduct of social life.

Special Structures

By *special structure* we mean a structure within a sociocultural system having a specialized function. The sum of the classes, or segments, of a society is exactly equal to the whole; society as a whole is subdivided into a number of classes or segments leaving no remainder. But a special structure is merely a differentiated *part* of the social whole, differentiated structurally and functionally; the sum of special structures is not equal to society as a whole. In biological systems a heart or stomach is a special structure. In sociocultural systems shamans, chiefs, kings, parliaments, police are special structures. In societies based upon ties of kinship the number of such structures is few and their development relatively weak. It is only on the higher levels of cultural development, especially in the cultures produced by the agricultural revolution and in the more recent systems of the fuel era, that specialized mechanisms of social integration and control become numerous or play a prominent role in the conduct of social life. Since the significance of special structures lies in their co-

[56] Firth, *op. cit.,* pp. 202–203.

ordinative, integrative, directive, and regulative functions, we shall discuss them under the heading of social control and integration, rather than here under social structure, or anatomy.

In this chapter we have considered the aspects of primitive sociocultural systems that Herbert Spencer liked to call "morphology and physiology," i.e., the structure and functioning of human social systems. We have viewed these aspects in evolutionary perspective as well as in a nontemporal context.

We have examined the various kinds of social segments found in stages of cultural development—families, lineages, clans, and moieties, as well as the so-called Australian marriage classes, or sections—and have endeavored to show how they have come into being and how they function in the system as a whole. We have discovered in the process of segmentation an important principle: segments are means of achieving larger organizations, on the one hand, and of intensifying internal cohesion, or social solidarity, on the other.

We have noted the various kinds of classes extant in primitive society. We have discovered the bases upon which they rest and terms in which they are distinguished and defined. The ways in which classes are related to one another were considered also.

The concept of special structure was introduced. But since such structures have functions of integration, regulation, and control almost exclusively, we reserved discussion of them for the following chapter.

Chapter 8   INTEGRATION, REGULATION,
AND CONTROL OF SOCIAL SYSTEMS

A society is more than a mere aggregation of individuals; it is an organization, a system. It is a complete and autonomous whole, rather than a part of a system. We would therefore call a tribe or a nation a society, but a clan, a guild of artisans, or a class of nobles would be but a part of a society. A society, or social system, is composed of parts—individuals, segments, classes, etc.—each of which is related to all the others, the relationship of part to part being determined by the relationship of part to whole. Societies may be human or subhuman, large or small, loosely or highly integrated. They may be homogeneous or highly differentiated structurally, specialized or unspecialized functionally. The concept of society embraces, therefore, the whole realm of living beings, plants as well as animals, and all social systems, from the simplest, such as a colony of single-celled organisms, to the most complex civilization in the world today—or tomorrow.

One of the basic questions in any general consideration of social systems is, *"What holds societies together?* Why do individuals form and maintain relationships with one another? How are they able to achieve unity among diverse and even conflicting elements?" For societies are made up of individuals, each of which has his own interests and is therefore opposed to each of his fellows at certain points, e.g., in the satisfaction of food and sex hungers. Moreover, some societies are composed of classes whose interests likewise differ and clash. How, therefore, are diverse and conflicting elements to be integrated into a stable and orderly system? And how is the continuity of such a system to be achieved? Finally, how and why do some social systems, specifically those of human primates, evolve from small, homogeneous structures to large, differentiated, and specialized structures? These are basic questions.

The problems of social organization confronting the sociologist are like, in kind, the problems with which the physical scientist or biologist has to deal. What holds a nebula together? Why do not the stars composing it diffuse uniformly throughout space? What holds the solar system together? A drop of water? Or a molecule or an atom? The nucleus of an atom is composed of parts held together by tremendous forces which are today but little understood. The atomic nucleus can be rent asunder, but only by the application of tremendous forces.

Turning to biology, a cell is a material, physicochemical, system. What holds it together? A cell is a tiny droplet of fluid encased by "jelled" membrane. Its integrity and its existence depend "largely on the different proportions of ions inside and without the cell." If one cuts an amoeba, swimming about in a "balanced" salt solution, with a microscopic glass knife, "protoplasm starts to flow out through the wound. As the sol comes in contact with the new ions it gels, a fresh membrane forms, the outflow stops, and in a short time the amoeba is entirely normal again. Now add extra potassium to the outside salt solution; again make a cut. The sol starts to pour out as before, but no gelation occurs. The protoplasm continues to stream out, spreads into the water and vanishes, until the amoeba is entirely dissolved." [1] What holds a colony of single-celled animals together? Why do they not live at random, each for itself? How are metazoans formed, and how are they able to evolve into higher forms?

We shall, of course, leave these questions to their proper students. We raise them only to place the study of social organization in its correct context. A society is a material system, an organization of material bodies. This is true whether we are dealing with oak trees, fungi, bacteria, sponges, ants, bears, baboons, or men. And the question "What holds systems together?" is as fundamental to sociology as it is to biology, chemistry, and physics. A force,[2] one might say, relatively weak in loose-knit societies, but powerful in highly integrated groups, holds living material bodies together. We have no name for this force unless we call it solidarity. In physics it is called gravitation in the realm of large bodies, attraction on the level of the minute. What its name, if any, is in biology, we do not know.

In primate societies the attraction between individuals is very strong. All primates live, so to speak, in a powerful gravitational field which not only unites them into a system, but which makes life apart from the system all but impossible. Apes and men alike normally die of loneliness in isolation. Solitary confinement is one of the most severe forms of penal discipline. In human societies, individuals may give their lives for

[1] R. W. Gerard, *Unresting Cells*, Harper & Brothers, New York, 1940, pp. 114–115.

[2] We are not indulging in empty metaphysical verbalism when we say "force." This word is merely the name of an aspect of the behavior of material systems. A solar, or galactic, system behaves in a certain way, and astronomers call it "gravitation." A social system of living material bodies behaves in a certain way, and we call it "solidarity." It is our job, as scientists, to observe, analyze, and interpret these forms of behavior in as objective and meaningful a way as possible.

the group. The "social gravitational force" is thus stronger even than that of life itself. It is our task, as scientific students of man, to render this force intelligible, to disclose its source and basis, and to show how it expresses itself in its manifold forms.

In a sense, it is pointless to ask, "Why does a body at rest remain at rest?" Or, "Why will a body in motion continue in motion forever and in a straight line unless . . . ?" Science has no answers to such questions other than to say that this is the way such bodies behave. Similarly, it is rather senseless to ask, "Why do living beings exert themselves to preserve their lives, both as individuals and as species?" Or, "Why do dead bodies remain dead; extinct species, extinct?" We raise these questions merely to dispose of them; they are not sensible scientific questions. This would, no doubt, be readily admitted by physicists and astronomers. It would be admitted, but probably much less commonly, in biology. There the tendency to regard the behavior of living beings in terms of purpose, cause, destiny, and goal is considerable, and some students would be rather loath to dismiss these questions as senseless or irrelevant. On the contrary, the "purpose of life" seems to some to be the only question of importance. The assertion that "the purpose of life is living" is to them not merely an empty tautology but an offensive doctrine as well. When we come to human societies, we find conceptions so anthropomorphic, so charged with mysticism, that the impersonal, nonanimistic attitude, now commonplace in physics, is sometimes rare or wholly wanting. It is a commonplace to regard an atom as a material system, composed of a proton nucleus and electrons. A polygynous primate family is also a material system, with a dominant male and a plural number of mates. In each case the system is to be explained in terms of the properties of its constituent elements, its organization, and its environmental context. The naturalistic point of view is of course now well established in physics; it is still relatively new in sociology. We still work with instincts, drives, psychic mechanisms, etc., not to mention free will and God Almighty,[3] to "explain" family organization.

Going from the family to such social systems as are labeled "de-

[3] Dogmas of the Roman Catholic Church such as the existence of God, a Supreme Being, divine revelation, original sin, and the fall of man are an integral part of the philosophy of ethnology of the Culture Historical school of ethnology, which for many years exercised considerable influence in America and Asia as well as in Europe under the leadership of the late Father Wilhelm Schmidt, S.V.D., and his coworker Father Wilhelm Koppers. See, for example, *Primitive Revelation*, 1939, by Father Schmidt; Koppers's *Primitive Man and His World Picture*, 1952. Sylvester A. Sieber, S.V.D., and Franz H. Mueller, M.C.S., American followers of Schmidt and Koppers, tell us that "after original sin . . . solicitude for one's daily bread became . . . a bitter necessity . . . the scarcity of food must be considered a punishment for sin. . . ." *The Social Life of Primitive Man*, B. Herder Book Company, St. Louis, 1941, pp. 73–74.

mocracy," "fascism," "communism," and "socialism," in contemporary thought, one finds himself almost wholly outside the viewpoint and habits of thought of science.

We shall attempt to treat human societies in the same attitude with which a physicist regards nebulae, stars, or atoms: as natural phenomena. In each instance material systems are involved, systems which may be studied and interpreted from the standpoint of structure and function. In each case explanation will consist in ascertaining the properties of things, in the observation of events, and in the formulation of generalizations or universals that will embrace the particulars.

A *society* is one aspect of the behavior of living material bodies; it is a form of behavior assumed by them. The nature of societies is to be seen in the fact that they are forms of behavior in which the living character of the component material bodies is maintained. In short, social organization is merely the interorganismal aspect of nutritive, protective, and reproductive behavior. To say, therefore, that a living species can live only if it does certain things is to say that it will form societies. Social organization is not merely a means of sustaining life; it is *a form* of life: of the life process itself.

There is more to life, of course, than social organization. Life is a form of motion, the form peculiar to material bodies having cellular structure and functions. Two aspects of vital motion may be distinguished: intraorganismal (motions within the living body itself) and extraorganismal (motions relating the living body to things outside itself). The extraorganismal aspect of motion may be analyzed into two categories also: the relations of an organism with other living beings with whom it forms a social system, and relations with elements in its habitat which are not incorporated into social systems. Social life, or social organization, is therefore the interorganismal aspect of the behavior of living material bodies. Societies vary widely, and these variations are made intelligible by noting the roles played by the intraorganismal and extraorganismal aspects of vital motion, respectively.

In some societies the intraorganismal aspect of behavior may play a relatively great, the interorganismal aspect an insignificant, part in the life of the individual and of the species. In others, the situation is reversed. There are situations in which a physiologic process, the nutritive, for example, is dependent upon social relationships (suckling mammals; the proletariat, whether employed or "on relief"). With regard to the human species, we shall see that there has been a growth, in absolute magnitude and relative importance, of the interorganismal factor throughout the whole course of cultural evolution.

The *why* of society or social organization is therefore clear. It is a way of sustaining and perpetuating life. Life may be made more secure and enduring by relationships between organisms. In reproduction, subsistence, and defense, the life, both of individual and species, is furthered by concerted action. We now wish to see *how* this is accomplished. Specifically, we wish to see how the social organism regulates and controls its component members so that all may be integrated into a whole.

In subhuman primate society, the individual members are held within the group by sexual attraction, by the method of nutrition, and by the safety and protection that group life affords its members. We have already analyzed this type of society and have demonstrated the operation of its determining factors and the results produced by them. We have seen, too, that articulate speech, which transformed the anthropoid into a man, provided a new means and a new basis of social organization. In addition to the impulses, reflexes, tropisms, gestures, signs, etc., of the lower primates, man has symbolic means of establishing relations with one another, and this means becomes of paramount importance in the human species. The peculiar and characteristic means of social integration and control in human society are therefore verbal rules and formulas. These find expression in many forms more or less explicit: philosophies, myths and tales, ritual, lore and legends, custom, codes of law, etc. This statement is neither inconsistent with nor unrelated to our conception of human beings as material bodies. Symbolic communication is, in a sense, a form of radiation: vibrations of one body affect another and influence its behavior. The fact that the *form* of the influence is symbolic does not deny or lessen the influence; it merely specifies its kind or nature. There are many kinds of influence exerted by one material body upon another. In the physicochemical realm we have gravitational, magnetic, electric, catalytic, etc., forms. In animate systems there are nutritional, sexual, aggressive and defensive influences which express themselves in tropisms, reflexes, or in patterns of response acquired through learning, or formed for the occasion by insight, understanding, and the creative synthesis of imagination, as exemplified by the problem solving of apes. The *form* of interorganismal influence within the human species and peculiar to it is *symbolic*. But symbolic interaction among human beings is merely a particular form of interaction among material bodies in general.

In Chapter 3, "The Nature of Social Organization," we considered some of the basic problems of social systems: the nature and basis of fundamental social processes, the factors that determine size of social group, etc. Now, however, we wish to discover how any given social system, particularly one within the human species, regulates itself, functions in an orderly and effective manner by controlling the behavior of its component parts. In order to discover these things for a particular social system we shall have to formulate generalizations valid for all social systems.

Any system is characterized by order and regulation. This is but another way of saying that we do not apply the word "system" to chaos. But the principles and bases of order vary, specifically, from one kind of system to another. What is it that gives order to a human society? Why does uniformity of behavior prevail rather than caprice or chaos? How does the system control the behavior of individuals so as to bring about uniformities in some instances, differences in others? Men behave like men, but unlike women. The system must articulate these differences with one another, as well as effect uniformities, in order to establish and maintain itself as a smooth-working, effective functioning whole. To discover how human societies do these things is our present task.

In answer to such questions as, "How does an atom of carbon regulate itself as a system?"; "How is order achieved?"; "Why do the electrons behave in a uniform manner?"; "How is the part controlled by, or subordinated to, the whole?"; the physicist might give such answers as these: An atom is an organization of different kinds of parts. "Different kinds of parts" means differences of structure, magnitude, and behavior: a proton is a different kind of thing structurally from an electron, and it behaves differently. Next, there is the number of parts. If an atomic nucleus has a certain number of parts, it is one kind of element; if another number, it is a different kind. Atoms of a given element may vary in the number of electrons they contain. These variations are called isotopes, and one isotope behaves differently from another in certain respects. Thus, we have three things to consider in the atom: the kinds of parts, the number of each kind, and the configuration in which they are placed and organized into a coherent whole. We can explain the behavior of the atom, both as a whole and with reference to its constituent parts, in terms of these factors.

Similarly with a living cell. It is composed of kinds of parts, of numbers of parts, and they are organized in a certain kind of configuration. A thing, taken by itself, is what it is; that is to say, an atom of carbon is an atom of carbon: it has a certain structure, mass, and magnitude. But in a *system*, a *thing* becomes a *part* and is therefore subordinated to the whole. Its behavior, e.g., the atom of carbon, is determined not only by its own composition and structure, but by its relationship to other parts of the system, by its place in the total context or configuration. The behavior of a carbon atom in a molecule of ethyl alcohol is not the same as its behavior in one of dimethyl ether. Both substances are composed of the same kinds of elements and the same quantities of each kind; the formula for each is C_2H_6O. But the arrangement of atoms in molecules differs, giving the substances marked differences in properties and behavior. The behavior of the part is thus a function of the configuration of the whole.

And so it is with multicellular organisms. Each is made up of kinds of parts, and these parts are arranged in a certain pattern, organized into a definite configuration. The part is subordinate to the whole. The behavior of the part is a function of the configuration of the whole as well as of its own properties. "If ectoderm cells," writes Novicoff, "were removed from a salamander embryo and transplanted over the mouth organizer of a frog embryo, they would develop into salamander structures—of the mouth; they would form teeth and not belly skin." [4] The relationship of part to part is determined by the relationship of part to whole.

The behavior of any system, therefore, whether considered as a whole or in terms of its constituent parts, is determined by three factors: (1) kind of parts, *kind* being described in terms of mass, magnitude, structure, etc.; (2) arithmetic number of parts, the number of units in each kind (the number of carbon atoms in a molecule or cell), and the number of kinds of parts (the number of kinds of atoms in a molecule or cell); and (3) the configuration in which the kinds and numbers of constituent elements are organized. We may write this as a simple formula:

$$S = K \times N \times C$$

A system, S, in its structure and function, as a whole and in its several parts, is a function of *kind* of things, K, *number* of things and categories, N, and *configuration* of organization, C. The system will vary as any one of these factors varies.

Let us turn now to social systems of primates. And let us recall the nature of the social organization of baboons as described by Zuckerman and summarized in Chapter 3, "The Nature of Social Organization." We noted that the size of the local group is determined by the factors of nutrition and of mutual aid in protection from enemies, especially the former. The size and composition of the family group are determined by attraction between the sexes, the dominance of the male sex, the prowess of the male in the struggle for mates, and so on.

But now we are concerned with the system as given. How is part related to whole? How and why does each individual behave in such a way so that collectively individuals constitute an orderly, effectively functioning whole instead of a chaotic mob?

We already have the answer: the behavior, both of the baboon troop

[4] Alexander B. Novicoff, "The Concept of Integrative Levels and Biology," *Science*, vol. 101, no. 2618, pp. 210–211.

and of the individual, is determined by kind of part, number of units and of categories, and the configuration in which all are organized.

A baboon is either a male or a female, old or young, strong or weak, fast or slow, etc. The proportion of the sexes may vary; so may the ratio of old to young. A male is a member of a family, either as an unweaned youngster or as the overlord of a family group, or he is a celibate male. In either case his behavior is determined by the social configuration in which he finds himself: family plus local group, or local group, composed of families and other celibate males. Thus, the behavior of a baboon social system, either as a whole or as any one of its parts, is determined by such factors as (1) age, sex, prowess, etc., of the individuals; (2) the number of individuals in the system, but more especially the proportions of male and female, old and young, strong and weak; and (3) the two kinds of social configurations, the family and the local, territorial group.

An individual will not voluntarily leave the group because he would deprive himself of food, if he were unweaned, as well as of protection from enemies. If he were an adult he would deprive himself of the opportunity for sexual satisfaction as well as of some protection from enemies if he left. Food, sex, and protection are the considerations that keep the individual within the local group. If, through reproduction, the group should outgrow the food resources of its territory, a number of individuals would break away and emigrate as a group, not individually.[5]

Within the local group, each individual has his behavior shaped and directed by the social configurations of family, or by the local group as a whole if he be a celibate male, or by both.

When we turn from subhuman primates to the human species, we note a profound and significant difference between these two categories. We may analyze the determinants of the social behavior of the lower primates into individual biological properties, on the one hand, and social context or configuration, on the other. But the social role in which the monkey or ape finds himself is determined by his biological properties. A male will have one role, a female another. The young and old, weak and strong, etc., will circulate and function in certain social orbits because they *are* young or weak. Social role here is a function of biological properties; the former is the dependent, the latter the independent, variable. In the human species, too, social role is dependent or contingent upon biological make-up to a certain extent; a suckling infant, a feeble old man, an adolescent girl, each will have a role determined in part, at least,

[5] Solitary apes have been reported. The reason for their lone existence is not clear. Perhaps they have been expelled by more powerful adversaries; perhaps they were abandoned when ill. According to W. Köhler, chimpanzees dislike exceedingly to be separated from their group: "They will risk their very lives to get back." *The Mentality of Apes,* Harcourt, Brace and Company, New York, 1925, p. 293.

by his or her respective biological properties. But in human societies there are many instances in which the biological factor is merely incidental to the social role of the individual, or plays no part at all. Within the class of normal adults, whether a person is a cook, a metal worker, freeman or slave, a weaver, a doctor, or a farm laborer may be wholly a matter of cultural determination. And in many situations in which a biological factor, such as sex, is relevant, it may be subordinated to the cultural factor or even overridden by it. Old men may care for babies; women may be excluded from pursuits for which they are qualified, for purely social reasons; and men may take the roles of women, and vice versa. We may generalize as follows: Among all subhuman species, social systems are, at bottom, biologically determined; they are functions of bodily structure and process. In the human species, there is, as we noted in Chapter 1, a generic relationship between the human species as a whole and culture as a whole. Culture is as it is because man is as he is; it would be different if man were biologically different. But "culture as a whole" is made up of an indefinite and a very great number of particular cultures, no two of which are alike. These differences among cultures, and the processes of culture change, cannot be explained biologically. Assuming the biological factor to be a constant, which we are justified in doing, and treating the environmental factor as a constant, which we may do for purposes of scientific analysis and problem solving, differences among cultures are to be explained culturologically, i.e., in terms of cultural factors themselves. Any human society, i.e., the network of interrelationships among human organisms, is a function of its extrasomatic tradition, culture, the biological and environmental factors being constant: $S = f(C)k$. We thus come to a very important point: there are two fundamentally different kinds of social systems, and they imply and require fundamentally different sociologies to interpret them. Subhuman sociology is a subdivision of biology; human sociology is a subdivision of culturology. This distinction is, unfortunately, not always recognized and appreciated by sociologists and social anthropologists.

In previous discussion we have emphasized orderliness, uniformity, and regularity as characteristics of all systems, social systems included. We have pointed out that unless these qualities were present we could not call an aggregation of things and events a *system*. System is the name of a kind of organization that *is* orderly, regular, and uniform to a certain degree and in certain aspects. A portion of reality that was iron one instant, salt the next, and a hodgepodge of material particles and radiation, or a bacterium, the next, would not be called a system; it would be half chaos, half miracle. Order, uniformity, regularity, continuity, etc., are therefore *given* with reality as we find it. This does not mean, of course, that order, etc., is everywhere, that order "is all." The very terms order, uniformity, etc., imply the absence or opposite of these qualities.

We may take, then, order, uniformity, regularity, continuity, etc., as properties of all systems. It will contribute to an understanding of human social systems if we consider what these qualities mean in terms of concrete experience and behavior.

There are many ways of making an arrow, of drawing a bow and releasing the arrow, of greeting a friend, catching a fish, seasoning a duck, dressing the hair, tending a child, or of burying the dead. But within a given social system, particularly among small ones such as those of preliterate peoples, we will find that there tends to be only one way of performing a certain operation. In short, we have customary ways of doing things: customs. *Custom* is the name we give to uniformities, regularities, continuities, etc., in cultural social systems.

The meaning of custom is to be discovered in the role it plays in human social systems. It means economy and efficiency, to begin with. To continue a technique once acquired is easier than to devise a new one. It saves both time and effort.[6] Once a suitable type of arrow release has been achieved, it is easier, more economical, and therefore more efficient socially, to continue to use it than to develop a new one. Five major types of arrow release have been used throughout the world. But they are not distributed at random or at the caprice or preference of the bowmen. Few, if any peoples, use more than one major type; and there are great areas of the world where only one method of release is found.[7] Novelty is expensive in terms of origin and development on the technological side, and costly also from the standpoint of learning by the individual. Moreover, novelty is disruptive. A people who is habituated to putting salt in tea might be disturbed by the use of sugar.

A consideration of novelty versus uniformity and regularity brings up the matter of prediction. All human social life is conducted in terms of anticipations, expectations, predictions. Orderly social life would be quite impossible without the ability to make realistic predictions. I know what to expect when I put flame to dry straw, put salt in water, or plant seeds in warm moist soil. Effective intercourse with the external world is made possible only because certain realistic predictions can be made. And predictions in this area are made possible by the uniform, regular, continuous, and repetitive aspect of the external world, as determined by

[6] "Custom makes for a powerful economy in the learning of an individual." E. Sapir, "Custom," in *Encyclopaedia of the Social Sciences*, vol. 4, The Macmillan Company, New York, 1930, p. 661.

[7] A. L. Kroeber, "Arrow Release Distributions," *University of California Publications in American Archaeology and Ethnology*, vol. 23, no. 4, pp. 283-296, 1927.

its own inherent properties. So also in the realm of human social relations: one must be able to anticipate, to predict, in order to act meaningfully. I must know, within a certain range of variation, how someone will act if I greet him, ask him for a match, clasp his hand, spit at or on him, kiss him, etc., if I am to have effective social intercourse with him. But in the sociocultural sphere there is no inherently determined response to a given stimulus. What is one to do when someone "bites his thumb" at you? Since realistic expectation and prediction are necessary to social intercourse, and since in the social realm inherently determined response to stimulus is lacking, in short, because uniformities, regularities, and continuities are not *intrinsic* in the realm of social ritual and intercourse, they must be established *ad hoc* to provide a basis for prediction. These regularities, uniformities, and continuities are *customs*.

Custom is therefore a powerful and effective means of social integration and regulation. It is a means of effecting regularity, uniformity, order, and continuity in social systems. Each part of the system is given its identity, and each part is geared to other parts and to the whole. Each baby born into the social system is molded by education and training and is fitted securely into the system. He is so conditioned by his training as to match the external and objective permanence of custom with his own inner fixity of attitude. Custom thus becomes so fixed as often to be called *rigid*.

In addition to the characteristics and advantages of custom that we have just set forth, there is still another: custom per se is a powerful means of promoting social solidarity—perhaps the most important quality of all social systems—by serving as a stimulus to arouse, and as a medium to express, group loyalty and allegiance.[8] A group does something in a certain way. In itself, perhaps, it is of no practical value; it may seem very trivial. It may be the custom of cutting or wearing one's hair in a certain way, a characteristic type of ornament or garment, a technique of using knife and fork, of carrying school books in a green cloth bag instead of a leather briefcase. These customs serve as social badges, means of identifying societies, or classes within social systems. They are external expressions of "we-ness" as distinguished from "they." They tell at a glance whether you are "one of us" or not. The observance of custom, said Sapir, "is a symbolic affirmation of the solidarity of the group."[9] The solidarity of a group may thus seek and find expression in some customary act or insignia. But there is action and reaction here as elsewhere. The customary act or insignia in turn stimulates and channels the sentiment of solidarity. It is a means of objectifying it,

[8] The Hopi Indians label deviations from custom ka-Hopi, i.e., not the Hopi way. But the deviation is not merely different; it is disapproved of because it is different.

[9] Sapir, *op. cit.*, p. 661.

and this objectification, this externality, makes easier and more effective the transmission of sentiments of solidarity from one generation to another.

Thus we see that an inquiry into the nature of custom, the origin, basis, and function of regularities, uniformities, and continuities within social systems, does much to answer the questions, "What holds human societies together?" and "How are they able to coordinate their component parts and integrate them into a coherent and smooth-working whole?"

Uniformities, regularities, and continuities are found everywhere, in systems of all kinds. Custom is merely the name of these attributes within the class of *cultural* systems. The concept *custom* thus serves to place sociocultural systems in a context as broad as science itself by indicating that they are but a subclass of all systems taken as a whole.

The concept of custom serves also to relate human social systems to those of other species. The uniformities, regularities, and continuities in the social life of subhuman species are sometimes termed the *habits* of the animals (or plants) in question. And it may be justly assumed that the social habits of man's immediate ancestors served as the basis of the primordial customs of mankind. It was the symbol, articulate speech, that transformed the habits of certain anthropoid species into human customs. In the history of man, therefore, customs are basic in an evolutionary sense, as they are in logical, functional analysis.

We turn now from a consideration of custom in general to subdivisions within this category, to special kinds of organization of customary behavior. We distinguish two such subclasses of custom, namely, *ethics* and *etiquette*. We define ethics as a set of rules designed to regulate the behavior of individuals so as to promote the general welfare, the welfare of the group. Etiquette is a set of rules which recognizes *classes* within society, defines them in terms of behavior, and so regulates the behavior of individuals as to keep them in their proper classes. In this way classes are kept distinct and intact; and means of articulating classes with one another in social intercourse are provided. The rules of ethics and of etiquette alike serve to integrate and regulate human social systems by determining the relationships between part and part and between part and whole. Let us turn first to a consideration of ethics.

Ethics. As just stated, we mean by *ethics* a code of rules the purpose of which is to regulate the behavior of individuals so that the welfare, or what is deemed to be the welfare, of the group will be fostered. We define *welfare* in terms of subsistence, health, protection from the elements, defense against enemies, etc.; in short, in terms of security and continuity of life. We qualify welfare with the phrase "or what is deemed to be the welfare" of the group because ethical rules are sometimes based upon unsound premises. For example, custom might require the killing of one or both twins at birth on the assumption that this would avert subsequent evil to the community. In this instance the ethical rule actually works an injury upon the group, but it is done in the belief that it is promoting its welfare. Every human society, as a social system, tends to maintain itself to maximum advantage, and it does this by attempting to regulate the behavior of each one of its component individuals so that this end may be attained. The particular process and mechanism by which society does this we call ethics.

In speaking of human welfare we may distinguish between the interest of the group as a whole, on the one hand, and the interests of individuals severally, on the other. The interests of the individual and of the group coincide, as of course they must, at many points. But they differ, and even conflict, at others. No system can permit an individual to wreak his aggressions at will upon other members of the community, nor does any human society allow its members freely to gratify their sexual appetites where they will, or to marry any person they please. Many, if not most, systems oblige certain individuals to share their food with others, and otherwise to subordinate their own needs to the welfare of the group. It is therefore at points where the interests of individual and group differ or conflict that the rules of ethics come into play.

There are only two major types of philosophy of ethics: the absolutistic and supernaturalistic, and the relativistic and naturalistic, conceptions of ethical values. In the supernaturalistic conception, "right" and "wrong" are absolute; a thing is right because it is right, or wrong because it is wrong. We find this conception expressed in our own culture in such beliefs as that it is wrong to tell a lie, or to drink a glass of wine, or to play cards on Sunday, etc., no matter what the context or consequences of the act may be. In the rationalistic conception of ethical values there are no absolute rights or wrongs. A deed is right or wrong depending upon whether it promotes or militates against the welfare of the group. Thus a deliberate misstatement of facts may be beneficial. A physician might aid the recovery of his patient by deliberately telling him things that were not true. If the patient's health is restored or his life saved by this lie, then it is good. If, however, a deed such as killing one's brother should injure the group as a whole, then it is bad. From the standpoint of scientific interpretation of human social behavior, we must, of course, take the view that ethical values are not absolutes, that they are purely naturalistic phenomena, and are always relative to the situation, that they are meaningless apart from context. The conception of ethical values as absolutes, whether supernaturalistic in character or not, can only be regarded as a delusion, a failure to understand the real nature of human behavior.

From the standpoint of this distinction between these two philosophies of ethics, we may make an interesting and pertinent comparison between the ethical systems of preliterate peoples and those of modern literate cultures, namely, that the ethical systems of the former rest upon premises, whether explicit or implicit, that are naturalistic to a greater degree than the ethical systems of modern civilized peoples. Among primitive peoples the distinction between relations between man and God, on the one hand, and between man and man, on the other, is sharper than in civilized cultures. Primitive peoples negotiate with their gods in order to obtain their good will and help in their struggle for existence with reference both to their natural habitat and to their hostile neighbors. But with regard to their own domestic social affairs, primitive peoples felt for the most part that they could manage them themselves without the interference or the help of the gods. The gods may require the savage "to do his duty towards them," Tylor observes, but "it does not follow that they should concern themselves with his doing his duty to his neighbor." [10] Thus an Indian might seek the aid of spirits in hunting, horticulture, medicine, or warfare, but not in his social relations with his fellow tribesmen. Virtually nowhere do we find that marriage or divorce is an affair of the gods in preliterate systems. Nor is the killing of a fellow tribesman, even a member of one's own family, an affair in which the gods have any concern. In primitive society, says Tylor, "if a man robs or murders, that is for the party wronged or his friends to avenge; if he is stingy, treacherous, brutal, then punishment may fall on him or he may be scouted by all good people; but he is not necessarily looked upon as hateful to the gods, and in fact such a man is often a great medicine-man or priest." [11] In civil society, on the other hand, there has tended to be a diminution of dependence of man upon the gods in his relations with his natural habitat—subsistence, medicine, etc.—but there has been a marked intrusion of the deities into the social affairs of mankind. Thus in our own system such things as lying, stealing, charity, homicide, marriage, and divorce have come to be matters in which the gods are vitally concerned.

The reason for this difference between the ethical systems of primitive peoples and those of civil societies is not difficult to discover. Primitive peoples were weak and ineffectual technologically and consequently relied upon the gods for help in their relations with the external world. But they were quite able for the most part to manage their own social

[10] E. B. Tylor, *Anthropology*, 1881, p. 368.
[11] *Ibid.*

affairs without resort to the spiritual world. Advanced literate, metal-lurgical cultures, on the other hand, are much more effective techno-logically, though even here appeals for spiritual aid continue. But the situation with regard to human social relations differs considerably. All civil societies are composed of two major classes: a small, dominant, ruling class and a large subordinate class of slaves, serfs, peasants, or proletariat. The interests of these two classes are antithetical at many points. The continuation of such social systems, the maintenance of their integrity, depends therefore upon the perpetuation of this relationship between the two classes: the dominant class must continue to rule and to exploit, and the subordinate class must be continued in a condition of subjection. The ruling class employs military force in the maintenance of its position of dominance, but force is not always effective and success-ful, as the innumerable uprisings of serfs and slaves make clear. The use of force is therefore supplemented with theology. The masses of the people are taught by the priests that they must be docile, patient, and humble, that they must endure privations and bitter labor, that they must not rise up against their masters but must submit to them peace-fully and even with good will. Tylor speaks of "a powerful priesthood" in "the great old-world religions" who are "the educators and controllers of society" and "moral teaching fully recognized as among the great duties of religion." [12] The message of the priests has a definite super-natural character: it is the will of God. "The gods take on themselves the punishment of the wicked," says Tylor, "the Heaven-god smites the perjurer with his thunderbolt, and the Nation-god brings sickness and death on the murderer." [13] The subordinate classes are thus made to feel that it is not merely their terrestrial masters whom they must serve and obey, but the eternal and almighty gods. This supernaturalistic system of ethics has, like naturalistic ones, its own sanctions. The masses are made to believe that if they fail to obey they will suffer divine wrath and punishment.

The late Sir James Frazer has supplied some interesting evidence bear-ing upon the difference between the ethical systems of tribal societies and those of the higher cultures. Early versions of the Ten Commandments, he points out, have to do almost wholly with the relationship of man to God, not with man's relationship to man. In one of the early codes which he cites there is not a single ethical commandment, ethical in the sense of governing the relationship of one member of a society to another. Instead, we find rules having to do with religious rituals and sacrifices: "The feast of unleavened cakes thou shalt keep. . . ." "The fat

[12] *Ibid.*, pp. 368–369.
[13] *Ibid.*

of my feast shall not remain all night until morning"; [14] etc. In later versions of the Mosaic code, however, we find such commandments as "Thou shalt not steal, commit adultery," etc. Tribal society had by this time been outgrown, and civil society with its state-church had taken its place. Theology had become an instrument of social control.

During the long course of the evolution of philosophy we have seen a gradual diminution of supernaturalism and a corresponding increase of naturalism. In the history of ethical systems, however, the opposite trend is to be noted: modern ethical systems tend to be more supernaturalistic than those of preliterate peoples. This fact might seem at first glance to contradict our general thesis of the evolution of culture. One might think that earlier ethical systems would be more "primitive," i.e., supernaturalistic, than later ones. But as we have pointed out above, a code of ethics is merely an aspect of a social system. It is merely a mechanism of social control. As social systems evolve, so will their ethical counterparts.

This brings up the question of "the evolution of morals." This phrase is a very misleading one and is based upon a number of false conceptions. It assumes first of all that ethical values are things in themselves, that one ethical value may be compared directly with another, and that we can say that the one is better or higher or worse or lower than the other. On this basis it has been assumed that there has been an evolution of ethical values, that they have, like axes, succeeded one another in a series of stages of development. Some students have asserted that extremely primitive peoples were defective or lacking in "a moral sense," that they were incapable psychologically of grasping the lofty moral conceptions that are supposed to prevail in advanced, i.e., our own, culture. Thus, Tylor speaks of the "dull-minded barbarian [who] has not power of thought enough to come up to the civilized man's best moral standard." [15] All these conceptions are unsound and unwarranted.

We have already examined the question of the nature of ethical values and have seen that a deed is good or bad only in terms of its context and consequences, not in terms of its own inherent qualities; that charity or lying may be either good or bad, depending upon whether it helps or harms the group. We have seen, furthermore, that the ethical systems of advanced literate cultures are supernaturalistic to a greater degree than those of preliterate cultures, which would mean retrogression rather than advance from the standpoint of a theory of "the evolution of morals." But ethical values are functions of social systems; they are determined, in final analysis, by technologies and habitats. Cultural systems have evolved, and it is proper to speak of the evolution of social systems. But

[14] Sir James Frazer, *Folk-lore in the Old Testament,* Macmillan & Co., Ltd., London, 1923, p. 362.

[15] Tylor, *op. cit.,* p. 407.

the only meaningful way in which we could speak of the evolution of ethics is in terms of the social systems of which they are functions. In this evolutionary process, the social systems are the independent, the ethical systems the dependent, variables.

It has sometimes been argued that the ethical advance of mankind can be measured by the different evaluations placed upon human life. In primitive society, according to one version of this view, life is cheap, babies may be smothered at birth, one's parents killed when they become old, and one's neighbors are not only killed as enemies but tortured before death. As culture progressed, according to this theory, human life became more and more valuable, until now, in our own culture, it is "sacred." Unfortunately most discussions of this thesis are not very realistic. They tend to overlook the reasons for homicide in preliterate cultures. It is not lack of a "moral sense" that causes a mother to smother her newborn babe, but lack of food. The same reason applies to the killing of old folks. Technological control over circumstances is weak and inadequate in many primitive cultures, and habitats are occasionally niggardly and harsh. Many times on low cultural levels there is not enough food for all and the group is faced with starvation. But who is to die? Not the able-bodied breadwinners, for if they starve the whole group will perish. The nonbreadwinners, therefore, the young and helpless, on the one hand, or the old and feeble, on the other, must be denied food. If it is a choice between young and old, the latter must be denied, for unless babies are fed, the tribe will not be perpetuated. The old people have already lived their lives and will die soon anyway. Therefore, in times of famine it may become a moral obligation to kill the old in order to feed the young, and it is sometimes felt to be more merciful to kill them outright than to allow them to die by inches. Sometimes, however, the young also are killed when there is not enough food.

Some primitive peoples have indeed been cruel in their treatment of captives, but it is doubtful if their methods of torture have been more brutal and ingenious than those employed by Christian culture in its Inquisition, heretic hunting, slaveholding, colonial exploitation, lynching, and even, one might say, in the treatment of common criminals such as pickpockets or horse thieves. Methods employed by modern police to extract confessions, or by the military to obtain "intelligence," are sometimes but little better, if at all, than the treatment of captives by primitive tribesmen. As for the "dignity of man" and the sacredness of human life, what is one to say of social systems that condemn the great majority to lifelong poverty and want, sometimes even in the midst of plenty? And when one considers modern systems of mass destruction of human life, the simple war parties of moccasined braves seem puny and insignificant in comparison. It would be rather difficult to make a convincing case for a higher evaluation of human life in modern nations as compared with primitive tribes.

To return to the notion that primitive peoples are psychologically incapable of grasping the lofty moral values that are supposed to animate our behavior, it has been assumed, on the one hand, that there *are* ethical values in the external world that may be grasped by the "moral sense," just as one might see minute or distant objects, or hear almost inaudible sounds. And on the other hand, it has been assumed that the moral sense of primitive man is weak, just as one's ears or eyes may be weak. Both of these assumptions are unsound. As we have already seen, there are no moral values, in the external world, to be grasped. And in the second place, there is no evidence to indicate that primitive man is any less sensitive than modern man in matters of ethics. From the standpoint of neuropsychological equipment, primitive man must be regarded as essentially like ourselves. And as regards his sensitivity to social pressures such as the esteem of his fellows or their ridicule, there is an abundance of evidence to indicate that primitive man is just as sensitive and responsive as his more civilized brother. Indeed, life in preliterate cultures, organized as it is in small groups, has a greater preponderance of intimate personal relations than does civil society, and hence stimulation and response in terms of praise and blame, esteem and ridicule, in short, in ethical matters of right and wrong, probably play a relatively greater part in primitive than in civilized societies.

The notion that every human being is equipped with a conscience, a mechanism that can perceive and appreciate moral values in the external world, is old-fashioned and invalid. "Conscience" is merely the name we give to man's responses to social stimulation in the ethical field. As Radcliffe-Brown has put it, "What is called conscience is thus in the widest sense the reflex in the individual of the sanctions of society." [16] The "still small voice of conscience" is then merely a mandate of the tribe, making itself felt through the viscera and brains of an individual human organism.

According to earlier conceptions of ethics and morality, some peoples were "more moral" than others. Here again we find the implicit assumption that a universal set of moral values exists in the external world and that this can serve as a standard by which the coefficient of morality, so to speak, of each people could be gauged. This assumed set of moral values turned out, of course, to be our own, and consequently every other people was judged in terms of our own moral standards. A people, therefore, that did not conform to the standards by which we pro-

[16] A. R. Radcliffe-Brown, "Sanction, Social," in *Encyclopaedia of the Social Sciences*, vol. 13, The Macmillan Company, New York, 1934, p. 531.

fessed to live was adjudged to be immoral. Thus a people that not only allowed but encouraged premarital sexual intercourse among its young men and women was adjudged to be immoral. From what has gone before, it is easy to see the unsoundness of this view. The ethical values of any people are relative to their own social, technological, and environmental situation, not to an assumed absolute and universal standard. This means that every people has its own ethical standards, its own ethical system.

There is one sense, however, in which one people might be said to be "more moral" than another. By *morality* we would mean the degree to which any people conform in actual practice to the ethical code that it professes to live by. If a people lives up to its ethical code to a high degree, then it is moral; if it does not, it is immoral to the extent that it fails. Thus we might distinguish degrees of morality; peoples would fail, in varying degrees, to live up to their respective ethical codes. However, we have as yet no adequate means of measuring the gap between profession and practice other than the impressions of observers. We know of no reason, however, for believing that primitive peoples are any more or any less moral than peoples in more advanced cultures. In short, we cannot speak of an "evolution of morality." Discrepancies between moral codes as enunciated by a people and its behavior with reference to them are due no doubt to dislocations of its sociocultural systems, caused by changes in habitat, technology, or relations with other peoples. In a highly integrated and stable culture we would expect to find a close correspondence between profession and practice in the field of morals, i.e., a high degree of morality. In poorly integrated and unstable systems, on the other hand, we may expect to find a low degree of correspondence, or *immorality*.

There is still another way in which ethical systems may be evaluated and compared, and hence considered from the standpoint of evolution of ethical systems. An ethical code is a means to an end—social welfare—just as medical techniques are means to an end. Could we not say, therefore, that one ethical system *as a means* may be better than another, i.e., promotes the welfare of its own group more effectively? And if this is so, could we not speak of the evolution of ethical systems, a course of development in which ethical systems—like axes or plows—are improved and become more effective as means of promoting group welfare as culture advances?

We must be on our guard here as elsewhere in comparative evaluations of ethical systems. The code of ethics of tribe A may promote the welfare of tribe A more effectively than the ethical code of tribe B serves its society. But it does not follow that tribe B would be better off with the code of tribe A than with its own, by any means; it might, and probably would, be worse off. Here again, it is important to realize that the meaning and value of a set of ethical values is relative only to its own sociocultural context.

But perhaps we could—if we had the data and the scientific techniques—determine a "coefficient of effectiveness" for each and every ethical system in its own sociocultural setting. An ethical system might, for example, contribute nothing to the welfare of its society, or perhaps even be injurious. Its coefficient of effectiveness, as a means of promoting the general welfare, would therefore be zero, or less. On the other hand, we can imagine a situation in which the ethical code is so well adapted to the needs of its society that any change would diminish its contribution. The coefficient of effectiveness here would be 100. And, of course, there may be variations between 0 and 100. We might, therefore, again assuming that we had the requisite ethnographic data and the appropriate scientific techniques, go from one sociocultural system to another, determining the coefficients of their respective ethical systems. Having done this, we could consider the question of a progressive development of ethical systems throughout the history of culture.

With regard to this problem, we may say, first of all, that we have neither the requisite information about the cultures of mankind nor the proper scientific techniques to undertake such a study of comparative evaluation. It is reasonable to assume that ethical systems vary in their contributions to the welfare of their respective societies; some must be well suited to needs, others less well suited. But we see no reason for believing that, in general, the ethical systems of modern, civilized cultures serve their respective societies any better than the ethical systems of preliterate cultures served primitive peoples. On the contrary, there is *some* indication—the relatively greater ingredient of supernaturalism in ethical systems of literate cultures—that the ethical codes of civilized societies are less effective in promoting the general welfare than are those of primitive peoples.

Taking the ethical systems of human history as a whole, however, one can perhaps discern an evolutionary trend, at least on recent and highest cultural levels. As we have already noted, the ethical systems of modern literate civil societies tend to be more supernaturalistic than those of preliterate peoples. But with the growth of science and rationalism in modern times, within the last few centuries and particularly since the triumph of Darwinism, there has been a gradual weakening of supernaturalistic sanctions and a corresponding growth of rationalism in the field of ethics. The old theological view that there is an absolute, universal, and divine set of ethical values and standards to which all peoples must conform is gradually breaking down. The naturalistic and rational view that "goods" and "evils" are always relative to particular situations is gaining ground. It is fairly obvious that adherence to a code of absolute values cannot promote the *general* [17] welfare as effectively as a code of relative values could. If an ethical system says that something is always good regardless of the circumstances, action in terms of this premise may produce actual harm instead of good. The trend from the philosophy of absolute values toward that of relative values must therefore be regarded as progressive. And there is indication that modern cultures are moving in this direction.

Etiquette. Every system is composed of divers parts. If the system as a whole is to maintain its integrity and to function effectively, each of its parts must maintain its own identity and each must be related to others so that all may function together smoothly and efficiently. Among the parts of which every social system consists are, as we have already seen, *classes.* A class, as we have defined the term, is one of an indefinite number of parts of a social whole, each of which differs from the others in composition and functions. Men, women, adults, children, married, widowed, divorced, etc., are thus classes. As we have just noted above, each class must maintain its own integrity, and each one must be articulated with the others if the social system as a whole is to function harmoniously and effectively. The means of accomplishing this is a code of rules that we call *etiquette.* A code of etiquette defines each class in terms of behavior and obliges each individual to conform to the code proper to his class. In this way the identity of each class is established and its integrity maintained. Furthermore, the behavior of an individual member of a class, as prescribed by the code of etiquette, serves not only to identify him with his own class but to prescribe the proper form of social intercourse with individuals in other classes. Thus a code of etiquette not only operates to preserve the identity and integrity of each class, but serves to relate classes to one another in an effective and efficient manner.

The rules of behavior imposed by the society upon the individual are enforced by social sanctions, such as adverse comment or criticism, ridicule, and ostracism.

The above propositions may be illustrated with a few examples. One of the universal classes in human society is that of *men.* This class, like every other class, is defined in terms of behavior: men are individuals who behave in certain prescribed ways; that is to say, they dress and wear their hair in a distinctive manner, engage in certain occupations, and in other ways behave in a manner prescribed by society. Each male individual as he comes to manhood is obliged to conform to the rules which serve to define the class *men.* If he fails to do this, he is punished. The usual

---

[1] It may, as of course it has in the past, serve the interests of a dominant ruling class, but not the welfare of the people as a whole, or even as a majority.

form of punishment is ridicule. If this does not succeed in bringing him into line, he will be ostracized. The class character of etiquette is clearly revealed in the social act of ostracism. Ostracism is a way of ejecting an individual from his class. He thus becomes a mere outcast or is relegated to another class. Thus a man who is ostracized by his fellows, i.e., ejected from the class *men*, would be relegated to some other class, either a special class of outcasts, or one of children, women, or men-women. We see, then, how the social mechanism of etiquette operates to regulate the behavior of individuals in such a way as to maintain the identity of each class and thus to promote the integrity of society as a whole.

The regulation of behavior by rules of etiquette has three aspects, positive, negative, and neutral; i.e., it requires certain things, prohibits certain things, and is quite indifferent to other matters. A woman, for example, may be obliged to wear a certain garment, or dress her hair in a certain way, as a means of identifying herself with the social class *women*. This identification is effected also by forbidding her to do certain things, such as smoking or riding horseback. Or the code may be quite indifferent to certain things, neither prescribing nor prohibiting them, such as playing the piano or drinking tea. It is important to note that, from the standpoint of etiquette, it does not matter what specifically is required, prohibited, or ignored, so long as external indications of class structure and membership are provided by customary prescriptions and proscriptions. It does not matter, for example, whether men are required to wear earrings or prohibited from wearing them. Nor need the code of etiquette take a stand for or against the wearing of earrings; it may be neutral and indifferent at this point. But if social classes are to be defined and made distinct and kept intact by obliging each individual to identify himself with his class, then some external signs are necessary. It is the business of systems of etiquette to provide these signs. In some cultures, as we noted earlier, there may be differences of vocabulary between men and women at certain points: men will use certain words or forms, women will use others. Sometimes fine distinctions are made between what is permitted and what is prohibited. In our own culture, for example, there was a time when women were permitted to smoke, but not while walking on the streets. Now female pedestrian smoking is tolerated, but women still may not smoke cigars. Also in our own culture, men are permitted to wear black, white, or tan shoes, but are not permitted to wear shoes of shell pink or robin's-egg blue. This aspect of rules of etiquette gives the appearance, superficially at least, of being capricious, and many persons who do not understand the nature and function of systems of etiquette are inclined to rail against them as being irrational, senseless, and therefore unnecessary. They fail to understand that society must have some way of assuring itself that men will behave as men, and women as women.

The effective operation of codes of etiquette provides society with a high degree of order and stability. All orderly social life, and indeed order in any kind of system, depends, as we have seen earlier, upon regularity in the occurrence of events. Regularity and repetition mean continuity and the possibility of making realistic anticipations and predictions without which orderly social intercourse is impossible. We are so accustomed to the numerous regularities and uniformities in our social life that we tend to take them for granted and fail to appreciate the contribution they make to our social existence. We can, for example, predict with a high degree of success how a lady, a priest, a policeman, professor, or just an ordinary citizen will behave in certain situations. Suppose, for example, we stop a pedestrian on the street and ask him to direct us to the city hall. We may be sure that in nine cases out of ten, providing he speaks our language, he will direct us or tell us that he does not know: "I'm a stranger here myself." Sometimes he will attempt to direct us even when he doesn't know. There are, however, innumerable other responses that he might make. He might strike the inquirer, or run, laugh, spit, sit down, take off his shoes, or any one of a thousand other possible responses.[18] Or, to take another example, when I go into my classroom I can be sure of the behavior of my students. I can tell in advance just how they will behave, at least within limits, and these very narrow ones. They in turn know exactly how I shall behave. I must be dressed in a certain manner. I must wear shoes. Irrelevant as shoes may appear to be to collegiate instruction in anthropology, they are nevertheless essential. I may come to class with my lecture unprepared, but not without my shoes. Wearing shoes is one of the things required by society of an individual of the class *professor*. Parents would not wish to have their children take courses from a man who did not wear shoes. Neither would the administration be likely to tolerate it.

All these things are of course taken for granted. But suppose we imagine a situation in which the students did not behave as students. Suppose a young man appears in class wearing lipstick or earrings. At first we think that it is part of a fraternity initiation; i.e., we refer the event to a context, a class, where this kind of behavior would be appropriate. But we learn eventually that it is not a part of a ritual of initiation but an individual idiosyncrasy. We know, then, that he is not a normal male college student. He has deviated from the strict norm of behavior required of members

[18] That responses of this sort do not exist only in the imagination, but sometimes actually occur, is indicated by a United Press dispatch from Glasgow, Scotland, which appeared in the *Ann Arbor News* on Mar. 30, 1950: "Patrick McCusker was arrested for disturbing the peace because he raised his hat to some women waiting for a street car. There were two white mice under the hat scampering around the top of his head."

of this class. And here comes the significant and important point: *we do not know what he will do next.* We can no longer predict his behavior. If he will wear lipstick or earrings, he may do almost anything. Similarly, if the professor should come to class one day without his necktie, but with an old bicycle tire around his neck, or take off his shoes during class and munch birdseed taken from his briefcase, the students would no longer be able to predict his behavior, and hence would not know how to conduct themselves with reference to him. A professor who would behave in this manner is unpredictable. And again we come to an important point: *a person whose behavior is unpredictable is potentially dangerous.* We have no way of knowing when he might poison others, throw acid in their faces, or otherwise injure them. People do run amok occasionally and shoot or stab people indiscriminately. It is not surprising that the gentleman in the preceding footnote was arrested. In short, if we are to have normal social intercourse, we must be able to predict the behavior of our fellows and they must be able to predict ours. Without the regularities and uniformities of custom, and the ability to predict which they make possible, we would have a chaos of individual whim and caprice.

It is easy to see, therefore, the great contribution made by systems of etiquette. They define the various classes of society in terms of behavior and oblige each individual to conform to the behavior proper to his class. We are thus assured that a man will behave as a man, a priest as a priest, a host as a host, and so on. We have uniformity and regularity and use these traits as a guide to our behavior. We know what to do and what to expect. Codes of etiquette also keep classes intact. If, therefore, adult males do not behave as men, then the class *men* disintegrates and goes to pieces. The whimsical and capricious professor in the example above removes himself from the category of professor. It may be countered at this point that many societies, our own for example, allow certain individuals to dress and behave pretty much as they please so long as they do not actually injure or obstruct social intercourse at any important point. It might be supposed at first blush that this constitutes an exception to, or refutation of, the general propositions regarding etiquette that we have made above, but this is not the case. Our society includes among its classes a class of eccentrics or of celebrities who are permitted many things denied to ordinary people—members of other classes. The class character and significance of eccentrics is frequently indicated by a common saying: "He is in a class by himself." But even eccentrics will not be tolerated unless their behavior is predictable, i.e., unless it conforms to the code for their class.

Our understanding of systems of etiquette is furthered by a consideration of penalties imposed for violations of the code. In many instances punishment consists of removing a person from one class and putting him into another. Thus an Army officer may be stripped of his insignia. The customary formula which expresses his violation of the Army code is "conduct unbecoming to an officer." Similarly, a clergyman who fails to conform may be unfrocked. A man who does not behave like a gentleman is put into the class of "boor." Small boys who do not conform to the patterns of their class become "sissies."

It is remarkable to note in the literature of sociology and cultural anthropology how little attention is paid to etiquette. One may look through the tables of contents of many works without ever finding a chapter on this subject. Yet the system of rules and sanctions that we call etiquette is one of the most powerful and important mechanisms of any society. The contribution made by a code of etiquette to the order, integrity, and effective functioning of a society is enormous. It is interesting to contrast the attention given to ethics with that given to etiquette. The literature on ethics is very extensive indeed. It is a characteristic trait of our own culture that so much attention should be paid to ethics and so little to etiquette.[19] An adequate scientific analysis of social systems, however, would place etiquette on a par at least with ethics. There is, as a matter of fact, some evidence that systems of etiquette are in many instances even more powerful and effective than ethics as means of regulating social intercourse. In the first place, violations of rules of etiquette are always punished, because such violations are always observed. An act committed in solitude does not come within the scope of etiquette, and hence cannot be a violation of its code. Those who violate rules of ethics, on the other hand, are not always punished. The violation may not be observed, or the violator may not be apprehended. Or, if caught, he may escape punishment. In our own society, for example, many offenders get off scot-free. But in the case of violations of rules of etiquette, punishments are certain, and often extremely painful.[20] No one wants to be "talked about." Ridicule is painful. To be "snubbed" is very hard to bear, and complete ostracism is virtually intolerable.

As suggested above, it is perhaps because our own society is so much

[19] Americans are an ethics-ridden people. They never tire of harangues on the subject of good and evil—and "sin." Moral crusades, to rid the nation of alcoholic beverages, or to purge the planet of some international Evil One or an odious form of government, seem ever to find favor with them. On the other hand, countless European visitors, both before and since De Tocqueville, Harriet Martineau, et al., have commented on the "bad manners" of *Homo sapiens Americanensis.*

[20] In ancient Peru, nobles who violated laws were commonly punished by public ridicule rather than by imprisonment, torture, or execution: "Inca law ... held that public ridicule and loss of office hurt a noble as much as exile or torture would a poor man, and that the prestige of the nobles as a class must be upheld." John H. Rowe, "Inca Culture at the Time of the Spanish Conquest," in *Handbook of South American Indians,* Smithsonian Institution, Bureau of American Ethnology, 1946, p. 271.

more concerned with etiquette than with ethics that we fail to appreciate systems of etiquette as powerful influences in our society and fail to recognize the contribution made by them. In other cultures, however, the significance of etiquette may be appreciated and its codes placed above those of ethics and law. Thus, for example, a European historian, after discussing the importance of social ritual in old Japan, remarks that "even in certain quarters in Europe, Ceremony has been a much more potent thing than Religion, while even now a breach of etiquette sometimes entails graver social penalties upon the offender than flagrant outrages on what is most vital in morality do in the highly moral and comparatively democratic British Empire under the sway of King Edward VII." [21]

With regard to the question of evolutionary development, the situation in the case of etiquette is essentially like that of ethics: we can discern no evolution of etiquette as such. Codes of etiquette, like those of ethics, are aspects of social systems; they are not something that can be evaluated independently and apart from their respective contexts. Some societies may emphasize rules of etiquette more than others or, more properly speaking, may exhibit more elaborate codes than others. In some respects, etiquette is more important, relatively speaking, in primitive cultures than in civilized societies; in other respects, however, it is less important. In primitive society, communities are relatively small, social intercourse is to a great extent intimate and personal, most of one's contacts are with relatives, friends, close neighbors, or acquaintances. Courts of law, police, and penal procedures are rare or lacking. In such sociocultural systems, therefore, codes of etiquette play a very prominent and important role in the regulation of social life. The extent to which primitive peoples are governed or dominated by the social forms of proper behavior has often been commented upon. On the other hand, the number and variety of classes are much greater in advanced civilized cultures than on tribal levels. In addition to the universal classes of sex, age, and marital status, there are occupational groups, professional classes, social strata, orders of nobility, etc. The need for rules to regulate the behavior of these classes is therefore very great. By and large, it would appear that the importance of rules of etiquette is approximately uniform throughout the various stages of cultural development.

A final word concerning the present status and possible future of codes of etiquette. As we have noted above, the requirements and prohibitions of codes of etiquette often seem not only capricious but irrational. Furthermore, some of them actually tend to decrease the welfare of individual members of society at certain points while working for the

[21] James Murdoch, *A History of Japan*, vol. 1, The Asiatic Society of Japan, Kobe, 1910, p. 159.

integrity and orderliness of the society as a whole. In some instances rules of etiquette make for economic waste. As Veblen pointed out, some of the marks of social status require "conspicuous consumption and waste." Food, clothing, and other goods are often wasted in order to satisfy the canons of good taste and status. Bodily discomfort is not infrequently caused by the observance of rules of etiquette. Tattooing, head deformation, the piercing of ears for pendants and of lips for plugs and labrets, scarification, corsets and stays, the binding of feet, high-heeled shoes, starched collars, etc., may cause pain and much discomfort. And in some instances one's health may be impaired, as, for example, when etiquette requires a person to wear clothing that is excessively hot or obstructs free respiration.

The discomforts and disadvantages that rules of etiquette work upon the individual, plus the apparently irrational and senseless nature of many articles of the codes, have caused many to regard "conventions" as but senseless survivals of an earlier and less rational era and have led them to the conclusion that they can and should be dispensed with. But such reasoning is individual-centered; it fails to realize that etiquette is a sociocultural process or mechanism. Etiquette is inseparable from classes, and class structure is and will remain universal in human society. Codes and conventions will therefore be with us always. But there is still this question: "Cannot systems of etiquette accomplish their purpose without promoting waste, bodily discomfort, or injury to the health—in short, are not *rational* systems of etiquette possible?" Here, as in the case of ethics, we see the possibility of change in the direction of the rational. We may be sure that social systems will continue to avail themselves of codes of etiquette as mechanisms of order and integration indefinitely. But when and as civilization becomes more rational and humane, it seems probable that codes of etiquette will be modified in this direction also.

Kinship systems. A kinship system is a powerful and effective mechanism of social integration and control, as we have already made clear in our earlier discussion of this subject. It should be pointed out here, however, that the rules which regulate kinship systems are those of both ethics and etiquette. On the one hand, the behavior of a person toward his relatives is regulated so that the general welfare of the entire group of kindred will be promoted. And, on the other hand, patterns of behavior proper to his various classes of relatives, affinal and consanguine, are prescribed.

Custom and law. One may draw a logical distinction between custom and law easily enough. Practically and empirically, however, it is sometimes difficult or even impossible to do so. The regularities, uniformities, and continuities of human social behavior that we have called *custom* are felt as moral imperatives by members of society. If a people dress in a certain way, refrain from eating certain animals or habitually eat them, paint their faces or blacken their teeth, there tends to be a feeling that one *ought* to do, or refrain from doing, these things and in the proper, i.e., customary, way. If all males in your society wear their hair long, or blacken their teeth, then you, an adult male member, *should* do likewise. To do so is to proclaim your oneness, your solidarity, with them; to do otherwise is to proclaim yourself different, a person who is not "one of them," which might mean in some instances a person who could not be relied upon in an emergency—perhaps even a traitor. Custom is right; therefore one ought to do what is customary.

Infractions or violations of customary regulations are punished, as we have seen, by ridicule, ostracism, and, in some cases, by retaliation by an injured party. But by whom is the punishment meted out? We may distinguish, logically, two agencies of punishment and discipline: (1) the *community in general,* i.e., an unspecified, anonymous, undifferentiated aggregation of fellow tribesmen or citizens, such as a local band, a village, or neighborhood; or (2) a special social or political mechanism, acting in the name of and by the authority of the society as a whole, such as a chief, council of elders, policemen and courts. In the one case we are dealing, by definition, with custom; in the other, with law. Law, therefore, is a special category of custom; a law is a custom the violation of which is punished by a society by means of a special social mechanism.

The foregoing logical distinction is valid as well as clear. But the practical application of the two concepts, law and custom, is not always easy. When will an act be considered an offense against custom and when against law? In our society, if a man should wear earrings, or a woman smoke a cigar in public, it is probable that neither would be arrested, although he or she might be; there are cases of this sort on record. Their deviations from social norms may be, and in all probability would be, punished as offenses against custom. But it is not likely that they would be considered as having violated a law. If, however, one should exceed a speed limit, or throw his garbage in the street, he might well be arrested as a violator of the law. How, then, are we to tell what is custom and what is law in the disciplinary and punitive functions of social systems?

By our definition, an offense is a violation of *law* if it is punishable by a society as a whole *by means of a special social mechanism.* If it is punished merely in general, by the community as a whole, but by the members of society rather than by and through some special instrumental means to which public authority and power are delegated, then the offense is against *custom.*

In connection with the question of punishable offenses, it would be well to distinguish between *crimes* and *torts*. A crime is an offense the punishment of which is a monopoly of the community, or social system as a whole. A tort is an offense which may be punished, or avenged, by the injured party. A crime is therefore a public matter; a tort, a private one, although the whole community may be vitally interested in it.

If *law* is distinguished from *custom* by the fact that the former involves the punishment of violations of the society's code of behavior by the public authority of the society exercised through a special instrumentality, then we must examine these instrumentalities.

As we have noted repeatedly, a society may be highly homogeneous, or generalized, structurally and functionally, or it may be differentiated structurally and specialized functionally. A biological organism, for example, may or may not have special structures, or organs, of locomotion, nutrition, etc. Similarly, a social system may or may not have differentiated and specialized structures for certain functions such as integration and regulation. In the operation of custom in general, there are no special social mechanisms; the society as a whole functions as a *system of custom*. A kinship system, for example, is but an aspect of the society as a whole. But in the case of law, of crime and punishment, the social system functions through special social structures or mechanisms. These are headmen, councils of elders, chiefs, shamans, priests, secret societies, clubs, etc., in societies organized on the basis of kinship, and the police, courts, prisons, etc., in civil societies.

The earliest human societies were, as we have seen, relatively small and discrete territorial groups, or bands, each of which was made up of families. It would be hardly proper to speak of structurally differentiated and specialized mechanisms of social regulation and control in these primordial societies. These social systems were regulated by custom in general, by the special systems of etiquette, ethics, and kinship. There were, however, rudimentary beginnings of such specialized mechanisms, namely, *headmen*. By this term we mean simply a man who, because of his superiority over his fellows, in terms of physical prowess, skill, force of character or personality, knowledge or wisdom, serves as a means of coordinating and directing the activities of his fellows on certain occasions. It should be noted that even if all men were absolutely equal in all their abilities, it would still be desirable, from the standpoint of security and survival, to have the activities of a number of associated individuals coordinated and directed, at certain times at least, by one person. Concerted, cooperative, group action may be more effective, in terms of food getting, protection, and defense, than individualistic effort. There are many occasions, in hunting, fishing, and in offense and defense, etc., in which success would be made more sure by directed, coordinated action. But to achieve this, there must be a means, a mechanism, of coordination and regulation. In the earliest of human societies this mechanism was the headman.

As we have just seen, headmen, leaders, would be necessary at times even though all men were absolutely equal in all respects. But of course men are not equal; on the contrary, they differ rather widely in many respects. We may assume, therefore, that in the earliest human societies—just as in those of their prehuman forebears—a few individuals stood out among their fellows because they possessed certain qualities or abilities in larger measure or in more intense form than the rest. They were the ones who took charge on certain occasions, who served to coordinate the activities of the group and to direct their efforts. They were like the individuals who spontaneously find themselves in a position of leadership on temporary occasions in our own society.

One commonly hears of head*men* among very primitive groups, such as the Eskimo, for example, but there are relatively few and infrequent allusions to head*women*. This is probably because the male sex is the dominant one in the human species, as it is in some subhuman primate species. The male, therefore, takes the predominant role as a rule in the principal life-sustaining activities of the group on very low cultural levels, namely, hunting and defense-offense. A man, rather than a woman, will be the head of the local group. Women differ in their qualities and abilities as men do, and some may stand out and exercise functions of integration and leadership on certain occasions and to a limited extent. But this hardly warrants the term "headwoman." The vital activities of the group are dominated by men; the leader must therefore be a man, a headman.

A *chief* is merely a formal recognition of the headman. There are various gradations of chieftainship in the spectrum of special mechanisms of integration and regulation. A headman may be said to be self-appointed and group-accepted. A formal and explicit recognition of this fact may be called *chieftainship*. Chiefs, too, may be self-appointed and group-accepted, or they may be selected by the group. The latter may be regarded as more advanced from the standpoint of social evolution because it represents a greater role for society as compared with the individual. The next stage would be hereditary chiefs rather than elective officers. A man chosen for the office of chieftain is likely to be superior to one who inherits the office, since a free choice would be made upon a basis of merit, whereas a hereditary successor to the office may or may not have the requisite qualities and abilities. The disadvantage of the principle of inheritance is somewhat lessened, however, by the fact that the office is usually confined to a certain lineage within which the selection can be made from a number of candidates. The advantages, however, of inheritance over selection in the office of chieftainship are very considerable. The principle of inheritance gives a greater degree of continuity to the office than does selection. This makes for a more orderly succession, and consequently greater stability of social order. Even in some advanced systems, such as that of the Ganda of Uganda, where succession to the office of king is supposed to be hereditary, the country falls into virtual chaos and anarchy upon the death of the king, as the various princes resort to force of arms to seize the throne. In this case the principle of succession by inheritance is not well established. Had it been, succession to the kingship would have been orderly and peaceful. The principle of inheritance of office makes, therefore, for a definite, peaceful, and orderly succession. It fosters a higher degree of integration and solidarity. The office of hereditary chief evolves eventually into that of king, as we shall see later.

Police. In some tribal systems, but relatively very few, the authority of the chief is backed up by the physical force of a body of policemen. The buffalo-hunting tribes of the North American Plains provide us with the best—if not the only—example of police in social systems based upon kinship. In their mode of life it is imperative that the members of the tribe conform strictly to a plan of concerted action at certain times, such as communal hunts and marches from one camp site to another. To disregard the plan and orders of the hunt chief might stampede the bison herd and deprive the camp of food; an unwise act while on the march might jeopardize the safety of all. In a number of tribes, therefore, the authority of the hunt, or tribal, chief is backed up by police, who may punish or kill offenders. The composition of the police force varies somewhat; usually they are one of several military societies into which the men of the tribe are organized.

These instances of political authority, supported by military force, are the first adumbration of the armies and militia of civil societies.

Councils are special mechanisms of social control in many sociocultural systems and on various levels of development, from the primitive aborigines of Australia to the intensive agriculturalists of the pueblos. They may be composed of the old men of the community as in Australia or of the mature men as in the Rio Grande pueblos. Or they may be made up of chiefs as in the case of some of the Plains tribes of North America. In any event, the council is a *part* of the community or tribe acting for the society as a whole.

Shamans and priests. In discussing shamanism as an example of division of labor, we noted that the medicine man has secular functions of social control in many cultures. He may act as watchdog over his fellow tribesmen to see that they do not violate custom or law. Priests, too, have these political functions. As a matter of fact, social control, especially keeping the subordinate classes in their place, docile and subservient, is a critically important function of the priesthoods in most of the civil societies of higher cultural levels, as we shall see later in the chapter on the state-church.

Secret societies function as special mechanisms of social control in some cultures, particularly in west Africa and parts of Melanesia. The Kachina society in some of the Southwestern pueblos also serves in this capacity. On ceremonial occasions, the societies appear, dressed as gods, and punish violators against custom.

We thus see what sort of special mechanisms of social regulation and control exist in tribal societies based upon ties of kinship. The Agricultural Revolution rendered social organization on this basis obsolete and replaced it with a different form in which the special mechanism of social integration, regulation, and control grew greatly in magnitude and power. This mechanism was the state-church. We shall deal with it at length later.

Chapter 9 ECONOMIC ORGANIZATION
OF PRIMITIVE SOCIETY

In previous chapters we have sketched the evolution of primitive culture from two principal standpoints, technological and social. In the latter category we have dealt with social organization in general and with kinship, division of labor, and social control in particular. We now undertake to trace the course of cultural development from the standpoint of economic organization. But what *is* economic? Unfortunately there is considerable confusion among cultural anthropologists on this point,[1] so we must deal with it at once before turning to primitive cultures themselves.

One can tell whether a given atom is hydrogen or not by looking at it, so to speak. If it has one electron revolving about its nucleus, it is hydrogen; if it has two, it is helium. Likewise, one can tell whether a species of animal is mammalian or not by observation: if it suckles its young it is mammalian; if it does not, it is not mammalian. But one cannot tell by looking at it, or by any other kind of examination, whether a given event is economic or not. Suppose *A* gives *B* an arrow. Is this an economic event? Suppose that *A* gives *B* an arrow and *B* gives *A* a string of beads in return, is the transaction an economic one? The answer is, it all depends.... When *A* gives an arrow to *B* it might mean that *B* is to succeed *A* as chief priest of the tribe. Or handing the arrow to *B* might be a challenge to fight, and the handing of beads to *A* by *B* might indicate an acceptance of the challenge, or an offer of indemnity. We would not wish to call these events economic.

Whether an event is economic or not depends upon the context in which we appreciate its significance. A thing or an event is just what it is,

---

[1] "There is no other aspect of primitive life," says Malinowski, "where our knowledge is more scanty and our understanding more superficial than in Economics. Hence misconception is rampant, and it is necessary to clear the ground when approaching any economic subject." B. Malinowski, *Argonauts of the Western Pacific*, Routledge and Kegan Paul, Ltd., London, 1922, p. 84. We do not feel, however, that Malinowski succeeded very well in clearing up misconceptions, as we shall note later.

a thing or an event. Whether a thing or event is an economic, moral, aesthetic, religious, or astronomical datum depends upon the context in which we observe it as a thing of significance. A Chinese porcelain vase is a Chinese porcelain vase, or, more precisely, a form and magnitude of glazed, fired clay is a form and magnitude of glazed, fired clay. But the vase may be significant to us in a variety of contexts: aesthetic (object of art), commercial (article of merchandise), scientific (an artifact), or legal (as exhibit A in a lawsuit).

Anything may be referred to any context. It might not always make sense—either common sense or scientific sense—to place any event in any context, but this is an entirely different matter. My writing these words can be meaningfully referred to an astronomic context: the energy expended has come from the sun, it has reached me via the process of photosynthesis and the substances of food, it is transformed by the process of metabolism (which gives us a physiologic context), and is expended in the operation of a mechanical device called a typewriter. Whether a thing or event is to be reckoned as economic or not depends, therefore, upon context. But what is an economic context?

An *economic context,* as we define the term, must have four characteristics. First of all, it must be sociocultural in character. Secondly, it involves the appropriation of things from the external world. Thirdly, these things are used to satisfy a need of human beings. And finally, human energy must be expended in making these things available for human consumption. Let us consider these factors in turn.

"Sociocultural" limits economic things and events to the human species; it excludes activities of birds, beavers, ants, and so on, that are more or less analogous to our own. If this seems arbitrary, it must be remembered that all definitions are arbitrary. Furthermore, there is a fundamental, qualitative difference between human and nonhuman behavior, as we noted in Chapter 1, "Man and Culture." Economic behavior is *social* as well as *cultural.* It is a process of interaction among persons; the Robinson Crusoes and Alexander Selkirks have no economic life. Merely picking and eating wild berries, or catching a fish and eating it, is not to be reckoned an economic activity: monkeys can pick berries, and otters can catch fish. Economic, then, by definition, must be both social and cultural.

In Chapter 1, "Man and Culture," we distinguished two kinds of needs of human beings: (1) those which can be served only by drawing upon the resources of nature, and (2) those that do not require things from the external world. Economic is concerned with the first of these two kinds of needs only. I may have need for consolation, and this need may be served by prayer or by a friend. But the need is not economic—by definition.

To be counted as economic, a thing or process must satisfy some human need. If one expended labor upon the appropriation and transformation of materials taken from nature, it would not be economic if the result was of no use or value to anyone.

Human labor, which may of course be supplemented by energy from nonhuman sources, must be expended in the satisfaction of needs with materials taken from the external world. Breathing air, smelling a rose, and admiring a sunset are not to be counted as economic activities because no labor is expended in the processes. If, however, the air were compressed, the rose used to make perfume, or the sunset reproduced on canvas, it could qualify as economic since each would require the expenditure of human labor.

Economic systems must be distinguished from technologic systems. The two are much alike: each is concerned with the appropriation of things from the external world by means of human labor and for the purpose of satisfying human needs. And in many ethnographic monographs we find a section, or a chapter, entitled "Economic Life," which is devoted to a description of the construction and operation of a loom, the manufacture of salt or pigments, or other like matters. The economic context is distinguished from the technologic context by the fact that the latter is characterized by *things* in terms of their inherent properties and in terms of their relations to one another: the properties of clay, for example, and tempering material, the tools and techniques in pottery making, and so on. The economic process, on the other hand, is characterized by *a kind of relationship among human beings:* giver, recipient; debtor, creditor; buyer, seller; or mutual sharing.

It is not difficult to distinguish one kind of context from another in logical analysis. But it is not always easy to determine the context in which a thing or event may have its chief significance—and, of course, it may be simultaneously significant in a number of contexts. We noted earlier that writing this chapter has significance in an astronomic context. But, we earnestly hope, this is not its chief significance. Some royalties may accrue to the author when the book is published, thus making the writing significant in an economic context. But this, too, is not the chief significance of the activity from the standpoint of the writer. For him, understanding culture and the communication of this understanding are the principal features of his labors.

Suppose Mr. and Mrs. X purchase a turkey, roast it and serve it, with all the customary accompaniments, at a dinner to which Mr. Y has been invited. Is this to be reckoned as an economic event or not? The answer is, it is not an either-or situation; it may be significant in both economic and noneconomic contexts, and these may vary widely in relative magnitudes. Let us suppose that Mr. and Mrs. X are wealthy, which makes the cost of the dinner a trivial matter to them. Further, Mr. Y is their nephew just returned from years of Army combat service. In this case, the economic significance of the dinner is negligible; the kinship factor, paramount.

But suppose that Mr. X is a young man with meager means and a slender salary and Mr. Y is his employer from whom Mr. and Mrs. X hope to obtain a promotion for Mr. X. Here the economic factor may well be uppermost.

When a young Crow Indian and his relatives give thirty horses to the family of a girl he proposes to marry, is this to be considered as an economic transaction? Although this custom is often referred to as "bride price," all ethnographers emphasize the fact that the wife thus obtained is not a chattel. But the transfer of the horses is not a small matter. If the marriage breaks up, the groom and his relatives may demand the return of the horses. We would rule, in this case, that this whole transaction is to be regarded primarily as a social affair, and only secondarily an economic transaction. The chief end to be served is to establish an alliance, a mutual-aid relationship, between two groups of relatives. The transfer of horses is merely a means, and not even an essential means, to this end.

We are face to face with a real and an important problem here. Merely because some sociocultural process has some obvious economic features, it does not follow that its chief significance lies in the context economic. It may be primarily a social ritual whose purpose is to serve psychic needs, such as conferring or transmitting an honor, and in which the economic factors are of significance merely as means to this end. It would be unfortunate, from the standpoint of an understanding of primitive culture or our own, to present and interpret a social ritual as an economic institution. We would not, for example, discuss marriage under the heading of "economics" because the bridal costume cost a considerable sum of money. But this is just what some ethnologists have done upon occasion. We shall cite two instances: the *potlatch* and the *kula*. Both have been treated as economic institutions by not a few ethnologists. It is true, of course, that both institutions contain economic elements, just as marriage may involve the purchase of a bridal gown. But both the potlatch and the kula, like the institution of marriage, find their chief meaning and significance in the context of social ritual; the economic factor is subordinate and is significant only as a means to the end.

The potlatch is an institution in the cultures of a number of Indian tribes of the Northwest Coast of America: the Kwakiutl, Nootka, and others. It involves the distribution of blankets by a person among his relatives. After a time, the relatives return these blankets plus many times more. This process is commonly characterized as "lending at a high rate of interest"; Benedict has termed it "usury." [2] The "underlying principle"

[2] Ruth Benedict, *Patterns of Culture*, Houghton Mifflin Company, Boston, 1934, p. 184.

of the potlatch, says Boas, "is that of the interest-bearing investment of property." [3] The vocabulary is that of economics, and the impression is conveyed that the institution is essentially an economic one. The "economic system . . . finds its expression in the so-called 'potlatch,' " Boas tells us.[4] Ruth Bunzel treats the potlatch as an economic institution.[5]

But to present the potlatch as an *economic* institution is to offer a distorted picture of the institution and a muddled conception of economic processes. The potlatch is primarily and essentially a social ritual.[6] Its chief purpose is to transfer, or to validate the transfer, of honors or prestige. It is a means of satisfying one of that class of needs that can be served without drawing upon the resources of the external world—except incidentally, perhaps, and then only as a means to an end. It is a social game, and it is no more made an economic institution by the "lending of property at interest" and the extravagant destruction of property at the feast than chess is made an economic activity because ivory chessmen cost money.

The same general comment may be made about the kula, so well described by Malinowski for the Trobriand Islanders of Melanesia and their neighbors.[7] In the kula, a group of people make a circuit of a number of islands exchanging shell arm bands for bead necklaces with their inhabitants. The kula "is concerned with the exchange of wealth and utilities," says Malinowski, "therefore it is an economic institution." [8] But his description of it makes it quite clear that it is not to be so considered according to our definition. "Kula exchange . . . can never be barter," he says, "a direct exchange with assessments of equivalents and with haggling." The natives, too, "sharply distinguish it from barter, which they practise extensively, of which they have a clear idea, and for which they have a settled term." [9]

The kula is a sociopsychological game. Arm bands are exchanged for strings of beads in a formal, ritual manner. The objects remain in circulation indefinitely, traveling a definite circuit among a number of islands, one kind going one way, the other in the opposite direction. Exchange takes place only between certain individuals, the kula partners. To par-

[3] Franz Boas, *The Social Organization and Secret Societies of the Kwakiutl Indians,* Report of the U.S. National Museum for 1895, p. 341.

[4] Franz Boas, "The North-western Tribes of Canada," *Report of the Sixty-eighth Meeting of the British Association for the Advancement of Science,* London, 1899, p. 681.

[5] Ruth Bunzel, "The Economic Organization of Primitive Peoples," in *General Anthropology,* Franz Boas (ed.), 1938, pp. 358–360.

[6] This fact is recognized by some who nevertheless treat it as "an economic institution."

[7] Malinowski, *op. cit.*

[8] *Ibid.,* p. 84.

[9] *Ibid.,* pp. 352, 96.

ticipate is a privilege; to hold one of the articles of exchange is an honor. Here, as in the potlatch, we have a game the purpose of which is to confer honor and distinction, a way of making life pleasant and interesting. The shells and necklaces are merely instruments with which the game is played. They are the visible, tangible expression of a game of make-believe. The objects acquire value from their use in the game. But it is the game that determines the significance of the objects, not the other way around. Malinowski, in trying to make this institution intelligible to us, likens the arm bands and necklaces to athletic trophies in American colleges. One group will win a metal cup in a contest and hold it until defeated by a rival, whereupon the cup changes hands. But this pattern as such is not properly to be designated as economic. To be sure, the cup can be referred to an economic context: it is an object produced by human labor from materials in the external world and used to satisfy human needs. But it is the manufacture and sale of the cups which is economic, not their use as trophies. Similarly the *mwali* of the kula, the objects which are exchanged, may be referred to the economic systems of the various tribes. But as kula elements as such, as counters in a social game, they are not economic elements.

From the standpoint of our analysis, there are logically only two major types of economic systems, although there may be in actuality any number of intermediate or composite systems. In one of these major types the factor that determines the system and gives it its distinctive character is the relationship between persons as human beings. In the other, the determinant is the relationship between goods as objects. We may illustrate these two types in the following way. In Figure 9–1, A and B are persons,

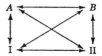

Figure 9–1. Analysis of the process of exchange.

I and II are goods produced by human labor and capable of satisfying human needs. At the outset, A owns I; B owns II. A and B exchange their goods so that in the end A owns II, B possesses I. The various interrelationships within this system, for it is indeed a whole economic system though expressed here in its simplest terms, are shown by the arrows in the diagram. A is related to the object he owns at the outset, namely, I. B is similarly related to II. The act of exchange, however, relates A to II; he becomes its owner. Similarly, B becomes related to I. But the act of exchange does more than this. It not only brings the two persons, A and B, into a specific relationship to each other; it brings the two objects, I and II, into mutual relationship as well. Thus, in this system, we have a network of interrelationships which bind together all the elements concerned into a unity. But what is the character of the unity, of the system? We have already supplied the answer: *the system will be dominated either by the relationship between persons (A and B) or by the relationship between goods (I and II).* This means that in the former case the relationship between goods is determined by, and is dependent upon, the relationship between the persons; in the latter, the relationship between persons is determined by and subordinate to the relationship between things. Thus we have systems that are not only different, but diametrically opposite. Let us illustrate with examples.

Let us suppose that A and B in the diagram are friends and neighbors of each other. I and II are shirts and sox, respectively, if you wish to refer the exchange to our society, or arrows and buckskin if the reference is to be to primitive culture. The exchange takes place because they are mutual friends and neighbors. This social relationship finds expression in the act of exchange: their friendship is reaffirmed. A and B are also related to both objects, I and II; each gives up the one and acquires the other. But there is more to this than relationships between persons and between persons and objects: I and II are brought into relationship to each other, as objects, by the act of exchange. If this is not at once apparent, it is because the relationship between the objects is obscured by the relationship between the persons, and this, in turn, is because the one relationship is subordinate to and dependent upon the other. In the example under consideration it is the relationship between persons that dominates the transaction and determines its character. But a relationship between the objects is established nevertheless. This is true despite the fact that there is absolutely no bargaining between A and B. But the objects are evaluated in terms of each other for all that. If A and B are of equal social status and equally able to give, a marked discrepancy in the values of I and II would be noted. The attitudes of A and B may vary in their reaction to this discrepancy, of course. A may be proud of the fact that he gave more than he received from B. There may be rivalry to see who can give most. Prestige may accrue from generosity or lavishness. Or A might be annoyed or hurt as a consequence of receiving much less than he gave. Or each may note with satisfaction that he received a value equal to that given. In any event, the objects I and II will be evaluated in terms of each other, which is to say that they are brought into relationship with each other by the act of exchange. Here we have, then, one type of economic system. It is determined by the relationship between persons as persons; the relationship between objects is subordinated to the relationship between persons.

Suppose, however, that *A* and *B* come together, not as friends and neighbors, but as owners of commodities (i.e., objects capable of satisfying human needs and produced by human labor). They exchange their respective goods, let us say yams (farm produce) for iron knives (manufactured articles). Naturally they do not make the exchange for the fun of it; each desires to derive some advantage from it. And since both objects represent and embody human labor, each wishes to derive as much advantage as he can from the transaction. The knife cost its maker so much labor. Yams will satisfy needs of the knife maker. He wishes, therefore, to obtain as much of yams for his knife (i.e., per unit of human labor) as possible. On the other hand, the yams have cost the farmer labor, and he wishes to get as many knives or as good a knife ("as much knife") for his yams as he can. Consequently each weighs the product of the other in terms of his own. They bargain; i.e., they balance one magnitude of value against another in terms of their need or desire. Finally the exchange is effected, and the farmer goes home with his knife; the artisan, with his yams.

A comparison of this example with the previous one will disclose many points of similarity or identity: two persons exchange articles with each other in each instance. In each act of exchange, persons are brought together in a social relationship; in each a relationship is established between the objects exchanged. These two types of exchange—or economic system—are alike in certain particulars, but in particulars only; as *whole systems* they are diametrically opposite. In the one transaction it is the relationship between persons that determines the nature of the system as a whole; in the other, it is the relationship between objects which gives the system its character. The one is personal, the other impersonal. And as in the one case the relationship between objects was concealed, or obscured, by the relationship between persons, so in the other, the relationship between objects tends to conceal or obscure the relationship between persons. In the case of the farmer and the artisan exchanging yams for knives in a face-to-face transaction, it is not difficult to recognize the existence of a social relationship between them, although even here the attention is likely to be so fixed upon the objects and the relationship that is worked out between them that the social relationship between the persons is apt to be undervalued, if not ignored entirely. In a world market, however, it is not so easy to see that a Navajo Indian in Arizona, a hundred miles from a railroad, is brought into social relations with the sheep rancher of Australia whose wool competes with his own on the market, or with the coffee picker of Brazil, the sugar grower of Cuba, the knife maker of Massachusetts, and so on, but such is the case nevertheless.

The systems which we have just described are, so to speak, pure systems; i.e., they are logically distinct, each is homogeneous, they are radically different—opposite, in fact. What we have described is, of course, a picture produced by logical analysis. This is not to say, however, that they are unreal; they are very real indeed. There are, or have been, systems in the real world of human beings that correspond with our two types exactly and point for point. But there have also been economic systems in some cultures which are not identical in all respects with either one of our types. This does not mean that our types, or categories, are inadequate; it simply means that there may be systems which are not pure in the sense of being wholly determined by a single principle. Some systems are the product of more than one principle; i.e., there are mixed as well as pure systems. Thus, certain systems which at bottom rest upon the economic relationship between goods are modified by legislation which requires transactions to take account of the person, or class of persons, involved. Sumptuary laws, for example, restrict the full and free operation of a socioeconomic system in terms of purely economic laws and considerations. In a free system, an ounce of gold would buy so much silk or ermine, no matter who owned the gold. But sumptuary laws might prohibit persons of a certain class from wearing silk, and hence keep the purchase of it from taking place. A sociological principle, one of class structure and prerogatives, is thus introduced into the economic system. Our own society during wartime presents another example: I buy gasoline for my car, paying hard cash for it. But no matter how much money I have and wish to spend for gasoline I cannot buy more than so many gallons a week. Similarly, one family can buy no more butter than another of equal size, even though it has ten times as much money which it would like to spend for food. All this, of course, disregards the so-called black markets. These illegal markets are simply the principle of the relationship between things asserting itself over the relationship between persons. History has, therefore, produced socioeconomic systems in which both kinds of principles are operative. They are mixed systems, and there may be a great variety of mixtures. But any system that does not correspond to either of our two pure types must be a combination of them.

Let us return now to the evolution of culture and see how our analysis of economic systems into these two major types will apply to specific societies and cultures.

We find only one type of economic system in societies based upon kinship ties. This statement is virtually tautologous, for societies based upon kinship could have no other kind of economic system than one in which relationships between persons took precedence over relationships between goods. To state the same proposition in reverse, a society whose economic system subordinated relationships between persons to relationships between goods would not and could not be based upon the personal ties of kinship. This is not to say that nowhere in preliterate societies do we find exchange taking place in terms of the values of the things exchanged rather than in terms of the social relationship between the persons making the exchange. We find markets and commerce among the nonliterate Incas and among many African nations. But these sociocultural systems have evolved so far that they have already outgrown some of the basic features of primitive society and have acquired some of the characteristics of civil society, such as monarchs and slaves. We may also find instances of commodity exchange among some primitive groups *under the influence of higher cultures*, such as certain groups in the Philippines or Melanesia. But *within* tribal society, based upon kinship ties, we find only the one type of economic system: the determination of the system by the relationship between persons. The economic system of primitive society is thus in complete harmony with the social system. Both are based upon personal relations, upon cooperation and mutual aid. In short, primitive society is characterized, as Morgan pointed out long ago, by liberty, equality, and fraternity. The type of economic system characteristic of civil society, however, is at bottom the exact opposite. It is impersonal, nonhuman, and nonmoral, which in terms of human welfare means inhuman and immoral. It is based upon competition and struggle, upon class subjugation and exploitation. The economic system of civil society is also in harmony with its own social system. Liberty, equality, and fraternity in civil society are conspicuous by their absence. But we shall hear more about this later when we come to a discussion of economics in modern society.

As we have just noted, the method of exchange of goods within primitive societies is, like the social system as a whole, based upon kinship ties. Between tribes, however, there was exchange of a different sort: commercial exchange. Intertribal commerce takes place on the basis of the relationship between the articles themselves rather than upon the relationship between persons; the relationship between persons is merely incidental to the relationship between the goods exchanged. The incidental character of the human relationship is set forth in a rather striking way in a form of intertribal exchange known as the "silent trade." Here the persons making the exchange never come into direct contact with one another at all; they do not even see each other. Members of one tribe place goods for exchange in a certain place in a neutral zone between the two tribal territories and then retire. Persons from the other tribe then take their goods to this place and leave them in exchange for those they find there. This does not mean, of course, that a social relationship between the two parties of the exchange has been done away with. It exists and operates just as truly as if they met face to face in exchange. But the incidental character of the interpersonal relationship, the fact that it is the relationship between goods that is paramount, is made clear in this form of trade.

Commodity exchange originated in intertribal intercourse rather than in intratribal socioeconomic processes. And all commercial and financial systems known in human history have grown out of the economic system that originated in simple barter between tribes. Such systems are, however, characteristic of civil society rather than of primitive peoples. We shall, therefore, reserve fuller discussion of economic systems determined by relationship between goods for a later chapter.

The economic organization of primitive society is virtually identical with its kinship organization. The mutual-aid group organized along lines of consanguinity and affinity had economic activities as its primary functions. The family was the first economic organization, as it was the first cooperative group. Economic organization was developed and enlarged as the cooperative kinship group was enlarged by extending the radius of kinship ties. In almost all primitive societies of the modern world, however, it is not the nuclear family, or even the extended family, that is the basic unit of the economic organization; it is the *household group*. This term is inappropriate in so far as it may be applied to societies in which there are no houses or other dwellings, but we have no better term. We mean by household group all those individuals whose food is prepared and served in common. The nuclear family as an independent and discrete unit is rare or wanting in primitive society; the extended family is much more the rule. But the household group would be distinguished from the extended family in that it might include persons who are relatives, but not actually members, of the extended family, such as a widow, widower, or orphan who has, through unusual circumstances, no place in a family of his own. The family, extended or nuclear, would form the nucleus and probably the major part of the household group, but supernumeraries, as indicated above, would swell its ranks. The household group is therefore a very important unit in the economic organization of a primitive tribe, since it is the principal organization of production, preparation, distribution, and consumption of food.

Cooperation in the production of food in the earliest stages of cultural development was possible in some pursuits but not in others. In some instances hunting and fishing could be carried on more effectively through cooperative action than by individual effort; sometimes cooperation was not possible or advantageous. In gathering wild plant food, cooperation was often not possible technologically. But even where the actual techniques of production did not require or could not employ to advantage the principle of cooperation, there was nevertheless some social regulation. We have already noted the division of labor along sex lines which made for cooperation and mutual dependence between men and women on a tribal basis and within each family as well. Thus, even though production had, in some activities, to be carried on individualistically so far as technology was concerned, there were a social organization and regulation of these and all other aspects of production.

In some very primitive tribes there is some social regulation of consumption (and consequently of production also) in terms of social classes. In aboriginal Australia, for example, children were not permitted to eat certain foods which their elders might eat. As they grew older the food taboos were removed, a few at a time, until they were permitted to eat virtually anything in their old age. In some tribes there may be sumptuary regulations for men and women as classes. Whether regulations of this kind can be assigned to the very earliest stage of social development or not is a question that we cannot answer, but it is rather unimportant. Their presence among the very primitive aborigines of Australia indicates that they are compatible with an extremely low degree of cultural development, and hence may be very ancient.

In the case of division of labor along the lines of sex in production, and in the regulation of consumption in terms of age (and perhaps sex) classes, we have examples of the socialization of production and consumption along tribal and class lines. It is within the realm of kinship relations, however, that we find the social regulation of these processes exerting its greatest influence in tribal society. And this regulation pertains to consumption to a greater degree, as a rule, than to production. The mode of production is determined to a considerable extent by the technological processes with which production is carried on, i.e., by such instruments as digging stick or plow, potter's wheel, forge, loom, etc. But the specific manner of distribution is determined by social considerations; and apart from a few class factors just noted, these are expressed by rules and regulations of the kinship system. In families and in local groups, both being bodies of kindred, the rules and patterns of kinship behavior determined how food was to be distributed. A man or woman was obliged to share food obtained through his or her efforts with certain categories of relatives. Proportions or quantities were governed also by customs of kinship, as we have already seen in the case of the Kurnai of Australia, cited in Chapter 6, "Kinship" (see pp. 119–120).

To be sure, we do not find among all primitive peoples such a neat set of detailed and specific rules of distribution as the Kurnai possessed. But there is no difference in principle: food is to be shared by relatives, and the distribution is regulated by custom. The essence of the economic system of the earliest stage of cultural evolution was, then, the production, distribution, and consumption of goods carried on primarily in terms of kinship systems, in terms of specific duties, privileges, and obligations between relatives, and secondarily, by rules of tribal organization which regulated such things as division of labor and consumption in terms of sex and age classes. We might say, therefore, that the economic system was virtually identical with the social system in general and the kinship system in particular.

Throughout the whole era of primitive society, i.e., from the origin of culture until the disintegration of society founded upon kinship ties and the beginning of civil society based upon property relationships, the principle of economic organization that we have just described prevailed. Development of this system consisted merely of the extension of reciprocity and mutual aid and the elaboration of social and economic structure. But no new element was introduced. Throughout primitive society, the processes of production, exchange, and consumption within societies were carried on primarily in terms of the kinship system and secondarily in terms of tribal classes.

Let us return briefly at this point to the question of contexts. When, earlier, we presented the Kurnai custom of dividing food among relatives (p. 120), we remarked that the custom was probably as significant as a means of fostering solidarity as it was in the economic context of subsistence. How, then, are we to regard the distributions and sharings of goods that are identified, in primitive society, with the kinship system? Are they to be regarded as economic institutions or as means of fostering social solidarity? The answer is: both. A Chinese vase may be an object of art, or a scientific specimen, *and* an article of commerce. There is a tendency toward economy and efficiency in the organization and operation of sociocultural systems; these characteristics have a biological survival value. One institution may, therefore, have more than one function and serve more than one end. We have already noted the great diversity of use to which human social evolution has put the union between the sexes in marriage. Customary division of labor between the sexes tends to promote economy and efficiency in the performance of certain occupations, and it also fosters solidarity by making each sex dependent upon the other.

And so it is with kinship-economic systems among primitive peoples: they foster solidarity, on the one hand, and serve economic ends, on the other. In the very earliest stages of cultural evolution, when technologies were crude and meager and the struggle for existence was intense, the economic significance of the kinship-economic system may have been uppermost, whereas in later and more highly developed cultures, with more effective technologies and a greater security of life, the solidarity function may have been of greater significance. But so much depends upon particular situations and circumstances that broad generalizations can mean but little. And in any event, even in the highest of primitive cultures organized upon the basis of kinship, the economic significance of mutual sharing along kinship lines was never lost. The truth of this statement is made evident by the occasional occurrence of crises: in times of want the sharing of food and other goods served as a means of social insurance, of social security. "The law of hospitality, as administered by the American aborigines," observed Morgan, "tended to the final equalization of subsistence. Hunger and destitution could not exist at one end of an Indian village ... while plenty prevailed elsewhere in the same village...." [10]

Having described the economic system of primitive culture in terms of the processes of production, exchange, and consumption, we turn now to another aspect, namely, property. By *property* we mean (1) something in nature that is capable of serving human needs and which has been incorporated into an economic system by a social device called *ownership;* (2) a thing taken from nature, the extraction or appropriation of which involves and requires human labor, and which thereafter functions in an economic context; or (3) human labor power, exercised or expressed in an economic context.

Ownership is a concept correlative or complementary to property: property is that which is owned; ownership is the tenure of property. By ownership we mean the incorporation of an item of property into an economic system in such a way as to permit someone, or ones, to use or consume it while at the same time denying this activity to others.

According to these definitions, deposits of coal, oil, and iron were not owned and did not become property until they were introduced into a system of human relationships that was economic. The atmosphere is not property, for the same reason. The "air" in radio communication and in aerial transportation may, however, become property. Land not held by any group of people is not property; no one owns it. The same observation will hold for bodies of water. A lake or river may be owned by a tribe or a nation. The high seas, however, are not so owned and are therefore not property.

Turning now to the third category of property, we mean by *human labor power* the capacity to do work, to expend energy to the end that a human-need-serving adjustment to the external world be made. "Human" in this connection means "cultural," dependent upon the use of symbols. Breathing is the appropriation of something from nature. It costs effort, and it serves a need. But property is not involved because the effort is not cultural; the process is biologic, not economic.

Property is a compound made up of two elements: a *thing* and *human*

[10] Lewis H. Morgan, *Houses and House-life of the American Aborigines,* 1881, p. 45.

labor, or *effort*. A thing is not property unless human effort is expended upon it; to take and to hold is, of course, in human society, an expenditure of human effort. Human effort is of no economic significance unless it is expended upon a thing. Thus property is made up of two things: $P = T \times L$, in which P is property, T the thing, and L labor, or effort. T and L imply each other and are inseparable in the context "property." We often overlook this, however, because of our tendency to think of property as consisting merely of things—of beads, axes, fields, lakes, perfumes, etc. But human labor power, too, may be called property as legitimately as things; it is an attribute of an organism that has been reared—fed, clothed, and housed—by an expenditure of human labor. Thus *a haircut* is human labor expended upon a thing. The barber owns his capacity to do work and sells it in the form of haircuts. A *service* is thus economically equatable with a thing.[11] Likewise, the industrial wage-worker sells his labor power in the labor market just as a farmer sells wheat or hogs in the commodity market.[12] We see, then, that human labor power is a form of property just as things are. A slave is both a thing and a form and magnitude of human labor power. He is a thing, as a horse or an engine is a thing. But it is because he is a source of energy that he is significant as a form of property. His master owns his ability to work, his labor power, just as he owns the horse or engine.

Let us turn now to the institutions of property found in primitive society. First of all, there is the land upon which the people live. This may be held in common by the tribe, or by subdivisions of the tribe such as local groups, clans, lineages, or households. Or a portion might be held in common, with the rest divided among units of the tribe. The word "held" is more appropriate here than "own" because the relationship between a tribal subdivision, such as a clan, and a piece of land that "belongs" to it is a right to use, to exploit, the land rather than ownership in our sense of the term. If the group ceases to use the land, it reverts to the public domain. There is no such thing as "absentee ownership" in primitive society. In line with this custom is the further fact that land is inalienable in primitive society; it cannot be bought or sold. The situation with regard to land and natural resources in primitive society may be summarized somewhat as follows: Land is owned by the tribe in the strict sense of this term; i.e., it is held and exploited to the exclusion of other tribes. Within the tribe, however, subdivisions

[11] We may not be accustomed to think of a haircut as a thing, or as equivalent to a thing. A pottery bowl, we say, is a thing; but it is merely the expenditure of human labor upon clay, just as a haircut is an expenditure of human labor upon hair. The two situations are exactly alike in this respect.

[12] The Ph.D. also sells his labor power in the market—unless he has independent means. The journal *Science* used to have a page of job advertisements which it called "The Market Place."

may have the exclusive right to use certain tracts of land or to exploit certain of its resources. That this is merely a right to use or exploit is indicated by two facts: the absence of buying and selling and the reversion to public domain upon lapse of use.

But whatever the particular customs of tenure or ownership may be, one fact stands out in bold relief in primitive societies based upon kinship: *everyone has free access to the resources of nature.* This is one of the most important and fundamental generalizations that can be made about primitive society as compared—or contrasted—with civil society. It is basic because the political character of a society, i.e., whether it is democratic, feudalistic, or communistic, is determined by the way in which man's relations to the resources of nature are socially organized. Let us see what this generalization means.

It means that in primitive society no class is obliged to submit to the dictates or terms of another class as a condition of exploiting the resources of nature. No institution stands between anyone or any class and the right to appropriate things from nature to satisfy their needs. No class is enabled to live by the labor of another. To live by the labor of others, a class, or group of classes, must have complete and exclusive property rights to the available resources of nature, i.e., rights which do exclude others from exploiting these resources for their own benefit. In primitive society we find exclusive rights to the use of certain natural resources, but these rights merely exclude one group from the resources held by another; they do not exclude the other group from nature itself. In civil society, by contrast, a certain class or classes own all the natural resources, or enough of them so that the nonowning class or classes can live only by working the resources of the owners, in the course of which the owners receive a portion of the product. In primitive society the right to use or exploit may be private and exclusive, but ownership is public, tribal, and inclusive; i.e., *everyone* has access to natural resources and the right to exploit them. In civil society, on the other hand, ownership is private and exclusive; i.e., nature's resources are not open to all members or classes of society but are held by some to the exclusion of others. Here, the only way in which the nonowning class can live is by working resources of the owning class and upon terms laid down by them. Thus we find that the basic property institutions in primitive society make for equality, equality of privilege and opportunity, and equality of obligation to labor and to support one's self. This means freedom, too, of course, since equality precludes the possibility of the rule or exploitation of one class by another. The fundamental property institution of civil society, however, is just the opposite. It makes for inequality, inequality of opportunity, and inequality of obligation. One class owns but does not work; another class works but does not own.

Freedom, consequently, exists only for the owning class, which is, of course, always a minority. Thus we see that the political character of society rests upon a basis of institutions of property and is determined by them.

We turn now to objects which have been appropriated from nature and made available for the service of human needs by means of human labor. Here we may distinguish between things to be consumed directly and things used as a means of further production, such as a hoe, fish net, or harness. Among things to be consumed directly we may distinguish those whose consumption is instantaneous, so to speak, such as food, drink, and cosmetics, and those consumed gradually, such as houses, clothing, masks, canoes, or beads. Here again we find great diversity. On the one hand, there are numerous classes of objects ranging from breechclouts to pyramids, and on the other, a great variety of customs of ownership. However, a number of generalizations may be made.

It may be said that in primitive society in general a person owns his own clothing and ornaments, tools and weapons. By *own*, as we specified at the outset of this discussion, we mean a system of social relationships which admits some and excludes others to the use or enjoyment of an object. When it is said, therefore, that a man owns a breechclout, it is meant that he has a right to wear it, whereas another does not. But here, as at other points in a discussion of property and ownership, we find that concepts taken from our economic system are not always applicable to customs of primitive society. Thus, a man might own something in a primitive community, but custom might oblige him to lend it to someone upon request. What meaning then can be attached to the term own? In some societies a person feels free not only to *borrow* (again a word from our culture) an article but to keep it. The theory is that if a man can afford to *lend* it he does not need it, and hence there is no point in returning it. There is so much borrowing and giving, through hospitality, friendship, kinship, etc., of personal property in primitive society that here again ownership borders upon the communal.

Among the Nama Hottentots, a well is said to belong to the man who dug it, but he may not refuse others permission to use it. Fishing sites among the Tolowa-Tututni are said to be "privately owned," but "ordinarily these were used freely by any person within the village group." [13] The winter house among the Polar Eskimo belongs to a family only while they are living in it. When they leave it in summer it becomes free to anyone who claims it in the fall. Here again we find that *our*

[13] Cora Du Bois, "The Wealth Concept as an Integrative Factor in Tolowa-Tututni Culture," *Essays in Anthropology: Presented to A. L. Kroeber*, Berkeley, Calif., 1936, p. 50.

concept of ownership is hardly applicable. It is not ownership, but right to use, that is significant.

In the use and consumption of goods, therefore, as in their production, we find in preliterate cultures a powerful and universal trend toward communism, toward mutual sharing. This is, of course, precisely what one would expect from what is known about the social system in general and the kinship system in particular. In a social system in which reciprocal and correlative duties and privileges prevail, in a society based upon the principle of mutual aid as a way of making life more secure, cooperation and communism in the production and consumption of goods would naturally follow.

The fact that in certain primitive societies wealth is employed as a means of achieving or maintaining social distinction does not alter what we have said above. In the Northwest Coast great rivalries were carried on in terms of wealth. But they were carried on by kinship groups, the members of which participate in terms of kinship rather than economics. Wealth is employed to humiliate or to vanquish a rival. But in so doing it is consumed, destroyed, or given away, so that the victor may emerge from the contest virtually propertyless. Everyone in this region has free access to the resources of nature, and wealth is not used to subjugate or to exploit, in an economic manner, any class or individual. There are similar rivalries elsewhere. In parts of Melanesia great quantities of yams are grown, only to let them rot after they have served to enhance their owner's social standing.

There are situations just the opposite of this in many primitive societies. A person may win social distinction by giving away all he has. In both instances, however, we have a social game in which the stakes are social distinction, the counters with which one plays are articles of property. But nowhere in the acquisition of wealth or in its destruction or giving away is there anything that would invalidate the general propositions we have set forth so far.

In some tribes headmen, or chiefs, make levies upon the common people for food or other goods. But in most cases, this is not a form of private property or of exploitation, but a public, communal transaction. The headman performs public, tribal functions, in the form of political, military, or ceremonial services. The contributions made to him support and sustain such services. Usually, too, the chief is required by custom to give a great feast at which the food is consumed for the most part by those who contributed it.

We might summarize our discussion of property among primitive peoples by saying that in general natural resources are collectively owned though often privately exploited by some group, almost never by an individual. There is so much sharing of food and other basic forms of wealth as to amount almost to communism.[14] Personal property is individually owned, but again the claims of relatives, the laws of hospitality and friendship, make ownership here, too, border on the communal. Communism and mutual aid in ownership, production, and consumption are the characteristics of economic systems of primitive society.

Since the conception of primitive society organized upon the basis of kinship that we have presented has been vigorously opposed by certain anthropologists, it might be well to consider some of the issues involved.

Herskovits has asserted flatly that "it has become a truism that there is no generic difference between primitive societies and literate ones."[15] Lowie, too, has insisted that civilized societies differ from primitive societies in degree only; there is, he argues, no fundamental difference between them.[16]

One of the chief targets of the opponents of cultural evolutionism was "primitive communism." We have already noted that the economic system of societies based upon kinship might fairly be called communistic and that Morgan used this term in describing their social life. But the antievolutionists almost never make clear and explicit what they are opposing when they attack "primitive communism," nor do they quote or cite any evolutionist who espoused such a theory.

Apparently the opponents of the theory of primitive communism took this theory to mean "no private property at all; everything was held in common in primitive society." None of the leaders of evolutionist theory ever held such a view, however. Morgan recognized clan, family, and individual rights to land. "A person might transfer or donate his rights to other persons," he writes, and one could bequeath these rights "to his gentile kin.... Personal property, generally, was subject to individual ownership."[17] Tylor observed that primitive peoples draw "the same distinction which our lawyers make between real and personal property";

---

[14] Cf. Morgan, *op. cit.*, for description of "communism in living" among the North American Indians: chap. 2, The Law of Hospitality; chap. 3, Communism in Living; chap. 4, Usages and Customs with Respect to Land and Food. See also Ruth Bunzel, "Economic and Social Life of the Zuni Indians," in *Introduction to Zuni Ceremonialism*, 47th Annual Report, Bureau of American Ethnology, Washington, 1932, pp. 474–480. Her characterization is very much like that of Morgan despite the fact that she was an adherent of the Boas school, which opposed most of Morgan's theories and conclusions.

[15] Melville J. Herskovits, *The Economic Life of Primitive Peoples*, Alfred A. Knopf, Inc., New York, 1940, p. 4; see also pp. 447–448.

[16] Robert H. Lowie, *The Origin of the State*, 1927.

[17] Morgan, *op. cit.*, p. 79, and *Ancient Society*, 1877, pp. 541–542.

that they recognized "private property" in game "when struck"; that they held land by clan and family; and that they recognized "personal or individual property." [18]

Thus we find clear and explicit recognition of individual personal-property rights in the works of the two chief exponents of cultural evolutionism. But so menacing did the theory of primitive communism become,[19] apparently, that members of three anthropological "schools" have felt called upon to scotch it. Lowie, of the Boas school, has attacked it repeatedly.[20] Malinowski, a leader of the Functionalist school, branded it "perhaps the most misleading fallacy there is in social anthropology." [21] Sylvester A. Sieber, S.J., and Franz H. Mueller, M.C.S., clerical followers of the Catholic (Culture Historical) school of anthropology led by Father Wilhelm Schmidt and Father Wilhelm Koppers, make it perfectly clear that in opposing the theory of primitive communism they are trying to undermine the socialist doctrines of Marx, Engels, Bebel, and others.[22] Lowie has been commended by Catholic scholars for his criticism of the theory of primitive communism, and through this, his opposition to socialist doctrines.[23] And Linton, an independent, branded the theory of primitive communism a "long-established myth." [24] It would appear that an effort was being made to "make the world safe for private property."

Opponents of primitive communism were not content to demonstrate the existence of genuine private property in primitive society. They went further and invented a spurious concept: *incorporeal property* which is privately owned. By incorporeal property is meant such things as an insignia of rank, the exclusive right to sing a certain song, or owner-

[18] E. B. Tylor, *Anthropology*, 1881, pp. 419–420.

[19] Because, no doubt, Karl Marx "adopted" Morgan's *Ancient Society*, and it became a socialist classic.

It might be recalled, also, that the great proletarian uprising, the Paris Commune, took place in the same year that saw the publication of Morgan's *Systems of Consanguinity and Affinity* and Tylor's *Primitive Culture*: 1871. Seven years later Pope Leo XIII issued his encyclical *Quod Apostolici Muneris*, addressed to the rulers of Europe, on the subject of "the plague of socialism."

[20] R. H. Lowie, *Primitive Society*, 1947, pp. 205–206, 231; "Anthropology and Law," in *The Social Sciences and their Interrelations*, William F. Ogburn and Alexander Goldenweiser (eds.), 1927; and *Social Organization*, 1948, pp. 131, 134, 144, 146.

[21] B. Malinowski, introduction to H. Ian Hogbin, *Law and Order in Polynesia*, Harcourt, Brace and Company, New York, 1934, p. xli. He flogs "primitive communism" unmercifully in his address at the Harvard Tercentenary Celebration, "Anthropology as the Basis of Social Science," 1936.

[22] Sylvester A. Sieber, S.J., and Franz H. Mueller, M.C.S., *The Social Life of Primitive Man*, 1941, pp. 362–363.

[23] See, for example, Joseph Husslein, S.J., Ph.D., *The Christian Social Manifesto*, 1931, pp. 65–66.

[24] Ralph Linton, in an advertisement of M. J. Herskovits's *The Economic Life of Primitive Peoples*, Alfred A. Knopf, Inc., New York, 1940.

ship of a dream or a magical spell. Lowie has developed the thesis of incorporeal property to a greater extent than anyone else, having contributed a special article on it as well as discussing it in his books.[25] But Boas and others have subscribed to this thesis also.[26] Lowie is not content with listing such things as the right of a certain individual to "limp and howl in a ceremony" as private property; [27] he includes also tribal political functions assigned to certain clans among various tribes in the category of "incorporeal property." [28]

In some instances, items of incorporeal property are hereditary, or are an integral part of the social structure of the tribe, such as the function of the Thunderbird clan among the Winnebago to make peace. In other instances incorporeal property may be "sold." These transactions are often discussed under the heading of "economics," just as the objects, rights, etc., are called "property." A little reflection and analysis, however, will show that both of these usages are unwarranted, or at best confusing and misleading. To call a magical formula obtained in a dream property is to confuse it with such things as an ax made from a piece of flint dug from a quarry, a canoe carved from a tree trunk, or a piece of buckskin. The two are radically different kinds of things: in the one case value derives from inherent properties of things in the external world plus an expenditure of human labor; in the other, value is of sociopsychological origin. To apply the term property to such diverse things as "the right to limp and howl in a ceremony" and to a stone ax is to breed confusion. One might as well call the right to wear the Purple Heart, or the right to write LL.D. after one's name, *property*. There are other rights than those of property; there are values that are not economic.

Lowie cites a case, known to him personally, of a Crow Indian who "bought" the right to use a special ceremonial paint from his own mother.[29] What can be the meaning of "bought" in such a transaction

[25] R. H. Lowie, "Incorporeal Property in Primitive Society," *Yale Law Journal*, vol. 37, pp. 551–563, 1928; *Primitive Society*, 1947, pp. 235–243; *Social Organization*, 1948, pp. 131–134; *Introduction to Cultural Anthropology*, 1940, pp. 281–282.

[26] F. Boas, "Anthropology," in *Encyclopaedia of the Social Sciences*, vol. 2, 1930, p. 83; Alexander Goldenweiser, *Early Civilization*, 1922, p. 137; Herskovits, *op. cit.*, pp. 348–350; Ruth Benedict, *Patterns of Culture*, 1934, p. 183; Ruth Bunzel, "The Economic Organization of Primitive Peoples," in *General Anthropology*, F. Boas (ed.), p. 358; E. Adamson Hoebel, *Man in the Primitive World*, 1949, pp. 344–345; and Raymond Firth, a British social anthropologist, alludes to it in "Property, Primitive," in *Encyclopaedia Britannica*, 14th ed., 1929.

[27] R. H. Lowie, *Primitive Society*, Liveright Publishing Corporation, Black and Gold Library, New York, 1947, p. 237.

[28] R. H. Lowie, *Social Organization*, Rinehart & Company, Inc., New York, 1948, p. 131.

[29] Lowie, *Primitive Society*, 1947, p. 239.

in a society where people are not only obliged by mores and custom to help and feed their own close relatives, but to be lavish in their generosity with visitors and guests? "A man is expected to give meat to any one who comes up as he is butchering a slain animal," says Murdock, in a summary description of Crow culture.[30] "Visitors are hospitably received ... and served immediately with ... food, no matter what time of day. Guests may take home with them any food that remains, and sometimes even ask for containers in which to carry it away." And yet a man must "buy" a ceremonial paint from his own mother!

Is it not rather plain that we are dealing here with two quite different kinds of situations? The production and distribution of food is an economic process; the "purchase" of "ceremonial paint" is a ritual, a symbolic process. In the one case, we are dealing with intrinsic values: the nutritive properties of the food. In the other, we are faced with make-believe values. According to the beliefs which attend the use and transfer of ceremonial paint among the Crow, the paint must be paid for if the whole transaction is to be effective and beneficial. The "payment" is a ritual way of validating the process of transfer. To call the right to use the paint "property" and its ritual transfer "purchase and sale" is effectively to confuse two fundamentally different categories of things and to make any sort of intelligent understanding of either impossible.[31]

The thesis that primitive society is fundamentally like civil society, differing in degree only, is expressed and supported by discussions of the use of *money* by primitive peoples.[32] This is unfortunate, since in most instances *primitive money* functions in contexts radically different from the financial and commercial contexts of our own culture. In a few preliterate societies, notably those subjected to the influence of higher cultures having genuine money, mediums of exchange are indeed used in commercial transactions. But for the most part, primitive money is not employed in economic contexts at all, but in a game of social intercourse in which social values—status, prestige—are transferred or vali-

[30] G. P. Murdock, *Our Primitive Contemporaries,* The Macmillan Company, New York, 1934, p. 276.

[31] Goldenweiser recognizes this fact, although he speaks of "immaterial property" along with others. In describing the Indians of the Northwest Coast, he says: "They talk property, live property, manipulate property, as lustily as any group of modern business men. *What property means to them is, nevertheless, something entirely different from what it means to us* [italics supplied]." Alexander Goldenweiser, *Anthropology,* Appleton-Century-Crofts, Inc., New York, 1937, p. 153.

[32] Benedict speaks of "currency of a complex monetary system" among the Indians of the Northwest Coast. *Patterns of Culture,* Houghton Mifflin Company, Boston, 1934, p. 184. Bunzel does likewise in "The Economic Organization of Primitive Peoples," p. 358. Hoebel calls the dentalium of California tribes, wampum beads of eastern North America, and even the "huge limestone wheels of Yap," "money." *Op. cit.,* p. 352.

dated by such means. The distinction between these two contexts, the economic and commercial, on the one hand, and the social, on the other, is drawn sharply by Du Bois in her analysis of the culture of the Tolowa-Tututni of California.[33] She distinguishes two "economies": a "subsistence economy" and a "prestige economy." By the former, she means "the exploitation of ... natural resources"; by the latter "is meant a series of social prerogatives and status values. They included a large range of phenomena from wives to formulae for supernatural compulsion ... mourners' privileges and innumerable personal dignities...." These two contexts are quite distinct, says Du Bois, and money functions in the context of social ritual rather than in matters of subsistence. Natural resources were plentiful and easily exploited. Food "was shared by the provident with the improvident within the village group. A successful hunter was expected to be liberal with his kinsmen.... The favorable environment made ... barter a minor activity"; and dentalia, or other forms of money, played virtually no part in it. But, in their prestige economy, they were definitely "money-minded": "they haggled and drove a hard bargain.... Money was serviceable in the purchase of social protection and prestige ... in maintaining familial status, but it entered hardly at all into the subsistence equation." In short, as Du Bois aptly summarizes: "Subsistence economy is divorced from prestige, and money operates in the latter realm."

We thus see that money in this culture is not money at all in our sense of the term; it is not a medium of exchange in commercial, i.e., economic, transactions, but an instrument employed in a social ritual,[34] a set of counters in a game of symbolic and psychologic values. It is unfortunate that the terms *money, economy,* and *purchase* are used to describe such definitely noneconomic, noncommercial, and nonfinancial culture processes.[35]

The thesis that the economic systems of primitive society are fundamentally like our own, differing only in degree, has been expressed or implied at other points also. Boas tells us that "the economic system of the Indians of British Columbia is largely based on credit, just as much as that of civilized communities."[36] Herskovits discusses wages, interest, and capital among primitive peoples.[37] Firth speaks of "a kind

[33] Du Bois, *op. cit.*, pp. 50–51.

[34] Bunzel observes that a kind of money used on Rossel Island was "used only in certain ceremonial exchanges...." "The Economic Organization of Primitive Peoples," p. 399.

[35] Cf. Firth, *op. cit.*, who distinguishes nicely between genuine and pseudo money.

[36] F. Boas, "The North-western Tribes of British Columbia," *Report of the Sixty-eighth Meeting of the British Association for the Advancement of Science*, London, 1899, p. 681.

[37] Herskovits, *op. cit.*

of capitalist enterprise" among the Maori.[38] Radin refers to the Indians of the Northwest Coast as "the Capitalists of the North."[39] But perhaps we have said enough in our previous discussions of incorporeal property and money to show how inappropriate these concepts and terms are to a description of tribal societies based upon kinship.

There are two basic types of economic system. In the one, property relations are subordinated to human relations; in the other, the opposite is the case. *Within* primitive societies, the economic system subordinates property relations to human relations, to human welfare. *Between* tribes, however, commercial relations obtained.

The economic system of primitive peoples is identified largely with the kinship system and is therefore characterized by cooperation, mutual aid, and sharing. The widespread custom of exchanging goods promotes solidarity. But it is also a means of sharing food and other goods in times of scarcity; it is a system of social security.

Private and personal property are institutions of primitive society as they are of our own, but use is emphasized rather than ownership in the sense in which the latter term is used in our culture. But the private ownership of natural resources or of means of production is never extensive enough in primitive society to exclude any class or any individual from the resources of nature: it is a fundamental fact of primitive society that everyone has free access to the resources of nature. This is the basis of the freedom and equality of tribal societies.

[38] Raymond Firth, *Primitive Economics of the New Zealand Maori*, E. P. Dutton & Co., Inc., New York, 1929, p. 82.

[39] This is the title of chap. 14 in Paul Radin, *The Story of the American Indian*, 1927.

Chapter 10 PHILOSOPHY: MYTH AND LORE

In our first chapter we distinguished technological, sociological, and ideological components of cultural systems. We have traced the course of cultural development from the standpoint of technology and of social organization. It is time now to turn our attention to ideologies.

The world of man consists of himself and of an external world in which he lives. Experience consists of the interaction of a living organism with the external world (which includes, of course, other organisms), on the one hand, and on the other of interaction of the component parts of the organism itself with one another. We thus distinguish extra- and intraorganismal aspects of experience. In the human species, experience is translated into concepts, and these concepts are expressed in symbol-word form. I have sensory experience of an object in the external world and translate and express this experience in concepts such as *red* or *hot*. Or I translate and express intraorganismal experience in concepts such as *tired* or *hungry*. Experience is expressed in the form of propositions, declarative statements that say something about something: grass is green, fire is hot, I am hungry. These propositions are the components, the units, of ideologies. For want of a better term we may call them *beliefs*.

In the human species great areas of experience, both intra- and extraorganismal, are translated into beliefs. We may distinguish two kinds of beliefs: the *is* kind and the *ought* or *should* kind. Fire is hot; ice melts. Adults should be kind to children; kids should not be seethed in their mothers' milk. We need a name for the sum and total of beliefs that any people has, and we shall use the term *philosophy* for this purpose.

There are two, and only two, major types of philosophy: (1) naturalistic and (2) supernaturalistic. All philosophies are the product of the interaction of two factors, the self and the external world. Things and events may be described or explained in terms of *themselves*, or they may be explained in terms of the self, the ego that is doing the explaining. Thus a shower of rain can be accounted for in terms of meteorological factors such as temperature, humidity, barometric pressure, air currents, etc.; i.e., it rains when these factors interact with one another, or are in conjunction with one another, in certain ways. This is a naturalistic interpretation of a shower. But one can account for rainfall by postulating a spiritual being who has control over precipitation and is, for one reason or another, disposed to shower the earth. This is the supernaturalistic type of interpretation. It consists of projecting the ego, the psychological processes of self, into the external world without being aware of this projection. The rain gods, witches, and devils of ideologies are merely the psyches of man projected into the external world without his knowledge or understanding of this fact, so that he believes they have an existence in the external world independently of himself. Supernaturalistic philosophies are the result of a failure to distinguish between the self and the not-self; naturalistic philosophies make this distinction.

Philosophy had its beginning in the origin of man and culture. It has evolved and become diversified as an integral part of cultural systems.

The philosophies of primitive peoples are predominantly supernaturalistic in character; they consist, for the most part, of myths. Primitive peoples possess a great deal of naturalistic, matter-of-fact knowledge, but such knowledge tends to exist and to function to a great extent on sublinguistic levels. Considerable genuine knowledge is required to make a chipped-flint ax or a bow. But there is little need to express this knowledge verbally, on the one hand, and it is often difficult to express, or to communicate, such knowledge verbally. How, for example, could one person tell another how to swim? Knowledge in such matters is best communicated by example rather than by precept. To be sure, knowledge about the properties of plants, minerals, and so on, may be communicated as lore from one generation to another. But even here, such knowledge is not usually formalized and made explicit as mythological knowledge is. Thus, while we recognize a significant naturalistic component in the philosophies of primitive peoples, their over-all complexion appears to be predominantly supernaturalistic—mythologic—in character.

The world of primitive man is divided chronologically into two parts: (1) the remote past and (2) the present and recent past. The former era is wholly mythological in character according to primitive peoples' conception; in it took place the great events of the origin, or formation, of the earth and the beginnings of man and his culture. It was an era of wonder working by supernatural beings. The present is a much more prosaic era. It contains gods and supernatural forces, to be sure, but they function according to fairly well established rules. It is the world we live in today where water runs downhill, fire consumes straw, the seasons follow each other in turn, and all men eventually die. The present recedes into the past until the limits of tribal memories are reached; then one enters the world of the mythical past, the Alcheringa era, as the Arunta of Australia call it. Legend reaches into the past as far as it can, but this is not far; and beyond this lies the land of myth.

In our culture today, philosophy—especially with a capital P—tends to be regarded as "something that one studies at college," as something that stands apart from everyday life. But in the lives of primitive peoples, philosophy is an integral part of their way of life, intimately related to everything they do. And, of course, the layman in our society today has a "philosophy of life." Philosophy has a number of functions in primitive culture; i.e., it does various things in sociocultural systems.

One of the functions of philosophies, primitive as well as modern, is to provide a means of adjustment to and control over the external world; i.e., it provides us with knowledge and tells us how to use it. This knowledge is of two kinds, as we have already noted, naturalistic and supernaturalistic. In primitive cultures the genuine knowledge functions largely on sublinguistic levels and to that extent is not a part of the tradition that we call philosophy. The use of philosophy among primitive peoples as a means of adjustment and control with reference to the external world is therefore primarily mythologic in character.

The myths of primitive man tell him everything he needs to know; they provide him with answers to all the fundamental questions of life and being. They describe the cosmos and tell how it was formed. The earth and all its inhabitants are likewise accounted for. The origin of man and the establishment of languages and customs are set forth in some detail; the acquisition of fire is frequently chronicled, and sometimes the origin of death is noted. The relationship between man and the spirit world is defined, and rules for man's conduct prescribed. From mythology man learns how to control the weather, cope with disease, overcome his enemies, and how to dispatch the dead on their journey to the afterlife. In some cultures one even learns from myths how to change the course of the sun across the heavens.

Myths of adjustment and control find expression through ritual and the use of paraphernalia. Magic becomes a pseudotechnology in medicine, hunting, warfare, weather control, and horticulture. Thanks to myth and ritual, primitive man becomes both omniscient and omnipotent—but only in make-believe.

Philosophy is an important means of serving man's psychic needs. We have already touched upon this in Chapter 1, "Man and Culture." Man needs courage in order to face the hazards and uncertainties of life. He needs to feel that he is of some significance, that somehow he counts in the cosmic scheme of things. He needs some assurance of success. And he requires consolation when he fails or when disaster overtakes him. Philosophies, in the form of mythologies or theologies, perform these services for man; they envelop him and hold him securely in a firm embrace.

The myths of primitive man serve to entertain him as literature does us. The stirring accounts of incidents in the mythical past, when gods performed their feats of wonder and interceded directly in the affairs of men, serve to entertain and beguile primitive man as well as to explain the world to him. Indeed, one of the principal functions of mythology is to entertain men in meager cultures on long winter evenings.

Philosophy is not merely, or even primarily, a conceptual process, as many people in our culture are inclined to believe. It is a *social* process as well, and a very important one it is. The verbal tradition that we call philosophy equips each growing child within its embrace with a uniform [1] set of beliefs, of ideas and ideals. It thus makes for uniformity of behavior, which is essential to coherent social organization and the effective conduct of group life. A philosophy not only provides people with information needed for action; it stimulates them to action, inspires them, and defines the goals for which they shall strive. A philosophy is therefore an important means of social integration. It is, so to speak, the peculiarly human connective tissue of society; it is something that anthropoids and all other lower species lack. And it is a means of stimulating people to action and of guiding their efforts toward philosophically defined objectives.

The sociological function of philosophy is clearly revealed in the process of educating the young. Growing children must be equipped with knowledge, or beliefs. They must be told what sort of a world this is and also how they should behave toward it. Some of this knowledge and belief is transmitted casually in the form of lore about items of habitat: plants, animals, earth materials, and so on. But in matters of greatest importance it is mythology that provides the information and the ideals. The boy or girl becomes acquainted with the gods; he learns their idiosyncrasies and how to communicate with them. Ideals of conduct are held up to them in myths: a certain course of action always brings retribution or disaster; another course spells success and reward. In Keresan mythology the ideal girl is always pictured toiling at her grinding bins, early in the morning; ideals appropriate to the young man are presented in sharp relief, also. Philosophy works for *morality*, in primitive society, as well as for social organization and solidarity.

Mythology is but the verbal component of a great complex that in-

[1] This uniformity is achieved, on the one hand, by the requirements of internal consistency which every philosophy must have and, on the other, by the social imperatives which demand uniformity as a basis for concerted action.

cludes ceremony, ritual, and paraphernalia as well. Rituals are ways of putting mythological knowledge into practice in curing disease, bringing rain, or raising corn. Great ceremonies are often dramatizations of episodes in the mythology, and as such they may have a profound effect upon the young: they communicate information to them and impress upon them the tribe's ideals and values. And for the mature, these ceremonies reanimate and reaffirm the tribal values. Ceremonies are means of promoting solidarity; all their participants are united and bound together by spiritual bonds as well as by social action. The sacred items of paraphernalia employed in ceremonies and rituals are visible, tangible expressions of belief and of spiritual value, and as such they are convincing. They stimulate emotion, reaffirm values, and unite individuals in a common sentiment. Ceremonies and their paraphernalia prove, in terms of primitive logic, the propositions expressed in the myths: the dramatizations of myths in dance, pantomime, costume, song, and paraphernalia can leave no doubt in anyone's mind of their genuineness and validity. No child who has ever witnessed the great Shalako ceremonies of the Zuñi Indians or the totemic ceremonies of the Arunta under aboriginal conditions can have failed to be impressed for life.

And, added to all this, the ceremonies are sources of entertainment and of aesthetic satisfaction. The beauty of the songs, the dramatic effect of the costumes and paraphernalia feed and nourish the aesthetic hunger of the people.

Philosophy, in primitive culture, is not merely belief; it is a way of life.

Nonmythologic knowledge and belief. Although the naturalistic, genuine knowledge—as distinguished from the pseudo knowledge of mythology—of primitive peoples is often not verbalized, or only slightly so, and consequently does not constitute a conspicuous part of the intellectual tradition, no account of the philosophies of primitive culture should ignore this important element.

We might define knowledge as an acquired ability to behave appropriately in a given situation. This definition would embrace the behavior of subhuman species, but it would rule out instinctive behavior. In this sense, apes have knowledge. And, as a matter of fact, they possess a rather considerable body of knowledge. They ascertain and appreciate the properties of all sorts of materials which they use in terms of these properties: sticks, stones, ropes, pigments for painting, tubes to blow through like trumpets, objects for ornaments, and so on. They learn how to use sticks as levers or to pole-vault with, stones as hammers, blankets as hammocks, and a host of other things.

Every living species, plant or animal, must be able to "behave appropriately in given situations" if it is to survive. This ability is either instinctive or learned, i.e., knowledge. Man, like all other species, must be able to behave appropriately to situations, and lacking instincts, he must provide himself with knowledge. Being endowed with the ability to symbol and equipped with language, he can accumulate knowledge almost indefinitely: his sensory experience is translated into concepts and is stored up in his verbal tradition. And it can be transmitted easily from one individual, one generation, or one people, to another.

Mythologic knowledge, by the very nature of mythology, cannot be tested by experience. The processes that create kachinas (i.e., semi-anthropomorphic spirits who bring rain to the Pueblo Indians) effectively prevent the testing of this concept by experience.[2] But the knowledge that is inherent in the effective exploitation of the resources of the earth to provide food, materials for clothing, tools, weapons, and ornaments *is* testable, as of course it must be; its very acquisition and use provide the test.

During the course of cultural evolution up to the Agricultural Revolution a very considerable amount of genuine, matter-of-fact knowledge was acquired and accumulated. Some of this knowledge was very widespread, much of it was locally restricted, depending upon the uniformity or diversity of local circumstances of habitat. The totality of these local knowledges is impressive and forms the foundation for the naturalistic philosophies of more advanced cultures and for the science of our culture. It will be interesting and instructive to pass in review these traditions of genuine knowledge in primitive cultures.

Primitive peoples knew their habitats intimately. They knew what useful resources it contained, where red ocher, clay, or flint might be found. They knew the distribution of flora and fauna and which species were useful or edible and which were useless or injurious. They knew the habits of local birds, animals, fish, and insects and how to take them for food and other uses. Eskimos were able to make topographic sketches of the territory within which they lived and traveled so accurately that they could be used to good advantage by arctic explorers.

Preliterate peoples possessed knowledge concerning the heavenly bodies and temporal and seasonal sequences. Constellations of stars were distinguished and named. Polaris was spotted, and the movements of planets followed. Even such a primitive tribe as the Ona of Tierra del Fuego

---

[2] This is not to say that the mind in primitive culture is impervious to evidence. It is not. But the "evidence" may well support the conceptions of mythology. It frequently *does* rain after a rain ceremony; patients of medicine men do recover in many instances. Thus we have evidence, and it may be convincing. But it does not provide an adequate *test*.

distinguished Sirius, Procyon, and Betelgeuse. Morning and evening stars received particular attention. They knew that there are twelve to thirteen lunations in a complete solar cycle; these "moons" were frequently named according to the time of the year—"new-leaves moon," or "first-snow-flurries moon." Seasons were distinguished according to latitude. Among some tribes systematic observations were made upon the sun. The Pueblo Indians of the Southwest, for example, had a special priest to observe the risings of the sun in order to determine the times of the solstices.

Virtually all kinds of tools were invented and developed by primitive peoples, such as knives, axes, scrapers, hammers, awls, needles, and so on. Machines, i.e., mechanical devices composed of moving and inter-related parts, such as the bow drill and pump drill, were occasionally developed. Tubular drill bits and abrasives were used. In the field of weapons, spears, harpoons, clubs, shields, and armor were developed. The atlatl, or spear thrower, the blowgun, and the bow and arrow are particularly ingenious devices. Hammocks were invented and used by the Indians of the Amazon. All techniques for producing fire known to man prior to the invention of matches in the early nineteenth century were developed by primitive peoples: percussion (flint and iron pyrites), friction (the fire drill and fire saw), and compression (the fire piston). The fire piston is an especially ingenious device. Tinder is placed in the bottom of a cylinder and is ignited by being raised to the kindling temperature by air compression. The principle involved here was later incorporated in the Diesel engine, where fuel is ignited in the cylinder by compression rather than by an electric spark. Rubber was manufactured by the American Indians and used as balls in games in Meso-America and to make enema syringes in Amazonia.

A great many techniques involving considerable knowledge were developed by primitive peoples in one culture or another. The manufacture of good pottery, the proper admixture of tempering material with clay and the subsequent firing, requires a great deal of knowledge and skill. Similarly the art of making buckskin requires an extensive knowledge of materials and techniques. The textile arts—carding, spinning, twining, twilling, weaving—require knowledge, skill, and apparatus. Bark cloth, made from the inner bark of mulberry or fig trees, beaten to almost paper thinness with corrugated mallets, was made in Polynesia and west Africa. Felt was made by various peoples of central Asia. The nonsubmersible kayak and the sealskin float used to retard the escape of harpooned sea mammals among the Eskimos demonstrate an understanding of physical principles. The snowhouse in the same cultures is also a remarkable exhibition of realistic knowledge and understanding, not to mention the utilization of the thermos-bottle principle in some of these houses. Some Eskimo groups sewed caribou skins together and suspended them from the walls and ceilings of their snow-houses, separating the two by a few inches. A layer of non-heat-conducting air is thus interposed between the skins and the snow wall, which is of course an example of the principle utilized in thermos bottles in our culture. The Eskimos also made and used goggles, with narrow slits instead of lenses, to protect them from the glare of sunlight reflected from the snow. Outrigger canoes are ingenious contrivances which utilize a number of mechanical principles.

In the field of chemistry, primitive peoples by and large amassed a considerable store of knowledge of materials and processes. They knew how to make paints and pigments, some of which had a quality and durability that have never been surpassed. They discovered the use of mordants, substances for fixing colors. One of the most remarkable chemical processes on primitive cultural levels is to be found in north-eastern South America. There, some tribes have learned to remove a deadly poison, hydrocyanic acid, from a species of manioc, which then becomes a staple article of diet. They have done this by a complicated process of grinding, drying, and leaching, which incidentally uses a most ingenious mechanical basketry device known as a cassava squeezer. How these primitive Indians ever discovered that they could separate a deadly poison from a plant otherwise nutritious is something to wonder at.

A great many poisons were known and used on preliterate cultural levels. The primitive Semang, and other peoples of Southeast Asia, used the lethal sap of the upas tree (*Antiaris*) to tip darts and arrows. Curare, made from the sap of *Strychnos toxifera*, was widely used in north-eastern South America. It paralyzes the respiratory muscles, causing death but leaving the carcass quite edible. Some peoples tipped arrows with a mixture of snake venom and liver. Hemlock and the Calabar bean among other poisons were also used to kill members of one's own society.

Many plant materials have been used to kill or stupefy fish so that they might be easily taken for food. The active, or significant, ingredient of some of these plants is saponin, a soaplike material that smothers the fish. Tannic acid or an alkaloid of some kind is the active agent in others. The aborigines of Australia drugged pools with pituri, an alkaloid, in order to stupefy and catch emu.

Chemical knowledge of many primitive tribes is expressed in other ways also. Tribes of the Northwest Coast of America chewed tobacco with lime, made by burning shells. In the Andean region coca leaves, and in Melanesia and Southeast Asia betel nuts, were chewed with lime in order to produce an effect the nature of which is not too well understood. According to one authority, lime helps to liberate "the arecoline alkaloid from the areca [betel] nut." [3] Also, lime acts as a gastric sedative and is an antidote for mineral and oxalic poisoning.

The Indians of the Andean highlands prepared corn for the manufacture of beer (*chicha*) by chewing it in order to institute a chemical process by the action of saliva upon the grain. Starch must be transformed into sugar before it can be fermented. Saliva contains an enzyme called ptyalin, which breaks down starches, first to simple dextrins, then to maltose, a crystalline sugar. In Polynesia, the kava root was chewed, no doubt for a similar reason, in the preparation of kava, a slightly intoxicating drink.

Agriculture and animal husbandry are the achievements of preliterate peoples. No new plant or animal has been brought under domestication by modern civilized peoples. On the other hand, a number of useful plants, cultivated by primitive peoples, have been virtually ignored by modern civilization: *Chenopodium* (quinoa) and oca, for example. Primitive peoples discovered the most suitable plants to domesticate and cultivate and devised effective techniques for their cultivation. They developed and improved cultivated plants by selective breeding and learned to increase yields by fertilization and irrigation.

All the kinds of foods known to modern civilization—starches, sugars, fats or oils, proteins, "greens," etc.—were known and used on preliterate cultural levels. This does not mean, of course, that the diet of every tribe was varied and well balanced; it merely means that modern civilization uses no kind of food that was not known to some primitive tribe somewhere.

In the preparation and preservation of foods, too, primitive peoples acquired a vast amount of knowledge and skill. Stone boiling and earth ovens exemplify their ingenuity and resourcefulness. Foods were preserved in a variety of ways. In arctic regions they were frozen. In other regions certain foods—fruits, vegetables, and meats—were preserved by drying. Sometimes they were sealed up airtight with tallow. In short, preliterate peoples devised virtually all the techniques known to us today for preserving food except the tin can and the airtight glass jar.

Medical diagnosis and practice among primitive peoples were not wholly magical by any means. They took a rational view of many ailments and attempted to treat them realistically in matter-of-fact ways. In certain cultures, broken bones were set with splints, tourniquets were used, poultices and bandages employed. Steam baths were used and massage practiced by many peoples. Bloodletting was a widespread therapeutic practice, as it was in European culture until quite recent times.

[3] Louis Lewin, *Phantastica, Narcotic and Stimulating Drugs*, P. H. A. Wirth (trans.), E. P. Dutton & Co., Inc., New York, 1931, p. 242.

Some tribes of South America administered enemas, using a rubber syringe for this purpose. In surgery, the Melanesians and Peruvians developed great skill in cutting out broken bones of the skull to relieve pressure on the brain. "In this delicate operation known as 'trephining,'" says Lowie, "they were more successful than European physicians of the Eighteenth Century." [4] The Peruvian surgeons also amputated feet with success; pictures on pottery bowls show men with an artificial foot, taking part, however, in a ceremony or dance. Doctors among the Ganda are said to have been able "to cure men partially disembowelled from spear wounds by washing the protruding intestines, forcing them gently back into the abdomen, and keeping them in place with a piece of gourd." [5]

The human heads, shrunk by the Jivaro Indians, might be mentioned in this connection, also, since they involve knowledge and skill in anatomical surgery and mummification. The Jivaro remove the bones of the head and reduce it to the size of a fist, retaining at the same time the original facial features. They are preserved by smoking—and perhaps other techniques—and kept as trophies.

Many plant materials were used by primitive peoples in nonmagical, or only partially magical, contexts in the treatment of ailments of many kinds. It is now known that many plants used by aborigines for medicinal purposes such as cascara, sweet flag (*Acorus*), *Angelica*, seneca snakeroot, sassafras, licorice, eucalyptus, etc., do have therapeutic value. It is exceedingly difficult, however, to determine what effect certain medicinal plants will have on patients because of the complexity of the chemical content of the plants, on the one hand, and the personal idiosyncrasies of individuals, on the other. In the use of plants for medicinal purposes, however, primitive peoples have discovered and recognized many important drugs, such as tobacco, cocaine, quinine, ipecac, hashish, peyote, datura, and fly agaric.

The roster of beverages among preliterate peoples demonstrates a very considerable knowledge of the properties of materials and of techniques of preparation. Many peoples have brewed leaves of plants to make "teas." The Pueblo Indians made a tasty and nutritious drink of corn which had been soaked and allowed to sprout, then dried, parched, ground, and used as we would use coffee. Coffee is indigenous in Abyssinia, but the origin of coffee drinking is not definitely known. It appears to have been introduced to Western culture by the Arabs about the sixteenth century. Whether coffee drinking was invented by a pre-

[4] R. H. Lowie, *Introduction to Cultural Anthropology*, Rinehart & Company, Inc., New York, 1940, p. 335.

[5] G. P. Murdock, *Our Primitive Contemporaries*, The Macmillan Company, New York, 1934, p. 542.

literate people or not is unknown, but it is interesting to note, in this connection, that the Ganda of Uganda did not drink coffee, but carried the beans—boiled, dried, and sometimes roasted—on their persons for occasional chewing. The Aztecs drank chocolate, made from the cacao bean, flavored with vanilla, honey, or pepper. Some tribes drink milk, fresh or fermented, from mares as well as from cows.

The saps of various trees, e.g., maple and palm, are drunk, fresh or fermented. A great variety of "wines," made from sap or fruit juices, are drunk by many peoples. The Hottentots drank an alcoholic beverage made by diluting wild honey with water and adding certain roots to promote fermentation. The Ganda made a mildly intoxicating beer of ripe bananas and millet flour. The Aztecs drank pulque, an alcoholic beverage made from the sap of the agave. We have already spoken of the kava drink of Polynesia and the maize beer, or *chicha*, of Peru. About the only advance made by modern civilization in the art of making liquors is the distillation process.

In the realm of music, primitive peoples have much to their credit. They developed musical systems and styles and advanced the vocal art as far as part singing. Their musical systems were often exceedingly complicated rhythmically—much more so than our own—but were relatively simple harmonically. Virtually all kinds of musical instruments known to the modern world today were invented and developed by primitive peoples: stringed instruments of all kinds, which incidentally may have originated in the musical bow; percussion instruments—drums, clackers, rattles; wind instruments—flutes, trumpets, pan pipes (our great pipe organs today are simply pan pipes enormously magnified).

Primitive peoples have some noteworthy achievements to their credit in ocean travel and navigation. Prior to the voyages of Columbus, the most extensive overseas voyages, as distinguished from coastwise travel, were made by the Polynesians. It is 2,500 miles from Rapa to Easter Island. Regular voyages between Hawaii and Tahiti, a distance of about 2,350 miles, were made. Their seacraft sometimes exceeded 100 feet in length. War canoes of Fiji could accommodate 200 men, warriors, and crew, and some Tahitian canoes are said to have seated as many as 300. Coastwise commercial craft of New Guinea, consisting of as many as seven to fourteen dugouts lashed together side by side, and measuring up to 59 feet long by 51 feet wide, could carry as much as 34 tons of cargo.

The Marshall Islanders devised and used some very ingenious navigational charts. They were frameworks made of the midribs of cocoanut leaves arranged in such a way as to indicate the location of reefs, ocean swells, and currents. The position of islands was indicated by cowrie shells tied to the frame.

The accumulated knowledge, skills, tools, machines, and techniques developed by primitive, preliterate peoples laid the basis for civilization and all the higher cultures. They invented and developed all the basic tools, weapons, and utensils. They developed the major arts and crafts, such as the ceramic and textile arts, and initiated the art of metallurgy. Food and fiber plants were brought under domestication by them, and they developed the techniques for their culture. They originated the domestication of animals.

Thus during the first hundreds of thousands of years of culture history, primitive peoples were acquiring realistic and matter-of-fact knowledge and originating and perfecting rational and effective techniques. This age-old process of accumulation and development culminated in the Agricultural Revolution, which, as we have seen, profoundly transformed the whole cultural tradition. It is indeed remarkable to see how close to the present day primitive peoples have come at many points on the technological level. Western civilization surpassed primitive techniques of making fire by mechanical friction or percussion only within the last 150 years. And the principle underlying artificial illumination —burning fuel with or without a container and with or without a wick —has been outgrown only within the last 75 years. As recently as 1850 in the United States, white frontiersmen as well as Indians were using the bow and arrow in buffalo hunting in preference to the best of firearms then available to them. And Tylor tells us that Russian troops armed with bow and arrow marched down the boulevards of Paris in 1815 in celebration of the defeat of Napoleon. Thus the bow and arrow, a mechanical triumph of preliterate cultures, has been rendered obsolete as a practical device only within recent years—almost within the memory of persons now living.

The philosophies of primitive peoples are composed of both supernaturalistic and naturalistic elements. In some situations the knowledge and techniques of supernaturalism are uppermost; in others, naturalism predominates. And in many instances both are mingled in varying degrees, and in accordance with the following rule: supernaturalism varies inversely with the extent and effectiveness of naturalistic control. In activities where man has little actual control, or where chance and circumstance play a prominent part, such as hunting, fishing, warfare, horticulture, curing sickness, or identifying persons guilty of offenses, recourse to supernaturalism will be great. In activities where man's control is extensive and effective, such as making a bow or chipping an arrowhead, making buckskin or pottery, resort to supernaturalism will tend to be meager and perhaps only perfunctory. The supernaturalistic and naturalistic components of primitive philosophies do not, therefore, stand separate and apart from each other or constitute distinct layers or strata. Rather, they intermingle with each other as two gases might in a chamber, and together they embrace and envelop the entire life of primitive man.

Technological and social determinants of philosophies. In Chapter 1 we set forth a theory of technological determination of cultural systems. Social systems and ideologies were seen as functions of technological systems. But since philosophies express experience, they must reflect the influence of social life as well as of systems of energy and tools. We shall review briefly the influence of technological and sociological factors upon primitive philosophies.

Fundamental in the experience of man is the "technology" of his own body: his bodily structure, erect posture, sense organs, etc. As a mere animal, man's experience would differ but little from that of an anthropoid ape. He would feel the same earth beneath his feet, see the same fields and hills and sky, hear the same songs of birds and the crashing of thunder; the same odors would assail his nostrils, the same tastes affect his palate. But as a human being, man's whole experience becomes tinged with culture. Everything that he does, thinks, or feels is conditioned by this extrasomatic tradition. Culture is interposed between him and the external world, and all his experience of it is refracted by this medium through which it passes.[6] Man cannot even see the same moon or stars that the ape beholds. To the ape they are merely points or areas of light, but to man they are characters in a story of creation that is suffused with wonder and awe. Plants and animals become beings that can be constrained with magic, and even the poorest stone may house a spirit. Culture has added a new dimension to primate experience.

As the culture, so the experience; as the experience, so the philosophy. And since every cultural system rests upon a technological basis, as of course it must since it is here and with these means that man and culture are articulated with earth and cosmos, both experience and the philosophy that reflects it will depend upon the technological component of the culture. A primitive technology means a primitive philosophy: mythology. A culture activated by human energy alone will differ from one in which the sun's rays are harnessed with the techniques of agriculture and animal husbandry.

Benedict has asserted that religion is independent of technology, that

---

[6] "No longer can man confront reality immediately; he cannot see it, as it were, face to face. Physical reality seems to recede in proportion as man's symbolic activity advances.... [Man] has so enveloped himself in linguistic forms, in artistic images, in mythical symbols or religious rites that he cannot see or know anything except by the interposition of this artificial medium." Ernst Cassirer, *An Essay on Man*, Yale University Press, New Haven, Conn., 1944, p. 25.

man "can *at any stage of technological development* create his gods *in the most diverse form* [italics supplied]." [7] But this is manifestly not true. In cultures where the superiorities of animals over man are manifest on every hand—in size, strength, speed, and special abilities like those of the cobra, skunk, seal, eagle, or mole—the attitude of man is not the same as it is in cultures where man's supremacy—thanks to his technology —is undisputed. In primitive cultures man did not consider himself both superior and unique, nor even *primus inter pares;* he was merely one of the animals and often so inferior that they became his gods. The prevalence of animal gods—the bear, snake, eagle, and coyote—on pre-literate, tribal cultural levels, the wide occurrence of half-man, half-beast gods in the cultures of the Bronze Age—such as gods with the heads of cats or birds, or the bodies of bulls or hippos, in Egypt and Meso-potamia—and the emphasis upon anthropomorphic deities in modern cultures cannot be without significance, although these correlations are not yet well understood.

The social experience of primitive man in societies based upon kinship is reflected in his mythologies. Not only are subhuman species his neighbors, they are often his friends and even his kinsmen. "I *am* a kangaroo," says an Arunta in identifying himself with his totem. And in myths and tales, lower animals and birds can assume the human form; all animals can speak and intermarry freely with man. In Christian cultures, by contrast, man alone has a soul and his nonhuman kin are degraded to the level of beasts. Apropos of Benedict's pronouncement about the independence of religion from technology and stages of social evolution, we may observe that no primitive culture is capable of having a deity who is "[Christ] the *royal* master" or "Great God our *King*," just as alphabets, keystone arches, and tempered steel are incompatible with Emu totems, Sun Youth, and Spider Grandmother.

Cultural systems are self-consistent, as they are coherent and integrated. A primitive society goes with a primitive technology, and both are reflected and expressed by a primitive philosophy.

[7] Ruth Benedict, "Anthropology and the Humanities," *American Anthropologist,* vol. 50, p. 589, 1948.

Chapter 11 *PRIMITIVE CULTURE*
AS A WHOLE

We have now traced the course of cultural development from its beginnings a million years ago until the eve of the Agricultural Revolution, less than ten thousand years ago. We have treated the evolution of culture from a number of standpoints—technological, sociological, and ideological—and in its functional and structural aspects. We shall now try to grasp this process in its entirety, to envision primitive culture as a whole.

We must begin with man's prehuman ancestors, from whom the two basic units of human society at its inception were inherited: the family and the local, territorial group. Articulate speech and the human use of tools were the means whereby anthropoid society was transformed into human society and the means by which man was eventually to acquire control over physical forces of nature and mastery over many species of plants and animals. Families were the building blocks with which the new society was to be constructed. To the narrow family function of sex was added a broader economic function and the all-embracing function of mutual aid. Families were united with one another by strong ties of marriage. Kinship became the basis of social organization. As society evolved under the impetus of increased technological control over nature, the processes of exogamy and endogamy operated to increase the size of the cooperative group of kindred while at the same time maintaining its solidarity and effectiveness. The radius of kinship was extended until the boundaries of the community were reached; eventually the whole tribe became a unified, integrated group of kindred living together on terms of mutual aid.

Custom in general and special codes of etiquette and ethics served to integrate and regulate societies. Classes were defined and kept intact by rules of etiquette; the general welfare was fostered by ethical rules. Division of labor and specialization of function marked the course of social evolution. Special mechanisms of integration, regulation, and control made their appearance in the evolution of culture, as they did

275

in biological evolution. Headmen, chiefs, shamans, and secret societies supplemented custom and codes to hold societies together and to enable them to function effectively.

The economic systems of primitive peoples were virtually identified with their kinship systems. The duties and rights of kinship were applied to customs of property. Individual rights were enjoyed, but the duty to share with one's kinsman was always present. Customs of hospitality and the codes of kinship created a system of sharing that was virtually communistic in character. This system of mutual aid and of sharing worked for social solidarity, on the one hand, and provided economic security for all, on the other. Resources of nature might be privately owned—or rather held, for right to use rather than absolute and exclusive possession characterized the economic systems of primitive cultures—but never so extensively as to exclude anyone from free access to nature. Everyone and every class in primitive society had free access to the resources of nature and to technological means of production. It was this freedom to exploit nature that made it impossible, in primitive society based upon kinship, for man to exploit man. Free access to nature and freedom to own and use the technological means of production provided primitive society with a secure and substantial foundation for freedom and equality: everyone was free to go to nature to obtain things to satisfy his needs; all were equal in this respect. The organization of society on the basis of kinship added "fraternity" to liberty and equality, thus forming the great triad which, as Morgan noted long ago, marks the institutions of tribal society.

Much of the knowledge of primitive peoples was mythological and make-believe, but they possessed an enormous amount of practical and useful knowledge as well. But myths, magic, and ritual are not to be despised and belittled by any means. They provided man with a courage and a confidence that he needed. They gave him a feeling of consequence in the cosmic scheme of things and made him feel that life was worthwhile. Myths and tales fed his mind and sustained his spirit with a food that was often sorely needed. Great and colorful ceremonies dramatized episodes in the mythology of a past filled with marvels and provided man with the riches and the satisfactions of the theater, in which he was alternately actor and spectator. Lesser magical rituals gave man the illusion of control, and this illusion was as precious as it was real: it provided a sense of power and security as a bulwark against fear and impotence.

The panorama of primitive culture is kaleidoscopic in its variety. A crude culture and an inhospitable habitat might well mean a harsh and wretched life for its inhabitants. Other cultures and habitats, however, might provide more than enough food for needs and leave ample time for leisure and the cultivation of the arts. Naturally, the cultures of primitive man were of little or no avail in times of natural catastrophe such as flood, drought, tornado, or earthquake. But in this respect they were but little more helpless than our own is today in similar circumstance. For the most part, primitive cultures could provide enough to eat in normal times and enough shelter for comfort. The very crude cultured aborigines of Australia were able to store up enough food in advance, so that they could devote themselves to drama and dance for days, or even weeks, on end. Myth and ceremony gave a richness to life that was not found among the masses during the Bronze Age, the Middle Ages of western Europe, or even among the industrial proletariat of modern times.

Probably the weakest and least effectual part of primitive cultures was their techniques for coping with sickness and disease. They did possess some genuine knowledge and some practical and effective techniques, as we have already noted in Chapter 10, "Philosophy." But except for relatively minor matters, these were of little avail. In many cultures the death rate among infants was appallingly high, and the hazards and vicissitudes of adolescence and adulthood took their toll, too. But in many societies, if one could survive the illnesses of infancy and childhood he, or she, had a good chance to live to a ripe old age. And the elimination of the weak and the biologically unfit by sickness and disease tended in many instances to produce a stock that won admiration and praise from European travelers for its physical excellence and even beauty. But ignorant and inclined toward magic as primitive peoples were, and crude and ineffectual as were their medical techniques and practices, they were not far below the peoples of western Europe as recently as the eighteenth century, as any history of medicine will make abundantly clear.[1]

However crude and ineffectual primitive cultures were in their control over the forces of nature, they had worked out a system of human relationships that has never been equaled since the Agricultural Revolution. The warm, substantial bonds of kinship united man with man. There were no lords or vassals, serfs or slaves, in tribal society. In social ritual one man might make obeisance to another, but no one kept another in bondage and lived upon the fruits of his labor. There were no mortgages, rents, debtors, or usurers in primitive society, and no one was ever sent to prison for stealing food to feed his children. Food was not adulterated with harmful substances in order to make money out of human misery. There were no time clocks, no bosses or overseers, in primitive society, and a two-week vacation was not one's quota of freedom for a year.

[1] See, for example, R. H. Lowie's *Are We Civilized?*, 1929, for a comparison.

Crude and limited as primitive cultures may have been technologically, and wretched and poor as life may have been for many—but far from all—peoples living in tribal organization, their social systems based upon kinship and characterized by liberty, equality, and fraternity were unquestionably more congenial to the human primate's nature, and more compatible with his psychic needs and aspirations, than any other that has ever been realized in any of the cultures subsequent to the Agricultural Revolution, including our own society today.[2]

[2] A veteran British ethnographer, Baldwin Spencer, once declared that the "life and treatment" of women in aboriginal tribes of Australia, who have about the lowest cultures observed by modern science, were "far preferable to those of hundreds and thousands of women in British slums." *Wanderings in Wild Australia*, vol. I, Macmillan & Co., Ltd., London, 1928, p. 200.

P A R T   T W O   *The Agricultural Revolution*
and Its Consequences

Chapter 12 THE AGRICULTURAL REVOLUTION

We come now to a most interesting and important period in the history of culture, namely, the first great cultural revolution. After about a million years of cultural development, during which time cultural systems were activated almost exclusively by energy from the human organism, a radical change took place: solar energy was harnessed in the form of plants and animals. The consequences were profound and comprehensive. Social organization was transformed from tribal society, based upon kinship, to civil society organized upon the basis of property relations. The ideological sector of culture, too, underwent change, but not as great as in the case of the sociological component.

Evolution and *revolution* designate ways in which the temporal-formal process expresses itself. It will be recalled that in Chapter 1 we distinguished a temporal-formal process as well as a temporal and a non-temporal, formal-functional process. The temporal-formal process is characterized by a chronological sequence of forms: one form grows out of one and into another. This process is usually called evolution, and we have so termed it in Chapter 1. But it will be useful and instructive to distinguish between quantitative and qualitative changes which may take place within this temporal-formal process. When the changes are quantitative we call the temporal-formal process evolution; when they are qualitative we call it revolution. When in the course of reproduction and descent a small primate species becomes a large primate species, we call it evolution. But when a qualitative change takes place, such as occurred in the origin of man with his new and unique ability to symbol, we call it revolution. Man is the child of the Primate Revolution. The terms evolution and revolution are applicable to systems, or systemic processes, only. Evolution is change within the framework and limits of a system. Revolution is a *radical* transformation of a system, the substitution of one principle, or basis, of organization for another.

As we have made clear, evolution and revolution are correlative and complementary concepts, not mutually exclusive or opposite. Both may characterize a single temporal-formal process. The evolution of writing has been punctuated by periods of revolutionary transformation, e.g., in the transformation of picture writing into rebus writing, and this in turn into alphabetic writing. Biological evolution has been characterized by such revolutionary innovations as lungs for breathing air, legs for terrestrial locomotion, or the emergence of mammals. In the evolution of culture the change from primitive society to civil society was revolutionary.

Changes of degree sometimes accumulate and culminate in changes of kind. Thus, additional quantities of heat applied to water will eventually transform it from a liquid to a vapor. Changes of degree in the nervous system of an anthropoid may eventually produce a brain capable of symboling. The transition from hieroglyphic to alphabetic writing, however, is not to be explained in this way. No amount of change within the framework of hieroglyphics would of itself produce the alphabetic principle. Although alphabetic writing grew out of hieroglyphic in a sense and to a certain extent, it would be wrong or misleading to explain the new principle as the result of quantitative change alone. There was a sudden and abrupt substitution of a new principle for an old one. Similarly, it may be said that no amount of change or growth within primitive society based upon kinship could ever have produced civil society based upon property relations. This was a sudden and abrupt change, a revolution.

We have just used the term *sudden* in characterizing revolutionary change, and there is more than a little justification for this; revolutions are sometimes sudden, abrupt, and swiftly executed transformations. The transformations from the autocratic government of Russia under the czars to the bourgeois, capitalist government under Kerensky, and this in turn to the Soviet regime under Lenin, were both sudden and revolutionary. The invention of the alphabet, which constituted a revolutionary transformation of the art of writing, probably took place suddenly.

But whether a transformation is to be described as swift and sudden or gradual is a relative matter. We do not believe that a primate species acquired and employed the ability to symbol in a matter of months or years. It took ages for neurological evolution to reach the point of symbolic expression. When a certain threshold was reached, the exercise of this ability can, we believe, be fairly described as abrupt and sudden. But these are relative terms, relative to the amount of time required to develop the neurological basis for symboling. We do not believe that articulate speech came into being overnight or within the span of a single generation. In the growth of an infant in the species *Homo sapiens* the threshold of the ability to symbol may be reached at an instant, but it requires time to develop and establish patterns of behavior based upon symboling. We may recall here that Helen Keller reached and crossed the threshold of symboling in an instant. But it took time to develop patterns of human behavior.[1]

The process of technological change in western Europe between A.D. 1500, say, and the end of the eighteenth century is customarily spoken of as the Industrial Revolution, yet it extended over a period of centuries. But this was a relatively short time compared with the four or five millennia of cultural development preceding that era. And so it is with the Agricultural Revolution. It required centuries, or even a few thousand years, but against the background of the vast ages of wild food and human energy, the transition to a domestic food supply and the harnessing of solar energy must be reckoned as both sudden and swift. Even five thousand years is but one-half of one per cent of the million or so years of cultural development.

Agriculture was not the result of a single discovery or invention. The theory that "the idea" of the cultivation of plants suddenly flashed across the mind of some man or woman long ago, evoked perhaps by the discovery that seeds thrown away from a meal had subsequently sprouted, and that the whole complex of agricultural techniques and practices grew out of this "idea," is simple and naïve. It is, of course, but an example of the anthropomorphic and psychologistic type of explanation of culture that has so long characterized the reflections of the folk and the layman. According to this point of view, to explain an element of culture, all you have to do is to invoke a hypothetical individual who first "got the idea" of the trait in question; the trait is regarded as the external expression of the idea. If an invention or discovery did not take place, it was because no one "had the idea." The sterility of such reasoning is obvious. Events are "explained" in terms of ideas. But the occurrence or nonoccurrence of ideas is not explained at all.

We are not to think of the origin of agriculture as due to the chance discovery that seeds thrown away from a meal subsequently sprouted. Mankind knew all this and more for tens of thousands of years before the cultivation of plants began. We know that primitive peoples of modern times, wholly without agriculture, have nevertheless an abundant and accurate knowledge of the flora of their habitats. They know that seeds sprout, that parched plants are revived by rain, that they grow better in one soil than another, etc. No tribe of the modern world, however primitive, is without a vast amount of realistic knowledge and understanding of the nature and behavior of plants in their locality, and we may therefore infer that prehistoric man, long before the origin of agriculture, possessed a like knowledge of his flora. The origin of agriculture was not, therefore, the result of an idea or discovery; the cultivation of plants

[1] Cf. Leslie A. White, *The Science of Culture*, 1949, pp. 36–39.

required no new facts or knowledge. Agriculture was simply a new kind of relationship between man—or more properly, woman—and plants.

All peoples use plant materials in one way or another. Man's prehuman ancestors undoubtedly subsisted in part, perhaps largely, upon plant foods, and it is a sound inference that all peoples, during the hundreds of thousands of years of human history, have used plants for food and also for other purposes. Even a people like the modern Eskimo, who subsist largely upon meat, nevertheless eat berries, leaves, lichens, etc., even salvaging plant material from the intestines of slain caribou for their mess.

We have, then, an intimate association between man and the flora of his habitat throughout the entire length of human history. And this intimate association meant knowledge and understanding of plants on man's part, as we have just indicated. At the outset of his career as a human being man was exploiting the wild-plant resources of his habitat, just as his anthropoid ancestors had done before him. Various tools and techniques were devised and developed for this purpose. Innumerable cultural systems have been quite capable of providing the human beings within their embrace with an adequate supply of food derived wholly from wild flora and fauna. Cultural systems relate man to habitat, and an equilibrium can be established in this relationship as in others. When an equilibrium has been established culturally between man and habitat, it may be continued indefinitely, until it is upset by the intrusion of a new factor, the disappearance of an old one, or a radical change in the cultural configuration. Agriculture began when the old equilibrium of hunting and gathering was upset, and a new type of adjustment, a new kind of relationship to local flora, became requisite to survival.

We have no adequate records of how, when, and where this new type of adjustment became necessary and took place. We do know, however, that man's whole relationship with plants involves two significant factors: human effort, or labor, on the one hand, and plant materials capable of serving human needs and obtained by the expenditure of human energy, on the other. There is a ratio $E:P$ between the expenditure of human energy and plant product. In the gathering of wild-plant food so many ergs of human energy are expended and so many calories of food are obtained. If natural resources are abundant, the amount of food obtained per unit of human energy expended will be large; if they are meager, the return will be small, the technological factor being constant.

In order to continue to exist, man must obtain from his efforts at least as much energy in the form of food as he has expended in putting forth these efforts; should he receive less he will eventually die of starvation. It is of course desirable from the standpoint of security and survival to obtain considerably more energy in the form of food than was expended in obtaining it. There have been, as we know, many cultural systems that have been able to make life secure for its human occupants by exploiting the wild-food resources of their respective habitats. Many have been able to do much more than to supply the bare necessities of life; they have provided surpluses which have made a considerable amount of art, ceremony, and recreation possible. Even very crude cultures like those of aboriginal Australia were able to do this.

But suppose the relationship between man and his wild-plant food supply undergoes change adversely to man. Population pressure upon food supply may be increased by immigration. Or the food supply may decrease as a consequence of meteorologic or physiographic change. In either case, the amount of food per capita per square mile will decrease if the technological factor remains constant. This will mean a decrease of amount of food produced per unit of human energy expended. If food is scarce in one's immediate vicinity, he may make up for the deficiency by foraging farther afield, but this requires more effort, more energy.

It may happen, therefore, that the amount of food obtained per unit of human energy expended may be diminished from one cause or another. When this occurs one or another of the following consequences must follow: (1) a lower standard of living, or, to express it in other words, cultural regression, (2) emigration, or (3) agriculture or animal husbandry or both.

In analyzing the energy relationship between man and plants—energy expended, plant food obtained—we must consider not only the amount of energy expended in human labor but the way in which it is expended as well. Gathering wild plant food is one way of expending human energy in food production; agriculture is another. *Agriculture* is merely the name we give to various ways of increasing man's control over the lives of plants. And the significant thing about this increase in control is that it may increase the amount of food produced per unit of human labor. The farmer with well-developed agricultural techniques can produce much more food per unit of human energy expended, or better, per man-year, than can the gatherer of wild plant food in all but the most abundant of wild resources.

At certain times and places in the course of culture history, the threat of a diminished food supply, coming from an increase of population pressure through immigration, or from a decline in local flora due to climatic or physiographic change, was met by various measures of cultural control over plant life, which, collectively, we call agriculture.

We are still faced with such questions as, "Why did agriculture begin, in the Old World, about 8000 B.C. rather than 50,000?" and "Why did it begin where it did rather than in other places?" These are questions of specific fact rather than problems of general theory, and we do not have enough facts to answer them at present. We must suppose that a certain degree of cultural development is necessary for the inauguration of an agricultural technology; we would not expect that a cultural system only 50,000 or 100,000 years above an anthropoid level could launch an agricultural way of life. But we see no reason why cultural systems of 50,000 B.C. (i.e., 950,000 years old) could not have been capable of originating agriculture as well as systems in 8000 B.C. (990,000 years old). We must look, then, to environmental—climatic and physiographic—factors and to the possibility of population movements, rather than to cultural factors, for the answers to these questions.

Childe and the Braidwoods have suggested that climatic change at the close of the last great Ice Age in the Old World, with its consequent changes in flora and fauna, affected cultural systems and set the stage for agriculture and animal husbandry, if it did not actually initiate these arts.[2] According to their theory, great areas of central Asia became desiccated after the retreat of the ice sheet—and there appears to be geologic evidence of this—causing their inhabitants to migrate to more suitable habitats. This migration increased the population, and consequently the pressure upon food supply, in the areas in which the migrants settled. The increased pressure upon food supply upset the equilibrium between need and supply, initiating attempts to *control* food supply through the use of new techniques—as well as, perhaps, the refinement or extension of old ones—to control the growth and reproduction of plants. This is agriculture.

Agriculture, then, is a matter of cultural control over the lives of plant species. And this control was not a matter of all or none, but a matter of kind and degree. We can observe beginnings of such control among many cultures usually—and quite properly—designated as nonagricultural.

First of all, no doubt, were the magical attempts at control. The totemic ceremonies of aboriginal tribes of Australia well exemplify this attempt to control the lives of certain plant and animal species and to increase the food supply thereby. Eventually, and at first sporadically and little by little, came rational attempts at control. Seeds might be sown, and then left to themselves: many tribes of the Great Lakes region in North America used to sow wild rice in marshes to increase the yield, but did nothing else until the harvest. Some wild plants were tended to help them in their

[2] V. Gordon Childe, *What Happened in History*, 1946, pp. 36, 41; Robert J. Braidwood, *Prehistoric Men*, 1948, pp. 72, 76–81. The Braidwoods have suggested that agriculture may not have originated in the fertile river valleys of the Old World as previously supposed, but on the "hilly flanks" of these regions. Linda and Robert J. Braidwood, "On the Treatment of the Prehistoric Near Eastern Materials in Steward's 'Cultural Causality and Law,'" *American Anthropologist*, vol. 51, p. 665, 1949.

struggle with nature. Irrigation preceded agriculture in some regions.[3] The first agriculture was nomadic, so to speak, in some instances. Seeds would be sown in the spring before leaving the winter encampment for the summer's hunt or grazing. Upon returning in the fall the crops, if any remained, would be harvested.

Increased concern with plant growth, more control over their way of life, resulted in increased yields. Labor spent in this way came to be more profitable, more lucrative, than effort confined to gathering natural produce only. Control became deliberate and systematic. New techniques were developed, and new tools invented. More and more plants, for textiles, drugs, and liquors, as well as for food, were domesticated. The best seeds were used for planting. Competing plants were eliminated or restricted by hoeing and weeding. Fields were fertilized; arid lands irrigated. The agricultural arts evolved in two stages: horticulture, or garden culture with the dibble and hoe; and agriculture, or field culture with the plow. In the earlier stage, the cultivation of plants was probably the work of women. As dependence upon garden produce increased, cultivation grew in importance and in many instances passed into the hands of men. This was true particularly where the plow was used. Thus the agricultural arts were developed. Beginning in Neolithic times, they had grown in the relatively short period of a few thousand years to maturity and had produced the great urban, metallurgical, literate, calendrical civilizations of antiquity.

The observations just made concerning the origin of agriculture will apply also to the origin of animal husbandry. The domestication of animals is not to be thought of as the result of an idea which flashed across some man's mind about 10,000 B.C. It was not the result of a sudden discovery, either of fact or of concept. Man had been living in intimate association with other animal species for hundreds of thousands of years. We know from studies of preliterate cultures of the modern world that even the most primitive of peoples have a great deal of accurate and detailed knowledge of the fauna of their habitats, and it is a reasonable inference that all tribes, thousands of years before domestication began, had a comparable knowledge of the animal species in their own localities. Animal husbandry, like agriculture, is most profitably to be regarded as a change in the relationship between man and the other animal species with which he was associated. The domestication of animals is merely the imposition and extension of cultural control over the lives of certain animal species.

It has often been assumed that the domestication of animals was moti-

[3] Cf. Julian H. Steward, "Irrigation without Agriculture," *Papers, Michigan Academy of Science, Arts and Letters,* vol. 12, pp. 149-156, 1930.

vated by rational and utilitarian considerations, and there is no doubt but that they played a part, perhaps the principal role, in the process. But there are reasons for believing that this is not the whole story. Some primitive peoples keep domestic animals or fowls for use in magical rituals, and domestication may, in some instances, have grown out of such practices. Again, some primitive peoples keep various animals—birds and reptiles as well as mammals—as pets. Domestication may have been initiated in this way in some instances. And with regard to utilitarian motives, we have already noted, in Chapter 2, that the ancestors of our domesticated sheep had no wool, or at least none suitable for textile purposes, and cattle were not milked until centuries after their domestication [4]—although, of course, both sheep and cattle could have been kept for meat.

It seems best, therefore, to assume that more than one factor, or motive, played a part in the domestication of animals. Furthermore, it seems reasonable to think of not one single occurrence of domestication, but of a few or several. In some instances magical or ritual reasons may have been uppermost. In others, as Morgan long ago suggested, it may have resulted from "the capture of the young of . . . animals and rearing them, not unlikely, from the merest freak of fancy." [5] But whatever factors may have established the symbiotic relationship between man and other animals in the first place, we may be sure that it was practical and utilitarian considerations that developed, expanded, and extended these relationships later, in the art of animal husbandry. The relationship between man and other species had of course been close and intimate for a very long time. Man had depended, in varying degrees, upon animals for food and other valuable and useful materials for hundreds of thousands of years prior to domestication. The exploitation and utilization of the fauna of a region is a form of control over nature exercised by man. The domestication of animals is merely an enlargement and an intensification of this relationship of control as the consequence of the introduction of a new principle: keeping animals alive for use instead of killing them for use. This change in the relationship between man and certain other animal species was no doubt brought about by the same factors which initiated and established agriculture.

In regions where both agriculture and animal husbandry were established, the latter did much to complement the former, as well as to make a distinctive contribution of its own. Beasts could be used to draw plows or vehicles and as motive power for irrigation pumps and grinding mills.

[4] R. H. Lowie, *An Introduction to Cultural Anthropology*, rev. ed., 1940, pp. 41, 51–52.
[5] L. H. Morgan, *Ancient Society*, 1877, p. 42.

Their dung could be used for fertilizer or for fuel. Livestock could be fed in part on cultivated plants. Meat and milk provided a stable and nutritious food supply in many cultural systems. Thus, in some regions, agriculture primarily or alone, in others, agriculture and animal husbandry together, provided the motive force for the First Great Cultural Revolution. We shall now trace the steps in this process. They follow one another naturally and logically.

The first link in the chain of consequences flowing from the new technology was an increase in food supply. When the photosynthetic process of capturing and storing energy from the sun was brought under cultural control, the amount of food produced per unit of human labor increased. This increase continued until the agricultural arts had reached maturity. With an increase in food supply, the population increased in numbers.

There had undoubtedly been increases in food supply during Paleolithic times, too, when wild animals and plants were the basis of subsistence. Improved tools, weapons, and techniques augmented the amount of food obtained. And an increase in population followed upon a more abundant supply of food. But social organization was changed little, if at all. Instead of greatly enlarging the size of the social unit, the group divided, a portion of the tribe broke away and formed a new tribe. This was made necessary, of course, by the mode of exploitation. In a wild-food economy, the human population of a given area cannot increase beyond a certain point: the limit of its food supply. A tribe might increase in good times, but when lean times came, a portion would have to leave the parent body and seek a livelihood elsewhere. Abundant evidence indicates that new tribes were formed in this way many times. This periodic division of tribes was compatible with their mobile, if not nomadic, mode of life.

When, however, the agricultural arts had been considerably developed, resulting in a substantial increase in amount of food produced per unit of human labor, and when this in turn increased the population, the people could remain in the same territory because its productive capacity had been increased. And until agriculture had reached a certain stage of development, the land would continue to produce more and more food per acre, as well as more per unit of human labor. The sedentary mode of life, made necessary by all but the most rudimentary forms of agriculture, also disposed the people to remain where they were.

With the development of the agricultural arts goes an increase in the productivity of human labor and an increase in population, both in absolute numbers and in density per square mile. But the political consequences of this increase in population may vary. They will depend upon a very important relationship: the ratio between man-hours spent in food production and calories of food produced.

In a wild-food economy the amount of food obtained varies to some extent with the amount of time spent in hunting, gathering, etc. A hunter may obtain more game by four hours of hunting than by only two. The same would hold for a woman gathering wild plant food. But the amount of wild food obtained is not proportional to the amount of time spent. Beyond a certain point, the amount of food obtained by additional man-hours diminishes with each additional hour. The hunter or plant gatherer may be able to obtain more food by working longer, but to do this he must go farther afield and therefore spend more and more of his time going to and from his camp, which time and labor are unproductive of food. Moreover, if hunters and gatherers exploit the resources of a locality faster than they are renewed by natural increase, additional time spent in food getting will actually and eventually *reduce* the food supply of the area, decreasing the number of calories per man-hour. In a wild-food economy, therefore, there is a limit, both to the absolute amount of food obtainable per capita per year and to the number of calories produced per man-hour.

With agriculture it is different. More food can be produced per unit of human labor, and more per square mile. And these rates can be increased as the agricultural arts are improved. But in agricultural systems the ratio between man-hours of labor expended and calories of food produced varies, and this variation is very significant for social and political organization. The population may be dense whether the amount of food produced per man-hour is great or small, but the structure of society will vary, depending upon the relationship between these two factors. If the food return per man-hour be low, there will be relatively little division of labor along occupational lines, little specialization of occupation and profession, possibly no class stratification at all, and no large population organized under one government. If, however, the yield per man-hour is high, there will be division of labor, specialization of occupation, and, when a certain point is reached, class stratification, a transformation from tribal to civil, or state, organization. Let us demonstrate these propositions with examples of (1) the rice-growing tribes of Luzon and (2) the agriculture of ancient Egypt.

The Ifugao and the Bontoc Igorot of Luzon grow rice as their principal crop by intensive agricultural techniques. So intensive is their cultivation that they are able to produce a very large amount of food per square mile. As a consequence of this, they are able to maintain a very large population per square mile. The density of population in some of the highly cultivated regions in Luzon is truly impressive for preliterate cultural systems: possibly as much as 2,000 per square mile of cultivated land.[6] The population of these areas is therefore much greater than could be supported anywhere by hunting and gathering alone.

But although the yield per square mile is high in Luzon, the yield per man-hour is low. A very large portion of the time of the adults, both men and women, is spent in agriculture, and even children are recruited for certain tasks. A small area of land will support a family,[7] but virtually all the labor time of the family is required to support itself. There is little or no surplus. It is not possible for a portion of the population to produce enough food for all. Consequently, it is not possible to divorce a portion of the population from agriculture and to occupy them with arts and crafts as vocations. There is, therefore, very little division of labor, little specialization of occupation, and virtually no class stratification among the Ifugao or the Bontoc Igorot. There are no large political units, there is no state.

In Luzon, then, we find an intensive agriculture but a relatively low degree of development of social organization, for the simple reason that the caloric return per man-hour is low.

In ancient Egypt and Mesopotamia, however, the situation was different. In these regions, as in Luzon, the amount of food produced per square mile was very large as compared with wild-food systems. But the caloric return per man-hour was large also. Consequently, it was possible for a portion of the population to produce enough food for all. A considerable portion of the population could therefore be drawn off the farms and put to work in arts and crafts as special occupational groups. And eventually society became divided into such classes as rulers, nobles, priests, scribes, craftsmen, serfs, and slaves. A large number of people were organized within a single political system, the state or nation. Thus we see that it is not merely and simply the practice of agriculture that is significant. It is the ratio between calories and labor time as well as amount of food per acre that counts.

It may well be true that a population, human or nonhuman, *tends* to

---

[6] The province of the Ifugao had an area of about 750 square miles, of which not more than 50 were cultivated. Cf. A. L. Kroeber, "Peoples of the Philippines," *American Museum of Natural History Handbook*, 8, p. 34, 1928. A portion, but only an insignificant percentage, of their subsistence is derived from hunting and by gathering wild plant food. Barton estimates that only 9.4 per cent of the subsistence of the Ifugao is derived from wild sources as compared with 84 per cent from agriculture, 4.2 per cent from animal culture, and 2.4 per cent from imports. R. F. Barton, "Ifugao Economics," *University of California Publications in American Archaeology and Ethnology*, vol. 15, no. 5, p. 398, 1922.

[7] Of 109 families included in a census made by R. F. Barton, only 20 held 2 acres or more, 40 held between 1 and 2, and 40 held less than 1 acre each. Barton, *op. cit.*, p. 412.

increase to the limits of its food supply, but this increase does not always take place in human communities by any means; there are other factors besides food supply that are significant for population increase. Some primitive peoples may find it necessary to spend almost all their time exploiting the resources of nature and processing materials for consumption, but certainly many tribes do not. Even in aboriginal Australia, where natural resources are not generally abundant and technologies are simple and crude, the natives had a great amount of leisure time for ceremonies and social intercourse. Indian tribes of British Columbia produced great quantities of food and other goods, only to destroy them in ceremonies. Many pastoral and horticultural peoples are able to produce enough to meet their needs in only a portion of their time. The Kuikuru, for example, a manioc-growing tribe of Brazil, were quite able to produce two or three times as much food as they were actually producing, according to Carneiro, who made careful measurements and calculations of their mode of subsistence.[8]

In the case of the Kuikuru, and other similarly situated tribes, it seems clear that, so far as subsistence is concerned, the population could have doubled or tripled and that all the social consequences of such increase—the separation of a portion of the population from food getting, the formation of occupational groups of specialized artisans, and the division of society into dominant and subordinate classes—could have taken place. But the sociocultural system of the Kuikuru was not moving in this direction. Enough food to meet needs was produced in a fraction of the working time, and then production ceased. The population was not increasing. An equilibrium had, apparently, been established, and it was maintained. Situations of this kind raise two important questions: (1) "Why does not the population increase?" and (2) "What will cause a people to produce more food than they need?"

Unfortunately, we do not have a satisfactory answer to the first question. Circumstances affecting fecundity and reproduction, endemic and other diseases, and doubtless other factors affect the relationship between birth rate and death rate.

With regard to the second question, it would seem that some sort of coercion is necessary to cause or induce a people to produce more than it needs. This coercion may be supplied by the conquest of one people by another; e.g., some European powers have increased production in their colonies by imposing a head, or a hut, tax upon the natives. But coercion may arise within an evolving sociocultural system itself. Coercion to increase production characterized the Agricultural Revolution. It was

[8] Robert Carneiro, *Subsistence and Social Structure: An Ecological Study of the Kuikuru Indians,* a doctoral dissertation, University of Michigan, 1957; see, especially, pp. 136, 142, 158–159, 222–223.

derived from both of these sources, extra- and intra-societal. The application of force by one people upon another is a fairly obvious operation and requires but little explanation. The genesis of coercion within a sociocultural system is much less obvious and requires considerable elucidation.

We may assume that in such regions as the Nile Valley and Mesopotamia, where civil society first appeared, the following situation obtained and this sequence of events took place: (1) Agriculture and animal husbandry made possible increased food production both (a) per acre and (b) per man-hour. (2) Pressure of population increase brought about increased food production, which in turn tended toward further growth of population. (3) The productivity of labor, i.e., amount of food per man-hour, increased as the agricultural arts and those of animal husbandry were developed. (4) As the density of population increased, society became structurally differentiated and functionally specialized; i.e., a portion of the productive members of society were divorced from food getting and their time and labor were devoted to various arts and crafts, thus forming occupational groups—weavers, potters, metal, stone, and leather workers, carpenters, and so on. (5) This development made a change of economic system necessary. (6) Concomitantly with the growth of population in size and density, and concomitantly with the structural differentiation and functional specialization of society, there was developed a special political mechanism, the state-church, which coordinated the various parts and functions, integrated them into a coherent whole which it regulated and controlled. It was this that provided the coercion necessary to cause a class of food producers to produce more than they needed or could consume. (7) The result was a division of society into a dominant, ruling class and a subordinate class. And hand in hand with the development of institutions of civil society, there was breakdown of tribal society. But let us describe this transformation a little more fully.

The advent of agriculture and animal husbandry was followed by an increase in population in some regions, if not in others. In the Nile Valley, Mesopotamia, the river valleys of India and China, and, in the New World, in Mexico, Central America, and the Andean Highlands, the growth of agriculture and of population proceeded hand in hand; birth rates did exceed death rates, for whatever reasons. As the productivity of human labor in agriculture increased, it became possible for a portion of the population to produce enough for all, and this portion decreased as the productivity of labor increased. Conceivably, one of the consequences of this could have been that each family, or each household, would divide its time between the fields and livestock, on the one hand, and various arts and crafts, on the other. But this would eventually have become practically impossible, and everywhere it would have been socially wasteful. As the various arts and crafts developed, it would have become impossible for each household to become a workshop for textile and ceramic manufactures, metalworking, brickmaking, leatherworking, and so on. And much of society's labor time would have been lost if such a thing had been attempted. Therefore, for practical and technological reasons and for reasons of social economy, the various arts and crafts became specialized industries. In such a way, society became differentiated along occupational lines into weavers, spinners, dyers, wood-, leather-, and metalworkers, masons, bakers, brewers, and so on.

A new principle of social organization was thus introduced: occupational. And as this new principle was extended, the old basis of kinship receded. There was, to be sure, a tendency for guilds of specialized artisans to become hereditary, and to that extent to retain kinship as an element of organization. But kinship was subordinated to occupation and was, moreover, confined within the limits of the guild, so that kinship as a basis of society's organization was diminished in magnitude and subordinated in importance.

Quite apart from coercion, the agriculturalists would produce more food than they needed after the formation of guilds of artisans, so that they could obtain manufactured goods in exchange for food.[9] Social, or political, coercion came later, and we shall deal with it shortly.

The division of society into occupational groups required a profound transformation of economic system. In tribal society, as we have seen, goods were exchanged, shared, and consumed in accordance with the rights and obligations of kinship ties. But in the new society this was no longer possible. The metalworker, potter, or weaver could not obtain food from his kinsmen since they would tend to be members of his own guild. And the various occupational groups were not related to each other by kinship ties; they were interrelated in terms of correlative, specialized functions. Obviously, a new kind of system of exchange and distribution of goods had to be devised to meet this situation. The type of economic system in which human rights and human welfare took precedence over property rights and which had prevailed in primitive society for ages had become obsolete. The new economic system would subordinate human welfare to property rights.

There are two kinds of intrasocietal economic systems in which relationships between persons are functions of relationships between goods. Both were brought into being by the Agricultural Revolution.[10] In the

---

[9] Many primitive peoples, or native populations, have increased their production when they had a chance—as the Kuikuru did not—to sell surpluses in a market and buy manufactured goods in exchange. This is a form of inducement, if not of coercion.

[10] It will be recalled that commercial exchange took place *between* tribal societies

one, the economic process is dominated and controlled by the political process, i.e., by the government. Production and distribution are regulated by the government and are carried on in terms of *class* and *status*. Mediums of exchange and markets are absent in this kind of system. In the other type of economic system, the economic process is allowed to function freely *as* an economic process; i.e., production and exchange of goods are carried on in terms of their economic values, with only enough governmental supervision to see that certain rules, e.g., those pertaining to honesty, are observed. Mediums of exchange and markets, agreements and contracts, characterize this kind of economic system.

There are no generally agreed-upon names for these two kinds of economic system. The system which allows great freedom for the economic process as such may well be called *commercial*. The governmentally controlled system has been called *socialistic:* e.g., the state-controlled economic systems of the ancient Incas,[11] of Germany under Hitler, and of the U.S.S.R. have been designated socialism, and trends in this direction in the United States have been so branded. These systems would not exemplify the conception of socialism held by Marx and Engels, however; in their socialist system, the state, which is regarded always as an instrument of class rule and oppression, will be nonexistent —it will have "withered away" or have been "dismantled" by the triumphant working class. And there are other objections to the term socialistic. We shall therefore simply refer to this kind of system as *state-controlled*.

The Incas of Peru provide us with a good example of the state-controlled type of economy; the Aztecs of Mexico, with the commercial type.[12] Both of these societies were organized along occupational lines, and each was divided into a dominant class and a subordinate class. In Inca culture, production and distribution were regulated by the government; goods were assigned by law to various classes and groups. In Mexico, on the other hand, there were markets and currency, and exchange of goods took place freely in terms of their respective values.[13]

---

prior to the Agricultural Revolution; but *within* social systems based upon kinship only the economic system that subordinated relationships between goods to relationships between persons prevailed.

[11] L. Baudin, "L'Empire socialiste des Inka," *Travaux et Mémoires de l'Institut d'Ethnologie*, vol. 5, 1928; see also George P. Murdock, *Our Primitive Contemporaries*, 1934, pp. 415, 430–431.

[12] The reader who is not familiar with the cultures of these peoples will find excellent and brief descriptions of them in Murdock, *op. cit.*, as well as descriptive accounts of many other cultures.

[13] This was qualified somewhat by sumptuary laws which prevented persons of certain classes from buying or using goods not proper to their station in life. But sumptuary laws may function in feudal societies as well as in commercially organized cultures.

Why the Agricultural Revolution produced a state-controlled system in one culture, or country, and a commercial system in another is a question for which we have no adequate answer. No doubt many factors are operative here, none of which can be singled out as the independent variable. The factor of integration appears to be very significant, however. If the transition from primitive to civil society takes place in a well-ordered, coherent fashion, then the chances of state control seem to be good. If, however, there is considerable disorganization in the process, the possibilities of freedom for business enterprise would seem to be improved. This is a subject that requires further study.

But both kinds of economic systems produced by the Agricultural Revolution are not only different from that which obtained in primitive society, they are its opposite: social relationships between persons become functions of economic relationships between goods.

The development of industries and the formation of guilds were followed by still other consequences that tended to break down the old kinship and tribal organization. With the exception, perhaps, of some feudal systems, commerce developed as a consequence of the growth of industries. Merchants would leave their homes and go abroad to manage their affairs. Skilled craftsmen occasionally went abroad, too, to find improved opportunities for the practice of their trade. In this way members of the tribe would become dispersed—the kinship organization would be weakened by geographic separation. Each nation would come to harbor merchants and craftsmen from other nations, and these people, being foreigners, would have no status in the tribal organization where they resided, even though they were performing significant functions in the community. About 1000 B.C. many Greeks went abroad as merchants and craftsmen, and similar classes of persons came to Greece. For a time these foreigners were so numerous in Athens that they constituted a political problem: they were residents in the city; they carried on important social and economic functions; yet, being foreigners and hence not members of the Greek clans, they had no political rights. In this way commerce and itinerant craftsmen tended to break down the old kinship organization: tribesmen and clansmen were being transformed into *citizens*.

As the kinship organization gave way under the impact of the developing agricultural technology, there was a tendency for kinship groupings to be replaced by territorial groupings as a basis of political organization. When genealogical ties, known or assumed, could no longer suffice to serve as the means and basis of social organization, some other principle had to take their place. This principle was the definite, explicit, and

substantial one of locality or area. We shall describe the territorial organization of civil society in our next chapter.

Public works and community functions were important factors in the
transition from tribal society to civil society. Even in some primitive
tribes such as the Keresan Pueblos of the Rio Grande Valley in New
Mexico, there are public works and community functions.[14] There was
a priest-chief who was the head of the tribe, or community. His household had to be supplied with wood. There was a community house in
which the tribal council held its meetings. But even more important, in
this respect, there was a community irrigation system. As culture evolved
under the impetus of a developing agriculture, public works multiplied
and grew in magnitude and special community functions increased in
number and importance. Houses must be provided and maintained for
administrators. Temples have to be provided and maintained for priesthoods. These public works and communal enterprises have to be supported by taxes or levies upon the people, and these operations require
special personnel to administer them. If there is irrigation—and it is
significant to note that this has been an important factor in the rise of
civilizations in both the New and Old Worlds—an administrative body,
clothed with great authority, must be in charge. We are moving toward
a political state and away from clan and tribal chiefs.

Special community functions and the lodging of power in the hands
of a few arise in another quarter also, namely, military defense and offense. As agriculture developed and industries flourished, wealth accumulated, and this incited nations to attack one another. "As property
increases," observed Tylor, "there appears with it warfare carried on as
a business." [15] Given the finite areas of rich river valleys and other arable
lands, it became not only profitable to wage war but necessary to do so
if a nation were to hold its own in international competition and rivalry.

In many primitive tribes every man was, or could be, a warrior, but
even on these levels of development specialization begins to appear: the
Opi, for example, constituted a special class of warriors among the
Keresan Pueblos. With the growth of large and dense populations during
the Agricultural Revolution, professional armies were developed. Warfare requires the concentration of virtually absolute power in the hands
of a very few. The conduct of a war results not only in the conquest of
a foreign people, but in the subordination of the common people at home,
who must yield to their military leaders in the interests of a common
defense. The spoils of war are distributed among the principal war cap-

[14] Cf., for example, Leslie A. White, "The Pueblo of Santa Ana, New Mexico,"
American Anthropological Association Memoir 60, 1942.
[15] E. B. Tylor, *Anthropology*, 1881, p. 225.

tains and civil administrators. The common people in the defeated country are subjugated, while those at home are subordinated to military and civil authority. Thus a wedge is driven deep into society, dividing it into a group wielding almost absolute power—a ruling class—and the great mass of common people whose function it is to provide the necessities of peace as well as the sinews of war.

The multiplication and growth of public works and the extension of community enterprises and functions—especially irrigation and warfare—as a concomitant and a consequence of the development of agriculture and animal husbandry, and the necessity of imposing taxes or other levies upon the masses of the population in order to support and maintain these public works and enterprises, led to the division of society into a ruling class, in whose hands great power was lodged, and the mass of common people, who were subordinated politically and economically to the administration of the dominant class. The old order of tribal society breaks down and gives way before the advance of civil society and the emergence of the political state.

The accumulation of wealth played a role in another respect, also: in the transformation of tribal society into civil society. In primitive society, as we have seen, wealth was shared during life and inherited widely by kinsmen after death. But in higher cultures where wealth is more abundant, and where clans or other kinship groups are larger and have less solidarity, the laws of exogamy weaken and finally give way in order to keep property within a lineage or clan. Morgan noted that the ancient Athenians modified their laws of exogamy to permit a man to marry a wealthy woman of his own clan so that her property might be kept within the clan: "Solon enacted that the heiress should marry her nearest male agnate, although they belonged to the same gens [clan], and marriage between them had previously been prohibited by usage." [16] And Moses, too, ruled in the case of the daughters of Zelophehad, that they should not marry outside their kin group for the same reason: "... Only to the family of the tribe of their father shall they marry," Moses decreed. "So shall not the inheritance of the children of Israel remove from tribe to tribe: for every one of the children of Israel shall keep himself to the inheritance of the tribe of his fathers." [17]

Wealth accumulated unevenly in society as kinship groups grew in size and diminished in solidarity. Families with greater wealth became increasingly disinclined to share it through inheritance with other family lines of lesser wealth. Consequently, the rules of inheritance were changed, and with this change the ancient classificatory system of re-

[16] Lewis H. Morgan, *Ancient Society*, 1877, pp. 548–549.
[17] Num. 36:5-9. Quoted by Morgan, *ibid.*, pp. 546–547.

lationship, which made every member of your tribe a close relative, became obsolete and was supplanted by the descriptive system of nomenclature.[18]

We have noted that two different kinds of social processes may be involved in the transformation of tribal society into civil society: a forcible, military process and a peaceful, economic—primarily monetary —process. And we have already described the way in which the military process functions and have noted the consequences of its operation: concentration of power in the hands of a few and the subordination or subjugation of the many. We now wish to indicate briefly how the peaceful, monetary process tends also to divide society into two classes: the rich and the poor. We shall describe the operation of this process more fully in Chapter 14, "Economic Structure of Higher Cultures."

In a society in which relations between persons are subordinate to relations between economic goods, the status of persons will be determined by the interaction of these economic entities. In a free, commercial, monetary economy, goods and money will circulate freely, exchanging with one another in terms of their respective values. This process is a competitive one, and in such a process the weak succumb to the strong. The big merchant can eliminate the little one. But the most significant expression of this process with reference to social structure is the practice of moneylending. Inequalities of wealth occur everywhere in human society. They are produced by differences of health, ability, initiative, sagacity, and by differences in circumstances, such as accident or misfortune. In primitive societies, however, these inequalities tend to be rectified by the obligation to share wealth with one's kinsmen, i.e., tribesmen, and to assist them when they are overtaken by misfortune. In an intrasocietal, commercial, and monetary system, on the other hand, these inequalities are accentuated: the poor become poorer; the rich, richer. This is how it works.

A person or a family group finds itself, for one reason or another, unable to maintain itself economically. They go, therefore, to the moneylender for help. The lender demands security and exacts interest, usually at a high rate. The circumstances which made it necessary for the unfortunate one to borrow may well make it impossible for him to repay the loan, or even to meet interest payments as they fall due. He thus sinks deeper into debt, and in some cultures he must become an indentured servant or a slave, or sell his children into slavery, before he is done with the usurer. Thus the free circulation of money in a competitive, commercial economy tends naturally and inevitably to divide society into

[18] This is Morgan's thesis, which he argues forcefully in *Ancient Society*, especially in Part 4, "The Growth of the Idea of Property."

the rich and powerful and the poor and weak. It goes without saying, of course, that such a system must have the endorsement of the government and be enforced, in the last analysis, by physical force. But a sociocultural system that has made moneylending possible almost always provides adequate safeguards to the lender.

We may now review the steps in the transition from primitive society to civil society and try to envision it as a whole. Populations increased in size and density as a consequence of increase in food production. Sheer increase in size of group put a heavy strain on the kinship organization, and eventually it tended to fall apart of its own weight.

The productivity of human labor increased as the agricultural arts advanced. This resulted in removing a progressively larger portion of the population from food raising and in organizing them into guilds of specialized artisans or occupying them with political, ecclesiastical, or military functions. This required the abandonment of the old economic system of mutual aid among kindred and the adoption of a feudal or a commercial system, depending upon which emphasis was uppermost in the transition, the military or the monetary process. Communal tenure of property gave way to private ownership. Inheritance laws were revised to exclude all but agnatic relatives, and this brought about a shift from the classificatory system of kinship to the descriptive system. The free circulation of commodities and money resulted in the division of society into debtors and creditors, and eventually into rich and poor.

Warfare also was a powerful and effective means of political transformation. The equality and democracy of tribe and clan were submerged by the exigencies of large-scale military competition for accumulated wealth and natural resources, and society was divided into a military and civil ruling class and a subordinate class.

The multiplication and growth of public works and community enterprises contributed further to the development of civil society. They required a special administrative personnel, which of necessity had to be clothed with power and which had to be supported by taxes or other levies. Here again, a cleavage was brought about within society: administrative functions backed by power, on the one hand, and a subordinate class that supplies labor and goods, on the other.

Maintenance of integrity is essential to any system, sociocultural or otherwise. If the new type of civil society that was being produced by the developing technologies of agriculture and animal husbandry were to be able to maintain and perpetuate itself, it would have to achieve and maintain integrity, and this would mean doing three things: (1) coordinating, correlating, and integrating the various parts and functions of which the new sociocultural system was composed, namely, the various public works and community enterprises such as irrigation, communal offices, temples, transportation, public markets, systems of currency, and so on; coordinating and integrating the various social structures that comprise the system as a whole, namely, the occupational groups—industrial, ecclesiastical, and military. (2) It would have to reconcile the two basic classes of society, the dominant, ruling class and the subordinate class, whose interests were not only different but opposite and conflicting at many points, and prevent the subordinate class from disrupting society and reducing it to anarchy and chaos through insurrection and civil war. And finally (3) it must maintain its autonomy and independence by successful military operations of offense and defense with reference to its neighbors. To accomplish all this, the new society would have to have a special mechanism, a special political device, for coordination, integration, regulation, and control. Such a special mechanism was developed. We shall call it the *state-church*.

The situation here is precisely comparable to that obtaining in biological evolution: as living organisms have evolved—at least among the phyla that have become mammals—they have become more and more differentiated structurally and more specialized functionally. Differentiation and specialization, on the one hand, require coordination, integration, and control, on the other. The coordinative, integrative, and regulative mechanism developed in phyla leading to mammals was the central nervous system. What the brain and central nervous system are to biological evolution, the state-church is to sociocultural evolution.

The institutions of primitive society broke down and gave way because they could not contain and accommodate the new technological forces introduced by the cultivation of plants and the domestication of animals. Kinship organization was not only adequate but ideal for sociocultural systems activated solely by human energy, and even for systems in which agriculture and animal husbandry were but little developed. But when these arts acquired considerable stature and magnitude, they exerted such pressures upon the sociopolitical system that eventually it could no longer withstand them. New institutions were constructed, or developed, as the old were broken down and cast aside. Apropos of the belief, held in certain quarters, that social revolutions are brought about by agitations of revolutionists, our study of the Agricultural Revolution would seem to offer much support for the following generalizations: No institution or sociopolitical system will give way and become abandoned as long as it is able to perform effectively a vital function; no new set of institutions, no new sociopolitical system, can be brought into being until technological conditions make it possible and until social conditions require it. In short, a sociocultural revolution cannot take place before its time; but when its time does come, it will take place. This is merely the application of the principles of cause and effect and of determinism to sociocultural phenomena as they are applicable to physical, chemical, or meteorological phenomena. It will not rain unless and until certain meteorological factors and processes are present and operative in a certain manner; when these factors and processes are in certain conjunction, it will rain (i.e., "precipitation is inevitable"). Finally, it may be added that the same forces and processes that destroy the old construct the new. These generalizations concerning revolutionary cultural change are as valid and as applicable to the world situation today as they are to the Agricultural Revolution.

As we have indicated repeatedly, the transformation of primitive society into civil society was not instantaneous: there were transitional stages. This fact will help to clarify an issue that has been much confused in American ethnological theory. Morgan argued that the institutions of primitive society were democratic, that they were incompatible with monarchy.[19] Critics of Morgan have retorted by pointing to sociocultural systems in Negro Africa that have both clans and a king, and having done this they imagined they had dealt evolutionist theory a mortal blow.[20] But nothing could be farther from the fact. Morgan's *societas* (primitive society) and *civitas* (civil society) are logically distinct and mutually exclusive categories, just as *reptile* and *mammal* are. But there may be transitional stages between primitive and civil society, just as there may be transitional stages between reptile and mammal. And these transitional stages do not in any sense render these logical categories or distinctions invalid. A monotreme is an animal that, in the course of biological evolution, acquired the mammalian faculty of suckling the young while at the same time it has retained the old reptilian faculty of laying eggs. In the same way, some of the Negro nations of Africa have acquired, in the course of sociocultural evolution, some of the institutions of civil society, such as a king, while at the same time they have retained some of the institutions of primitive society, such as clan organization. Far from constituting a refutation of cultural evolutionist theory, these mixed systems are made intelligible only in terms of it, i.e., as transitional systems.

[19] See, for example, Lewis H. Morgan, "Montezuma's Dinner," *North American Review*, vol. 122, 1876, as well as *Ancient Society*.

[20] See, for example, R. H. Lowie, *Primitive Society*, 1920, pp. 389–390. Lowie speaks of Morgan's characterizations as "palpable nonsense."

Chapter 13 THE STATE-CHURCH:

ITS FORMS AND FUNCTIONS

The concept of the state-church. Civil societies are characterized by a number of diverse parts and specialized functions, on the one hand, and a special mechanism of coordination, integration, and control, on the other. This special mechanism should have a name, and we have decided to call it the *state-church.* We do this because this mechanism always has both a secular and civil aspect and an ecclesiastical aspect; *state* and *church* properly designate *aspects* of this coordinative, integrative mechanism rather than separate entities. Unless we coin a new term we must rely upon usage, and state-church seems to be the most suitable term that usage affords.

The situation here has a close parallel in physical theory. For a very long time it was thought that *time* and *space* were separate entities. With the development of the theory of relativity, time and space were recognized, not as entities, but as aspects of something for which there was, and still is, no better designation than space-time. Similarly, state and church have long been regarded as separate entities. With the development of culturological theory, however, it is now plain that they are but aspects of something for which we have no better term than state-church. The special coordinative, integrative mechanism of political control in civil societies is everywhere marked by a civil, political, and military aspect, on the one hand, and an ecclesiastical, clerical, and theological aspect, on the other.[1]

State and church may be one structurally, as they were in many cultures of the Bronze Age; or they may be structurally quite distinct, as they are in the United States today; or they may overlap in varying de-

[1] It is interesting to note that the dual character of the mechanism of integration and control in civil society is explicitly recognized by the Roman Catholic Church: "God has divided the government of the human race between two authorities, ecclesiastical and civil, establishing one over things divine, the other over things human." Quoted from an encyclical of Leo XIII by Pius XI in the latter's encyclical "On the Christian Education of Youth," *New York Times Current History,* vol. 31, p. 1097, 1930.

grees. Originally, i.e., with the advent of civil society, the church and the state were one, as Herbert Spencer astutely observed many years ago.[2]

"In Africa," writes Radcliffe-Brown, "it is often hardly possible to separate, even in thought, political office from ritual or religious office. Thus in some African societies it may be said that the king is the executive head, the legislator, the supreme judge, the commander-in-chief of the army, the chief priest or supreme ritual head, and even perhaps the principal capitalist [sic] of the whole community. But it is erroneous to think of him as combining in himself a number of separate and distinct offices. There is a single office, that of king, and its various duties and activities, and its rights, prerogatives, and privileges, make up a single unified whole." [3]

Among the Keresan Pueblos, the cacique is the head of a political organization that is both sacred and secular; he is a priest as well as a chief. Among the Natchez of the Gulf Coast, the head of the sociopolitical system was both king and god. In Mexico at the time of Cortez the ruler was distinguished from the priesthoods, but the ruler was no doubt considered divine. In ancient Peru, the head of the state and the head of the church were brothers, or uncle and nephew; and the former was a god, or descended from the sun god. In Egypt, the pharaoh was for ages god, priest, and king, at least in theory. In practice, the pharaoh had of necessity to delegate the worship of the gods to priests, who acquired thereby so much autonomy as virtually to constitute a church structurally distinct from state.

In the early urban cultures of Mesopotamia, "priestly and secular functions no doubt rested in one and the same person." [4] In ancient Sumer, "church and state were so bound together that those exercising authority formed a theocracy, functioning on the one hand religiously and on the other secularly." [5] The kings of Assyria were priests originally, and they "retain their priestly functions through all periods of the kingdom." [6] "Church and State are one in India." [7] In Greece during the Iron Age the king was also a priest. Many pagan ruling families of Scandinavia reckoned their descent from Nordic deities, even as the

---

[2] "...Originally Church and State are undistinguished." Herbert Spencer, *Principles of Sociology*, vol. 3, 1896, p. 125, in a chapter entitled "Church and State."

[3] A. R. Radcliffe-Brown's Preface to *African Political Systems*, M. Fortes and E. E. Evans-Pritchard (eds.), Oxford University Press, London, 1940, p. xxi.

[4] Morris Jastrow, *The Civilization of Babylonia and Assyria*, J. B. Lippincott Company, Philadelphia, 1915, p. 271.

[5] Ralph Turner, *The Great Cultural Traditions*, vol. 1, McGraw-Hill Book Company, Inc., New York, 1941, p. 287.

[6] Jastrow, *op. cit.*, p. 468, footnote 148.

[7] A. M. Hocart, *Caste: A Comparative Study*, Methuen & Co., Ltd., London, 1950, p. 67.

modern Japanese trace their Emperor to divine ancestry. Caesar was Pontifex Maximus as well as emperor in imperial Rome; Augustus likewise served as the head of the state religion.

The *state* aspect of the mechanism of integration and control of civil societies is, perhaps, more apparent, or obtrusive, today than the *church* aspect. But there were times during the Middle Ages when the church was the more prominent. Also, there is a tendency on the part of many people to think of the church as a "religious" institution only. If, for example, one consults the *Encyclopaedia of the Social Sciences* for an article on "Church," he is requested to "see Religious Institutions." The church is indeed a religious institution from the standpoint of the individual human psyche. But from the standpoint of sociocultural systems, it would be more proper to call it a political institution. In some civil societies there is no organized priesthood or special ecclesiastical structure. This, too, might tend to obscure the ecclesiastical component of the state-church. It should be remembered, however, that state and church, as we are using these terms, do not necessarily label discrete entities, but rather *aspects* of the mechanism by which civil societies are integrated, regulated, and controlled; they are the names of two categories of factors, or components, that comprise the mechanism of integration and control in its totality. We have already noted the fusion of the secular and the ecclesiastical in some systems, but it will be profitable to consider their relationship in some detail in two great non-Western cultures, namely, Islam and China.

The state-church in Islam. Islam has no priesthood. There are men who devote themselves to theology, but they are merely learned men, not priests. The men who conduct religious services at the mosques are laymen. No human being can invoke divine punishment upon another, nor grant him divine mercy or salvation. But this does not mean that religious elements were lacking in the institutional means with which society under Islam was integrated, regulated, and controlled. They were, on the contrary, numerous and powerful.

Church and state were fused in the person of the caliph in Islam. Allah created "the office of sovereign and demands obedience to all of the latter's commands that do not conflict with Muslim law." [8] "Historically the Caliphs are the successors of Muhammad in the rule of the whole Muhammadan state"; [9] they are "vicars of the Prophet." The only valid law of Islam is the sacred law given out by Mohammed; jurisprudence is, in reality, a branch of theology. And the chief duty of the caliph is the enforcement of holy law. The caliph "was the supreme re-

[8] H. E. Barnes, *History of Western Civilization*, Harcourt, Brace and Company, Inc., New York, vol. 1, 1935, p. 527.

[9] Sir T. W. Arnold, *The Caliphate*, Oxford University Press, New York, 1924, p. 199.

ligious head of Islam," writes Barnes, "and the caliphate was a theocracy to a degree rarely matched in any other historic government." [10] Joseph Schacht has summarized the composition and structure of Muslim society as follows: "Islam then permeated both state and civilization, impressing them with a unified religious stamp. . . . Islam became a combination of a religion and an ideal of a state and of a civilization." [11]

Thus we see that, although Islam is without an organized priesthood or ecclesiastical hierarchy, religious elements are powerfully operative in the integrative and regulative processes of the sociocultural system. The state is, in a very real sense, a church also.

The state-church in Chinese culture. Like Islam, China has not possessed an organized priesthood, but again like Islam, religious elements have played a prominent role in the integration, regulation, and control of sociocultural systems in China.

In the first place, the emperor derived his authority from Heaven. Confucius emphasized, in his teachings, the duty of a subject to his ruler. During the Han period Confucius "was deified and worshipped, his disciples receiving sacrifices with him." [12] In 140 B.C., Han Wu Ti officially adopted Confucian principles as the policy of the state. Sacrifices at the tomb of Confucius began early in the Han era. By A.D. 37, the worship had become official. In A.D. 59, Han Ming Ti ordered that sacrifices should be paid to Confucius in the government schools. The influence of Confucius was felt in the government in yet another way, namely, through scholars who were not only influential in governmental administration, but in religious contexts as well. "Han scholars," says Turner, "formed a kind of priest class, and in many respects the Han empire was a glorified priestly monarchy." [13] During the Tang dynasty, "temples to Confucius were erected in all cities of the empire." A Taoist emperor attempted to bestow the title of *ti*, "god-emperor," upon Confucius, but failed. In more recent times the Manchu emperors patronized the Confucians and obtained their support. And during the Republic (1911–1927), an attempt was made to make Confucianism a state religion. [14]

The religious and ecclesiastical aspect of the mechanism of integration and control is thus seen to be very significant in Chinese culture, as in

[10] Barnes, *op. cit.*, pp. 524, 527, 529.

[11] Joseph Schacht, "Islam," in *Encyclopaedia of the Social Sciences*, The Macmillan Company, New York, 1932, pp. 339–340.

[12] John K. Shryock, *The Origin and Development of the State Cult of Confucius*, Appleton-Century-Crofts, Inc., New York, 1932, p. 43. Our discussion of this point is based largely on Shryock.

[13] Turner, *op. cit.*, vol. 2, pp. 838–839.

[14] Shryock, *op. cit.*, pp. 217, 229–230.

Islam, despite the absence of an organized priesthood, or of a formal "church" in the political sense in which we know this institution in Christian Europe.

It would be easy to demonstrate that state and church are but two aspects, or kinds of components, of the special mechanism of integration and control in Western, Christian culture, also. Early church councils made decisions that had the "force of law. Thus the character of the Church as a State institution voiced itself in them." [15] The church of the Middle Ages "was essentially an organised state," according to Flick.[16] And Hayes has enumerated the political powers of the Popes as "supreme lawgiver, supreme judge, and supreme administrator." [17] But an examination of the state-church in western Europe lies outside the province of this volume.

Class structure of civil society. There were two main classes in civil society, the dominant class and the subordinate class, but each of these may be divided into subclasses. The dominant class was composed of the political rulers, priests, and military men. Very often, as we have seen, the king was also a priest. Sometimes, too, the king was the head of the military organization. In some states there was a class of nobles who constituted a rural aristocracy and who ruled over districts of the kingdom. The development of military technology—the introduction first of bronze, later of iron, weapons and the introduction of horses and chariots—led to the formation of military aristocracies. In regions where the commercial, as distinguished from the feudal, type of economy prevailed, a merchant class sometimes rose to power. The independent businessman had become an important figure in society in Hammurabi's time. And in Babylon mercantile oligarchies became powerful enough to rival the priestly and military classes.

The subordinate class consisted of those who produced wealth by means of their labor. They may be divided, first of all, into an urban and a rural working class. The former were craftsmen of various kinds; the latter were agriculturalists. The rural working class was composed of free peasants in some instances; of serfs or slaves, in others. Where a free peasantry existed they were subjected to taxation, which took from them virtually all their produce except that which was required for bare subsistence. The serfs were bound to the soil, and the slaves were mere chattels.

[15] Article, various authors, "Church History," in *Encyclopaedia Britannica,* vol. 5, 1929, p. 679.

[16] A. C. Flick, *The Rise of the Mediaeval Church,* G. P. Putnam's Sons, New York, 1909, pp. 603–604.

[17] C. J. H. Hayes, *A Political and Social History of Modern Europe,* vol. 1, 1916, pp. 116–117.

The earliest specialized craftsmen were workers in temple workshops, where they might be serfs or slaves. In cultures where the commercial type of economy existed, an urban working class developed to provide wares for an expanding commerce. In many instances they were organized into brotherhoods or associations, under the supervision of a royal overseer. The tendency was first to pay craftsmen their wages in kind, i.e., in food and other goods, which they could use only for their own consumption. Later, in the Iron Age, workmen came to be paid money wages.

Slavery, too, seems to have had its beginning in temple organizations, but later the institution became widespread in both urban and rural industries. There were various kinds of slaves: (1) domestic, or household, slaves; (2) craftsmen attached to temples or to royal or noble households; (3) gangs of slaves who worked upon public works such as pyramids, canals, temples, etc.; and (4) agricultural slaves. Conquest and subjugation in war was the earliest source of slaves and continued to be such for a long time. Later a slave trade developed, with raiders capturing persons and selling them into slavery in other lands. The great merchants of Babylon, for example, used to purchase large numbers of slaves from Semitic tribesmen who had captured them on raids. As the commercial type of economy developed, and especially as a consequence of usury, the ranks of slavery were recruited from children who were sold by their parents to pay debts.[18]

A deep and fundamental cleavage thus ran through all civil societies. On the one hand was a class of kings, nobles, priests, and warriors who ruled; on the other were the rural and urban workers who might be "free" or might be serfs or slaves. In any event, they were the wealth-producing class, and virtually all their produce, over and above that required for a bare subsistence, was drawn off by means of taxes, corvées —forced labor—or by simple appropriation.

The property basis of civil society. We shall discuss this subject at greater length in our next chapter, "Economic Structure of Higher Cultures," but it is worthy of note here that the class structure of civil society is merely a political reflex of economic institutions. The dominant, or ruling, class has a virtual monopoly of wealth, as it does of political power. It either possesses it outright or it acquires it by taxation, forced labor, or levies. It may own the human producers of wealth as well as the resources and the technologic means of production. The subordinate, or working, class, on the other hand, are the producers of wealth, but retain but a portion of it for their own consumption.

It is interesting to note, in this connection, an instance of the political

¹⁸ Cf. Turner, *op. cit.*, vol. 1, pp. 297–300.

organization of a nation upon the basis of wealth. One of the provisions of the constitution of Solon, *ca.* 594 B.C., was the division of the citizenry into four classes upon the basis of wealth, each class having political functions commensurate with its wealth.

Territorial organization of civil society. Sir Henry Maine divided human social evolution into two great epochs: primitive society based upon ties of kinship, and modern society organized on a territorial basis. "The history of political ideas begins," he says, "with the assumption that kinship in blood is the sole possible ground of community in political functions." He speaks of the introduction of the principle of local contiguity as a revolutionary innovation. The "idea that a number of persons should exercise political rights in common simply because they happened to live within the same topographical limits was utterly strange and monstrous to primitive antiquity." [19]

Morgan expressed essentially the same views. He, too, divided all human societies into two major types: *societas* and *civitas*. *Societas* embraced those sociocultural systems that we have been calling primitive, or tribal. These societies, said Morgan, "were founded upon persons, and upon relations purely personal." The system which he called *civitas*, or the state, was founded "upon territory and upon property." [20]

We hold this distinction to be valid today despite criticism to which it has been subjected.[21] Lowie accepts the Maine-Morgan distinction between kinship in blood and local contiguity as principles of political organization, but denies that these categories characterize primitive and civil societies, respectively. The territorial factor, he argues, is significant in the political organization of primitive peoples, and he traces the development of the state throughout primitive society from "primeval" beginnings.[22] Lowie fails, however, to produce any society that is organized throughout upon the basis of kinship ties that also recognizes, in Maine's terms, "political rights in common simply because they happened to live within the same topographical units." [23] And we have already called attention to the fact that foreigners, residing per-

[19] Sir Henry Maine, "Primitive Society and Ancient Law," chap. 5, *Ancient Law*, 1861.

[20] Lewis H. Morgan, *Ancient Society*, chap. 1, 1877.

[21] Notably by Robert H. Lowie, in *Primitive Society*, 1947, pp. 390–396, and in his *The Origin of the State*, 1927. Morgan's categories and their evolutionary sequence are accepted, however, by Radcliffe-Brown: "Indeed, we may agree with Morgan that the passage from lower forms of civilization to higher forms such as our own was essentially a passage from society based on kinship to the state based on political organization." "Some Problems of Bantu Sociology," *Bantu Studies*, vol. 1, October, 1922, pp. 40–41.

[22] Lowie, *The Origin of the State*.

[23] Maine, *op. cit.*

manently in Athens, had no political rights at all because they were not members of Greek kinship groups (the *gentes*).

While we do not admit that local contiguity ever constituted a principle of political organization in tribal society based upon kinship, we believe that we can discover in primitive society some of the antecedents of territorial political organization. To reduce a great mass of data to a single statement, we believe it fair to say that in the transition from tribal society to civil society, localized kinship groups became territorial units in the political system.

Localized clans are not uncommon in many primitive societies. And even in tribal villages where all clans live together in a single community, there is often spatial distinction between one clan grouping and another. After all, people must live somewhere, and this results, in some instances, in a close correspondence between kinship grouping and place grouping. As tribes and clans grow larger and larger, the ties of kinship weaken, as we have noted repeatedly, and the kinship organization tends to fall apart of its own weight. As the kinship factor wanes, the territorial factor waxes. By the time a special mechanism of coordination, integration, and administration has been developed and kinship has been supplanted by property as the basis of social organization, it is territorial unit, rather than kinship group, that becomes significant as a principle of political organization.

The Ganda of Uganda were organized into some thirty exogamous, patrilineal clans. Since the Ganda numbered almost a million people, most of the clans had several thousand members. A clan of this size would be too unwieldy to be significant or effective in the conduct of social life, so they were divided into subclans. Each subclan had its own district which was administered by a chief. But the nation as a whole, which was ruled by a king who wielded absolute power, in theory at least, was divided into ten districts, each of which was administered by a chief, or "earl," appointed by the king. Each district was divided into subdistricts, which were administered by subchiefs of various grades, also appointed by the king. Much of the kinship organization was preserved in the clans, or rather the subclans, and was significant in the daily life of the common people. But with regard to the organization and administration of the nation as a whole, it was territorial organization that was functionally significant.

We find territorial units in the political organization of some cultures, where there are indications that these units were once kinship groups. This is the case of the *calpulli* of the Aztecs. There are indications that they were originally exogamous, patrilineal clans, but by the time of the Spanish conquest they had become "localized in separate districts...

each with its own temple and cult, council house and officials. . . ." [24] The twenty *calpulli* districts were the component parts of the four quarters into which Mexico was divided for governmental purposes. Similarly the *ayllu* of the Inca empire was, apparently, an exogamous, matrilineal kinship group which became a standardized unit of one hundred male heads of households. Each *ayllu* had a definite territory. A "tribe" was composed of 10,000 male heads of households, and four tribes constituted a "province"; the provinces of the empire were grouped into four "quarters," each ruled by a viceroy. The kinship organization was transformed into a territorially organized political system. [25]

In the evolution of political organization in ancient Egypt, clans were transformed into territorial groupings called *nomes*, as Turner interprets the evidence: "With the development of the nomes as territorial administrative areas . . . tribal organization was replaced by territorial rule." [26] In ancient Greece, four tribes became unified in a single political structure, Attica, about 700 B.C. The population was divided into three classes, according to wealth. To facilitate the raising and maintenance of military and naval forces, Attica was divided into forty-eight districts, or *naukraries*, twelve for each of the four tribes. About two centuries later, the trend from kinship to territorial organization was carried further by the reforms of Cleisthenes. He abolished the four Ionian tribes and substituted ten new and wholly artificial "tribes" in their stead. Membership in these tribes was based upon residence in the *deme*, a village or township of Attica, or a section of Athens itself. According to Aristotle's *Constitution of Athens*, Attica was further divided into three geographical regions: urban and suburban, inland, and maritime. Each region was subdivided into ten *trittyes*. Each tribe had three *trittyes*, one located in each of these three regions. Furthermore, artisans and merchants who had migrated to Attica and had settled there, but who, up to this time, had had no political rights because they were outside the kinship organization, were now given citizenship by the reforms of Cleisthenes. Here again we see kinship organization giving way and territorial organization taking form.

The territorial organization of modern nations is made manifest in units such as states, counties, townships, shires, Congressional districts, and so on.

---

[24] George P. Murdock's summary description of Aztec culture in *Our Primitive Contemporaries*, The Macmillan Company, New York, 1934, p. 372. Murdock calls the *calpulli* "clans," however. See L. A. White's discussion in *Pioneers in American Anthropology*, vol. 1, 1940, pp. 27–30, 40–43.

[25] Murdock, *op. cit.*, pp. 410, 415–416.

[26] Turner, *op. cit.*, vol. 1, p. 180.

Political forms: monarchy, feudalism, democracy. The political systems of civil society have a variety of forms which, however, may be grouped roughly under the rubrics of monarchy, feudalism, and democracy, or parliamentary forms. Little need be said of the monarchical form since it is very common and rather well understood. A single individual, a king, stands at the head of the political organization of the state. He may also be a priest; he may be the head of the armed forces. His power may be virtually absolute, or it may be qualified by a council of nobles or by a parliament. The characteristic of the monarchical form is *centralization of power.*

The feudal form is distinguished by decentralization. It may have a king, but if so his power is limited, or perhaps merely nominal. Feudalism is characterized by a number of local, territorial nobles, often a military aristocracy, who, under the nominal authority of a king, or independently and in their own right, rule their respective demesnes.

We can point to no instance of the democratic, or parliamentary, form of government among the great cultures of the Bronze Age and only a few during the Iron Age; parliamentary government is essentially a characteristic of the modern era of Western culture. There are, however, a few examples of democratic, or republican, forms of government in the cultures of ancient Greece and Rome. We shall cite an example of the former.

Athenian democracy began with the constitution of Solon, *ca.* 594 B.C. This document divided the citizenry into four classes based upon wealth and admitted the lowest class to political rights—to sit in the Assembly and on juries, to participate in the election of magistrates, etc. The chief offices in the executive, judicial, and religious spheres were, however, open only to the wealthiest citizens. The reign of the tyrant Pisistratus and his two sons was followed by another constitutional reform authored by Cleisthenes, *ca.* 502 B.C. The state was organized territorially; it was divided into a hundred or more districts called demes. Every Athenian citizen became a member of a deme and exercised political rights by virtue of this membership. The state was administered by a Council of Five Hundred, which was composed of men selected by lot from candidates elected by the demes. Any citizen was eligible to sit in the Council. Then there was an Assembly which consisted of "the entire citizenry over twenty years of age" and which "met regularly ten times a year." [27] Under the constitution of Cleisthenes, Athens was governed by elected officials. There was no property qualification for office, and, under Pericles, officials were paid for their service, making

[27] Turner, *op. cit.*, vol. 1, p. 470; our account of Athenian democracy is drawn largely from Turner.

it possible for poor citizens to hold office. The Assembly could try officials on charges of treason, impiety, or improper performance of their duties, and if convicted, they could order punishment in the form of fines, exile, or death.

Democracy in ancient Athens did not mean that all men were equal politically by any means. Even though "the development of democracy had given power to the poor citizens," says Turner, "the chief functionaries of the state were, almost without exception, members of the noble and wealthy landowning families."[28] Furthermore, only *citizens* had political rights, and this class constituted only about 55 per cent of the population. The other classes were slaves, 36 per cent, and the metics, or foreigners, who comprised about 9 per cent. The metics could not vote or hold office or become members of the priesthood. They could not own land, or ask the state for relief in times of dire need. Even their children were regarded as illegitimate. They were, however, obliged to pay taxes such as were levied upon citizens and an additional metic tax. Failure to pay the latter tax reduced the metic to slavery.

Function of the state-church. The function of the state-church, in a word, is the preservation of the integrity of the sociocultural system of which it is a part. This means, as we have seen, coordination and control of parts and regulation of the system as a whole. The integrity of civil social systems is threatened from two directions: outside and inside. If a sociocultural system is to preserve its identity and integrity, it must defend itself from its enemies abroad. But sometimes the best *de*fense, in international relations as well as in prize fighting, is *of*fense. This means, then, that the state-church must mobilize the resources—people and materials—of its own sociocultural system from time to time and employ them in military effort of offense and defense, in short, in warfare. The integrity of a social system may be threatened from within as well as from without. All civil societies are composed of classes with conflicting interests. In every instance there is the dichotomy of a minority ruling class with a virtual monopoly of wealth or political power or both, and a majority of the population held in bondage of one sort or another, economic or political or both. And in many societies there is competition and rivalry among the upper classes for the position of supremacy.

The struggle between dominant and subordinate classes has been chronic and perennial in civil society. The lower classes—the slaves, serfs, industrial proletariat—periodically try to better their lot by revolt and insurrection. If the social system is to be kept intact, if it is not to explode in violence and subside in anarchy, the relationship of subordina-

[28] *Ibid.,* p. 471.

tion and superordination between the classes must be maintained; in other words, the subordinate class must be kept in a condition of subjection and exploitation. It is the business of the state-church to see that this is done.

The subjugation of the masses, and the attitudes of dominant and subordinate classes toward each other, have been graphically described by Turner: [29]

"In the alliance of the priest class and the military class [i.e., the secular arm of the state-church] religious duty, legal right, and force were fused, and the original peasant-village attitude of acquiescence to the overworld of spirits was elaborated into a subservient manner toward earthly superiors. As the masses became servile, the priestly and military classes became lordly and arrogant. They looked upon labor as degrading and explained the refinements of life which their exploitation of the masses made possible as the result of their own superior mental and moral qualities. To the subservience of the exploited masses they opposed a patronizing insolence and declared the masses fit for no better lot than working to support their betters. They suppressed the resistance of the masses by a ferocity which, while maintaining their domination, only made the masses more brutal. Urban cultures taught both the power-holding groups and the powerless masses the utility of the resort to violence for political purposes."

In addition to preserving the integrity of its own sociocultural system against enemy attack from abroad and from revolt and insurrection from within, the state-church has other functions of internal organization, regulation, and control. These have to do with the tremendously important process of transmitting culture from each generation to its successor, namely, *education*, with relationships between persons in marriage and the family, with crime and punishment, property relations, public health, social welfare, means of transportation and communication, and so on. We now wish to consider these functions of the state-church in their specific and concrete manifestations. We shall do this first from the standpoint of the state, then of the church.

The State

War. All states maintain military, and some have naval, forces for the purpose of waging offensive and defensive warfare with their neighbors. In this respect they are all alike; they differ in the ways in which this is done, and we may note a few specific instances. Probably the most common method of raising an army is by levies or conscription;

[29] *Ibid.*, vol. 2, p. 1283.

this has been the practice of ancient and modern societies alike. Another method much in vogue has been the use of mercenaries.

In some instances, the head of the state is also the head of the army and actually leads or accompanies it on its campaigns. It appears that the Egyptian pharaohs once led their armies in person. Eventually, however, a professional military class develops and takes over the actual conduct of military affairs. Sargon of Akkad, in the third millennium B.C., seems to have been the first to establish a permanent military force. We learn from the code of Hammurabi that a special military class existed in Babylonia.

Some states made use of spies as "distance-perceptors" for the armies and military intelligence for the government. The merchants of the Aztecs, for example, used to serve as spies among the peoples with whom they traded.

Material resources as well as manpower are mobilized by the state. We have already taken brief note of the consequences of war. A portion of the population of the defeated nation may be taken home by the victors as slaves; Sargon of Akkad "introduced the practice of enslaving the entire populations of subjected cities." [30] There may be annexation of conquered territory, in which case the vanquished may be kept on the land as serfs and vassals. The victor appropriates the wealth of the vanquished in varying degree, and in diverse ways—as loot, spoils, trophies, or levies. This wealth is commonly distributed among the ruling class of the conquering nation: members of the ruling family and the government, the church and priesthoods, and military leaders. Warfare tends to maintain and even to intensify the class structure of nations. Peoples of the vanquished nation are subjugated. The masses of the victorious nation have become subordinated to absolute rule as a condition of waging war, while the ruling class becomes enriched and more strongly entrenched in power.

Class struggles. The lot of the subordinate class is often a hard one, and excessive privation and toil, coupled frequently with harsh and brutal treatment, incite them to revolt. Slave revolts, insurrections of serfs, uprisings of peasants are chronic and periodic occurrences in civil society.

An insurrection of the masses took place in Egypt as early as 2200 B.C., according to Moret and Turner.[31] Another uprising occurred during

---

[30] *Ibid.*, vol. 1, p. 298.

[31] Alexandre Moret, *The Nile and Egyptian Civilization*, 1927, pp. 224-231; Ralph Turner, *op. cit.*, vol. 1, pp. 185-186, 301-302. H. Frankfort, however, says that there is no evidence of "any trace of revolution in three thousand years of recorded

the Twentieth Dynasty. "Both had their origin in the failure of the ruling classes to permit the masses to have sufficient food," says Turner, "and both were accompanied by disorder, murder, and robbery." [32] Iranian peasants rose against the priests and nobles in the Mazdakian revolt about A.D. 500, seizing land and cattle and transforming their villages into communistic communities. There were uprisings of peasants and miners in China under the early Han emperors. In Sparta, secret agents circulated among the *helots*, one of the two servile classes, to search out and kill "anyone who was disobedient or showed signs of possessing superior intelligence." [33] A quarter of a million slaves rose in revolt in Sicily in the second century B.C. They were starved into submission, and thousands of them were crucified. A slave revolt in Italy led by Spartacus in 73 B.C. was eventually put down on the field of battle; 6,000 of his followers were crucified along the Appian Way. These are but a few examples of the countless insurrections and uprisings throughout the length and breadth of civil society for centuries on end.

It is the business of the state, the secular arm of the special mechanism of integration and control in civil society, to put down these insurrections in order to preserve the integrity of the nation within which they occur. And the sternest measures are employed in this process; mass executions are the rule. Sometimes, of course, the state does not succeed in quelling a revolt, or, at least, it does not remain unshaken by it. The first great revolt in Egypt "destroyed the power of Memphis," says Turner, and the second, in the Twentieth Dynasty, "weakened the position of Thebes, the capital of the empire.... Upper Egypt never recovered from this disaster...." [34] The disruptive effect of insurrection, on the one hand, and the role of the state in putting down revolts, on the other, are made crystal clear by these examples.

Blood revenge and private wars. In primitive society an injury or a death was avenged by the injured party or by his kinsmen. And in case the actual culprit could not be found for punishment, revenge could be inflicted upon members of his family. In short, in tribal society, venge-

---

history" in ancient Egypt. "There were strikes and demonstrations [sic] in the Theban necropolis in Ramessid times when rations fell a month behind time. But there is no trace of any political movement against the existing order. On the contrary, the people showed their affection for the institution of kingship...." H. Frankfort, *Ancient Egyptian Religion*, Columbia University Press, New York, 1948, pp. 31, 43.

[32] Ralph Turner, *The Great Cultural Traditions*, vol. 1, McGraw-Hill Book Company, Inc., 1941, p. 302.

[33] *Ibid.*, p. 467.

[34] *Ibid.*, p. 302.

ance was an affair among kin groups, a private right rather than a public, tribal prerogative. On higher cultural levels, where property is more abundant and is coming to be more significant in social relations, the rule of a life for a life, an eye for an eye, becomes commuted into money, and the wergild is established in a series of gradations corresponding to the seriousness of the offense.

With the advent of civil society private vengeance becomes outlawed, and the state assumes an exclusive right to kill. This applies both to personal vengeance and private "wars," such as used to be fought by Scottish clans. Blood revenge had been outlawed in the ancient Aztec and Inca states, and in Negro African monarchies such as those of the Ganda and the Dahomeans. The state had exclusive jurisdiction over crimes in ancient Egypt and Mesopotamia. The outlawing of private vengeance and wars is one of the best indications that could be cited of the achievement of full status of civil society. It is interesting to note, however, that this point was reached rather late among Germanic peoples and in England. "As late as 1439," according to Munroe Smith, "the schöffen (criminal judges) of Namur declared in a judgment: 'If the kin of the slain man will and can avenge him, good luck to them, for with this matter we schöffen have nothing to do.'" [35] And as recently as the fifteenth century in England, a private war was fought between two noblemen and their followers.[36] One of the leaders was killed, and a money payment was made to his widow by his opponent. This appears to have been the last instance either of private war or of wergild in England.[37]

State and property. Given the class character and property basis of civil society, it is easy to see that property rights must be protected by the state-church. There must be some means to protect the property-holding classes in the possession of their wealth; and there must be ways of appropriating the economic surplus from the working class. These ways and means are political and are employed by state and church alike. We have already had occasion to take note of the relation of the state to property in our previous discussion of civil society in general. It has long been recognized that one of the basic functions of the state is to establish and to maintain an economic system. "Governments, institutions,

[35] Munroe Smith, *The Development of European Law*, Columbia University Press, New York, 1928, p. 30.

[36] In the tenth century King Edmund attempted to stop private wars by making them illegal. "It was a turning point in English history" when he did this, says Tylor, "but it was not stopped at once.... Long after the mere freeman ceased to go to war with his neighbors, there were nobles who stood to their old right." E. B. Tylor, *Anthropology*, 1881, pp. 418–419.

[37] *Ibid.*, p. 419.

and laws," observed Morgan, "are simply contrivances for the creation and protection of property." [38] Similarly, the distinguished German sociologist Tönnies remarked that "societies and states are chiefly institutions for the peaceful [sic] acquisition and for the protection of property." [39] This is the view of the Roman Catholic Church also, as set forth by Pope Leo XIII in his encyclical "On the Condition of Labor." In a section headed "The State Should Protect Private Property," he says, "It must be borne in mind that the chief thing to be secured is the safeguarding, by legal enactment and policy, of private property."

Class structure rests upon property relations in civil society, and the state undertakes to maintain both. In some cultures, however, the stability of class structure is threatened by economic processes. It might happen, for example, that some members of the "lower classes" might acquire enough wealth to enable them to wear clothing or ornaments characteristic of the upper classes. If this should happen, the position and prerogatives of the upper classes would be threatened, and there is no telling how far the elevation of the lower classes might go. To prevent this assault upon class structure and the privileges of the upper classes, some societies have resorted to sumptuary laws. A sumptuary law prevents one from consuming or displaying his wealth as he pleases; it is a political device for keeping an economic process in check. Ordinarily, of course, there is no need for legislative controls; the lower classes are usually unable to afford everything they need, to say nothing of luxuries. But when economic conditions place luxuries in the hands of some members of a subordinate class, the state may have recourse to legislation to preserve the class structure of the society. Among the Incas, for example, the common people "could wear only the coarser garments of llama wool, the finer fabrics of alpaca and vicuña wool being reserved for the nobility. Forbidden to them, also, were the choicer food delicacies, the more intoxicating beverages, and coca. They might wear wisps of straw or wool in their ears, or small pendants of wood or clay, but not larger earrings of dearer materials. They could adorn themselves with neither gems, feathers, nor the gold and silver rings, arm bands, anklets, and breast ornaments of the upper classes." [40] In pre-Columbian Mexico, it was a capital offense for an Aztec commoner "to build a stone house or to wear cotton clothing or ornaments of gold and precious stones." [41] Silk clothing was an exclusive privilege of princes and the aristocracy in

---

[38] *Extracts from the European Travel Journal of Lewis H. Morgan*, Leslie A. White (ed.), Rochester Historical Society Publications, vol. 16, 1937, p. 269.

[39] Ferdinand Tönnies, "The Problems of Social Structure," *Proceedings, Congress of Arts and Sciences*, 1904, vol. 5, p. 839, 1906.

[40] Murdock, *op. cit.*, p. 419.

[41] *Ibid.*, p. 378.

China in early Han times, and sumptuary legislation was enacted to keep a rising merchant class from wearing it.[42] We find sumptuary legislation in western European culture, also. In England under the Tudors, for example, "no man under the degree of a lord is to wear any cloth of gold or silver, sables.... Velvet of crimson or blue is prohibited to any one under the degree of a knight of the garter.... Coming to the lowest class, no serving man is to use above 2½ yards in a short gown or 3 in a long one; and servants of husbandry, shepherds, and labourers, not having goods above £10 in value, are forbidden to wear cloth exceeding 2s. the yard, or hose exceeding 10d. the yard, under pain of three days' confinement in the stocks." [43]

Punishment of theft. As a means of safeguarding the property foundation of civil society, the state punished theft with severity. Among the Aztecs thieves were enslaved. Petty theft in the Inca state was punished by flogging; theft from the state was punished by death. The Ganda killed a thief if caught in the act; otherwise he was mutilated. In the great urban cultures of the Bronze Age death or mutilation was the usual punishment for theft. Whether drastic punishment acted as a deterrent or not is a question for which we have no adequate answer. But whether it did or did not, it was employed for this purpose. And the frequently lethal reprisals imposed by the state certainly kept many persons from committing the offense a second time.

Irrigation. Irrigation is of necessity a communal enterprise. Even in some primitive tribes we find irrigation carried on by the community under the direction of a tribal administrator.[44] Irrigation was a state enterprise in aboriginal Peru and Mexico. And one of the principal functions of the state in the great urban cultures of the Bronze Age was the irrigation of the fields; their economy depended primarily upon it, and consequently their whole political and social system rested upon this foundation.

State monopolies. In many of the ancient cultures of the Bronze Age the state undertook to conduct or to administer certain industries or to monopolize the commercial exchange of certain goods. Merchant classes were not prominent in societies of the early Bronze Age, and therefore it was necessary in many instances for the state to exercise industrial and commercial functions.

[42] Turner, *op. cit.*, vol. 2, pp. 815, 821.
[43] W. E. Hooper, "The Tudor Sumptuary Laws," *English Historical Review*, vol. 30, pp. 433–434, 1915.
[44] See, for example, Leslie A. White, "The Pueblo of Santa Ana, New Mexico," *American Anthropological Association Memoir* 60, 1942, pp. 105–106.

In ancient China, for example, the state held, at various times, monopolies of such resources and manufactures as forest products, salt manufacture, iron, shellfish beds, fermented drinks, etc.[45]

"In Mauryan India, Han China, Sassanian Persia, the Hellenistic kingdoms, and imperial Rome the state, i.e., the politically organized ruling class, kept industrial enterprise mainly in its hands. The state monopolies were established more as a means of raising revenue, directing labor, and controlling prices than as a way of organizing capital, and except in mining, metalworking, and textile making the state enterprises were principally of the kind known as public works—the building of walls, roads, aqueducts, canals, embankments, palaces, and temples. Such enterprises were conducted as state undertakings, partly because only the state could finance them and partly because the necessary labor force could be commanded only by political authority." [46]

Money, markets, weights and measures. The state came to exercise influence upon the economic processes of civil society through its supervision of markets and weights and measures and through its eventual monopoly of the right to coin and issue money. We find markets supervised by government officials among the Aztecs of Cortez' day and in some of the Negro African monarchies.

Roads and travel. Integration of a sociocultural system requires means of communication and transportation, and we find the state functioning in this field, also. The Aztecs had a system of well-kept roads; streams were spanned by wooden or suspension bridges. Couriers were stationed at posts along the roads. It is said that fresh fish was brought daily from the Gulf of Mexico to the capital for Montezuma's table. In pre-Columbian Peru two main highways, one coastal, the other inland, traversed the Inca empire from north to south, and a network of crossroads radiated out from the capital, Cuzco. Courier stations were located every two or three miles, and messages could be transmitted speedily: the distance between Quito and Cuzco, 1,300 miles, was negotiated in ten days. In Uganda, a network of excellent roads, sometimes more than 12 feet wide, connected the residence of the king with those of his principal chiefs, and those in turn with the lesser chiefs. In the Macedonian empire policed highways, provided with shelters, traversed the land. The royal road from Sardis to Susa, 1,500 miles, required two weeks' travel time. In China, prior to the Han dynasty, a vast system of roads radiating out from the capital, Hsien Yang in Shensi, was constructed by the king; it gave him a great advantage over the feudal nobles

[45] M. Granet, *Chinese Civilization*, 1930, pp. 87–88, 113.
[46] Turner, *op. cit.*, vol. 2, pp. 1259–1260.

and assisted materially in unification of land and government. And finally, Rome was outstanding in the construction of roads. In Trajan's time there were 47,000 miles of highway. Caesar once made a journey of 800 miles in ten days. Many Roman roads were paved, had inns, road guides, and signposts.

Government and the individual. The process of coordination, integration, and control of a sociocultural system must concern itself with the individual as the irreducible unit of its structure. The state supervises and controls the life of an individual in general, and it applies special pressure upon him at various points, such as birth, marriage, military service, and death. The individual is subject to laws with respect to class status, property, theft, and other offenses. But perhaps the state's greatest concern with the individual has to do with his education and training.

Education. In our society, and from the standpoint of scholars, learning and education are intellectual activities dedicated to the search for truth and the transmission of these truths to others. From the standpoint of a sociocultural system, however, education is a political process; it is a means of social integration and control. From an anthropological point of view, education is the process whereby the culture of one generation is passed on to the next; it is the way in which society imposes customs, beliefs, attitudes, ideals, and patterns of behavior upon individuals. The process of education may be formal or informal, and the latter is likely to be the more effective in shaping one's life because it is more continuous, more pervasive, and is an integral part of everyday life. The conception of education as a political process was well expressed by Aristotle: "Of all things that I have mentioned that which contributes most to the permanence of constitutions is the adaptation of education to the form of government.... That education should be regulated by law and should be an affair of the state is not to be denied. *The citizen should be moulded to suit the form of government under which he lives* [italics supplied]." [47] He praised the Lacedaemonians because "they take the greatest pains about their children, and make education the business of the state." [48]

There is little state concern with the education of the masses in the ancient Bronze Age cultures, although even among the Aztecs we find

[47] Aristotle, *Politics*, book 5, chap. 9, p. 1310a; book 8, chaps. 1 and 2, p. 1337a.

[48] Over two thousand years later Napoleon Bonaparte expressed much the same view: "Of all political questions that (of education) is perhaps the most important. There cannot be a firmly established political state unless there is a teaching body with definitely recognized principles." I. L. Kandel, "Education, Public," in *Encyclopaedia of the Social Sciences*, vol. 5, The Macmillan Company, New York, 1931, p. 415.

district schools for the sons of commoners. In ancient Egypt, during the Old Kingdom, there were schools attached to the palace to train young men in such practical affairs as writing, mathematics, engineering, medicine, etc. "Education consisted solely of the practically useful equipment for an official career." [49] In ancient India the ecclesiastical influence in education was great, but there were relatively secular schools for instruction in practical matters. Also, in some instances, emperors were patrons of universities, and some scholars exercised considerable political influence. In China, education became an integral part of the political organization of the state. A knowledge of the classics was necessary to ennoblement in the time of Wu Ti (second century B.C.). For centuries one had to pass an examination before he could be appointed to political office, so that, as Counts has observed, China was ruled by scholars.[50] This system also had the effect of securely binding "the entire learned group to the throne." [51] In Japan during the Nara period (about eighth century A.D.), the primary aim of education was to train men for official posts.[52]

Ancient Greek society had a pronounced secular emphasis—Aristotle does not even mention priests in his list of occupational groups or classes. The chief concern was with the relation between the individual and the state, not between man and God. Plato's *Laws* and *Republic* and Aristotle's *Politics* and his studies of constitutions indicate the focus of interest in Greek social life and thought. Education, therefore, was to be a concern of the state. According to both Plato and Aristotle, education should be regulated by the state authority; it should be compulsory for free citizens and uniform for all.

Education in Rome in early times was confined largely to the family; later, elementary schools were established. Under the empire the rhetorical schools were gradually organized into a state system.

Summary of the state's functions. We have now seen how the state, by means of such governmental machinery as kings, lords, viziers, and ministers, assemblies or parliaments, courts, police, and penal institutions, integrates, regulates, and controls much of the life of civil societies. They defend them against aggression from abroad and from insurrection within.[53] And they carry on or regulate many intrasocietal

[49] J. H. Breasted, *History of Egypt*, rev. ed., Charles Scribner's Sons, New York, 1909, p. 100.

[50] G. S. Counts, "Education, History," in *Encyclopaedia of the Social Sciences*, vol. 5, 1931, p. 404.

[51] Turner, *op. cit.*, vol. 2, p. 831.

[52] F. Brinkley, *A History of the Japanese People*, 1915, p. 214.

[53] "Within the state, the social order, whatever it may be, is maintained by the punishment of those who offend against the laws and by the armed suppression of

processes—of communication, transportation, irrigation, public health and welfare, finance and commerce, punishment of crime, education, etc.—which are essential or desirable to the effective functioning of the society. The goal or objective of these endeavors is security, continuity, and the effective functioning of the sociocultural system.

The Church

Having surveyed the functions of the state as a mechanism of integration, regulation, and control, let us now turn to the church. If, as we have premised, state and church are but two aspects, or segments, of the special integrative and regulative mechanism of civil societies, then we should expect to find that the functions of the church, and the role that it plays in the social organism, are fundamentally like those of the state. This, as a matter of fact, is what we do find, as the following will show.

In a word, the function of the church in civil society is to preserve the integrity of the sociocultural system of which it is a part by (1) offensive-defensive relations with neighboring nations, (2) keeping the subordinate class at home obedient and docile in order to prevent disintegration as a consequence of insurrection and civil war, and (3) carrying on intrasocietal processes of various kinds, such as agriculture, irrigation, handicraft industries, business transactions, public works, and in influencing the lives of individuals by means of education and rituals.

Everywhere in civil society the clergy—the higher clergy, at least—is a part of the ruling class, and as such exerts great political influence or authority and enjoys prerogatives of great wealth. As we have already noted, there is often a very close relationship between the head of the government and the priesthoods; the ruler himself is not infrequently a priest. And where this is not the case, the priests invariably advise the rulers on matters of policy. The two head priests of the Aztecs "advised the king and council on matters of war and public policy." [54] The head of the church in aboriginal Peru was the brother or the uncle of the Inca, the head of the government. In Egypt the rivalry between pharaoh and the priesthoods eventually led to the domination of the throne by the latter. And "the Assyrian autocrats ... did not embark on any public action without consulting her [Ishtar's] priests." [55] In Greece and Rome

---

revolt. Externally the state stands ready to use armed force against other states, either to maintain the existing order or to create a new one." A. R. Radcliffe-Brown, Preface to *African Political Systems*, M. Fortes and E. E. Evans-Pritchard (eds.), Oxford University Press, London, 1940, p. xiv.

[54] Murdock, *op. cit.*, p. 390.

[55] Turner, *The Great Cultural Traditions*, vol. 1, McGraw-Hill Book Company, Inc., New York, 1941, p. 292.

the priests exerted much political influence, but they "were too closely identified with the secular ruling classes to develop independent power." [56]

War. It may safely be said that no war can be fought without recourse to the supernatural. In civil society it is the business of the clergy, as it was of the medicine man in tribal cultures, to mobilize the population for military purposes. The principal god of the Aztecs was Uitzilopochtli, the god of war, and his priest was one of the two heads of the ecclesiastical hierarchy. Military expeditions were led by priests and the idols of gods. And one of the chief functions of war among the Aztecs was to obtain captives for the temple sacrifices. In Egypt and other ancient cultures of the Old World, victory in war was a gift of the gods: "Amon has given to me his victory," declared Rameses II after the battle of Kadesh. And consequently, the gods must be rewarded by gifts to, or a division of the spoils of war with, the priesthoods.

Class structure. The priesthoods of the urban cultures of antiquity were an integral part of the class structure of civil society, and consequently they accepted this class structure as they accepted their own existence. The masses were on one side; the rulers, military leaders, and priests were on the other; this was in accordance with the will and plan of the gods, and therefore it was a religious duty to maintain and perpetuate the system. Far from opposing slavery, it appears that "at first slaves were probably confined to the temples" where they worked as agricultural laborers or as handicraftsmen.[57]

Social control: education and worship. As we noted earlier, in our discussion of ethics, whereas the gods did not intrude into the domestic affairs of primitive peoples, they became very much concerned with the behavior of the masses in civil societies; that is to say, the priesthoods employed theology and ritual to instill obedience and docility into the minds of the masses and make them loyal to the established order. The military force of the state was not enough to cope with the chronic and ever-recurring threat of insurrection, civil war, and anarchy; the resources of the church must be employed to this end also. So it was that the priests taught the masses, and validated these teachings with the wonders and mysteries of religion, that they should accept, and even defend, the established order. For the Egyptians, the universe was a moral order established by the sun god, Re, and their social ideal involved "a full acceptance of class status, the inferiority of labor, and poverty as the ordinary condition of common men; these, indeed, were aspects of the

[56] *Ibid.*, vol. 2, p. 1256.
[57] *Ibid.*

divine moral order." [58] Buddhism taught men and women to be content with their lot and station in life. The teaching of Confucius "devoted its whole attention to making people recognize their betters with distinction," according to Ku Chieh-kang, "and that is certainly a most advantageous theory to an autocratic despot." [59] More recently, the Roman Catholic Church has recognized the utility and function of religion as means of preventing insurrection by "subduing the souls of men." [60]

Church and property. In keeping with its role as a component of the special mechanism of integration and control in civil society, the church possesses and enjoys great wealth. The ruling class possesses a virtual monopoly of wealth as well as of political power, and the higher clergy is a significant part of the ruling class.

"Man lives but by the grace of God" expresses an attitude found in virtually all cultures. Man cannot live by his own efforts alone; he must have assistance from the spirit world. So it is that even in the crudest cultures, subsisting wholly upon wild foods, sacrifices are made to the gods in return for their help. First-fruits offerings are made in early horticultural societies. Eventually this gratitude and recompense are extended to the human representatives, or vicars, of the gods: the priests. In some tribal societies, such as the Pueblos of the American Southwest, priests receive at least partial support. The priest-chief of the Keresan Pueblos owns all the land, in theory at least, and as the earthly representative of Iatiku, the Mother, he is supported by the community.[61] In the early urban cultures brought forth by the Agricultural Revolution, the land was owned by the god who was represented by a priesthood or by a king, who might also be a priest, or by both. A portion of produce must therefore go to the priesthood or to the king as "payment" for the use of the land. As the Agricultural Revolution progressed, kings and nobles and priesthoods came to possess more and more land and wealth derived from the arts and industries.

[58] Turner, *op. cit.*, vol. 1, pp. 213–214; see also pp. 313, 323 for comment upon the role of priests in general in maintaining class rule.

[59] Ku Chieh-kang, "History," in *The Chinese Year Book*, Shanghai, 1935, p. 45.

[60] "Only too well does experience show that when religion is banished, human authority totters to its fall...when the rulers of the people disdain the authority of God, the people in turn despise the authority of men. There remains, it is true, the usual expedient of suppressing rebellion by force; but to what effect? *Force subdues the bodies of men, not their souls* [italics supplied]." Encyclical of Pope Benedict XV, *Ad Beatissimi*, as quoted by John A. Ryan, D.D., and Francis J. Boland, C.S.C., in *Catholic Principles of Politics*, The Macmillan Company, New York, 1940, pp. 135–136.

[61] See L. A. White, "The Pueblo of Santa Ana, New Mexico."

Among the Aztecs, the priests "lived in ease and often in luxury, supported by large landed estates, rich contributions of tribute, and a continuous stream of sacrificial donations." [62] In ancient Peru, the land was divided into three parts, one of which was cultivated for the benefit of the temples and priesthoods. The temples possessed considerable wealth. The principal one, the Temple of the Sun, "had a golden garden, where trees and plants, fruits and flowers, birds and insects were all of gold, and where grazed a herd of golden llamas under a life-sized golden shepherd." [63]

The church owned vast wealth in ancient Egypt. We learn from the Harris Papyrus [64] that at about the time of Rameses III (1198–1167 B.C.), the temples owned over 107,000 slaves, or about 2 per cent of the population; about 750,000 acres of land, or about 15 per cent of all the tillable land in Egypt; about 500,000 head of cattle; a fleet of 88 ships; 53 workshops and shipyards; and all this in a land of "less than 10,000 square miles and some five or six million inhabitants." (Massachusetts has an area of 8,266 square miles and in 1940 a population of 4,316,721 inhabitants). At one time the Temple of Amon, at Thebes, alone held over a half million acres of land, 81,322 men, 421,400 head of livestock, 83 boats, and 65 villages.[65] The temples of Mesopotamia were also wealthy.

Temples became centers of business and industry. The temple of Baü, in Lagash, a city of ancient Sumer, employed wage workers—paid in barley—and possessed slaves as well. Bakers, brewers, spinners, smiths, and agricultural laborers, as well as officials, clerks, and priests, were its occupational groups. It owned its own equipment: "metal tools, ploughs, plough animals, wagons and boats.... [It also possessed] breeding stock, including a stud bull imported from Elam." [66] In Mesopotamia, according to Childe, the temple was "not only the center of the city's religious life, but also the nucleus of capital accumulation. The temple functions as the great bank; the god is the chief capitalist of the land. The early temple archives record the god's loan of seed or plow animals to cultivators, the fields he has let to tenants, wages paid to brewers, boatbuilders, spinners, and other employees, advances of grain or bullion to traveling merchants. The god is the richest member of the community." [67] The temples of Babylon also functioned as banks. The Igibi bank, ca.

[62] Murdock, *op. cit.*, p. 391.

[63] *Ibid.*, p. 427.

[64] Breasted, *op. cit.*, pp. 491–492.

[65] A. Moret, *The Nile and Egyptian Civilization*, 1927, p. 333.

[66] [V.] Gordon Childe, *What Happened in History*, Penguin Books, Inc., New York, 1946, pp. 87–88.

[67] V. Gordon Childe, *Man Makes Himself*, C. A. Watts & Co., Ltd., London, 1951, p. 124.

575 B.C., "acted as buying agent for clients, loaned on crops, attaching them in advance; loaned on signatures and on objects deposited, and received deposits on which it paid interest." [68] The "oldest decipherable documents from Mesopotamia are . . . the accounts of the temple revenues kept by the priests." [69] The *contract* as a legal device for business transactions was invented by Sumerian temple officials; it was used in rental of fields, houses, oxen, and boats.[70] And the temple-bank of Babylon used negotiable instruments in its loan business: "Warad-Ilisch . . . has received from the sun-priestess Iltani, one shekel of silver by the Sun God's balance. This sum is to be used to buy sesame. At the time of the sesame-harvest, he will repay in sesame, at the current price, *to the bearer of this document* [italics supplied]." [71]

The church often shares with the state and the military in the spoils of war. In ancient Egypt, "the booty collected both in Syria and Ethiopia went to enrich the god Amon as much as it did the kings themselves; every victory brought him the tenth part of the spoil gathered on the field of battle, of the tribute levied on the vassals, and of the prisoners taken as slaves. . . . The Pharaohs, perpetually called upon as they were to recompense one or another of their servants, were never able to retain for long their share of the spoils of war. The god [i.e., the priesthoods], on the contrary, received what he got for all time, and gave back nothing in return. . . ." [72]

The church was sometimes more tenacious than the state in other respects also: in Egypt under Rameses III, "while the poor in the employ of the State were starving at the door of an empty treasury, the storehouses of the gods were groaning with plenty, and Amon was yearly receiving over 205,000 bushels of grain for the offerings at his annual feasts alone." [73]

Our review of the church has made it plain that its functions parallel those of the state very closely. There are, to be sure, differences of detail; we have found, for example, no instance in which the church has undertaken the construction of roads. But in the major functions of waging war, in keeping the subordinate class docile and obedient, and in performing important functions in agriculture, irrigation, industry,

[68] "Banking, History of," in *Encyclopaedia Britannica*, 14th ed., vol. 3, 1929, p. 67.
[69] Childe, *Man Makes Himself*, p. 124.
[70] Turner, *op. cit.*, vol. 1, p. 282.
[71] "Banking, History of," *loc. cit.*
[72] G. C. C. Maspero, in *History of Egypt, Chaldea, Syria, Babylonia and Assyria*, A. H. Sayce (ed.), vol. 5, The Grolier Society, Inc., New York, 1903, p. 80.
[73] Breasted, *op. cit.*, 1942 ed., p. 496.

business, and finance, the church performs essentially the same functions as the state.

The state-church stands forth, therefore, as the special mechanism of coordination of parts and processes of sociocultural systems produced by the Agricultural Revolution; it is the secular-ecclesiastical means of their integration, regulation, and control.

Chapter 14   ECONOMIC STRUCTURE
OF HIGHER CULTURES

As we noted in Chapter 9, "Economic Organization of Primitive Society," there are only two basic types of economic system: (1) one in which relationships among items of property are functions of relationships among human beings, and (2) a system in which relationships among persons are functions of relationships among items of property. Or, to put it in another way, one system subordinates human social relationships to property relationships; the other subordinates property relationships to human relationships. It is unfortunate that neither economists nor anthropologists have names for these two fundamental kinds of economic system. The system which subordinates property relationships to human social relationships is the only kind that exists *within* primitive societies based upon kinship, although the other exists in intertribal commercial relations. The economic system that subordinates human social relations to property relations is the one that characterizes all civil societies, although vestiges of the primitive system remain among small groups of relatives, friends, or neighbors.

All civil societies are organized upon the basis of property relations. This means that all the classes that are characteristic of civil society, as distinguished from primitive, tribal society—kings, nobles, lords, priests, guilds of specialized artisans and other occupational groups, merchants, bankers, usurers, debtors and creditors, employers and employees, freemen, serfs, and slaves—are the social expression of economic organization. Social and political structures are the reflexes of economic structures. Nobles are persons possessed by wealth, by landed estates. Freemen are those who are neither possessed by wealth nor possess any by means of which they can live. Wageworkers are persons who sell their ability to work in the labor market; the entrepreneur, the employer, is the other pole of this axis. A prostitute is a kind of commodity. A serf is an adjunct of landed property. A slave is a piece of property in human form. A thief is the human expression of illegal property transactions. A beggar exemplifies parasitism in the realm of economics.

Property is the foundation of civil society; its forms and processes are the morphology and physiology of the body politic. It is the common denominator into which all social classes above the tribal level of social development can be translated. The status of every individual, every class, is a function of property relations. Everything has the form or function of property; one is himself an item of property or is a property owner. In civil society property is the measure of all men.

Because the economic systems of primitive society place human relationships—human rights and human welfare—above property relations and rights, they are human, or humane, ethical, and personal systems. And to the extent that they are organized in terms of kinship, the economic systems of tribal cultures are fraternal. The economic systems of civil society, on the other hand, subordinating as they do human rights and human welfare to property rights,[1] are impersonal, nonhuman, and nonethical in character. These traits translated into terms of human experience are impersonal, inhuman, or inhumane, and unethical. All the suffering, indignities, and degradation that come from slavery, serfdom, prostitution, usury, dependence upon wages, unemployment, wars of conquest and expropriation, colonial rule, and exploitation are inherent in the economic systems of civil society. In commercial systems, anything may be bought or sold: a woman's chastity, a judge's honor, a citizen's allegiance. There is no crime however heinous that men will not commit in obedience to their economic systems.[2] And the unethical nature of civil society's economic systems corrupts and blights the higher classes as well as the lower. The usurer is made avaricious as his victim is impoverished; the slaveowner becomes callous and hypocritical and even sanctimonious; the landlord is not ennobled by the eviction of widows and orphans; the great colonizer would have the oppression and anguish of millions of natives on his conscience, were he able to retain one; the great industrialist must derive satisfaction from a wretched and impoverished working class.

Although all the economic systems of civil society subordinate human relations to property relations, we may distinguish two kinds of these systems: (1) one in which the economic process of production and dis-

[1] An officer of the law may, in the line of duty, shoot and kill a man who has broken into a store in the dead of night to steal food to feed his hungry children. This is, of course, perfectly consistent with the property basis of civil society: if the social order rests upon private property, then theft is a blow struck at its very foundations, and no society can or will tolerate this kind of an attack.

[2] According to *Statistical Abstract of the United States*, 1953, 93.5 per cent of all crimes committed in 1951 were crimes against property, i.e., robbery, theft, embezzlement, etc. And this does not include murders committed during holdups or to collect life insurance. Nor does it include the sale of narcotics to juveniles.

tribution is controlled and regulated by the government, and (2) the system in which the economic process is allowed to function freely *as an economic process*, with only enough governmental supervision and control to ensure that it is carried out in accordance with certain rules. In other words, the processes of production, exchange, and distribution take place in terms of the economic values of the things involved, in terms of wages, prices, buying and selling, lending and borrowing; the government supervises and polices this activity to prevent dishonesty, cheating, defaulting on debts and contracts.

We have previously cited the empire of the Incas as an example of the government-controlled kind of system, and the Aztecs as an example of the relatively free commercial process. Among the great urban cultures of the Bronze Age, Egypt was for a long time a good example of state control of economic process, while Babylonia exemplified the commercial system. Under the Ptolemies the "whole economic organization of Egypt was built up on the principle of centralization and control by the Government, as well as the nationalization of all production in agricultural and industrial life. Everything was for the State and through the State, nothing for the individual...." [3]

In Mesopotamia, on the other hand, rights of private property and of individual business enterprise were established by the Sumerians and extended by the Babylonians. "In Hammurabi's time both land and chattels could be bought, sold, loaned, leased, pledged, bequeathed, and contracts covering any of these actions were enforceable by law. In other words a system of freehold property had evolved, i.e., possessors had rights of use and disposal without hindrance by any religious or political authority." [4] The free commercial system flourished in ancient Greece, also.

We have already advanced a theory to account for the development of these two different kinds of economic systems in the transition from primitive to civil society (see pp. 294–296). At this point we wish merely to call attention to the way each operates with reference to the class division of society. It is *class status* that characterizes the state-controlled system: certain people are serfs, peasants, or slaves; others are priests or nobles. The statuses of these classes are integral features of the political structure, and their weal or woe as a consequence of the operation of the economic system is determined by class status, which is

[3] M. I. Rostovtzev, "The Foundations of Social and Economic Life in Egypt in Hellenistic Times," *Journal of Egyptian Archaeology*, vol. 6, p. 164, 1920.

[4] Ralph Turner, *The Great Cultural Traditions*, vol. 1, McGraw-Hill Book Company, Inc., New York, 1941, p. 280. Turner adds that "it must be remembered, however, that not all property, especially land, was held under this private right; in fact, much land was held by the king, the temples, and the nobles...."

fixed and cannot be changed. In the free commercial system, however, it is *contract* that gives society its distinctive character. It is the possession of money that gives one person, or class, power over another in taxation, rent, moneylending, the wages system, and buying and selling. Subordination and exploitation are achieved by class status in the one system, by free contract in the other. In either case, however, the system is backed by the authority of the state.[5]

Land tenure. Land was unquestionably the most important factor in the economic systems of Bronze and Iron Age cultures. And indeed it remained so, with perhaps a few exceptions, until the Industrial and Fuel Revolution got under way in western Europe after the discovery of America. The great urban cultures of antiquity were based upon the intensive cultivation of the land. The institutions of land tenure were therefore of the greatest importance.

In primitive society based upon kinship the land belonged to the tribe; i.e., the title, so to speak, was held by the tribe, even though portions of the tribal territory might be held and used by family, or other kinship, groups. As we approach the threshold of civil society, however, there is a tendency for title to be held by the head of the political-religious system as the earthly representative of a god. Thus at Acoma, a Keresan Pueblo in New Mexico, the cacique, who stood for the earth mother, owned all the land in theory, although in practice he was obliged to allot unused land to anyone who asked for it.[6] In Buganda, East Africa, all land—except clan burial grounds—belonged to the king, who allotted it to officials and favorites. In Dahomey the king owned, in theory at least, not only all the land, but all the people, too, together with their possessions.

In the early civil societies the land belonged to a god who was represented by the king-priest. The Sumerians called their king-priest the "tenant farmer" of the god, and each year his "lease" was renewed. The Pharaoh held all the land of Egypt, presumably for a god. Where kings and priesthoods were different and distinguishable components of the state-church, they had their own lands. Lands were allotted to nobles and to military commanders in return for service. For a long time land

[5] This difference in economic systems of the Bronze and Iron Ages finds its parallel in the history of modern western Europe. Feudalism was a state-controlled system in which subordination and exploitation were determined by fixed class status. Feudalism was succeeded by capitalism, in which subordination and exploitation were achieved by the power of money expressed in free individual enterprise. This is the significant "passage from status to contract" about which Sir Henry Maine wrote so illuminatingly in *Ancient Law*, 1861.

[6] Leslie A. White, *The Acoma Indians*, Forty-seventh Annual Report, Bureau of American Ethnology, 1932.

continued to be held in feudal tenure, and it is not known precisely when the first sale of land took place. Eventually, however, land was freed from the feudal forms of tenure and entered the stream of commerce, along with products of the workshop. As early as Hammurabi's time (*ca.* 1940 B.C.), at least, as we have already noted, land was freely bought and sold.

Manufacturing industries. While agriculture was the principal industry in all the great cultures of the Bronze and Iron Ages, manufacturing increased in magnitude and significance as the Agricultural Revolution developed and diverted more and more of the population from food producing to the arts and crafts. Among these, the ceramic, textile, and metallurgical industries stood out as basic in the economic structure, but there were countless others, ranging from baking and brewing to the manufacture of perfumes and jewelry.

Industries grew up in both kinds of economic system, the state-controlled and the free commercial. We do not know the history of the development of the industrial system of ancient Mexico, but it apparently developed as a free economic enterprise, for Cortez found a great number of guilds of specialized craftsmen who produced goods on their own account, which they sold in an open market. The industrial system of the ancient Incas, on the other hand, was controlled by the state. In both Egypt and Mesopotamia, industry grew up in workshops attached to royal households and temples. There were a few independent craftsmen in Egypt who were free to sell their wares in the market, but this practice was much more extensive in Mesopotamia. In Babylonia, free craftsmen were paid wages, first in kind, later in money. Slaves and serfs were also employed in industry, especially in royal and temple workshops; in Greece, slaves were sometimes engaged in industries carried on by individual entrepreneurs. One finds the beginnings of a factory system in Greece, in which as many as twenty workmen might be employed. And division of labor was carried to such an extent in Greek workshops that cutting and sewing, in the manufacture of sandals, would be done by different workmen.

Commerce: its origin and development. Production for use precedes production for exchange everywhere in the course of cultural development. Production for use alone obtains among the Old World monkeys and apes of the present day, and we have every reason to believe that this was the case in the first era of human culture history. We find intrasocietal exchange of goods among modern primitive peoples, and we may assume that this is a very primitive and early practice. But, as we have seen earlier, this sort of exchange takes place on a basis of kinship and of friendly relations, not upon a commercial basis. We find no commercial exchange of goods *within* societies until we reach the horizons of civil society, or in some instances where the kinship organization of tribal society has been disrupted by the impact of a higher culture and the use of money or the practice of barter has been introduced.[7]

Commercial exchange originated in intersocietal relations. The basis of intertribal commerce is fairly plain. The geographic distribution of natural resources—of plants, animals, minerals, and other earth substances—is far from uniform; one tribe may have an abundance of certain resources and a meager supply of others or none at all. It is therefore advantageous for local groups to exchange the products of their respective territories with one another. Peoples on the seacoast may trade fish for garden produce with inland groups. Intertribal trade in shells, furs, feathers, ochers, jade, amber, ivory, turquoise, salt, obsidian, flint, etc., may take place as a consequence of inequalities of distribution of natural resources.

Commercial intercourse between local groups must have occurred very early in the course of cultural evolution. In modern times we often find a lively and extensive trade among peoples with very crude cultures, such as the aboriginal tribes of Australia, or the Semang of the Malay peninsula. And archaeological evidence points to extensive trade in prehistoric times. In aboriginal North America, for example, we find numerous instances of intertribal trade. Copper from the Lake Superior region is found in Ohio or even farther south. Obsidian from the Rocky Mountain region is found far to the east of the Mississippi River. Shells from Florida are found in northern New York. The Pueblo Indians of the Southwest obtained macaws from Mexico or farther south, possibly in exchange for their turquoise. In Europe, in Paleolithic times, seashells and bones of sea fish are found in the Dordogne (west-central France). In the Neolithic, shells from the Mediterranean are found in the Rhineland. Beads made of amber from Jutland have been found at Mycenae, and implements of the early Bronze Age found their way to Scandinavia from Mediterranean countries.

[7] The Bontoc Igorot and the Ifugao of Luzon are cases in point. They are very simple, primitive societies, with virtually no specialized mechanisms of political integration and control. Yet they use bundles of rice as money and lend rice at interest. Cf. A. E. Jenks, "The Bontoc Igorot," *Philippine Islands Ethnological Survey*, vol. 1, 1905; and R. F. Barton, "Ifugao Economics," *University of California Papers in American Archaeology and Ethnology*, vol. 15, no. 5, pp. 385–446, 1922. But these cultures have been strongly influenced, directly and indirectly, by Spanish culture, and their intrasocietal use of rice as money may well be the result of this influence. According to Jenks, "The Spaniard left his impress on the Igorot of Bontoc pueblo in no realm probably more surely than in that of the appreciation of the value of money" (p. 153). Similar observations would apply to some aboriginal cultures in Melanesia.

Production, i.e., the extraction or appropriation of materials from nature, for exchange undoubtedly preceded manufacture for exchange in the course of cultural development. But we do find manufacture for exchange on rather primitive cultural levels nevertheless. Thus in Luzon one pueblo may specialize in the manufacture of salt, another in bronze axes or gongs, and a third in rice sieves or transportation baskets. In the northwest Amazon, the Witoto tribe specialized in the manufacture of baskets, the Boro in blowguns, the Carajone in poisons, the Menimehe in pottery.

In intertribal commerce one value is exchanged for another, so many fish for so many yams, a basket for some obsidian. The exchange is not consummated, however, until the values are equally balanced. *A* will not exchange his fish for only three yams, let us say; he insists upon receiving four. If *B* is willing to give four, the exchange takes place; otherwise it does not. Each person determines for himself what will be a suitable equivalent for his article of trade. But his judgment is based upon or determined by a number of objective factors. One of these is the amount of labor, either of production or of manufacture, or both, that his own article has cost him. He will demand more in trade for an article that has cost him two hours of labor than for one that cost him only one. The amount of labor required to put a commodity on the market is affected by the degree of abundance or scarcity of the material in the habitat concerned, the technological factor remaining constant. If fish or berries are scarce, or if the yield of yams is poor, more labor will be required to produce a given amount than if they are abundant, in nature or in yield. Consequently, they will have a greater value to the producer, and he will demand more for them in exchange. The factor of scarcity or abundance in nature is of primary importance in the *productive* process, i.e., in the extraction or appropriation of materials from nature. To the degree that manufacturing, i.e., processing, enters into the preparation of the commodity for the market, the factor of natural abundance or scarcity declines in significance. The labor that goes into the manufacture of a glazed and painted pottery bowl is more significant, as a rule, than the natural abundance of clay.

We may define the exchange value of an article of commerce as that property which has been determined by the amount of labor required for its production. This amount, in turn, is determined by the technological means of production and manufacture, on the one hand, and by the natural abundance or scarcity of material, on the other. Value of product is proportional to the amount of labor, or energy, expended in its production, other factors being constant. But the labor of production may be expressed in different ways, and the values produced will vary accordingly. The labor may be expended with varying degrees of skill; the technological means employed may vary in efficiency; and the labor may be expended upon a single product or upon many. We are dealing here with differences that may properly be termed qualitative: one potter is better, i.e., more skillful, than another; one ax is better, i.e., more efficient, than another. But these qualitative differences can be reduced to a common denominator of quantity. A superior pottery bowl made by a highly skilled worker can be equated, in exchange, with a definite number of inferior bowls made by less skilled craftsmen. And in any community, the skills of the various workmen can be reduced to an average, so that the skill of any craftsman may be reckoned as a fraction—greater or less than one—of the average. So it is with the technological, or tool, means of production: some may be more efficient than others, but all can be reduced to an average in terms of which each one can be evaluated. And finally, the amount of labor energy expended can be lavished upon a single object—a finely carved blade or vase—or distributed over several products. The *value* of the product in any case will vary as the various factors of production or manufacture vary. We may express the whole situation in the following formula:

$$En \times Sk \times Ef = VP = VP_1 = VP_2$$

in which En is amount of energy, measured in ergs or calories, expended; Sk is skill of workman; Ef is efficiency of tools; VP is value of product; P_1 is a single product; P_2 is a dual, or plural, but definite and finite, number of products.

The value of the product will vary as the amount of energy, or the degree of skill of workman, or degree of efficiency of tool, varies, other factors being constant. In any community with a homogeneous culture, the factors of skill and of technological efficiency can be reduced to averages, so that we may say: *on the average, the magnitude of value of a product will be proportional to the amount of human labor, or energy, expended in its production.* Turning to the other side of the equation, the energy may be expended in the manufacture of one product or of several, but in either case the value will be the same: $VP_1 = VP_2$.

Returning now to the process of exchange, we have said that an act of exchange equates one value with another of equal magnitude. I know how much labor the yams or the shell beads that I offer in trade have cost me, but how do I ascertain the value of the yams that I receive in return? The answer is simple: I ascertain this by bargaining, by haggling over the price. If the fish have cost him little, he will offer more when I refuse to trade, just as I will offer more or less, depending upon the labor cost of my article of trade. Through haggling and bargaining, each party to the exchange reaches the maximum of his offer to the other; and, naturally, no exchange takes place unless they can agree. Thus we see that the exchange is an equation of values, measured in terms of human labor as conditioned by scarcity and abundance of natural resources and by the technological means of production. In the last analysis, it is *labor*, as represented by, and stored up in, commodities that is exchanged, unit for unit.

We may test this theory with the following example. In the seventeenth century, let us say, a European gives an American Indian a string of glass beads and receives an otter skin in return. A popular, i.e., European, view has it that this is a very unequal exchange, that the European obtains a beautiful and valuable fur for virtually nothing. But is this an adequate interpretation of the transaction? If the beads have cost the European little labor, so has the otter skin cost the Indian little. If the fur is prized for its beauty, so are the glass beads. One must be careful, however, in this connection to distinguish an exchange of gifts from commerce. A European may upon first contact with a tribe receive lavish gifts in return for a few bolts of red calico and a bit of copper wire. And, as we know, there are social situations in many cultures in which each tries to outdo the other in generosity. In commercial intercourse, however, primitive peoples are not slow to learn to measure values by haggling. In free trade there is competition among buyers. If one European trader will not give a certain number of beads for an otter skin, the Indian can refuse to trade —which leaves the European with expenses only and no profit—or take his fur to another trader. In this way, the Indian soon obtains a maximum return for his furs.[8] And as game is depleted, more labor is required to produce a given number of furs, and the Indian's price goes up. Here, also, we have exchange of value for value, measured in terms of human labor, and conditioned by the technological means of production and by the abundance or scarcity of supply.

We have been analyzing the conditions and circumstances within which intertribal exchange takes place. But this does not mean that because some articles are bartered in this way, any one may be. Exchange will take place only within limits set by the social and ideological (or spiritual) values of the groups in question. Sentiments, attitudes, taboos, etc., may inhibit or stimulate trade. A tribe may prize parrot feathers but place no value on those of the blue heron, though both may be equally scarce;[9] they may

[8] Quite primitive peoples are quick to accustom themselves to the ways of commerce, to equating one value with another, to haggling, to an appreciation of the effect of abundance or scarcity upon price, etc., as ethnographers, travelers, and others can testify.

[9] The author has taken beautiful blue heron feathers to the pueblos of New Mexico, where they were not accepted even as gifts. Parrot and eagle feathers were much prized, however, and Indians were willing to make a considerable return for them. It was the same with seashells; some kinds were highly prized, others were of no value to them at all.

prize beef but loathe pork. The labor theory of value cannot tell us what things will be valued, which ones loathed, and which regarded with indifference. These can be discovered only empirically, not in any *a priori* fashion. But once a thing is prized, its value in exchange may be measured in labor, conditioned, as we have said before, by the factors of technology and abundance or scarcity.

Commercial exchange originated in intertribal, or interlocal-group, relations and at a very early period in the history of culture. Throughout the great era of primitive society intrasocietal exchange took place, but it was carried on in personal terms: of kinship, hospitality, or friendship. With the advent of civil society, as a consequence of the development of the agricultural arts, commercial exchange becomes established as an intrasocietal process, for reasons which we have already noted. Among the great urban cultures of the Bronze and Iron Ages, this process finds its highest expression in a professional merchant class and in a system of banking. This means *money*. Let us turn, then, to the absorbing account of how this great instrument of civilized societies originated and developed.

Evolution of money. The method of barter is quite adequate for commercial exchange of goods on low cultural levels, but as higher levels are approached this method becomes increasingly unsatisfactory. So long as only a few commodities are involved and each owner can readily exchange his commodity for something that he wants in a direct face-to-face transaction, the barter method of exchange works very well. On higher cultural levels, however, and particularly in the case of intrasocietal commercial exchange where the number of kinds of commodities is relatively great, the system of direct barter becomes very cumbersome. The holder of a commodity might not readily find someone who has just what he wants to obtain in exchange.[10] If, therefore, the commercial process could be generalized instead of remaining on a particularistic basis, that is to say, if particular use values could be easily transformed into value-in-general, the process of commercial exchange would be much expedited. This is precisely what took place; and the result was the origin of mediums of exchange, or currency.

An article of commerce has two *forms* of value: *use value* and *exchange value*. The use value of shell beads is their property, or ability, to satisfy a need by serving as an ornament; the use value of yams is that property which enables them to serve a need by nourishing me. The exchange value of beads or yams is their ability to command a value, in magnitude

[10] The "Ifugao who has three or four death blankets...and who wants to trade them for a jar, probably has a pretty hard time finding another man who has a jar and who wants to barter it for three or four death blankets." Barton, *op. cit.*, p. 427.

equivalent to their own, in a commercial process of exchange: five units of value of beads will exchange for five units of value of yams—magnitudes of value being measured, as previously noted, in amount of labor necessary to produce or manufacture them. Thus, we distinguish *particular* values (use values) and *value-in-general* (exchange value).

In barter one particular use value is exchanged for another particular use value. But as we have already seen, this process is clumsy and limited; one cannot always readily find someone who has the article one wants and who is willing to exchange it for what one has to offer. Consequently, as the commercial process develops, some commodities—particular use values—become forms and magnitudes of value-in-general as they enter the process of exchange and function as such therein; i.e., the shell beads are use values before they enter the commercial process. But upon entering it, they become forms and magnitudes of value-in-general. As such they can be exchanged freely and readily for any kind of commodity. Now, one can exchange any kind of commodity for shell beads and then use the beads to buy any kind of commodity: a use value is taken to market, exchanged for value-in-general, which is then exchanged for a use value, which is withdrawn from the commercial process, taken home, and used or consumed. The process of exchange has become generalized; the evolution of currency has been achieved.

A medium of exchange is a vehicle of commercial intercourse, but this does not mean that it is a simple device. As a matter of fact, it is a rather complicated thing and possesses a number of properties which condition its use and determine the course of the evolution of such mediums. In addition to being a vehicle or instrument of exchange, it is also a measure of value. When a person takes his commodity to market and sells it, i.e., receives for it a medium of exchange, this medium must indicate the magnitude of the value of the commodity sold, and, in turn, the magnitude of value of the medium of exchange will again be equated with a commodity when an article is purchased with it. Thus a medium of exchange measures the value both of articles sold and of articles purchased. These measurements are expressed numerically, as so many units of something, such as cattle or cowrie shells, or as so many measures, e.g., ounces of some material such as gold.

A medium of exchange is a means to an end, and means vary; some are better than others. A great variety of things may serve as mediums of exchange, and since they vary in their properties and characteristics some will be found to be more suitable as measures of value and as vehicles of exchange than others. First of all, a medium of exchange must be a use value, at least in the early stages of the development of commerce. A person would not exchange an article of value for something unless it had value too. A medium of exchange must therefore have value; this is its cardinal feature. The first articles to become mediums of exchange were particular use values; they were capable of satisfying some human need, and they had been produced or manufactured by the expenditure of human labor. But if a medium of exchange must have value, and if value accrues from the expenditure of labor, then anything upon which labor had been expended could have value if it could also serve a need. A medium of exchange serves a need. If, therefore, human labor is expended in the production or manufacture of something that can serve as a medium of exchange, and a medium of exchange only, it will have all the requisites of such an instrument. In some cultures, strings of laboriously manufactured perforated shell disks fill these requirements and are used as mediums of exchange and for no other purpose. Thus we distinguish two kinds of mediums of exchange: (1) those that serve because they are capable of satisfying a need quite apart from commerce, such as cacao beans, bundles of unthreshed rice, or cattle; and (2) those that were designed and manufactured to serve *as* mediums of exchange, and which are enabled to do so because they are repositories of human labor that has been expended in their manufacture. The second kind represents a more advanced stage of development than the first. It should be kept in mind, however, that the expenditure of human labor is the basis and source of value in each case.

To be effective as a measure of value, a medium of exchange must be readily divisible, or exist in the form of small units; otherwise variations in magnitude of value cannot be easily expressed. Gold is readily divisible into a number of small pieces or can readily be combined into large ones. Cowrie shells are small units of value which can easily be multiplied to express large values. Thus precious metals like gold, shells, or strings of beads or dogs' teeth can easily measure numerous and fine gradations of value. Cattle are serviceable for relatively large values, but not for small ones, since one cannot divide a cow in half without destroying her, both as a cow and as a permanent medium of exchange.

To be effective in commercial intercourse, a medium of exchange should be movable and easily handled. Hay, unless it is baled, would therefore not be suitable, nor would very large stones or tree trunks. And, of course, immovable houses, growing trees, etc., would be quite impossible. Cattle, cowrie shells, metals are useful as mediums because they are readily movable.

A medium of exchange should also be relatively durable and imperishable. Fresh berries or milk, eggs, etc., are therefore not suitable.

Finally, a medium of exchange should possess value in rather concentrated form, since otherwise it would be difficult and laborious to move about. Wampum beads would be better than pieces of unworked flint, copper or gold better than clay, buckskin more suitable than building timbers. Diamonds contain value in concentrated form, but they are not readily divisible. We see, then, that a medium of exchange must have a number of properties and characteristics if it is to serve efficiently and effectively as a vehicle of commercial intercourse.

A great many different kinds of use values have become mediums of exchange within the commercial process. Cowrie shells have been widely used in Africa. The Bontoc Igorot used bundles of unthreshed rice. Wampum beads became currency in commerce between Indians and European colonists in North America. Strings of dogs' teeth were used in Melanesia. The Aztecs used sacks of cacao beans, copper ax blades, and quills of gold dust. Cattle and sheep—especially the former, from which we get the word *pecuniary,* from *pecus,* cattle—have been used as currency in many cultures.

In the great arena of commerce various things have competed with one another as mediums of exchange. In this competitive process the mediums with the greatest defects and shortcomings have tended to be eliminated, while the most effective ones have tended to survive. Some mediums have had one defect, others another. Cattle were too large to be used in small payments, were not easily divisible, and were relatively perishable. Tobacco and rice also were perishable. Shells did not contain value in sufficiently concentrated form, and so on. Diamonds possess value in concentrated form, are easily handled, and are virtually imperishable, but they are not suitable at all from the standpoint of divisibility. Out of this process of rivalry among materials the precious metals, gold above all, emerged as the best all-around medium of exchange. First of all, gold is a value in and of itself as a material for the manufacture of jewelry and utensils, and for other uses, such as in dentistry. Also it is a repository of human labor. Since much labor is required to produce gold, it contains value in highly concentrated form. It is easily handled and moved about and may be divided or combined in any quantity. Finally, it is virtually imperishable. It thus combines to a high degree all the virtues of an effective medium of exchange and a minimum of defects and shortcomings.

Naturally, the emergence and triumph of the precious metals as mediums of exchange had to wait upon technological development. It was not until the metallurgical arts could produce precious metals in quantity that they could be habitually used as mediums of exchange. Once, however, this step had been reached, gold and silver, particularly, and some of the baser metals such as copper, lead, and nickel, virtually replaced all other materials as mediums of exchange.

As we noted above, a medium of exchange must be a definite magnitude of value itself, such as a thousand cowries, a fathom of stringed beads, a cow, etc. The value of precious metals as mediums of exchange must also be determinable and measurable. One must know whether the gold is pure or not, and the amount of metal also must be determined by weight or measure. In early and primitive uses of metals as mediums of exchange, gold dust could be measured in standard units and the purity of nuggets could be assumed or taken on faith. But in a more extensive and systematic use of precious metals, it became the practice of merchants to stamp the metals with their seals to certify their purity. Cappadocian texts of about 2200 B.C. speak of sums of metal "of my seal" or "of your seal." Specimens of "sealed lead," used extensively in payment of fines about 1400 to 1200 B.C., have been found in Assyria, and blobs of silver bearing seal marks have been discovered in Crete of the twelfth century B.C. These metallic mediums were probably weighed, however, at each transaction.

The next step in the evolution of money was coinage. The Lydians of western Asia Minor are usually credited with this invention, which took place about the eighth century B.C. The first coins were of electrum, a natural mixture of gold and silver, and stamped, at first on one side, later on both sides. The Greeks were quick to follow the lead of the Lydians, Aegina, Corinth, and Athens, adopting the practice during the seventh century B.C. At first, coins were weighed like bullion, but before long they "passed by tale," i.e., were accepted at their face value. At the outset, coins were struck and issued by individual citizens, by merchants and moneylenders, but soon coinage became a monopoly of the state.

But the evolution of coinage did not stop here. If the state is to guarantee the value of a metal object used as a medium of exchange, it need not contain within itself the full value that it represents. In other words, a coin may stand for a value or be redeemable by an actual value instead of containing that value itself. This means that a coin need not be pure gold or silver. However useful gold is as a medium of exchange, it is relatively soft and wears away readily. Coins of pure gold would therefore deteriorate rather rapidly through usage. If, however, the use of coins as values is backed by a government, they may be made of alloys rather than of pure metals. They are thus much more durable, and if backed by the real value of gold, they have the values of gold. Very early in the history of coinage we see the substitution of tokens or symbols for values themselves. This substitution is carried still further in the issuance and use of paper money. Here a piece of paper serves as a medium of exchange without having any value in and of itself at all. It merely stands for a value and is redeemable in real value, i.e., gold. Paper money was used as long ago as the tenth century A.D. in China. Pieces of leather were also used as money by the Chinese, and in 1122 a doge of

Venice issued leather money to his troops, promising to redeem them later.

When weights and purities of metals were guaranteed by public authority, the state assumed a monopoly over money, its coinage and issuance, its regulation and control. This power over money is of course intimately related with the function of the state as the regulator of certain economic processes of the social organism as a whole. We refer here to such matters as taxation and the expenditure of moneys for public services and public works. In this function the state may be obliged to balance receipts against expenditures, and this, as the history of public finance reveals, is not always an easy task. It is, as a matter of fact, a chronic difficulty of states to obtain revenues large enough to meet their needs and requirements. Since the state has control over money it has found that it can help to balance revenues with expenses by changing the value of money. Thus it may acquire large debts with money of high unit value and pay them off with money of low unit value. Debasement or devaluation of money is an old trick in public finance. It was practiced by the ancient Greeks and Romans, and all states of modern times have recourse to it as the need arises.

Money as power and as process. Money emerged from mediums of exchange in general. And mediums of exchange were originally use values. We have, then, a process of evolution, a temporal sequence of forms: use values (corn, axes, cattle, etc.) become commodities; certain commodities (e.g., cattle) acquire new functions and become mediums of exchange; one particular medium, gold, emerges from the others and becomes money; and finally, tokens are substituted, in use and circulation, for gold.

We find differentiation and specialization in the evolution of commerce as in other evolutionary processes, such as the evolution of technology or in social evolution. The process of commercial exchange begins with commodities only; it becomes differentiated eventually into money, on the one hand, and commodities, on the other. Differentiation within the process of the circulation of commodities itself means, or brings about, a corresponding differentiation in society. Just as specialization of function and differentiation of structure within the process of the evolution of tools produce a corresponding differentiation of social function, forming groups of metalworkers, potters, brewers, weavers, steamfitters, a brotherhood of railroad trainmen, etc., so does differentiation within the process of commercial exchange produce a corresponding social differentiation. As money becomes distinguished from commodities, money owners —bankers—emerge and assume definite form as a class.

There were banks in Babylonia as early as 2000 B.C. And temples also functioned as banks, as we have previously noted. An early document reads: "Two shekels of silver have been borrowed by Mas-Schamach... from the sun-priestess Amat-Schamach. He will pay the Sun-God's interest. At the time of the harvest he will pay back the sum and the interest upon it." [11] As early as 575 B.C., private banking had taken the lead in Babylonia. The Igibi bank of Babylon, to which we have already referred (p. 326), has been compared with the Rothschilds of nineteenth-century Europe.[12]

Banking was well established in Greece by the fourth century B.C. There were both private and state banks. In ancient Rome, some of the temples functioned as banks, and there were also private but not state banks.

Money owners lend out their money at interest. Rates of interest vary: The charge was 20 to 25 per cent in ancient Babylonia; 15 to 33 per cent in Sumer. Hammurabi fixed the legal rate at 20 per cent. In ancient Greece, rates varied from 12 to 24 per cent; 50 per cent was not unusual in the Roman provinces.

Moneylending has important social consequences. Individual moneylenders may occasionally lose money, but as a class they invariably gain. As a rule the reason for borrowing money—except in the case of borrowing to establish an industrial or commercial enterprise—is an inability to hold one's own in a ruthless, competitive, exploitative socioeconomic system; one borrows as a drowning man cries for help. But if one is already sinking economically, how is he to repay the loan *plus* interest, which may range from 20 to 80 per cent? The fact is that the very circumstances that oblige a person to borrow money often make it impossible to repay it at high interest rates. The result is that he is pushed farther down the economic ladder, into bankruptcy or economic bondage in one legal form or another. One of the most common and widespread forms of slavery is that which springs from an inability to repay a loan or pay a debt.

Thus we find the social consequences of moneylending to be to make the poor poorer and the rich wealthier—an exemplification of the Biblical saying, "For whosoever hath, to him shall be given, but whosoever hath not, from him shall be taken away even that he hath" (Matt. 13:12). This quotation would serve as an appropriate inscription above the doors of moneylenders. Lending money at interest tends to divide society into two classes, the rich and the poor, the powerful and the weak. It is a means of concentration of wealth into the hands of the few, of expropriation of the many.

[11] Elmer Mantz, "Banks, History of," in *Encyclopaedia Britannica*, 14th ed., 1929, p. 67.
[12] *Ibid.*

Business enterprise carried on within a money economy, whether in agriculture or in manufacturing, tends to subordinate and subjugate the working class. "Assyria, for example, was originally a nation of free farmers," Turner has observed. But with the growth of cities and the rise of a money economy, farming for profit expanded. "Higher profits could be made by slave labor ... great estates grew, many free peasants became landless workers [not being able to compete with slave labor], and serfs and slaves increased in numbers." [13]

In manufacturing, money gives its possessor the power to control. It enables him to own the means of production and to buy, either as chattel slaves or as wageworkers, the labor power necessary for production. Ownership and monetary control give him possession of the profits that accrue from the enterprise.

Money is power, economic and political power. It is value, human labor, in concentrated form. The possession of great wealth gives the possessor immense power over others. With it he can possess himself of the means of life, the resources of nature, and the technological means of production. And he can compel, through the institution of slavery or the wages system, others to work for him, and thus create more wealth for him. Money is one of the two great instruments of class division and class rule; the other is physical force.

Evolution of markets and merchandising. By *market* we mean a place to which people customarily come at certain times to exchange goods. The earliest markets were, as we have seen, places where members of different local groups or tribes met to exchange goods. Intersocietal markets appeared on very early cultural levels, but it is not until we reach the higher cultures that we find markets within societies. When a certain stage is reached in social evolution, when differentiation of social structure and specialization of function have reached a certain point because of the evolution of the technological means of production, markets make their appearance within social systems. The Aztecs of Mexico, the Ganda, Dahomeans, and other peoples of Africa had markets, for example, but they were not found on lower cultural levels. The market is therefore a process of making general in distribution and consumption that which is particular in production. It is a means of relating parts of society— specialized structures in the process of production—to one another and of integrating them all into a coherent whole.

We may speak of the evolution of markets and of merchandising as a social process, and we find differentiation of structure and specialization of function here as elsewhere in the evolving culture process. In the early

[13] Ralph Turner, *The Great Cultural Traditions*, vol. 1, McGraw-Hill Book Company, Inc., New York, 1941, p. 295.

stages, each person is both buyer and seller. He comes to the market with his own commodity, and in the case of barter, the act of selling his commodity is also the act of buying another. With the emergence of mediums of exchange as special mechanisms of commercial intercourse, however, the acts of selling and buying are distinguished from one another; the production and sale of goods as a social process becomes distinguished from the purchase and consumption of goods. And paralleling the distinction between money, on the one hand, and commodities, on the other, is a social differentiation within the commercial process. Just as money evolves as a special economic mechanism of commerce, so do merchants evolve as a special class within society. A merchant is, so to speak, a medium or vehicle of exchange in human form; that is to say, he is the intermediary between the producer who brings his commodity to market for sale and the consumer who comes to the market to buy; he is a human repository with whom the seller deposits his commodity where it will remain until a buyer comes along. The merchant thus becomes an important mechanism of coordination and integration in society. He correlates a many-sided process of production with an equally varied and pluralistic process of consumption; he becomes a key figure in the metabolic processes of the body politic. We shall touch upon the significance of this function later.

As we have previously noted, the economic systems of civil society are impersonal, nonhuman, and nonethical, which, in terms of *human* relationships and values, means impersonal, inhumane, and unethical. Nowhere are these characteristics exhibited more clearly than in the market place and in merchandising. In Homeric times "the chief merchants of the sea...were also the chief pirates"; in the *Odyssey*, Nestor asks Telemachus, as a matter of course, if he is a trader or a sea robber.[14] The early Phoenician merchants kidnaped children as they traded, "profitably combining commerce with robbery." [15] "From the earliest to comparatively modern times the peoples through whose hands international trade has passed have been partly merchants and partly robbers." [16] Merchant and pirate "for a long period are one and the same person," observes Nietzsche, and "even today mercantile morality is really nothing but a refinement on piratical morality." [17] Lying, cheating,

[14] John L. Hammond, "Commerce," in *Encyclopaedia of the Social Sciences*, vol. 4, 1931, p. 3.
[15] George W. Botsford and Charles A. Robinson, Jr., *Hellenic History*, 3d ed., The Macmillan Company, New York, 1948, p. 36.
[16] Hammond, *loc. cit.*
[17] Oscar Levy (ed.), *The Complete Works of Friederich Nietzsche*, vol. 7, *Human, All-too-Human*, Paul V. Cohn (trans.), part 2, T. N. Foulis, Edinburgh and London, 1911, pp. 200–201.

misrepresentation, and stealing are natural and normal features of the commercial process.[18] A market is an arena in which commodities meet as competitors; each tries to get the better of the other; that is to say, in the process of merchandising each seller strives to get the highest price for his commodity and each buyer endeavors to pay as little as possible for his. In short, economic gain and advantage is the thing that dominates this process. Human values and virtues have no part in it. Thus we find cheating of all kinds, short weight, misrepresentation of commodities, the substitution of inferior for superior goods, adulteration, and, where money is used, systematic shortchanging.

Since markets are public places and perform public social functions, a public authority comes to exercise some supervision, regulation, and control over markets in fairly early stages of development. In Mexico at the time of Cortez we learn that government officials circulated about the market place to check up on weights and measures and to try disputes. In Uganda, the king appointed officials to supervise markets, to keep order, settle disputes, levy fines—and, incidentally, to collect a tax of 10 per cent on all sales.

Division of labor and specialization of effort increase efficiency in production, and therefore effect an economy of social labor time. Specialists are more skillful and efficient in the process of production than are Jacks-of-all-trades. One hundred thousand men divided into a dozen or so guilds, each of which is devoted to a particular craft, will produce a greater total product in a given time than these same hundred thousand persons devoting themselves equally to each of the crafts in question. Division of labor and specialization of effort mean, therefore, an increase in efficiency, an economy of time, increased productivity of labor, a greater magnitude of social product—in short, an all-around advantage to society.

Merchants are specialists who perform a special function in society, and the consequences of their efforts are the same as the consequences of division of labor and specialization of effort in general: they save time, promote efficiency of social effort. Just as social time is economized by having one or a few priests perform the functions of worship for many thousands of laymen, so do certain societies save time and effort by having a few merchants carry the bulk of the

[18] "Here Commerce springs, the venal interchange
   Of all that human art or Nature yield;
   Commerce! Beneath whose poison-breathing shade
   No solitary virtue dares to spring,
   But Poverty and Wealth with equal hand
   Scatter their withering curses."
      Percy Bysshe Shelley, *Queen Mab*, canto v, l. 38.

burden of the circulation and exchange of commodities. Instead of each producer hunting out the consumers, and each consumer hunting out the producer of the commodity he wants, producers and consumers alike go to the merchant and buy and sell through him. The merchant is thus the great clearinghouse between production and consumption. In his function as circulatory mechanism in the commercial process he plays an important role in society as a whole, and this importance derives from the fact that he effects economies in social labor time. This is true whether the merchant is sedentary or itinerant. In the one case he saves the time of both buyers and sellers by providing a place to which they can come and readily transact their business. The itinerant merchant saves society time by relieving each buyer and each seller of the necessity of making a trip to market for a small purchase or sale. Suppose, for example, each of ten farmers has a goose to sell. To take it to the market and return would require of each farmer a half day, let us say. This would mean five man-days of time. The merchant, let us suppose, could circulate among the farmers and buy the ten geese in one day. Thus four man-days of society's time have been saved.

We now come to a very interesting and significant point. The merchant performs a public service. He effects savings in society's labor time. But the advantages of this economy do not accrue to society in general, but to the merchant privately. This is an important point and one that is often overlooked. The merchant is able to perform a public service only because of a certain type of social organization. The merchant did not bring this type of social system into existence; on the contrary, he is a product of it, not its cause. From the standpoint of society in general the merchant is merely the *means* by which *society* effects its economies. It is really *the system* that effects the economies rather than the merchant. But the economies and advantages that accrue from this division of labor and specialization within society do not accrue to society in general, but to the merchant in particular. In short, we have a public function eventuating in private gain. The merchant is therefore getting something to which he is not entitled from the standpoint of the social system in general.

We may illustrate this point with the following example: A society may assign a man to stand guard at the intersection of an arterial highway and a railroad track to warn motorists of approaching trains. This guard is a specialist in the true and literal sense of this term: he performs a special social function; he is an expression of the division of labor within society. He saves motorists time by relieving them of the necessity of slowing down or stopping to see if it is safe to cross the tracks. More than this, he saves lives and property. By producing and using this specialist, therefore, society saves a great deal of time, much property, and many human lives. But in this case the savings and advantages are distributed throughout society in general; they do not accrue to the watchman privately. If, however, the watchman could arrogate unto himself the savings and advantages that accrue from his services, he would be in the position of the merchant who derives private advantages from a public function.

What is the significance of this peculiar position in which the merchant finds himself? The answer is fairly plain: he acquires private wealth at public expense. As we have tried to make clear, we do not deny that he performs a public service. On the contrary, we have emphasized just this fact. Nor do we wish to minimize the importance of this service; we have insisted upon its magnitude and value also. The point that we are trying to make is that the merchant is, from the standpoint of the social system, merely an instrument of a social process, that the economies that are effected through him are made possible by a certain type of social structure. But the economies and advantages that are effected through this particular form of division of labor and specialization of function are not returned to their source, namely, society, but flow into the private pockets of the merchant. Needless to say, we are not passing a moral judgment here. Society has evolved as it has, and things being as they are, it could not have evolved otherwise. We are neither praising the merchant for his public service nor blaming him for his private appropriation of economies socially effected. We are merely trying to analyze the merchandising process and to make it intelligible.

We may compare and contrast the merchant's function in society to other public services, such as a water, sewage, or postal system, telephones and telegraphs, municipal or cross-country railways, etc. All these are public services; they are social processes, circulatory systems in the body politic. Water and sewage systems are usually, but not universally, publicly owned and operated. The same is true of postal systems. Telephones and telegraphs may be publicly or privately owned. Railways are often privately owned, although they, too, may be owned and operated by a government, municipal or national. Merchandising is like all these in being a public service. It differs, however, in that the merchant sells *things* rather than services. The ownership of goods is an integral part of the system of private property. He therefore is considered to "have a right" to sell his own property and to pocket any profit that he can make. The postal service merely carries mail. It buys labor power to carry on these services. But the clerks and carriers who perform this service are not entitled privately to appropriate the social advantages accruing from their labor, because they have sold their labor to a buyer who thereupon becomes entitled to the full product of this labor. The tendency of railroads to be privately owned is due to the fact that a large investment in equipment is required, and this may be provided by private enterprise. The merchant always appears in the market with his own goods, and he is therefore permitted to keep any and all profits from his enterprise. The trend of social evolution appears definitely to be in the direction of public, governmental regulation and control of more and more general social processes. It is probably merely a matter of time before all will be brought within the orbit of public, governmental control, if not ownership.

With social economies flowing into the private accounts of merchants, they tend to become wealthy as a class. To be sure, many a merchant fails. Risks attend his profession as they do others. He may be robbed of his goods, or they may be destroyed by fire or storm. But the merchant class as a whole accumulates wealth as it continues to derive private advantage from public service. In addition to the above-mentioned risks which merchants individually take, there is the further hazard of being eliminated from the merchandising process by competition. Merchants are engaged in a ruthless competitive struggle with one another, and the stronger eliminates the weak. We therefore find not only accumulation of wealth in the merchant class, but a tendency toward concentration as well. Competition in merchandising tends inevitably toward monopoly.

There is another method, too, by which the merchant acquires wealth, namely, by the exploitation of slave or wage labor. At a certain stage of cultural development merchants become large enough to hire helpers or to buy slaves to perform the labor attendant upon the circulation of commodities. Both slave and wage laborers produce values in excess of their subsistence or wages. Since the merchant owns the slave outright, and owns also the labor power which he has purchased from the wage earner, he is entitled to all the fruits of their labor, and since, as we have just noted, these exceed in varying proportions the return made to slave and worker in the form of subsistence or wages, the merchant derives an advantage at their expense. As the merchandising process grows, and as larger merchants eliminate smaller ones, the advantage derived by exploitation increases. The small merchant who has no slave and hires no helper does his own work and exploits no one. The large merchant, however, who in the past had many slaves, or who today hires hundreds or thousands of relatively low paid workers, is engaged in exploitation on a large scale.

To summarize at this point the principal features of the merchant's role in society, we would note, first, that he derives private advantage from a public function, and hence acquires private wealth at public expense. Secondly, he acquires wealth by the process of exploitation, either of slave or of wage labor. Thirdly, competition within the merchandising process tends to concentrate merchandising, and the wealth accruing therefrom, into fewer and fewer hands. The effects of merchandising as a social process are therefore twofold: concentration of wealth, on the one hand, and expropriation, on the other, a tendency toward monopolies of wealth and power.

As we have noted earlier, intergroup and interregional trade is almost as old as culture itself. It is reasonable to suppose that it grew and expanded as culture in general developed, that it was much greater during Neolithic than in Paleolithic times. And, certainly, there is abundant evidence that commerce expanded enormously in volume, and perhaps in distance traveled, during the Agricultural Revolution. Great caravan routes were established in eastern, central, and southwestern Asia; trade was carried along sea routes in the Black and Mediterranean Seas, and even out into the Atlantic northward as far as Britain; and land routes connected Scandinavia, by way of the Danube, with eastern Mediterranean and Black Sea countries. "Beads of East Mediterranean faïence, such as were fashionable about 1400 B.C., reached southern England," according to Childe, and "it is highly probable that Cornish tin and Irish gold were brought to Greece in return. Amber from Denmark was certainly traded to Greece and Crete along a well-marked route across Central Europe...." [19] Silk from China reached the Mediterranean by overland routes during Han times, and an overseas trade was established between China and India. Egyptian traders went to Crete and to ports in Syria. Merchants had become a prominent and important social group in Mesopotamia before the time of Hammurabi. Greek and Roman trade was extensive, the latter extending as far as Britain by the first century of the Christian era. But perhaps the greatest traders of the ancient world were the Phoenicians. They busily plied the Aegean and Mediterranean, founding colonies as they went. They reached Gaul and Spain, and even pushed through the Straits of Gibraltar and skirted the coast of west Africa.

Merchants were never significant as a class in ancient Egypt because of the prominence of the state and the priesthoods. But in other regions they sometimes rose to great prominence. This was especially true in Mesopotamia, where they became important as early as the third millennium B.C. Mercantile oligarchies arose in Babylon and became powerful enough to rival the priests and military classes in political influence. The great mercantile cities of the Phoenicians, such as Tyre, Sidon, and Byblos, were ruled by mercantile oligarchies.

As we have already noted, many kinds of commercial and legal de-

[19] [V.] Gordon Childe, *What Happened in History,* Penguin Books, Inc., New York, 1946, p. 164.

vices such as contracts, promissory notes, negotiable instruments, and leases were in common use in the great commercial regions. Partnerships were commonly employed by merchants of the Mediterranean countries as a means of augmenting their power or security, and joint stock enterprises spread throughout the Mediterranean, and possibly to India. In China, businessmen formed associations, under state control, in both trade and industry.

The breakup of tribal society based upon kinship was attended with confusion and violence. There was competition and struggle for natural resources—fertile lands, especially—and for accumulations of wealth produced. Out of this confusion, competition, and struggle political-military rulers and priesthoods arose to power, the one through physical force, the other by means of supernaturalistic influence and control. Sheer possession of the land became the basis of power. This power was extended to the production of wealth and to control over wealth produced. The result was class division and class rule: a ruling class with a monopoly of control over natural resources and the means of production and a monopoly of military and political power; and a subordinate class whose lot was one of production, privation, and political impotence.

Agriculture was the principal industry throughout the era of the great urban cultures of antiquity, but manufacturing became increasingly important as the Agricultural Revolution reached its fulfillment. The state and the priesthoods were the original entrepreneurs, both in agriculture and in manufacturing, but as the Agricultural Revolution developed, a civil and secular class of businessmen developed. Eventually even land became private property which could be bought and sold.

The development of markets and money and an enormous expansion of trade and commerce followed upon the growth of industry. Merchants and bankers, as social classes, came into being as social expressions of diversification and specialization within the commercial process, the one being a reflex of commodities, the other of money. In some of the later cultures of the Bronze and Iron Ages, these merchants and bankers rose to great prominence and political influence.

Wars, conquests, and imperialism marked the development of the great cultures of the Agricultural Revolution. International competition and conflict became intensified as cultures developed within the rather fixed and finite limits of natural resources. Continued and repeated destruction as a concomitant of chronic warfare, and the ruthless exploitation of conquered lands through slavery, tribute, and taxation, eventually brought about the decline and downfall of one nation and empire after another. Technological development in industry and in warfare made possible and produced great nations and empires. But the political systems in which this cultural development found expression were not suited to stability, peace, and productive industry in the long run. Directed toward subjugation and exploitation at home, and conquest and spoliation abroad, the economic bases of these great cultures were undermined one after another, until, with the collapse of the Roman state, the era of the great cultures produced by the Agricultural Revolution came to an end.

Chapter 15   THEOLOGY AND SCIENCE

This chapter should properly be entitled "Philosophy," since it is concerned with the ideological component of the great urban cultures produced by the Agricultural Revolution. But we already have a chapter with this title. We are therefore entitling it "Theology and Science," since these terms designate the two most significant features of the intellectual sector of these cultures.

The philosophies of primitive cultures were composed, it will be recalled, of mythologies, on the one hand, and matter-of-fact knowledge, on the other. The Agricultural Revolution transformed *mythology* into *theology*, and it developed specialized intellectual disciplines and traditions which eventually became *sciences*.

An important consequence of the Agricultural Revolution was the differentiation of the intellectual cultural tradition into two components: (1) an upper-class, literate, and more or less systematized and coherent tradition; and (2) a lower-class, illiterate, and unsystematized and incoherent tradition. This differentiation of intellectual traditions is, of course, a consequence of the social differentiation into upper and lower classes. In civil societies the literate tradition was in the hands of educated classes, principally priests, but including scholars, businessmen, and sometimes military men as well. Little is known regarding the intellectual life of the masses in such cultures as those of ancient Egypt, Babylonia, India, and China, but it may be supposed that it consisted of beliefs characteristic of the tribal societies that preceded them. It is also reasonable to suppose that the rich and virile mythologies of tribal cultures underwent considerable disintegration and deterioration during the transition to civil society. This assumption is quite in keeping with the degradation of status and standard of living that the masses of the population experienced as a consequence of the Agricultural Revolution.

Mythology and theology are fundamentally alike in philosophic conception and point of view. Both are supernaturalistic interpretations of the world and of human experience. In theology, as in myths of primitive peoples, we find the same kinds of stories of gods, demons, and heroes;

354

of floods, diversification of races and languages, and of waters that bestow everlasting life.

We would distinguish theology from mythology chiefly by the characteristic that the former is reduced to writing, while the latter lives as an oral tradition. Secondly, a theology is likely to be a more systematized organization of religious belief, legend, and history into a coherent whole than is the case with mythology. "The most significant contribution of the Ancient Near East to our social heritage," says the Oriental scholar McEwan, "is the systematization and generalization of primitive thought. Spirits were arranged in a hierarchy; magical powers were ordered in categories relative to significant natural phenomena such as stars and seasons; forms of divination were excogitated in terms of variations in organs and other ominous data. Generalization of the supernatural was the result of a wider experience of the natural processes, a development largely incidental to the practice of agriculture." [1]

Ideas and emotions were expressed in pictures or designs in primitive cultures, but the Agricultural Revolution produced systems of true writing, i.e., a continuous, coherent, intellectual process, objectively comprehensible, reduced to visible markings made upon one kind of material or another. The meanings of the so-called picture writing of primitive peoples were discrete and episodic: a picture might stand for an object, an event, or an organization of perceptions, beliefs, and emotions. Thus a rough sketch of a bear might mean that the one who drew it saw a bear, or it might represent a dream in which all the beliefs, realistic and magical, associated with the bear, together with an attitude of respect for power, an emotion of awe or of totemic affiliation, might be expressed. Also, a pictograph of a bear might mean one thing to one person but have quite a different meaning for another; its meaning is in part subjective. With true writing, on the other hand, we have set down in visible form a representation of an organization or a flow of ideas, and in such a form as to ensure a uniform interpretation of meaning by all readers.

True writing comes into being with the development of urban life and has been taken by some to be one of the most significant indications of the attainment of *civilization*. Thus, both Lewis H. Morgan and Edward B. Tylor cite writing as the boundary line between barbarism and civilization. And writing has been extolled by countless scholars for its supposed contributions to the development of civilization. We have no wish to belittle the role of writing in the evolution of culture, but we believe that its importance has been much exaggerated. Writing in itself is not a culture builder. It was the development of agriculture—the har-

[1] Calvin W. McEwan, "The Oriental Origin of the Hellenistic Kingship," *Oriental Institute Studies in Ancient Oriental Civilization*, 13, p. 3, University of Chicago Press, Chicago, 1934.

nessing of solar energy in the form of plants and animals—that produced civilization, of which writing was a significant element; it was not writing that produced civilization. In reducing the mythologies of primitive peoples to writing, no fundamental, or even appreciable, change in philosophic principle or outlook was effected. On the contrary, this reduction tended to stabilize these beliefs as sacred revelations and thus make change and progress less likely to occur.

Much time and diligence were required to learn to write the complex and cumbersome systems of the Bronze Age, and consequently writing itself became a profession. Although learning was identified with writing, the ability to write, itself, became a specialty. Schools were attached to temples for the purpose of teaching youths this difficult art; the mark of extreme proficiency was the ability to take dictation. Probably much less than 1 per cent of the population in these ancient cultures could write, and among the literate the priests were in a great majority. But the art was gradually extended to others: to "scribe commanders" in the Egyptian armies, to foremen of labor battalions, and to merchants.

The art of writing helped to order, to systematize, and to make explicit much of the social, economic, and political life of the urban cultures of antiquity. Codes of various kinds defined rights and obligations of social classes, laid down rules of proper conduct, specified penalties for crimes of varying degrees, and standardized knowledge and techniques in various activities. Writing thus served effectively as a means of social organization, integration, and control, both diachronically and synchronically.

We have already noted, in previous chapters, that theology became an instrument of class rule in civil society, and we may merely remind our readers of this fact here. The priesthoods and the temples were symbols and expressions of power, terrestrial as well as divine. They had custody of sacred objects, and it was they who performed the religious ceremonies and rituals. All this would tend to impress upon the masses a conception of the world and of their place in it. And what this place was, was made obvious enough.

Any philosophy is, among other things, a guide to life and action. Astrology was one of the most noteworthy philosophical developments of the ancient urban cultures. Early in the third millennium B.C. Sumerian priests had discovered that some stars—actually, planets—move across the heavens in fixed paths comparable to those of the sun and the moon. These planets and the sun and moon were identified with gods, and, it was thought, their movements expressed their wills or influences. From the discovery that the movements of these heavenly bodies could be predicted came the notion that one could foretell terrestrial events. Thus arose a comprehensive and systematic philosophy and a class of specialists: astrologers. The zodiac—a band in the heavens surrounding the earth, divided into twelve parts, each of which was identified with a constellation—was invented and became an important astrological concept. The movements of the planets, both with reference to one another and to the signs of the zodiac, acquired prophetic significance, and it became the business of priestly astrologers to observe and interpret these movements and conjunctions. "If Venus approaches the constellation of Cancer there will be respect for law and property in the land; those who are ill will recover, and pregnant women will have easy confinement" is an example of this kind of knowledge and endeavor.[2]

Astrology in the ancient world was primarily a Sumerian and Babylonian development, but it readily diffused from Mesopotamia to other regions. It invaded Greece about the beginning of the fourth century B.C., and within a hundred years it had penetrated almost all fields of thought; it provided a principle, cosmic necessity, which tended to unify Greek science, religion, and ethics. In Mesopotamia astrology had been largely limited to predicting national, or public, events; in Greece it acquired significance for the individual citizen, and the casting of horoscopes became a reputable profession. In China, every emperor kept a court astrologer along with other diviners. He observed winds and clouds as well as heavenly bodies; five kinds of clouds and twelve kinds of winds were distinguished.

Divination in various forms constituted an important part of philosophy and practice in the cultures of the Bronze and Iron Ages. Originally divination was based upon the concept that the will of the gods is expressed in various ways which can be observed and interpreted. Eventually, however, divination came to express little more than a conviction that one kind of event will be followed by another. Hepatoscopy, or divination by means of the liver, was elaborately developed by the Babylonians; Turner calls it "the most complex body of learning built up in an early urban culture."[3] Hepatoscopy rested upon the belief that the will of the gods was revealed in various distinguishable features of the liver. Schools were established to teach this art, and little clay models of livers, like models of organs used in modern medical schools, were employed in instruction. Chinese culture was permeated with divination in many forms: oracle bones, scapulimancy, and geomancy. And the Romans had their augurs, haruspices, and pontifices who read the future in the flight of birds, the cackling of sacred fowls, or the intestines of fowls.

The Greeks placed great reliance upon their oracles as guides to conduct. Zeus was consulted at Dodona, Apollo at Delphi, and other gods at six other major oracles.

[2] Cited by Ralph Turner, *The Great Cultural Traditions*, vol. 1, McGraw-Hill Book Company, Inc., New York, 1941, p. 166.

[3] *Ibid.*, vol. 1, p. 165.

The theologies of the great urban cultures are characterized by a trend toward anthropomorphism. Spirits, or gods, among primitive cultures may have human form, but certainly many of them do not. Birds, mammals, and reptiles of all kinds are found in the pantheons of primitive peoples. But as we approach the highest cultures produced by the Agricultural Revolution, we find a progressive tendency to represent the deity in human form. Angels in Christian theology have wings, and Satan is depicted with horns and a tail, but God has the form of a man, and his only begotten Son *was* a terrestrial human being.

Spirits or gods are conceptual expressions of significant attributes of the world that man lives in. These attributes may be forces or powers like fire or the winds, a principle like fertility, or a quality like evil or truth. In primitive mythologies, the gods are very often natural phenomena that express, simply and directly, these forces, qualities, or attributes. The sun, moon, and earth become deities. Birds and animals, mythical and actual, may be deities also: bear, snake, coyote, thunderbird, eagle, horned or feathered water snake, and others. Natural phenomena may be personified also in primitive mythologies, such as Whirlwind Old Man or Sun Youth; the Chuckchee personify the cause of syphilis.

Gods are the supernaturalization of factors that significantly affect the lives of men. These factors vary with habitat and degree of cultural development. In primitive, preliterate cultures the most significant factors are the forces of nature. In civil societies the most significant factors tend to become sociocultural. In primitive cultures, the forces that pressed hardest upon man and determined his weal and woe were those of nature: the sun, wind, and rain; disease germs; powerful predators, or an abundance of game. In civil societies, the significant forces are social: economic and political. The privation, hunger, toil, bondage, or technological unemployment of the masses of civil society are not due to nature's niggardliness or hostility; they are features of a social system. The power, wealth, and ease of the upper classes may be ascribed to the favor of the gods, but if so this favor is made manifest and expressed in a kind of social system. The existence of slavery, serfdom, levies, usury, and taxation is to be attributed to a kind of social system, a type of society produced by intensive cultivation of cereals with plow and oxen, rather than to forces of nature. There may be gods of war in civil society, but battles are always fought by men who are commanded by kings and blessed by priests; and it is human beings, organized in political and military systems, who kill, conquer, and subjugate one another.

In the great urban cultures of antiquity, therefore, the most significant factors affecting the lives of the people, great and small alike, were those of *society*, of sociocultural systems in their technological and institutional aspects. Society and god became one. The almighty, immortal, and ethical power that is civil society was expressed in the conception of a deity in the heavens and in the person of a ruler on earth. Sometimes the king was only the earthly representative—the "tenant farmer," as he was sometimes called—of the deity; sometimes he was a god himself or the descendant of a god. Society, god, and ruler are a triad of concepts that constitute a unity; they are but three expressions of the same phenomenon. Eventually the concept of one supreme deity emerges.

How, then, are the half-human, half-beast gods of Egypt, Mesopotamia, and India to be interpreted?

It is indeed tempting to interpret them as transitional stages between zoomorphism of primitive cultures and the anthropomorphism of civil society. There is considerable support for the theory that the people of Egypt were organized into totemic groups before the advent of the Agricultural Revolution. As kinship groupings gave way to territorial organization in the *nomes*, the totemic animals may have become district deities. And as political power became concentrated with the rise of cities and monarchies, some of these animal deities may have become municipal or national deities, and in the course of the enlargement of their jurisdiction and their identification with government and personal rulers, their zoomorphic heritage may have been modified by the growing influence of political power in human form. This theory seems plausible, and certainly it is suggestive, but an adequate test of it is yet to be made.

Theologies are expressions of social experience as conditioned by habitat and technology. The theologies of the great Bronze and Iron Age cultures are complex affairs, being the resultants of the influence of many factors such as warfare, agriculture, the sequence of the seasons, political organization, and the exercise of power and authority, together with survivals of the mythologies of their tribal antecedents. No adequate study of the great religions produced by the Agricultural Revolution has been made, as far as we know, that attempts to interpret them in terms of the ecological, technological, social, and political factors of which they are expressions. Such a study is sorely needed, but cannot be undertaken here. We can merely indicate a few of the lines upon which such an inquiry might be undertaken.

The principal characteristic of the Agricultural Revolution is, of course, *agriculture*, and we might then expect to find this fact reflected in the great religions brought forth by the extensive and intensive cultivation of plants, especially the cereals. And this is precisely what we do find. Virtually all the great civilizations of antiquity had agricultural deities.

Isis was a goddess of grains; it was she who discovered wheat and barley and showed the Egyptian people how to grow them. When the Greeks learned of her they identified her with their Ceres. Osiris, the husband of Isis, personified cultivated cereals, at least in some contexts.

Ishtar, the great Babylonian goddess, represented the reproductive processes of nature. Tammuz, her husband, or lover, was a grain god. Attis is often represented as the god of trees, but in Phrygian mythology he appears definitely as a god of vegetation. He was beloved by Cybele, the great Asiatic goddess of fertility. Dionysus, too, was a god of trees in general, but he was also a god of agriculture and of cereals. He was the first to use oxen to draw plows. When the Greeks learned of the Semitic corn god Tammuz, they mistook his title, *adon*, "lord," for a proper name and adopted him under the name Adonis. He figured as a corn god in Greek religion. Chief among the earth gods of ancient China were Hou T'u, the ruler of the soil, and Hou Chi, god of cereals.

The theme of death and resurrection of gods as representative of the dying of nature in winter and her revival in spring was widespread in these ancient religions; it is associated with Osiris, Attis, Dionysus, and others.

Even Jesus Christ is associated with cereals, or at least with bread. He was born at Bethlehem, "the House of Bread," and he tells his followers that he "is the bread of life." And perhaps it is not mere coincidence that Christ was born at Bethlehem, where once stood a grove sacred to the cereal god, Adonis.[4]

There are other similarities, too, between Christian theology and those of other cultures. The death and resurrection of Jesus follow a widespread pattern. Mary, the mother of Jesus, was a virgin, as was Nana, the mother of Attis. And pictures of Isis suckling the infant Horus so resemble later paintings of the Madonna and Child that "it has sometimes received the adoration of ignorant Christians."[5] And the eating of Christ's body in the form of a wafer is duplicated in literally countless other cultures in which corn spirits are eaten in the form of bread.

Theologies reflect political organization and exercises of power and authority as well as agriculture and the succession of the seasons. We can cite only a few instances of this for ancient Egypt as suggestive of what an adequate study of Bronze Age cultures might do in this respect.

In ancient Egypt, as we have already noted, many localities had their own gods. As kingdoms arose, erstwhile local deities became national gods. And when Egypt becomes unified, one god rules the pantheon. Originally, Horus, the falcon-headed god, was a local deity of Damanhur in the Delta. Later, his residence was moved to Buto in the Delta and to

---

[4] Cf. Sir James Frazer, *The Golden Bough*, abridged ed., The Macmillan Company, New York, 1931, p. 346.

[5] *Ibid.*, p. 383.

Hieraconpolis, the two capitals of Lower and Upper Egypt, respectively. When Egypt became unified, Horus became the ruler of the entire country and had his seat at Heliopolis.[6]

The cult of Re, the sun god, became the official state religion of Egypt with the founding of the Fifth Dynasty. So great was his prestige that other gods, through their priests, became identified with him. Thus Amon, originally a local god of Thebes, became Amon-Re. And even the priests of the crocodile god, Sobk, who originally had no connection whatever with the sun, began to address him as Sobk-Re. In ancient Egypt, as Breasted has shrewdly observed, theological thinking was "brought into close relationship with political conditions." [7]

The struggle between Akhenaten (Ikhnaton), "the Heretic King," and the priesthoods of Egypt during the fourteenth century B.C. found its expression in theology.[8] The emergence of the doctrine of monotheism was a means employed by the pharaoh to oppose the priests: Aton, the disk, or sun, god, was declared to be the only god, and the pharaoh was his chief priest; the other deities were declared to be nonexistent, and therefore Akhenaten attempted to close their temples and abolish their priesthoods. It was an attempt, says Moret, to "break the power of the priests of Amon lest they should dethrone the kings." [9] He also makes the shrewd observation that "this appropriation of the property of the temples shows us what lay beneath the religious revolution, *the economic and political objects of the rupture* [italics supplied]." [10] In this bitter struggle between the two components of the special mechanism of integration of the nation, state and church, the pharaoh and his one god, Aton, were defeated. The victors razed the temple of Aton, and inscriptions pertaining to the "heresy" were expunged from monuments and public buildings. The god Amon, through his priests, triumphed.

The change from nationalism to imperialism, too, is reflected in Egyptian theology. In the Pyramid Age the sun god ruled only Egypt, and in the hymns of the day we find him standing guard at her frontiers "where he builds the gates which restrain all outsiders from entering his inviolable domain." But after Egyptian forces had conquered foreign lands and established an empire, the supreme god of Egypt became the

[6] Turner, *op. cit.*, vol. 1, p. 196.

[7] James H. Breasted, *A History of Egypt*, rev. ed., Charles Scribner's Sons, New York, 1909, p. 359.

[8] See Leslie A. White, "Ikhnaton: The Great Man vs. the Culture Process," *The Science of Culture*, 1949, for a thorough examination of this period in Egyptian culture history.

[9] Alexandre Moret, *Kings and Gods of Egypt*, G. P. Putnam's Sons, New York, 1912, p. 45.

[10] Alexandre Moret, *The Nile and Egyptian Civilization*, Alfred A. Knopf, Inc., New York, 1927, p. 324.

Lord of the Universe. As Breasted has observed, "monotheism is but imperialism in religion." [11]

All the great religions of the world today, with the possible exception of Islam, may be regarded as the products of the Agricultural Revolution. Confucianism, Taoism, Buddhism, Hinduism, Zoroastrianism, and its offshoot Mithraism were all developed during the closing centuries of the pre-Christian era. We know of no adequate study of any of these religions which interprets it in terms of the social conditions which it reflects, to say nothing of a comprehensive sociological interpretation of them all as a general theological expression of a type of culture. Our understanding of the social and political origins of Christianity is much greater than for the other great religions, but even here much remains to be done.

The social history of Christianity indicates clearly that it began as a lower-class social movement and that it got under way during the disintegration of the Roman Empire, in short, in a time of social unrest and crisis. It seems more than probable that some of these conditions attended the origin and development of the other religions. The legend of the Golden Age, expressed in the account of the Garden of Eden in Judeo-Christian theology, was widespread in the ancient world. As we have previously suggested, this may be a nonliterate folk memory of the era of primitive society based upon kinship and mutual aid. The struggles, toil, misery, and privations of the masses of civil society may be accounted for in part by the concept of sin, which figures prominently in some of the religions preceding Christianity; that of the Babylonians, for example. And in many of the ancient religions a messiah, or savior, was to come and reclaim mankind, to bring about salvation, and to establish the brotherhood of mankind as well as the kingdom of heaven. Krishna in Hinduism, the Buddha of Mayahana Buddhism, and Mithra are some of the Saviors that preceded Jesus Christ.

Beginnings of science. In Chapter 10, "Philosophy: Myth and Lore," we surveyed the genuine, matter-of-fact knowledge of primitive peoples, as distinguished from their pseudo knowledge of mythology, and found it to be both extensive and varied. Primitive peoples actually knew a great deal about a great many things: plants and animals, principles of mechanics, chemical processes, foods and drugs, and the behavior of heavenly bodies.

As a consequence of the Agricultural Revolution and the division of society into upper and lower classes, the intellectual life becomes stratified

[11] James H. Breasted, *The Development of Religion and Thought in Ancient Egypt,* Charles Scribner's Sons, New York, 1912, pp. 312, 315.

also into "high" and "low" traditions, to use Ralph Turner's apt terms. The upper classes acquire a monopoly of learning as well as of wealth and power. Learning becomes a profession, and learning-in-general becomes diversified into specialties of various kinds. In this way the various sciences, philosophy, and mathematics had their beginnings as distinguishable intellectual pursuits.

In astronomy the Egyptians mapped the heavens, drew up lists of stars, and grouped stars into constellations. They identified the polestar and oriented some of their structures with reference to it, apparently. The two sides of the Great Pyramid, for example, deviate but slightly from true north. The movements of the heavenly bodies were systematically observed and recorded. The Egyptian priest-astronomers had worked out a calendar based upon the sun's movements as early as 4226 B.C. The year consisted of 360 days, plus 5 added at the end of the year.

Egyptian mathematicians and scribes developed a system of notation for numbers; they had a sign for a number as large as one million, but lacked a sign for zero. They calculated the areas of rectangles and triangles by correct methods and were able to compute the volume of a truncated pyramid. They had a fair approximation of the value of pi (π).

Medicine was a highly specialized art and profession in ancient Egypt. The temples of the god of medicine, Imhotep, became medical schools. There were three kinds of medical men: physicians, surgeons, and exorcists. Systematic medical treatises were written, and some of them have been preserved. The Kahun Papyrus (ca. 1900 B.C.) deals especially with diseases of women. The Edwin Smith Papyrus (ca. 1600 B.C.) is a treatise on surgery; it classifies cases with reference to the way they might respond to treatment. Egyptian physicians had a fair knowledge of anatomy, but very little of physiology. The brain is described in the Edwin Smith Papyrus, and the author realized that injuries to this organ affected other parts of the body. Most of Egyptian medicine rested upon supernaturalistic conceptions of disease, but at least one notable break with this philosophy is recorded in the Ebers Papyrus (ca. 1550 B.C.): attempt is made to explain various ailments in terms of the behavior of the "vessels" of the heart.

The Sumerians were computing the areas of rectangles by multiplying length by breadth before 3000 B.C. The Babylonians had achieved complete mastery of fractions by 2000 B.C. and had a value of 3 for π. There was a complex medical literature in Sumeria before the second millennium B.C., with some treatises describing and classifying diseases, others which indicated cures as well. The Babylonians had professional surgeons in Hammurabi's time; fees for operations were specified in his Code. Babylonian medicine was dominated, however, by magical considerations. In astronomy, too, the supernaturalistic point of view prevailed generally;

the chief object was to determine the influence of heavenly bodies upon terrestrial affairs. This concern, together with the attempt to predict the incidence of this influence, led the Babylonian priest-astronomers to systematic observation of the sun, moon, and planets and to record their observations. This, in turn, led to effective techniques for predicting eclipses and foretelling the times of new and full moons. The gnomon, a device which indicates the position of the sun by its shadow and "one of the first scientific instruments," was invented by the Babylonians.[12]

The development of science in India was influenced to some extent by Greek culture, and possibly at an earlier date by the cultures of Mesopotamia. Some noteworthy developments took place, however, in the cultures of India, especially in mathematics, where the concepts of "void," "unlimited space," and "infinite time" were formulated. Our modern mathematical notation, "Arabic numbers," and the concept of zero were developed in India. Progress was made, too, in philology and grammar.

The development of the sciences in China is less well known than their growth in Mesopotamia or Egypt. It is known, however, that the course of development in China paralleled roughly the experience of the great culture centers to the West. A mathematical treatise of 150 B.C. dealt with problems of algebra and geometry as well as arithmetic; it also elucidated the extraction of both square and cube roots. Chang Heng (ca. 78–139), a distinguished astronomer, determined the value of π as the square root of 10. He also identified and classified stars: 320 large and 11,520 small ones. Heavenly bodies were systematically observed, and records of observations were kept; the first eclipse was recorded in 775 B.C.; a comet was noted in 613 B.C. A star chart had been compiled by the third century B.C. In physics, or "natural philosophy," the Chinese distinguished five basic elements of which everything was composed: fire, water, earth, wood, and gold. Life, it was believed, originated in the water and developed through a series of stages, eventually producing human beings. When a person died his body decomposed into the five elements. The "Internal Classic," or "Canon of Medicine," compiled in late Chou times, expounded a naturalistic theory of disease. This point of view was upheld by other distinguished physicians; Pien Chao (fl. ca. 255 B.C.), for example, asserted that if a person believed in sorcerers he could not be cured by a physician.[13]

With the advent of the Han Dynasty (202 B.C.–A.D. 220), however, there was a resurgence of supernaturalism and traditionalism, a "reorientation of Confucianism, the elaboration of Taoism, and the acceptance of Buddhism, [which] disintegrated the secular outlook and rational

[12] Turner, op. cit., vol. 1, p. 257.
[13] Turner, op. cit., vol. 2, pp. 842–846.

methodology which, although they were never clearly developed in the philosophies, might have produced a science if social and economic conditions had strengthened them ... [eventually] science became identi-fied with the Chinese low intellectual tradition, while the Chinese high intellectual tradition developed mainly as a body of ritualistic and decora-tive learning." [14]

We find the beginnings of science among the urban cultures of the Bronze Age, but not true science. On the one hand, there is still a con-siderable admixture of supernaturalism in the concern with nature and disease, and, on the other, the solution of specific, practical problems dominates the intellectual process with but few exceptions; there is rela-tively little exercise of the intellect for its own sake, little search for understanding and truth as goals in themselves. Both Babylonian and Chinese mathematicians, however, constructed problems with no other purpose, apparently, than to demonstrate techniques for solving them. The following is an example from "Arithmetical Classic," a Chinese treatise of the third century A.D.: [15] "There are three sisters, of whom the eldest comes home once in every five days, the middle in every four days, and the youngest in every three days. In how many days will all three meet together?"

Analysis of the cosmos into five basic elements and the dichotomy of *yin* and *yang*, in Chinese metaphysics, are likewise steps in the direc-tion of scientific theory. The observations and calculations of the Babylonian astronomers, even though tinged with astrological concep-tions, provided the Greeks with the essential materials for their scientific achievements and conceptions.

When we come to the ancient Greeks, however, we find a mature, pure, explicit expression of the scientific outlook. This does not mean, of course, that Greek thought in general, or even much of their scientific thought, had been purged of supernaturalism; much of this outlook per-sisted in science and flourished on its periphery and within its interstices. But we do find a free, self-conscious, and deliberate attempt to see nature directly, without recourse to religion or the tradition of the ancients, and to interpret what they saw in nonanimistic, naturalistic terms.

To be sure, Greece built largely upon the foundations laid in Egypt and Mesopotamia. It is said that Thales was half-Greek, half-Phoenician, and that he had studied geometry in Egypt. Pythagoras, too, is said to have learned this branch of mathematics in the Nile valley. And, as previously noted, the achievements of the Greek astronomers would have been impossible without the contributions of Babylonia.

[14] *Ibid.*, vol. 2, pp. 848–849; see also Fung Yu-lan, "Why China Has No Science," *The International Journal of Ethics*, vol. 32, 1922.

[15] Quoted by Turner, *op. cit.*, vol. 2, p. 843.

The achievements of the Greek scientists in astronomy, zoology, and medicine are too well known to need recounting here. But they went much farther than the physical and biological sciences; they invaded the realm of the social and cultural sciences as well. They were the first to put man himself within the matrix of nature and to study him and his institutions as natural phenomena. Herodotus was the father of ethnology as well as of history. Plato analyzed sociocultural systems in logical, if not in culturological, terms. And Aristotle applied the modern comparative method to the study of political systems in his work *The Constitutions of Athens*. It was Aristotle, too, who recognized thinking as a special kind of intellectual activity, as something that, like everything else, could and should be the object of scientific analysis and interpretation. He organized rules of reasoning into a coherent body of formal logic and catalogued, in "Sophistic Errors," various kinds of invalid reasoning. With the Greeks, science, as a comprehensive system of thought and a distinctive point of view, was born.

It used to be the custom to explain the phenomenal achievements of the Greeks in terms of their inherent intellectual genius. We now know, however, that they built largely with materials inherited from Mesopotamia and Egypt. But they did more than that; they went farther than their predecessors, and there are certain factors in the Greek situation which help us to understand their superiority. Greece was a small country, or rather, a number of small, autonomous city-states. Domination by an autocratic state-church, by rulers and priesthoods, which had been characteristic of great oriental nations, was lacking. Here for the first time in the history of civil society representative government was achieved, even though far less than a majority of the people were represented. All too often in Egypt, Mesopotamia, and China was it necessary for thinkers to tailor their reflections to fit national political exigencies or powerful priestly traditions; subordination of thought to national political considerations was a characteristic of most of the great cultures of the Bronze Age. But in Greece, for the first time, the situation in terms of topological, geographical, ecological, and sociocultural factors was favorable to freedom for the mind—and even in Greece, Socrates was put to death for corrupting the young.

Chapter 16 SUMMARY

Man was born of the Primate Revolution; culture is the product of symboling.

We have called the kind of sociocultural system developed by primordial man *primitive society*, or *primitive culture*. It was activated by the energy of human organisms almost exclusively. Because the amount of energy obtainable from this source is small—about one-twentieth of a horsepower per capita in a self-reproducing society—the cultures developed upon this basis were simple, crude, and limited in their possibilities for development. Cultural development could take place only within the limits set by the source of energy. But within these limits cultural advance could be effected by technological improvements.

Man has been called a self-domesticated animal. The process of domestication began with the origin of culture, with the inauguration of rules of conduct for individuals, with the subordination of individual right to general welfare, the origin of ethics. It is true that man subsisted upon wild foods as did other animals, but even here the art of cooking elevated him above the beast.

The type of social system developed during the human-energy era was unquestionably the most satisfying kind of social environment that man has ever lived in. By this we mean that the institutions of primitive society were the most compatible with the needs and desires of the human primate, the most congenial to his nature and temperament. In primitive society all men were brothers, or kinsmen. All were free. Everyone had free access to the resources of nature. And all were equal; no one held another in servitude or bondage.[1] Mutual aid characterized these primitive societies. Production was carried on for use, and human rights and welfare were placed above property rights and institutions.

The cultures of primitive man were almost infinitely varied. The life of primitive man was precarious and wretched in some cultures; quite

[1] Bitter enmity might exist between tribes, and captives of war might be brought home to be tortured and killed or allowed to live and be treated like dogs. But these were foreigners; they were not members of the society into which they were forcibly inducted.

secure and bountifully endowed in others. Fighting and killing did take place occasionally between local groups or tribes, but organized and large-scale homicide was unheard of. The greatest struggle was with nature: with the elements, with predators, but above all with disease. And it was in the medical sector that primitive cultures were weakest.

The life of primitive man was hard, drab, and dull in some instances. But in others it was comparatively easy, with much leisure time for the development and enjoyment of the arts. Rich mythologies fed his mind and provided him with entertainment. And the artistic life of many primitive cultures—in music, drama, dance, costume, ritual, and paraphernalia—was exceedingly rich, colorful, and emotionally satisfying.

No culture can develop beyond the limits of its energy resources, and the cultures of primitive man would have been circumscribed by the boundary of human energy for ages without end had not some means been developed for augmenting energy resources for culture building by harnessing solar energy in a new way and in a new form. This was accomplished by the domestication of animals and by the cultivation of plants, especially the cereals.

The Agricultural Revolution was indeed a revolution in every sense of the word and in all the sectors of cultural systems. It provided a new kind of technological basis for cultural development; it profoundly transformed man's social life; and it created a new way of interpreting experience: science.

Civil societies were organized territorially upon the basis of property relations. The resources of nature and the technological means of production became private property. Social relations became functions of property relations; every class, every individual became an expression of an institution of property—lord, vassal, serf, slave, and free craftsman alike. The lot of the masses was one of arduous and unremitting toil, privation, personal degradation, and an impoverishment of the intellectual and artistic life. The ruling class became harsh, indifferent, cruel, and arrogant; after all, they were the terrestrial representatives of the gods. City-states grew to become great nations, and these expanded into empires.

The arts and crafts, however, enjoyed great and rapid progress with the advent of agriculture. The origin of metallurgy was the most significant advance in this respect, but the beginnings of glass, the invention of porcelain, the introduction of silk, and many other things marked the development of cultural systems in their material aspect. Great temples, tombs, and pyramids were constructed, and the Chinese built the Great Wall.

In the intellectual arts, writing, calendars, and systems of weights and measures were achieved, and the foundations of mathematics and the sciences were laid. The great religions of the world arose and took form as supernaturalistic philosophic reflexes of the technologies and social and political systems of the Bronze Age.

Some 990,000 years of cultural development elapsed before agriculture and stock raising were begun in a few restricted areas of the Old World. Only about 8,000 years passed between the beginning of agriculture and the fall of Rome. It took only three or four thousand years to transform primitive tribal systems, activated by human energy and subsisting upon wild foods, into great urban cultures sustained by the intensive cultivation of cereals. But with the achievement of the great urban, literate, metallurgical, calendrical cultures, the curve of cultural development leveled off—for reasons which we set forth in our chapter on "The Agricultural Revolution." The foundations of these great cultures were laid between, say, 5000 and 3000 B.C. The specific achievements were "artificial irrigation using canals and ditches; the plow; the harnessing of animal motive-power; the sailboat; wheeled vehicles; orchard-husbandry; fermentation; the production and use of copper; bricks; the arch; glazing; the seal; and—in the earliest stages of the revolution—a solar calendar, writing, numeral notation, and bronze." [2] But between 2600 and 600 B.C., says Childe, "few contributions of anything like comparable importance to human progress" were made.[3]

The great cultures of southwestern Eurasia flourished from about 4000 B.C. to the beginning of the Christian era. They were first developed in the Fertile Crescent—in the valleys of the Nile and the Tigris and Euphrates Rivers. For something like three thousand years nations and empires rose and fell in Egypt and Mesopotamia. But eventually these great political structures crumbled, and new nations and empires arose in the West, first in Greece, then in Rome. The crest of the wave of cultural development has been moving westward ever since the Pyramid Age.

The great cultures of antiquity were produced and sustained by intensive agriculture, but they were carried on by exploitation and conflict. There were subordination and occasional insurrection of the masses at home, and chronic warfare and subjugation abroad. Great cities were built upon the ruins of their predecessors; nations and empires rose, only to fall to pieces through internal weaknesses or sink beneath the blows of a younger and more virile neighbor. The last of the series was in some respects the greatest: Imperial Rome. But there is a limit to territory, to lands and peoples. When these have been conquered, the peoples subjugated or enslaved, and the countryside drained of its wealth

[2] V. Gordon Childe, *Man Makes Himself*, C. A. Watts & Co., Ltd., London, 1951, p. 227.
[3] *Ibid.*

by levies and taxation, the end of the imperial road has been reached. The disintegration of political structures does not mean, however, a loss of culture. All the cultural achievements, the inventions and discoveries, the knowledge and techniques persisted after the ties of political systems had been loosed. The empires of Thutmose, Sargon, Darius, and Alexander went to their graves like the great men who led them; but no culture was lost in the ebb and flow of the imperial tides.

During the centuries when Greece shone at her brightest and Roman rule was extended far and wide, crude tribes or nations lived in the forests and on the plains of central and western Europe, and on islands offshore to the northwest. They were sturdy people, but uncouth and crude-cultured. A few refinements of Mediterranean lands had reached them through channels of trade, but rough skin clothing, war clubs, and iron sickles measured the quality of their technology, while barbaric gods were worshiped in sacred groves and semimystical runes anticipated the dawn of literacy. With the collapse of Roman military might, the bulwarks against barbarism were leveled, and Europe became a violent and chaotic proving ground of peoples and cultures. Migrations, war, and pillage became chronic; peoples pitted themselves against one another; and streams of culture flowed and eddied about in confusion. Eventually a modicum of order and stability was established. The rural strongholds of feudalism gave way to cities with their guilds, industries, merchants, and bankers. Important inventions followed one another in the textile industry, and significant advances were made in metallurgy. Then one day a wisp of smoke was seen on the English horizon, weaving about uncertainly and without much vigor. It was coming from a Newcomen engine. A few mutations later, the engines of Boulton and Watt were coming out of the Works at Soho and going into cotton mills, iron foundries, and the hulls of ships. The Age of Steam had dawned. But the story of the Fuel Revolution, and of the institutions of Democracy and Capitalism that were its social matrix, must be told in a succeeding volume.

INDEX

Du Bois, C., slavery, 201-202
Durkheim, E., 10
 explanation of social facts, 26n.
 on incest, 88
 quoted, 13
 on shamanism, 198
 social facts are things, 15n.

Economic exchange, 242-244, 335-338
Economic systems, based on kinship, 245-
 250
 of civil society, 294-295, 330-332
 commercial, 295
 of primitive peoples, 247, 259-260, 276
 state-controlled, 295
 types of, 242-245
Economics, defined, 238-239
 distinguished from technology, 239
 pseudo, 240-242
Education, political process, 321-322
 and social control, 324-325
Eggan, Fred, on kinship terminology, 134
Endogamy, and anthropoid family, 85-86
 and fraternal polyandry, 112
 and levirate, 111-112
 in literate cultures, 113
 and social evolution, 107-109
 and solidarity, 105, 106, 114
 and sororal polygyny, 112
Energy, concept of, 40-41
 life and, 33-38
 universal concept, 33
Energy sources, cultivated plants, 45-48,
 285-289
 domesticated animals, 45-48, 285-289
 human organism, 41, 43
 wind, water, fire, 43-44
Entropy, 34-35
Environment, role of, 50-52
Ethics, 216-225
 evolution of, 220-221, 224
 and morality, 222-223
 and supernaturalism, 217-220
Etiquette, 225-231
 and class structure, 225-226
 evolution of, 230
 neglect of, by social science, 229
Eunuchs, 185, 191-192
Evolution, of culture, 29-31
 defined, 29-30
 distinguished from history, 30
 of ethics, 220-221, 224
 of etiquette, 230
 of kinship systems, 134-136
 of money, 338-343
 and revolution, 281-283
 social, and articulate speech, 76

Evolution, social, and clan, 155-156
 and endogamy, 107-109
 and incest, 114-115
 and incest taboos, 90
 and kinship systems, 138, 141
 and moieties, 161-162
 and sex, 79, 99-100
 and thermodynamics, 144-145
 of writing, 355
 (See also Cultural evolution)
Exchange, economic, 242-244, 335-338
Exchange value, 335-336, 338-339
Exogamy, and clans, 102, 111
 and endogamy, 102-107
 among anthropoids, 102-103
 cooperative group, 103-106
 inseparable, 101, 105-107
 and incest, 88-89, 94
 and interfamilial cooperation, 91-94
 and size of cooperative group, 104

Family, based on sex, 76
 economic basis of, 95-97
 economic functions of, 76
 human, 79-81
 cooperative group, 80-81
 functions of, 79
 origin of, 79
 prehuman, 79, 90-91
 endogamous character of, 85-86
Feudalism, 312
Fire, significance of, 43-44
Firth, R., 31n.
 on incest, 89
 on primitive economics, 259-260
 on pseudo money, 259n.
 on slavery, 201, 203
Fison, L., on Kurnai, 119-120
Flick, A. C., on medieval church, 307
Food production, and coercion, 292-294
 and cultural evolution, 293
 and division of labor, 290-291, 293
 and population increase, 289-293
 per square mile, 289-291
 per unit of labor, 289-291
Forde, C. D., 31n.
Fortes, M., 31n.
Fortune, R., on incest, 89
Frankfort, H., 315-316n.
Franklin, B., on dowry, 98n.
Frazer, J., on ethics, 219-220
 on exogamy, 102
Freud, S., on culture building, 97
 on economic motive, 97
 on incest, 88-89
 and ethics, 91n.